The Big Book of Keto Diet for Beginners 2018

Written by: Jamie Stewart

Copyright © 2018

Warning-Disclaimer

Contents

Introduction 3

Vegetables & Side Dishes 11

Poultry 37

Pork 64

Beef 91

Fish & Seafood 118

Fast Snacks & Appetizers 145

Vegan 171

Eggs & Dairy 197

Desserts 224

Other Keto Favorites 250

INTRODUCTION

Doubtless, every person must eat in order to exist. However, eating simply to keep life in the body is not enough for the human race. Our body must be supplied with an adequate amount of essential nutrients that are needed for its growth, cell regeneration, and working power. What kind of food should we eat to supply our cells with the necessary building material? There is a jungle of information out there, so knowing what constitutes a healthy diet can be a tricky part of your food intake. Almost everyone agrees that a well-balanced diet is the key factor that contributes to a healthy and productive lifestyle. In other words, you should eat all major types of nutrients: protein, carbohydrates, and fats.

Furthermore, the cooking of food is another important factor in creating a well-balanced and healthy diet. Many studies have shown that people who regularly cook at home are more likely to meet dietary guidelines. When you follow a special dietary regimen and you have to track your nutrient intake, cooking at home is the best choice. If you follow a ketogenic diet, the right cookbook is exactly what you need.

The Ketogenic Diet in a Nutshell

The keto diet is a low carbohydrate, high-protein, and high-fat diet.

According to Wikipedia, ketosis is a "metabolic state in which some of the body's energy supply comes from ketone bodies in the blood, in contrast to a state of glycolysis in which blood glucose provides energy." Put simply, your body uses ketones for energy instead of glucose and consequently, it becomes a fat-burning machine. You can do this by simply avoiding sugar and starchy foods, and eating meat, protein food, healthy fats, and vegetables instead. Sounds fantastic? Yes, it is fantastic but you should follow some general rules in order to stay healthy during your diet. Health is a priceless wealth, isn't it?

In general, you should eat low-carb food. When following a ketogenic diet, there are foods you can eat, foods that you can eat in moderation and some foods that are strictly off-limits. For instance, the macronutrient ratio falls into the following ranges: 60–75 percent of calories from fat, 15–30 percent of calories from protein and 5–10 percent of calories from carbs. Use these recommendations as a guideline, you still have to stay within your macronutrient ratios, track your calorie consumption as well as keep an eye on the amount of cholesterol in your food.

Here're examples of ketogenic food to get an idea of what to eat:

MEAT & POULTRY – pork, beef, veal, goat, lamb, duck, chicken, turkey and goose.
FISH & SEAFOOD – fat fish, scallops, crab, lobster, mussels, clams, squid, and oysters.
DAIRY PRODUCTS – cheese, full-fat sour cream, Greek-style yoghurt, heavy whipping cream.
EGGS – fried, poached, deviled, hard-boiled, and scrambled.
VEGETABLES – non-starchy veggies such as asparagus, broccoli, cauliflower, cucumber, tomatoes, garlic, Brussels sprouts, zucchini etc. You can also eat canned and pickled vegetables but you must be careful about added sugar.
FATS & OILS – butter, ghee, avocado, organic oils.
NUTS – most of the nuts as well as unsweetened nut butters.
FRUITS – apples, banana, berries, dates figs, grapes, citrus fruit and so on.
Almost without exception, if you stick to the general rules and your meal plan, you'll shred pounds easily and effortlessly.

Top Five Benefits of a Keto Diet

1) **A genius way to regulate hunger and satiety while losing weight in the process** – When you avoid carbs, your body start burning stored fat as the primary energy source. It will automatically cause weight loss.

2) **Increased energy** – You will also have more energy because your body breaks down fat instead of carbs. If you observe an energy content of nutrients, you can see that carbohydrates contain 4 calories in each gram. A gram of protein provides 4 calories too, but a gram of fat contains even 9 calories.

3) **Mental clarity** – Due to the reduction of glucose, your brain starts using ketones as fuel, and the level of toxins decreases. It will improve your concentration and increase your productivity.

4) **A natural way to lower your triglycerides** – As you probably already know, your body converts excess calories into triglycerides and they are stored in your fat cells. Increasing an intake of unsaturated fats automatically leads to a reduction in blood triglyceride levels. Unsaturated fat-packed foods are nuts, seeds, avocado, vegetable oils, and peanut butter. Fatty fish such as salmon, mackerel, tuna, herring, and sardines are well known for their ability to lower triglycerides. Experts recommend eating fatty fish once or twice a week because it can reduce the risk of stroke.

5) **Reduced insulin levels** – When you eat carbohydrates, they are broken down into glucose (a type of blood sugar). High blood sugars are toxic and your body starts producing insulin as a response; it actually elevates your blood sugar levels. Insulin is responsible for bringing the glucose into your cells so your body will use it as energy. When there's too much glucose, insulin stimulates your liver to store excess glucose for later use. From the above, it is clear that cutting out carbs can lower blood sugar and insulin levels.

A Few Tips and Tricks for Success with a Ketogenic Diet

1) Keep it simple – If you have little time but you want to prepare keto meals for you and your family, you can still succeed. This recipe collection is chock-full of recipes that take 15 minutes or less to prepare. In addition, you can watch your carbohydrate intake because every recipe includes nutritional information.

As a matter of fact, the ketogenic diet requires a little pre-planning to ensure you're making healthy choices during your diet. Stock your pantry with products that will help you stay on track with your weight loss goals. Don't be confused by all these fancy-schmancy products. Simply purchase real foods which are listed in the table below. A well-stocked pantry is a must while reducing your favorite carbohydrates, especially sugars.

2) Go at your own pace – If you are feeling a little overwhelmed, stop, take a deep breath, and learn to listen to your body. Make your own meal plan and set your own weight loss goals. Everyone is different, even people of the same weight can have very different Basal Metabolic Rate (BMR). Stop comparing yourself to others.

Do you have a few excess pounds? Who cares? You are beautiful just the way you are. Always be yourself, be unique and watch what happens. Consequently, from a "big picture" standpoint, you will start losing your weight.

When it comes to the ketogenic diet, bear in mind that it is a journey, not a final destination, it should be an enjoyable lifestyle, not struggling and starving.

3) Get regular exercise – Many studies have shown that there is a link between regular exercise and happiness! Doubtless, exercise burns calories, boosts your metabolism and helps release toxins. Find an activity that fits into your lifestyle, whatever it is – running, jogging, walking, stair climbing or something else.

4) Stay hydrated – Drinking enough water will speed up your metabolism. It may sound cliché but it is an undeniable fact. Moreover, you should be drinking more water on a keto diet so those eight glasses of water are not enough. When you are in ketosis, your body loses more water in the form of urine. Therefore, reach for soups, full-fat yogurt and smoothies. If you have a hard time drinking water, add a few drops of lemon to it. Besides that, you should replenish your electrolytes by consuming homemade bone broth.

Easy Ketogenic Cooking

"The only real stumbling block is fear of failure. In cooking, you've got to have a what-the-hell attitude."
— Julia Child

Food and cooking are extremely important parts of different cultures all over the world. Although people have been cooking from ancient time, a modern cooking is a form of art that is constantly revamping itself with new techniques and diet regimens.

Cooking at home requires skills, willingness and confidence, but this is one of the most important things you can do for your health. Starting is the hardest part of anything, but it's easy to turn cooking at home into a habit. These recipes contain the ingredients that are available everywhere and are quick to prepare. You will explore 100 of the best keto recipes ever! Once you get the hang of it, you can experiment and come up with your own flavors.

The recipes presented in this cookbook are diverse, starting from traditional, classic dishes, to contemporary innovations. Hence, here you would be having simple soups and dipping sauce, along with more complicated casseroles and desserts. This recipe collection is comprehensive enough to teach anyone about keto diet. Regardless of whether you are a newbie or not, these recipes will make their way to your table with results that satisfy. Do not forget to add a heaping spoonful of love to every recipe!

ULTIMATE KETO FOOD LIST

Cheese

American

Blue Cheese

Cheddar

Cottage Cheese

Cream Cheese

Feta

Gouda

Mozzarella

Parmesan

Provolone

Ricotta

Swiss

Fats & Oils

Almond Butter, Oil

Avocado Oil

Butter

Cocoa Butter, Oil

Coconut Oil

Fish Oil

Flax Seed Oil

Grape Seed Oil

Hemp Seed Oil

Macadamia Oil

Full Fat Mayonnaise

Olive Oil

Walnut Oil

Dairy & Dairy Substitutes & Eggs

Almond Milk (unsweetened)

Coconut Cream

Coconut Milk (unsweetened)

Greek Yogurt

Sour Cream ((full-fat)

Soy Milk (unsweetened)

Whipped Cream (unsweetened)

Eggs

Fish & Seafood

Anchovy

Bass

Carp

Flounder

Haddock

Halibut

Mackerel

Salmon

Sardines

Sole

Tilapia

Trout

Tuna

Clams

Crab Meat

Lobster

Mussels

Oysters

Shrimp

Squid

Flours, Meals & Powders

Acorn Flour

Almond Flour

Almond Meal

Cocoa Powder

Coconut Flour

Flax Seed Meal

Protein Powder

Psyllium Husk

Sesame Seed Flour

Splenda

Poultry

Chicken: Breast, Legs, Wings

Duck

Goose

Quail

Turkey: Breast, Ground, Bacon

Seeds

Chia

Flax

Hemp

Pumpkin

Safflower

Sesame

Sunflower

Nuts

Almonds

Brazil Nuts

Coconut

Hazelnuts

Macadamias

Pecans

Pistachios

Walnuts

Fruits

Avocado

Blackberry

Blueberry

Cranberry

Lemon

Lime

Green Olive

Raspberry

Strawberry

Rhubarb

Tomato

Vegetables

Arugula

Asparagus

Bok Choy

Broccoli, Broccoli Rabe

Cabbage

Cauliflower

Celery

Chard

Chicory Greens

Cucumber

Eggplant

Endive

Fennel

Garlic

Green Bean

Jalapeno

Lettuce: Green Leaf, Romaine

Parsley

Radish

Spinach

Soy Bean

Zucchini

Artichoke

Brussels Sprouts

Carrots

Celery

Kale

Kohlrabi

Mushrooms

Okra

Onion

Peppers: Sweet or Hot Red, Sweet Yellow

Pumpkin

Snow Pea

Spaghetti Squash

Turnips

Meat

Corned beef

Ground beef, 70-90% lean

Beef, Hot Dog/Frankfurter

Beef Tongue

Beef Ribs

Beef Roast

Beef Sausage

Beef Steak

Filet Mignon

Beef Rib Eye

Beef Round

Beef Sirloin

Beef Strip Loin

Bologna (pork, beef, chicken)

Lamb, Chops

Pepperoni (pork, beef)

Pork Bacon

Pork Chops

Ham

Liverwurst

Pork Loin

Prosciutto

Sausage

Veal

Venison

VEGETABLES & SIDE DISHES

1.Broccoli and Baby Bella Mushrooms Delight............ 12

2. Roasted Turnips and Bell Peppers 12

3. Paprika Mushrooms with Coconut Flour Naan....... 13

4. Zoodles with Mushroom Sauce 13

5. Kohlrabi with Thick Mushroom Sauce...................... 14

6. Spinach and Strawberry Salad................................... 14

7. The Best Family Squash Stew..................................... 15

8. Japanese-Style Enoki Mushrooms
with Sesame Seeds... 15

9. Classic Creamy Cauliflower Soup 16

10. Grilled Zucchini with Herbed Sauce 16

11. Buttery Mixed Greens with Cheese 17

12. Cheesy Broccoli Casserole 17

13. Family Vegetable Bake 18

14. Easy and Yummy Cabbage with Bacon 18

15. Ground Turkey and Cheese Stuffed Tomatoes......... 19

16. Refreshing and Nutty Spring Salad 19

17. Spicy Cremini Mushroom Stew 20

18. Sour Cream Cabbage Soup 20

19. Vegetables à la Grecque 21

20. Roasted Asparagus with Feta Cheese 21

21. Chinese Cabbage Stir-Fry 22

22. Creamy and Easy Greek-Style Salad 22

23. Coleslaw with Sunflower Seeds 23

24. Spicy Vegetarian Delight 23

25. Cucumber and Cheese Balls 24

26. Yummy Oven-Roasted Asparagus 24

27. Roasted Vegetables with Spicy Sour Cream Dip...... 25

28. Stuffed Chanterelles with Prosciutto 25

29. Bell Pepper Casserole with Appenzeller................... 26

30. Sautéed Green Beans with Tapenade......................... 26

31. Sautéed Spinach with Cottage Cheese 27

32. Sunday Vegetable Patties.. 27

33. Sautéed Broccoflower with Blue Cheese Sauce 28

34. Slow-Roasted Cherry Tomatoes with Parmesan...... 28

35. Buttered Savoy Cabbage with Scallions.................... 29

36. Cabbage with Ham and Fried Eggs............................ 29

37. Colorful Vegetable and Broccoli Rice....................... 30

38. Bok Choy with Shrimp... 30

39. Spring Artichoke Salad with Feta Cheese 31

40. Sautéed Chicory with Pistachios............................... 31

41. Two-Cheese, Mushroom and Cauliflower Casserole 32

42. Spinach and Cheddar Breakfast Muffins................... 32

43. Gruyère Cheese and Kale Muffins............................. 33

44. Family Pizza with Spring Vegetables 33

45. Roasted Carrots with Green Peppercorn Sauce 34

46. Mushroom and Caciocavallo Stuffed Peppers.......... 34

47. Baked Avocado with Bacon and Cottage Cheese..... 35

48. Cabbage "Noodles" with Turkey Sauce 35

49. Keto Pasta with Alfredo Sauce.................................. 36

1.Broccoli and Baby Bella Mushrooms Delight

Ready in about 20 minutes
Servings 4

Broccoli is a powerhouse of many valuable nutrients. It fights cancer, boosts your immune system, and reduces many allergic reactions. Baby Bella mushrooms are a great source of vitamin B5, vitamin B3, copper, and selenium.

Per serving: 235 Calories; 20.9g Fat; 9.5g Carbs; 4.8g Protein; 2.7g Sugars

Ingredients

1/2 stick butter, room temperature
1/2 head broccoli, cut into small florets
10 ounces baby Bella mushrooms
1 teaspoon garlic, minced
1/3 cup chicken broth
1/3 cup whipping cream
1 teaspoon tarragon
1/2 teaspoon kosher salt, or more to taste
1/4 teaspoon crushed red pepper flakes
2 tablespoons Parmesan cheese
1/4 cup mayonnaise, preferably homemade

Directions

- Melt the butter in a skillet that is preheated over a moderate flame. Now, add the broccoli and mushrooms and cook until the mushrooms are slightly shriveled.
- Add the garlic and continue cooking until fragrant, stirring constantly.
- Add the broth, whipping cream and seasonings; cover with the lid and reduce the heat to medium-low. Cook an additional 10 minutes, stirring occasionally, until most of the liquid has evaporated.
- Stir the Parmesan cheese into the mushroom mixture until everything comes together. Plate and serve with mayo. Enjoy!

2. Roasted Turnips and Bell Peppers

Ready in about 35 minutes
Servings 6

Turnips is loaded with vitamins B1, B3, B5, B6, A, C, E, and K as well as minerals such as potassium, iron, manganese, copper and calcium. It contains omega-3 fatty acids too.

Per serving: 137 Calories; 11.1g Fat; 9.1g Carbs; 1.2g Protein; 5g Sugars

Ingredients

1 ½ pounds turnips, cut into wedges
1 bell pepper, sliced
1 fresh jalapeño, minced
3 tablespoons ghee, cubed
1 teaspoon dried marjoram
1 onion, thinly sliced
1 garlic clove, minced
2 tablespoons olive oil
1 teaspoon salt
1/2 teaspoon freshly ground black pepper
1/2 teaspoon cayenne pepper

Directions

- Begin by preheating an oven to 425 degrees F. Lightly grease a baking dish with a nonstick cooking spray.
- Toss the turnips and bell peppers with the remaining ingredients.
- Roast the turnips and peppers for 25 to 35 or until they're softened. Taste, adjust the seasoning and serve warm. Bon appétit!

3. Paprika Mushrooms with Coconut Flour Naan

Ready in about 20 minutes
Servings 6

These naans are a little bit crunchier than classic flour flat bread. In addition, they are easy to make and kid-friendly!

Per serving: 281 Calories; 21.4g Fat; 17.1g Carbs; 6.4g Protein; 0.1g Sugars

Ingredients

3/4 cup coconut flour
1/2 teaspoon baking powder
2 tablespoons psyllium powder
A pinch of salt
8 tablespoons coconut oil, melted
1 egg plus 1 egg yolk, beaten
1 pound cremini mushrooms, thinly sliced
1 teaspoon kosher salt
1 teaspoon smoked paprika

Directions

- In a mixing bowl, combine coconut flour with baking powder, psyllium and salt; mix to combine well.
- Add 6 tablespoons of coconut oil, egg and egg yolk; add the hot water to form a dough; let it rest for 10 minutes at room temperature.
- Now, divide the dough into 6 balls; flatten the balls on a working surface.
- Heat up a pan with 1 tablespoon of coconut oil over a medium-high flame. Fry naan breads until they are golden.
- Then, heat the remaining 1 tablespoon of coconut oil in a nonstick skillet. Sauté the mushrooms until tender and fragrant; season with kosher salt and paprika.
- Serve with naan and enjoy!

4. Zoodles with Mushroom Sauce

Ready in about 15 minutes
Servings 4

Here's a completely new way to eat your zucchs! Zoodles are funny and delicious!

Per serving: 85 Calories; 3.5g Fat; 11.4g Carbs; 5.8g Protein; 5.5g Sugars

Ingredients

2 zucchinis
2 tablespoons avocado oil
1 tablespoon shallots, minced
1 teaspoon garlic, minced
1 pound mushrooms, chopped
2 ripe tomatoes, chopped
1 cup chicken stock
1 teaspoon dried basil
1/2 teaspoon dried oregano
1/4 teaspoon chili powder

Directions

- Firstly, cut off the ends of each zucchini. Make zucchini noodles by using your spiralizer, a julienne peeler or mandoline.
- Now, bring a pot of lightly salted water to a boil; cook your zucchini noodles for one minute. Reserve.
- In the meantime, heat avocado oil in a large-sized pan over a moderate flame. Cook the shallot and garlic for 2 minutes. Add the mushrooms and cook an additional 3 minutes.
- Now, stir in the remaining ingredients; cover the pot and bring the mixture to a simmer over a medium-low heat. Cook until everything is warmed through.
- Top your zoodles with the prepared mushroom sauce and serve immediately. Enjoy!

5. Kohlrabi with Thick Mushroom Sauce

Ready in about 25 minutes
Servings 4

Use a vegetable peeler to peel off the tough outer leaves of the kohlrabi. Its mild flavor pairs perfectly with other vegetables and different sauces.

Per serving: 220 Calories; 20g Fat; 8.3g Carbs; 4g Protein; 3.1g Sugars

Ingredients

3/4 pound kohlrabi, trimmed and thinly sliced
3 tablespoons butter
1/2 pound mushrooms, sliced
1/2 cup scallions, chopped
1 garlic clove, minced
1 teaspoon sea salt
1/2 teaspoon ground black pepper
1/4 teaspoon red pepper flakes
1 ½ cups double cream

Directions

- Parboil kohlrabi in a large pot of salted water for 7 to 9 minutes. Drain and set aside.
- Warm the butter over medium-high heat. Sauté the mushrooms, scallions, and garlic until tender and fragrant.
- Season with salt, black pepper, and red pepper flakes.
- Slowly stir in double cream, whisking continuously until the sauce has thickened, about 8 to 12 minutes.
- Pour the mushroom sauce over the kohlrabi and serve warm.

6. Spinach and Strawberry Salad

Ready in about 10 minutes
Servings 4

Spinach, avocado, and strawberries are tossed with a high-quality brie cheese for a quick vegetarian dinner or an elegant appetizer.

Per serving: 190 Calories; 17.6g Fat; 6.6g Carbs; 4.3g Protein; 1.4g Sugars

Ingredients

4 cups baby spinach
1/2 cup strawberries, hulled and sliced
1 cup avocado, pitted, peeled and sliced
2 tablespoons olive oil
1/2 lime, freshly squeezed
1/2 teaspoon kosher salt
White pepper, to taste
1/3 cup brie cheese, crumbled
2 tablespoons fresh basil leaves, chopped

Directions

- Pat the spinach leaves dry and transfer them to a salad bowl.
- Add the slices of strawberries and avocado.
- Now, make the dressing by whisking olive oil, lime juice, salt and white pepper. Dress the salad and top with crumbled cheese.
- Serve garnished with fresh basil leaves. Bon appétit!

7. The Best Family Squash Stew

Ready in about 35 minutes
Servings 6

Vegetables are an extremely important part of every healthy diet, but when it comes to the keto diet, we find ourselves a bit confused. However, the more you learn about a keto diet, the more you know about combining food. For example, Butternut squash contains 2.1 g carbs per 1 ounce.

Per serving: 113 Calories; 7.9g Fat; 9.7g Carbs; 2.8g Protein; 1.6g Sugars

Ingredients

1/2 stick butter
2 shallots, chopped
1 teaspoon garlic, finely chopped
6 ounces butternut squash, chopped
1 celery, chopped
2 tablespoons fresh cilantro, roughly chopped
1/2 teaspoon sea salt
1/4 teaspoon ground black pepper, or more to the taste
1/4 teaspoon smoked paprika, or more to the taste
1/2 teaspoon chili powder
1 pound ripe tomatoes, chopped
2 tablespoons red wine
1 bay leaf

Directions

- Melt the butter in a stock pot over a moderate heat. Now, sauté the shallots and garlic until fragrant, about 4 minutes.
- Add the eggplant, celery and cilantro; cook an additional 5 minutes.
- Stir in the remaining ingredients; reduce the heat to a medium-low and let it simmer, covered, for 20 to 25 minutes.
- Serve with cauliflower mash. Bon appétit!

8. Japanese-Style Enoki Mushrooms with Sesame Seeds

Ready in about 15 minutes
Servings 3

Treat yourself and your beloved ones to this exotic dish that features amazing Enoki mushrooms. Did you know that wasabi powder can protect you against bacterial infections?

Per serving: 103 Calories; 6.7g Fat; 8.9g Carbs; 2.7g Protein; 1g Sugars

Ingredients

1 ½ tablespoons ghee, room temperature
1 cup scallions
2 cloves garlic, smashed
1 (7-ounce) package Enoki mushrooms, trim away about 1-inch of the root section
1/2 teaspoon salt
1/2 teaspoon Sansho Japanese pepper
1/2 teaspoon wasabi powder
2 teaspoons oyster sauce
1 tablespoon black sesame seeds

Directions

- Melt the ghee in a wok over a moderately high heat. Now, sauté the scallions and garlic for 5 minutes, until they are softened.
- Stir in the mushrooms and cook an additional 4 minutes. Remove from heat. Season with salt, Japanese pepper, and wasabi powder.
- Afterwards, add the oyster sauce and stir to combine well. Garnish with toasted sesame seed and eat warm.

9. Classic Creamy Cauliflower Soup

Ready in about 20 minutes
Servings 4

Is there anything better than thick and creamy soup during winter weekdays? Serve warm with kale chips. So good, right?

Per serving: 260 Calories; 22.5g Fat; 11.1g Carbs; 7.2g Protein; 4.5g Sugars

Ingredients

3 cups chicken broth
3 cups cauliflower, cut into florets
1 cup almond milk, unsweetened
1 cup avocado, pitted and chopped
1/4 teaspoon Himalayan rock salt
1/4 teaspoon freshly cracked mixed peppercorns
1 bay leaf

Directions

- Simmer the chicken broth over a moderate flame. Add the cauliflower and cook for 10 minutes.
- Turn the heat to low. Add the remaining ingredients and cook for a further 5 minutes.
- Puree the mixture using an immersion blender. Bon appétit!

10. Grilled Zucchini with Herbed Sauce

Ready in about 15 minutes
Servings 4

Warm, grilled zucchini with a homemade tangy sauce fitting for light dinner or a party appetizer. Be inspired and try sprinkling in a pinch of hot paprika or chili powder.

Per serving: 132 Calories; 11.1g Fat; 7.1g Carbs; 3.1g Protein; 2.3g Sugars

Ingredients

1 pound zucchini, cut lengthwise into quarters
1/4 cup avocado oil
1 teaspoon granulated garlic
1/2 teaspoon cayenne pepper
Salt, to taste
For the Sauce:
3/4 cup sour cream
1 tablespoon fresh cilantro, chopped
1 teaspoon fresh rosemary, finely chopped

Directions

- Start by preheating your grill to a medium-low heat.
- Drizzle zucchini slices with avocado oil. Sprinkle with garlic, cayenne pepper and salt.
- Place your zucchini on a lightly-greased grill. Grill your zucchini about 5 minutes per side or until they are tender and slightly browned.
- Meanwhile, make the sauce by mixing all of the sauce ingredients. Serve warm with the sauce on the side.

11. Buttery Mixed Greens with Cheese

Ready in about 25 minutes
Servings 5

Doubtless, leafy greens are among the healthiest foods in the world. They can help lower cholesterol levels, protect bone health and boost your immunity.

Per serving: 160 Calories; 10g Fat; 9.1g Carbs; 11g Protein; 1.4g Sugars

Ingredients

1 tablespoon butter
2 garlic cloves, chopped
1 bunch of scallions
2 pounds mixed greens, trimmed and torn into pieces
1/4 cup chicken broth
1 tablespoon apple cider vinegar
1 teaspoon cayenne pepper
1/2 teaspoon salt
1/4 teaspoon black pepper
1 cup Colby cheese, shredded

Directions

- Melt the butter in a large pan over a moderately high heat. Sauté the garlic and scallions about 2 minutes or until tender and aromatic.
- Stir in mixed greens and chicken broth; continue to cook until the leaves are wilted and all liquid has evaporated, about 13 minutes.
- Now, add apple cider vinegar, cayenne pepper, salt and black pepper. Remove from heat.
- Sprinkle with shredded cheese and serve immediately. Bon appétit!

12. Cheesy Broccoli Casserole

Ready in about 25 minutes
Servings 3

What are you up to this mooring? This ketogenic breakfast is both, light and fulfilling.

Per serving: 195 Calories; 12.7g Fat; 10.7g Carbs; 11.6g Protein; 2g Sugars

Ingredients

3 tablespoons avocado oil
1 shallot, minced
1/2 teaspoon garlic, minced
1 head broccoli, cut into small florets
3 eggs, well-beaten
1/2 cup half-and-half
1/2 teaspoon dried basil
1/2 teaspoon turmeric powder
Kosher salt and cayenne pepper, to taste
2 ounces Monterey Jack cheese, shredded

Directions

- Preheat your oven to 310 degrees F.
- Melt avocado oil in a pan over a moderate heat. Now, sauté the shallots and garlic for a few minutes. Stir in the broccoli florets and cook until they're tender. Transfer the mixture to a lightly greased casserole dish.
- In a separate mixing bowl, combine the eggs with half-and-half, basil, turmeric, salt and cayenne pepper.
- Pour the egg mixture over the broccoli mixture. Bake for 20 minutes or until set. Check the temperature with an instant-read food thermometer. Serve warm topped with cheese.

13. Family Vegetable Bake

Ready in about 1 hour
Servings 4

Here's one of the easiest keto casserole to make for an easy, no-stress family dinner. We opted for Taco seasoning but you can toss in whatever spices and herbs you have on hand!

Per serving: 159 Calories; 10.4g Fat; 12.7g Carbs; 6.4g Protein; 5.1g Sugars

Ingredients

1 large eggplant, cut into thick slices
1 tomato, diced
1/2 garlic head, crushed
1 medium-sized leek, sliced
1 celery, peeled and diced
1 Habanero pepper, minced
1 teaspoon Taco seasoning mix
2 tablespoons extra-virgin olive oil
1 tablespoon fresh sage leaves, chopped
1/3 cup Parmigiano-Reggiano cheese, shredded

Directions

- Place the eggplant in a medium-sized bowl; sprinkle with salt and let it stand for 30 minutes; now, drain and rinse the eggplant slices.
- Meanwhile, preheat your oven to 345 degrees F. Spritz a casserole dish with a nonstick cooking spray.
- Mix the vegetables along with seasoning, olive oil, and sage in the prepared casserole dish.
- Roast the vegetables approximately 20 minutes. Scatter shredded cheese over the top and bake an additional 10 minutes. Serve right away!

14. Easy and Yummy Cabbage with Bacon

Ready in about 20 minutes
Servings 6

There are many recipes for the classic cabbage side dishes, but this is one of the tastiest that you have ever tried. If you are able to use smoked bacon, the result will be even better!

Per serving: 259 Calories; 18.1g Fat; 8.6g Carbs; 15.5g Protein; 4.2g Sugars

Ingredients

1 tablespoon lard
1 large-sized head of red cabbage, shredded
1 carrot, finely chopped
1/2 pound bacon, chopped
1 bouillon cube
1/2 cup water
1/2 teaspoon cayenne pepper

Directions

- Melt the lard in a pan that is preheated over a moderate heat. Now, cook the cabbage and carrot until they are tender,
- Add the remaining ingredients, reduce the heat to a medium-low and cover the pan. Let it simmer for 10 minutes more.
- Taste, adjust the seasonings, and serve right away!

15. Ground Turkey and Cheese Stuffed Tomatoes

Ready in about 25 minutes
Servings 4

If you are tired of your dinner rotation, try these stuffed tomatoes. Everything is better stuffed with turkey and cheese!

Per serving: 413 Calories; 28.2g Fat; 7.8g Carbs; 35.2g Protein; 4g Sugars

Ingredients

4 tomatoes
1 tablespoon olive oil
1/2 pound ground turkey
1/2 cup scallions, chopped
1 garlic clove, smashed
1 tablespoon fresh parsley, chopped
1 teaspoon fresh rosemary, chopped
Seasoned salt and ground black pepper, to taste
1 cup Monterey Jack cheese, shredded
1 cup Romano cheese, freshly grated
1/2 cup chicken stock

Directions

- Slice the top off of each tomato. Discard the hard cores and scoop out the pulp from the tomatoes with a small metal spoon.
- Now, heat the oil in a cast-iron skillet that is preheated over a moderately high heat. Brown turkey meat for 3 to 4 minutes; reserve.
- In the same skillet, sauté the scallions and garlic until they are just tender, about 4 minutes. Add reserved beef and tomato pulp; sprinkle with fresh parsley, rosemary, salt, and pepper.
- Arrange tomatoes in a casserole dish. Divide the stuffing among tomatoes and top with cheese.
- Pour chicken stock around tomatoes and bake in the middle of the preheated oven at 360 degrees F, approximately 18 minutes. Bon appétit!

16. Refreshing and Nutty Spring Salad

Ready in about 5 minutes
Servings 4

A rich and fresh salad is always a good idea! Prepare this amazing, nutritious salad and make the most of the spring season!

Per serving: 184 Calories; 16.8g Fat; 9g Carbs; 2.1g Protein; 3.4g Sugars

Ingredients

1 medium-sized head lettuce, torn into bite-sized pieces
1/2 pound cucumber, thinly sliced
1 large-sized carrot, grated
1 cup radishes, thinly sliced
2 spring onions, sliced
1 ounce macadamia nuts, chopped
1/2 lime, freshly squeezed
3 tablespoons peanut oil
1 teaspoon chili sauce, sugar-free
1/2 teaspoon red pepper flakes, crushed
Coarse salt, to taste
1 tablespoon sesame seeds, lightly toasted

Directions

- Add the vegetables along with macadamia nuts to a large salad bowl. Toss to combine.
- In a small mixing dish, thoroughly whisk the lime juice, peanut oil, chili sauce, red pepper and salt.
- Dress the salad and serve sprinkled with toasted sesame seeds.

17. Spicy Cremini Mushroom Stew

Ready in about 30 minutes
Servings 4

This is a recipe you will be making again and again. It is best served with lots of cauliflower rice!

Per serving: 133 Calories; 3.7g Fat; 8.7g Carbs; 14g Protein; 2.4g Sugars

Ingredients

1 tablespoon olive oil
1 cup shallots, chopped
1 teaspoon chili pepper, finely minced
1 teaspoon garlic, minced
1 celery, chopped
2 carrots, chopped
1/2 pound Cremini mushrooms, chopped
2 ½ cups bone broth, low-sodium
1/4 cup dry white wine
1/2 cup water
2 ripe tomatoes, crushed
Salt and ground black pepper, to taste
1/4 teaspoon ground ginger
1/2 teaspoon ground allspice
1/4 teaspoon ground cinnamon
2 bay leaves
1/2 cup fresh basil, chopped

Directions

- Heat the oil in a large heavy pot that is preheated over a moderate flame. Now, sweat the shallots, peppers, garlic, celery, carrots, and mushrooms approximately 8 minutes.
- Add the broth, tomatoes, and seasonings, except for basil; bring to a boil. Now, turn the heat to a medium and let it simmer for 18 minutes, stirring periodically.
- Serve in individual bowls, garnished with fresh basil leaves. Bon appétit!

18. Sour Cream Cabbage Soup

Ready in about 25 minutes
Servings 4

You won't be able to resist this hearty soup that is sure to please. Make sure to use full-fat sour cream in this recipe.

Per serving: 185 Calories; 16.6g Fat; 7.4g Carbs; 2.9g Protein; 2.1g Sugars

Ingredients

1 ½ tablespoons butter, melted
1 leek, chopped
2 garlic cloves, minced
2 carrots, chopped
1 cup cabbage, shredded
1 green pepper, chopped
4 cups water
2 bouillon cubes
1 cup sour cream
Fresh tarragon sprigs, for garnish

Directions

- Warm the butter in a large pot over medium flame. Sauté the leeks until just tender and fragrant. Now, add the remaining vegetables and cook for 5 to 7 minutes, stirring periodically.
- Add the water and bouillon cubes; cover partially and cook an additional 13 minutes.
- Blend the mixture until creamy, uniform and smooth. Stir in the sour cream; gently heat, stirring continuously, until your soup is hot.
- Ladle into individual bowls and serve garnished with fresh tarragon. Bon appétit!

19. Vegetables à la Grecque

Ready in about 15 minutes
Servings 4

This authentic Greek sauté can be adapted according to what is in season. Feel free to top these amazing vegetables with Greek cheese like Halloumi.

Per serving: 318 Calories; 24.3g Fat; 9.1g Carbs; 15.4g Protein; 5.7g Sugars

Ingredients

2 tablespoons olive oil
2 garlic cloves, minced
1/2 cup red onion, chopped
1/2 pound button mushrooms, chopped
1 cup cauliflower, cut into small florets
1 medium-sized eggplant, chopped
1 teaspoon dried basil
1 teaspoon dried oregano
1 rosemary sprig, leaves picked
1 thyme sprig, leaves picked
1/2 cup tomato sauce
1/4 cup dry white wine
8 ounces Halloumi cheese, cubed

Directions

- Heat olive oil in a saucepan over a moderately high heat. Now, sauté, garlic for 1 to 1½ minutes.
- Now, stir in the onion, mushrooms, cauliflower, and eggplant; cook an additional 5 minutes, stirring periodically.
- Add the seasonings, tomato sauce, and wine; continue to cook for 4 more minutes. Remove from heat and divide among individual plates.
- Serve topped with Halloumi cheese and enjoy!

20. Roasted Asparagus with Feta Cheese

Ready in about 15 minutes
Servings 6

Asparagus and soft white cheese combine very well! Serve as a side dish or a complete vegetarian meal.

Per serving: 128 Calories; 9.4g Fat; 6.5g Carbs; 6.4g Protein; 3.3g Sugars

Ingredients

1 ½ pounds asparagus spears
2 tablespoons butter, melted
2 green onions, chopped
2 garlic cloves, minced
Salt and black pepper, to the taste
1 cup feta cheese, crumbled
1/2 cup fresh parsley, roughly chopped

Directions

- Preheat an oven to 420 degrees F.
- Drizzle the asparagus with the melted butter. Toss with green onions, garlic, salt, and black pepper.
- Place the asparagus on a lightly-greased baking pan in a single layer. Roast for about 14 minutes.
- Scatter crumbled feta over the warm asparagus spears. Serve garnished with fresh parsley.

21. Chinese Cabbage Stir-Fry

Ready in about 15 minutes
Servings 4

Chinese cabbage, also known as pak-choi, contains 2.18 grams of carbohydrates per 100 grams of vegetable. For this recipe, use a dry crispy wine like Chardonnay, Sauvignon Blanc, Albariño, Pinot Blanc or Pinot Grigio.

Per serving: 53 Calories; 3.7g Fat; 3.2g Carbs; 1.7g Protein; 1.3g Sugars

Ingredients

1 tablespoon sesame oil
2 spring onions, sliced
3/4 pound Chinese cabbage, cored and cut into chunks
1/2 teaspoon ground cumin
Salt, to taste
1/4 teaspoon rougui (Chinese cinnamon)
1/2 teaspoon fennel seeds
1/2 teaspoon Sichuan peppercorns, crushed
1 tablespoon tamari sauce
1/2 teaspoon chili sauce, sugar-free
2 tablespoons Chardonnay
1 tablespoon oyster sauce

Directions

- Heat the oil in a pan over medium-high heat. Now, sauté spring onions until translucent. Now, add the Chinese cabbage and seasonings.
- Cook about 3 minutes or until the cabbage leaves are wilted. Add tamari sauce, chili sauce, and Chardonnay; cook for a further 4 minutes, stirring often.
- Stir in oyster sauce and cook an additional minute. Serve warm in individual serving bowls.

22. Creamy and Easy Greek-Style Salad

Ready in about 15 minutes + chilling time
Servings 4

Accompany your festive dinner with this creamy and crunchy salad! This salad is so refreshing, so yummy, you will be delighted.

Per serving: 318 Calories; 24.3g Fat; 9.1g Carbs; 15.4g Protein; 5.7g Sugars

Ingredients

1 cup Greek-style yogurt
1 teaspoon garlic, minced
1 tablespoon fresh lime juice
1 teaspoon fresh or dried rosemary, minced
2 green onions, thinly sliced
4 cucumbers, sliced
6 radishes, sliced
Sea salt and ground black pepper, to taste
4 Boston lettuce leaves

Directions

- In a mixing bowl, thoroughly whisk Greek-style yogurt, garlic, lime juice and rosemary.
- Toss green onions, cucumbers, and radishes with prepared yogurt dressing; season with salt and pepper to taste and toss to coat well.
- Divide Boston lettuce leaves among four serving plates. Mound well-chilled salad onto each lettuce leaf and serve. Bon appétit!

23. Coleslaw with Sunflower Seeds

Ready in about 10 minutes + chilling time
Servings 4

If you want a multi-colored coleslaw, use a combination of green and red cabbage. Pine nuts and raisins in a small amount work well here, just watch your carbohydrate intake.

Per serving: 242 Calories; 20.5g Fat; 15.2g Carbs; 1g Protein; 4.1g Sugars

Ingredients

3/4 pound Napa cabbage, cored and shredded
1 large-sized carrot, shredded
1 cup mayonnaise
1 teaspoon coarse ground mustard
1/2 cup fresh parsley leaves, loosely packed and coarsely chopped
1 teaspoon celery seeds
Salt and ground pepper, to taste
2 tablespoons sunflower seeds

Directions

- Add the cabbage and carrots to your salad bowl. Now, stir in the mayonnaise, mustard, parsley, celery seeds, salt, and pepper.
- Gently stir to combine all ingredients. Allow it to sit for 3 hours in the refrigerator. Serve sprinkled with sunflower seeds.

24. Spicy Vegetarian Delight

Ready in about 15 minutes
Servings 4

If you prefer a more authentic Mexican flavor, you can make your own enchilade sauce. It is also budget-friendly because you can freeze leftovers for later.

Per serving: 290 Calories; 21.7g Fat; 17.5g Carbs; 10.6g Protein; 3.7g Sugars

Ingredients

2 tablespoons olive oil
2 small-sized shallots, chopped
1 garlic clove, minced
1 pound cremini mushroom, sliced
1/2 teaspoon salt
1/2 teaspoon ground black pepper
1 cup tomatillo, chopped
4 eggs
1/4 cup enchilada sauce
1 medium-sized avocado, pitted and mashed

Directions

- Heat olive oil in a saucepan over a moderate flame. Now, cook the shallot and garlic until just tender and fragrant.
- Now, add the mushrooms and stir until they're tender. Season with salt and pepper; stir in chopped tomatillo.
- Stir in the eggs and scramble them well. Top with enchilada sauce; serve warm with avocado slices.

25. Cucumber and Cheese Balls

Ready in about 25 minutes
Servings 2

These balls are so refreshing and light but they will fill you up for sure. Serve as an appetizer or a light dinner with a piece of fat fish.

Per serving: 133 Calories; 9.9g Fat; 6.8g Carbs; 6g Protein; 3.1g Sugars

Ingredients

1 ounce blue cheese
1 ounce Neufchatel
1 medium-sized cucumber, chopped
1 tablespoon fresh parsley, chopped
2 tablespoons walnuts, chopped

Directions

- Drop the chopped cucumbers into a colander; sprinkle with a pinch of salt. Let it stand for 20 minutes in the sink; press your cucumber firmly to drain away the excess liquid.
- Thoroughly mix the cheese, cucumber, and parsley in a bowl.
- Shape into 4 balls and roll them in chopped walnuts. Refrigerate until ready to serve.

26. Yummy Oven-Roasted Asparagus

Ready in about 20 minutes
Servings 4

Oven-roasted asparagus is crispy, flavorful and adorable! For a vegan version, just skip the bacon bits and save even more calories.

Per serving: 48 Calories; 1.6g Fat; 4.4g Carbs; 5.5g Protein; 2.1g Sugars

Ingredients

1 pound asparagus spears
Salt and freshly ground black pepper, to your liking
1 teaspoon onion powder
1/4 teaspoon cumin powder
1/2 teaspoon dried thyme
4 tablespoons bacon bits

Directions

- Start by preheating your oven to 460 degrees F.
- Toss asparagus spears with the salt, black pepper, onion powder, cumin powder, and thyme. Arrange them on a baking sheet.
- Spritz with a nonstick cooking spray. Bake for 8 to 10 minutes; turn them over and bake an additional 8 minutes.
- Serve garnished with bacon bits and enjoy!

27. Roasted Vegetables with Spicy Sour Cream Dip

Ready in about 45 minutes
Servings 4

This easy fresh from the oven dish, featuring a colorful array of vegetables and tangy dipping sauce, makes an amazing family main dish. Serve with Mesclun salad and enjoy!

Per serving: 357 Calories; 35.8g Fat; 8.2g Carbs; 3.4g Protein; 2.2g Sugars

Ingredients

2 carrots, cut into sticks
1 celery stalk, cut into sticks
1 red bell pepper, sliced
1 green bell pepper, sliced
1 red onion, sliced into rings
1/4 cup olive oil
1 garlic clove, minced
1 tablespoon fresh parsley, minced
1/2 teaspoon paprika

For the Spicy Sour Cream Dip:
1 ½ cups sour cream
2 tablespoons mayonnaise
3/4 teaspoon Dijon mustard
1 jalapeño pepper, finely minced
1 tablespoon lime juice
Salt and black pepper, to taste
2 tablespoons sage leaves, chopped

Directions

- Preheat your oven to 390 degrees F. Line a baking sheet with parchment paper.
- In a mixing dish, toss the carrots, celery, bell pepper, onion, olive oil, garlic, parsley, and paprika.
- Arrange vegetables on the baking sheet and roast about 40 minutes; be sure to stir halfway through.
- Combine all ingredients for the sour cream dip; whisk until everything is well incorporated. Serve with roasted vegetables and enjoy!

28. Stuffed Chanterelles with Prosciutto

Ready in about 25 minutes
Servings 6

Chanterelles mushrooms are a powerhouse of protein, vitamins, and minerals. They can improve your memory, decrease the risk of type 2 diabetes and help reduce skin problems such as irritation, redness, and inflammation.

Per serving: 98 Calories; 5.8g Fat; 3.9g Carbs; 8.4g Protein; 0.5g Sugars

Ingredients

6 medium-sized Chanterelles, stems removed
3 teaspoons sesame oil
1 tablespoon Worcestershire sauce
Coarse salt and ground black pepper, to your liking
3 slices of prosciutto, finely chopped
2 tablespoons fresh cilantro, minced
1 teaspoon fresh rosemary, minced
2 ounces Asiago cheese, grated

Directions

- Start by preheating your oven to 355 degrees F. Line a baking sheet with a piece of parchment paper.
- Rub sesame oil and Worcestershire sauce on mushroom caps. Season them with salt and pepper.
- Now, combine the prosciutto, cilantro, rosemary and cheese; mix well. Stuff the mushroom caps and bake for 18 to 22 minutes.
- Adjust the seasonings and serve immediately. Bon appétit!

29. Bell Pepper Casserole with Appenzeller

Ready in about 1 hour
Servings 4

Make this healthy and delicious alternative to the traditional casserole recipe. Looks like the perfect family meal!

Per serving: 408 Calories; 28.9g Fat; 13.6g Carbs; 24.9g Protein; 6.5g Sugars

Ingredients

8 bell peppers
3/4 pound Appenzeller, shredded
2 red onions, thinly sliced
1 garlic clove, crushed
6 whole eggs
1/3 cup sour cream
Sea salt and ground black pepper, to taste
1 teaspoon smoked paprika

Directions

- Preheat an oven to 470 degrees F. Arrange the peppers on a baking sheet in a single layer.
- Bake the peppers in the preheated oven until the skins are browned and blackened, about 20 minutes.
- Turn them over and bake another 10 to 15 minutes. Remove your peppers from the oven; cover with a plastic wrap and allow them to steam for 1 hour.
- Then, remove the skins, stems, and seeds. Place 4 peppers in a lightly oiled casserole dish.
- Top with half of the shredded Appenzeller; add a layer of sliced onions and crushed garlic. Place another layer of roasted peppers, followed by the remaining Appenzeller.
- In a mixing dish, whisk the eggs with sour cream, salt, pepper, and paprika. Pour the mixture over the peppers. Cover tightly with a piece of foil and bake about 20 minutes.
- Next, remove the foil and bake another 20 minutes. Serve warm.

30. Sautéed Green Beans with Tapenade

Ready in about 15 minutes
Servings 4

Tapenade is a piquant Provençal sauce that pairs perfectly with rosé wine. You can keep it in your refrigerator for 3 days.

Per serving: 183 Calories; 16.1g Fat; 9g Carbs; 3.2g Protein; 1.8g Sugars

Ingredients

1 pound green beans
1 tablespoon sesame oil
1 celery stalk, shredded
1 garlic clove, smashed
1/2 teaspoon smoked paprika
Flaky sea salt and ground black pepper, to taste

For Tapenade:
1/2 cup Kalamata olives
1 ½ tablespoons capers
2 anchovy fillets
1 tablespoon fresh lemon juice
3 tablespoons extra-virgin olive oil

Directions

- Put green beans in the steamer basket over the boiling water; steam approximately 4 minutes or until crisp-tender.
- Heat sesame oil in a sauté pan over a moderate flame. Add the celery and garlic; sauté an additional 4 minutes, stirring periodically.
- Season with paprika, salt, and black pepper.
- Puree all the ingredients for tapenade in your food processor. Serve immediately with sautéed green beans. Bon appétit!

31. Sautéed Spinach with Cottage Cheese

Ready in about 10 minutes
Servings 4

If you are a vegetarian and you are new to the ketogenic diet, you might be wondering what type of foods you could eat. This recipe offers an answer so keep it in your back pocket.

Per serving: 208 Calories; 13.5g Fat; 11g Carbs; 14.5g Protein; 1.2g Sugars

Ingredients

1/2 stick butter
2 garlic cloves, minced
2 pounds spinach leaves, rinsed and torn into pieces
1 teaspoon salt
1/2 teaspoon cayenne pepper
1/4 teaspoon turmeric powder
1 cup cottage cheese

Directions

- Melt the butter in a Dutch oven and sauté the garlic until it's just browned.
- Add the spinach leaves, salt, cayenne pepper, and turmeric powder; cook another 2 to 3 minutes over a moderate heat, adding a splash of warm water if needed.
- Next, turn the heat on high, and cook for 1 to 2 minutes more, stirring often. Taste and adjust the seasonings.
- Serve topped with cottage cheese.

32. Sunday Vegetable Patties

Ready in about 15 minutes
Servings 6

Cheddar is the perfect cheese for the low-carbohydrate kitchen. It works wonderfully with these patties. And remember – the harder the better!

Per serving: 153 Calories; 11.8g Fat; 6.6g Carbs; 6.4g Protein; 3.1g Sugars

Ingredients

2 medium-sized zucchinis, shredded
2 carrots, shredded
1 small-sized celery stalk, shredded
2 tablespoons parsley, chopped
1 white onion, finely chopped
1 garlic clove, finely minced
1 cup cheddar cheese, grated
2 tablespoons olive oil
1 egg yolk
Salt and black pepper, to taste
Lemon wedges, to serve

Directions

- Start by preheating your oven to 360 degrees F. Line a baking sheet with parchment paper.
- Now, press the shredded vegetables firmly to drain away the excess liquid. Then, thoroughly combine all ingredients, except for lemon wedges, in a mixing bowl.
- Shape the mixture into 12 patties and bake for 5 minutes per side. Serve with fresh lemon wedges and enjoy!

33. Sautéed Broccoflower with Blue Cheese Sauce

Ready in about 30 minutes
Servings 6

This delicious side dish features crispy broccoflower with the garlic and curry powder, served with delicate blue cheese.

Per serving: 159 Calories; 12.3g Fat; 8.2g Carbs; 5.7g Protein; 2.2g Sugars

Ingredients

2 pounds broccoflower, trimmed and broken into small florets
1 ½ tablespoons sesame oil
2 green onions, chopped
2 garlic cloves, smashed
1/4 teaspoon curry powder
Flaky sea salt and freshly ground black pepper, to taste
1/2 teaspoon fresh ginger root, minced
1 tablespoon fresh cilantro, chopped

For the Blue Cheese Sauce:
1 ½ tablespoons ghee
1/3 cup double cream
1/2 cup blue cheese, crumbled
1/4 teaspoon freshly cracked mixed peppercorns

Directions

- Place broccoflower in a large pot of boiling water; parboil for 2 to 3 minutes. Drain well.
- Heat sesame oil in a sauté pan over a moderately high flame. Sweat green onions for 2 minutes. Stir in the garlic and cook until fragrant, about 1 to 2 minutes.
- Now, stir in broccoflower along with curry powder, salt, pepper, and ginger. Continue to sauté, stirring constantly, for 2 to 3 minutes.
- Add a splash of water, cover and cook 6 minutes longer, or until it is softened.
- Next, warm ghee in a pan over a moderate heat. Add cream and stir until thoroughly heated; now, fold in blue cheese and freshly cracked peppercorns.
- Stir until your cheese is completely melted. If it is too thick, pour in 1 to 2 tablespoons of water and stir to combine.
- Serve garnished with fresh cilantro and the blue cheese sauce on the side. Bon appétit!

34. Slow-Roasted Cherry Tomatoes with Parmesan

Ready in about 25 minutes
Servings 4

As the name implies, these tomatoes are roasted in your oven gently and slowly, while absorbing amazing aromas of fresh herbs and high-quality, nutty cheese.

Per serving: 247 Calories; 19.8g Fat; 8.3g Carbs; 11g Protein; 5.2g Sugars

Ingredients

1 ½ pounds cherry tomatoes, halved
1/4 cup olive oil
1 tablespoon Worcestershire sauce
1 tablespoon white wine vinegar
1 teaspoon garlic, minced
Sea salt and freshly ground black pepper, to taste
1 spring of fresh rosemary, chopped
2 sprigs of fresh thyme, chopped
1 cup Parmesan cheese, freshly grated

Directions

- Preheat the oven to 400 degrees F.
- Place the tomatoes in a broiler-proof ceramic baking dish. Drizzle the tomatoes with olive oil Worcestershire sauce, and vinegar.
- Sprinkle with the garlic, salt, pepper, rosemary and thyme. Top with Parmesan cheese.
- Roast for 20 to 22 minutes, until the tomatoes begin to caramelize but not split. Bon appétit!

35. Buttered Savoy Cabbage with Scallions

Ready in about 20 minutes
Servings 4

Comforting and irresistible, this cabbage saute is loaded with nutrients. Savoy cabbage, scallions, and butter are definitely a match made in heaven!

Per serving: 142 Calories; 11.6g Fat; 8.7g Carbs; 2g Protein; 4.4g Sugars

Ingredients

1/2 stick butter, melted
1 bunch scallions, chopped
1 garlic clove, minced
1 pound Savoy cabbage, outer leaves discarded, cored and shredded
1 large-sized carrot, thinly sliced
1/4 teaspoon fresh ginger root, grated
1/2 teaspoon sea salt
1/2 teaspoon mixed peppercorns, freshly cracked
1/4 cup chicken stock
1 tablespoon dry white wine
1/3 teaspoon mustard seeds
A pinch of nutmeg

Directions

- Melt the butter in a pan over a medium-high flame. Now, sauté the scallions and garlic until they're just tender and fragrant.
- Stir in the cabbage, carrots, and ginger; cook for 10 minutes, stirring occasionally.
- Add the remaining ingredients and cook an additional 5 minutes. Test to check if Savoy cabbage is done to your liking. Enjoy!

36. Cabbage with Ham and Fried Eggs

Ready in about 15 minutes
Servings 4

Have you ever had a sauteed cabbage for breakfast? It's time to try something new! A crisp-tender red cabbage with chopped ham and fried eggs is your next favorite breakfast under 200 calories.

Per serving: 173 Calories; 10.6g Fat; 5.6g Carbs; 14.2g Protein; 2.1g Sugars

Ingredients

2 tablespoons bacon fat
1 cup spring onions, minced
1 garlic clove, minced
2 cups red cabbage, shredded
1 bay leaf
1/2 teaspoon salt
1/2 teaspoon ground black pepper
4 rashers of ham, chopped
2 teaspoons dry red wine
4 eggs

Directions

- Heat 1 tablespoon of bacon fat in a nonstick skillet over a moderate flame. Now, sauté the onions and garlic until just tender.
- Then, add the cabbage and cook, stirring continuously, until tender or about 5 minutes. Add the bay leaf, salt, pepper and chopped ham. Add the wine and cook an additional 3 minutes.
- Heat the remaining 1 tablespoon of bacon fat in another skillet. Crack the eggs into another skillet and cook to desired doneness.
- Divide prepared cabbage among four serving plates; top with fried egg and serve immediately.

37. Colorful Vegetable and Broccoli Rice

Ready in about 20 minutes
Servings 4

If you can make cauli rice, you should try broccoli rice. Use a food processor or box grater for this purpose. Add some colorful veggies and enjoy!

Per serving: 126 Calories; 11.6g Fat; 5.4g Carbs; 1.3g Protein; 2.5g Sugars

Ingredients

1 head broccoli, broken into florets
1/2 stick butter
1/2 yellow onion, chopped
1 garlic clove, minced
1 red bell pepper, chopped
1 Aji Fantasy chili pepper, minced
1/2 celery stalk, chopped
Salt and ground black pepper, to taste

Directions

- Blitz the broccoli in your food processor until it has reached a rice-like texture.
- Now, melt the butter in a sauté pan over a moderate heat. Sweat yellow onion for 2 to 3 minutes; stir in the garlic and cook until slightly browned and fragrant.
- After that, add the peppers and celery; cook an additional 4 minutes or until they're just tender. Add broccoli "rice" and season with salt and pepper.
- Cook for a further 5 minutes, stirring periodically. Serve warm and enjoy!

38. Bok Choy with Shrimp

Ready in about 15 minutes
Servings 4

Transform an ordinary vegetable such as Bok choy into a completely new keto dish with this appetizing recipe. Toss it with sautéed shrimp and enjoy a delicious weeknight meal.

Per serving: 171 Calories; 8.4g Fat; 5.8g Carbs; 18.9g Protein; 2.1g Sugars

Ingredients

2 tablespoons sesame oil
2 garlic cloves, crushed
1 ½ pounds Bok choy, trimmed and thinly sliced
1 (1/2-inch) piece ginger, freshly grated
1 tablespoon oyster sauce
Salt and ground black pepper, to taste
1 teaspoon cayenne pepper
10 ounces shrimp, peeled and deveined

Directions

- Heat 1 tablespoon of sesame oil in a sauté pan over a moderate heat. Now, cook the garlic until it is just browned.
- Stir in the Bok choy and ginger. Add the oyster sauce, salt, black pepper and cayenne pepper. Cook for 5 minutes, gently stirring. Transfer to a serving platter and reserve.
- Now, heat the remaining tablespoon of sesame oil in a clean sauté pan. Cook the shrimp, stirring periodically, until they are just pink and opaque, about 3 minutes.
- Serve with reserved Bok choy, garnished with lemon wedges.

39. Spring Artichoke Salad with Feta Cheese

Ready in about 25 minutes
Servings 6

Freshly roasted artichokes and flavorful Mediterranean cheese combine very well! Serve as a side dish or a complete vegetarian meal.

Per serving: 146 Calories; 9.4g Fat; 12.1g Carbs; 5.8g Protein; 2.5g Sugars

Ingredients

2 tablespoons extra-virgin olive oil
3 artichoke hearts, defrosted
1 teaspoon coarse salt
1/2 teaspoon freshly ground black pepper
1 cup white onions, peeled and finely chopped
2 tablespoons lime juice, freshly squeezed
1 ½ teaspoons brown mustard
3 tablespoons champagne vinegar
1/2 pint grape tomatoes
1/3 cup baby green oak lettuce
1/3 cup red Swiss chard
1/3 cup arugula
1/3 cup butter lettuce
3 tablespoons capers, drained
1 roasted poblano pepper, sliced thin
1/2 teaspoon dried basil
2 ounces Kalamata olives, pitted and sliced
4 ounces feta cheese, crumbled

Directions

- Start by preheating your oven to 350 degrees F. Line a baking sheet with parchment paper or a silicone mat.
- Arrange artichoke hearts on the prepared sheet pan and drizzle with olive oil. Season your artichokes with the salt and pepper and roast for 18 to 23 minutes.
- In the meantime, thoroughly combine the onions, lime juice, mustard and vinegar in a mixing dish; mix to combine well.
- Transfer the cooled artichoke hearts to a serving bowl; dress with the prepared vinaigrette.
- Toss with the remaining ingredients, except for feta cheese. Serve well chilled, garnished with crumbled feta. Enjoy!

40. Sautéed Chicory with Pistachios

Ready in about 10 minutes
Servings 4

Chicory greens can help improve your digestion and reduce heart diseases. It is a valuable source of vitamin A, vitamin C, vitamin E, and vitamin B6, as well as minerals such as magnesium, zinc, manganese, calcium, and potassium.

Per serving: 65 Calories; 4.7g Fat; 5.7g Carbs; 2.1g Protein; 1g Sugars

Ingredients

2 heads chicory greens, outer ribs discarded and cut into pieces
3 teaspoons olive oil
1 teaspoon garlic cloves, minced
2 green onions, chopped
Salt and pepper, to taste
1/2 teaspoon hot red pepper flakes
1/4 cup shelled pistachios

Directions

- Cook chicory in a pot of boiling salted water about 5 minutes. Drain well.
- Dry the pot and heat olive oil over moderately high heat until it shimmers. Add chicory, garlic and green onions.
- Season with salt, black pepper and red pepper flakes; sauté until the leaves are wilted.
- Serve garnished with pistachios. Bon appétit!

41. Two-Cheese, Mushroom and Cauliflower Casserole

Ready in about 35 minutes
Servings 4

Get ready for this fabulous combination of ingredients! Brown cremini mushrooms and cauliflower go perfectly with an aged goat cheese and cream cheese, while Piri piri sauce gives your casserole an extra kick!.

Per serving: 275 Calories; 21.3g Fat; 7.3g Carbs; 14g Protein; 2.6g Sugars

Ingredients

2 tablespoons lard
1 cup chicken stock
4 eggs, lightly beaten
1/2 cup sour cream
1 cup chive & onion cream cheese
1 cup aged goat cheese
1 tablespoon Piri piri sauce
1 teaspoon yellow mustard
1/2 pound brown cremini mushrooms, thinly sliced
1 teaspoon fresh or dry rosemary, minced
1/2 teaspoon coarse salt
1/3 teaspoon freshly ground black pepper
1 large head cauliflower, cut into florets

Directions

● Start by preheating your oven to 360 degrees F. Then, spritz a casserole dish with a nonstick cooking spray.
● Next step, melt the lard in a pan that is preheated over a moderate heat. Cook the stock, eggs, sour cream, cheese, Piri piri sauce and mustard in the pan until heated through.
● Layer cremini mushrooms and cauliflower on the bottom of your baking dish. Season with rosemary, salt, and black pepper.
● Pour saucepan mixture over the top. Bake for 25 to 35 minutes and serve warm. Bon appétit!

42. Spinach and Cheddar Breakfast Muffins

Ready in about 30 minutes
Servings 6

These savory muffins are a great choice for the perfect start to your busy day. Serve with fried bacon and enjoy!

Per serving: 252 Calories; 19.7g Fat; 3g Carbs; 16.1g Protein; 2.6g Sugars

Ingredients

1 cup full-fat milk
8 eggs
2 tablespoons vegetable oil
1/3 teaspoon salt
1/4 teaspoon ground black pepper, or more to the taste
1 cup spinach, chopped
1 ½ cups cheddar cheese, grated

Directions

● Preheat your oven to 350 degrees F.
● In a bowl, mix the milk, with eggs and oil. Add the remaining ingredients. Mix well to combine.
● Add the mixture to a lightly greased muffin tin.
● Bake for 25 minutes or until your muffins spring back when lightly pressed.

43. Gruyère Cheese and Kale Muffins

Ready in about 25 minutes
Servings 6

It's going to be the best muffins ever! Try them and enjoy their wonderful taste!

Per serving: 275 Calories; 15.8g Fat; 7.2g Carbs; 21.6g Protein; 1.4g Sugars

Ingredients

5 eggs
1/2 cup full-fat milk
Sea salt, to taste
1/2 teaspoon dried basil
1 ½ cups Gruyère cheese, grated
10 ounces kale, cooked and drained
1/2 pound prosciutto, chopped

Directions

- Start by preheating your oven to 360 degrees F. Spritz a muffin tin with a cooking spray.
- Whisk the milk, salt, basil and cheese in a mixing bowl. Toss in kale and prosciutto. Spoon the batter into each muffin cup (3/4 full).
- Bake for 20 to 25 minutes and serve with sour cream.

44. Family Pizza with Spring Vegetables

Ready in about 25 minutes
Servings 4

This fresh low-carb pizza features the tang of two kinds of cheese as well as the freshness of spring vegetables such as baby lettuce, red and green chard, green oak, frisee, etc.

Per serving: 234 Calories; 16.1g Fat; 11.1g Carbs; 13.6g Protein; 5.5g Sugars

Ingredients

For the Crust:
A spray coating
1 pound cauliflower
1/2 cup Edam cheese
4 medium-sized eggs
1/4 cup heavy cream
1 tablespoon basil-infused oil
Salt, to taste

For the Topping:
1 cup spring mix
3/4 cup tomato sauce, sugar-free
2 tablespoons chives, finely chopped
1 tablespoon fresh sage
1/4 cup Kalamata olives, pitted and sliced
1 cup mozzarella cheese

Directions

- Cook the cauliflower in a large pot of salted water until it is just tender; cut into florets and add the remaining ingredients for the crust.
- Then, preheat your oven to 380 degrees F; add an oven rack to the middle of the oven. Lightly grease a baking pan with a thin layer of a spray coating.
- Spread the crust mixture onto the bottom of the prepared baking pan. Bake for 15 minutes or until the crust is firm and golden.
- Remove from the oven and add the remaining ingredients, ending with mozzarella cheese; bake until the cheese has completely melted.
- Add a few grinds of black pepper if desired and serve immediately.

45. Roasted Carrots with Green Peppercorn Sauce

Ready in about 40 minutes
Servings 6

Carrots are full of nutrients and flavors. They go perfectly with creamy, peppery sauce like this one with green peppercorns, cognac, and cream.

Per serving: 183 Calories; 14.2g Fat; 9.1g Carbs; 2.6g Protein; 4.2g Sugars

Ingredients

1 ½ pounds carrots, trimmed and halved lengthwise
2 tablespoons butter, melted
1/4 teaspoon freshly grated nutmeg
1/2 teaspoon celery salt
1/4 teaspoon freshly ground black pepper
2 tablespoons apple cider vinegar
1 tablespoon green garlic, minced

For the Sauce:
2 tablespoons butter
1/2 cup green onions, minced
3 tablespoons Cognac
1 ½ cups beef broth
1 cup whipping cream
2 tablespoons green peppercorns in brine, drained and crushed slightly

Directions

Preheat your oven to 425 degrees F.
- Toss carrots with butter, nutmeg, celery salt, black pepper, vinegar and green garlic.
- Roast, stirring once or twice, until carrots are softened, about 35 minutes.
- Meanwhile, melt 2 tablespoons of butter in a pan over a moderately high flame. Sweat the onions for 2 minutes.
- Add Cognac and bring it to a boil for 2 minutes. Pour in beef broth and let it boil another 4 minutes.
- Lastly, stir in the cream and peppercorns; turn the heat to medium. Continue to simmer until the sauce is thickened and thoroughly warmed.
- Serve with roasted carrots and enjoy!

46. Mushroom and Caciocavallo Stuffed Peppers

Ready in about 30 minutes
Servings 6

These simple but endlessly crave-worthy peppers are both elegant and rustic. The secret lies in the simple approach – fresh button mushrooms, tomato sauce and mellow Caciocavallo cheese.

Per serving: 319 Calories; 8.8g Fat; 5.6g Carbs; 10.3g Protein; 8.5g Sugars

Ingredients

2 tablespoons avocado oil
1 shallot, chopped
1 teaspoon garlic, minced
3/4 pound button mushrooms, chopped
1 teaspoon Pimento
2 tablespoons fresh chives, chopped
1 teaspoon caraway seeds
Salt to taste
6 bell peppers, seeds and tops removed
1/2 cup Caciocavallo cheese, grated
1/2 cup tomato sauce

Directions

- Preheat your oven to 380 degrees F. Heat the oil in a pan that is preheated over moderately high heat.
- Sauté the shallots and garlic until the shallot softens. Stir in the mushrooms and cook an additional 4 minutes or until the mushrooms are fragrant.
- Add pimento, chives, caraway seeds and salt; stir until everything is heated through.
- Place the peppers in a foil-lined roasting pan; fill them with the mushroom stuffing. Top each pepper with Caciocavallo cheese.
- Afterwards, pour the tomato sauce over everything. Bake for 18 to 23 minutes or until cheese is lightly browned. Enjoy!

47. Baked Avocado with Bacon and Cottage Cheese

Ready in about 25 minutes
Servings 6

This is the perfect blend of savory flavors that will delight your taste buds. You can substitute prosciutto for bacon and Ricotta cheese for Cottage. Enjoy!

Per serving: 255 Calories; 21g Fat; 8.3g Carbs; 10.8g Protein; 0.4g Sugars

Ingredients

3 medium-sized ripe avocados, halved and pitted, skin on
2 eggs, beaten
3 ounces Cottage cheese
2 tablespoons fresh chives, chopped
3 ounce cooked bacon, crumbled
Salt and pepper, to taste
1/4 teaspoon smoked paprika

Directions

- Preheat your oven to 390 degrees F. Place avocado halves in shallow ramekins.
- In a mixing bowl, thoroughly combine the other ingredients. Divide the mixture among avocado halves.
- Bake for about 20 minutes and serve right away!

48. Cabbage "Noodles" with Turkey Sauce

Ready in about 20 minutes
Servings 4

The Aleppo pepper, also known as the Halaby pepper, has a sharp but fruity flavor. With its moderately hot flavor, Aleppo pepper will add a delicate touch of heat to this turkey sauce.

Per serving: 236 Calories; 8.3g Fat; 8.1g Carbs; 29.9g Protein; 4g Sugars

Ingredients

1 pound white cabbage
2 slices bacon
1 yellow onion, chopped
1 garlic clove, minced
3/4 pound turkey meat, ground
1 Aleppo chili pepper, minced
Sea salt and ground black pepper, to taste
1/2 teaspoon cayenne pepper
1/2 teaspoon dried oregano
1/2 teaspoon dried basil
1/4 teaspoon bay leaf, ground

Directions

- Remove any loose outer leaves of your cabbage. Now, spiralize your cabbage and reserve.
- Bring a pot of lightly salted water to a rolling boil; parboil cabbage for 3 minutes, until crisp-tender; drain.
- Heat a nonstick skillet over a moderately high heat. Now, cook the bacon for 3 to 4 minutes, crumbling with a fork; reserve.
- Now, cook onion and garlic in pan drippings until tender. Add turkey meat and chili pepper; cook until the meat is browned. Sprinkle with seasonings and stir to combine.
- Then, add the cabbage and bacon back to the skillet. Serve warm and enjoy!

49. Keto Pasta with Alfredo Sauce

Ready in about 30 minutes
Servings 4

If you are new to the ketogenic diet, you might be wondering what type of pasta you could eat. This recipe offers an answer so give it a try!

Per serving: 614 Calories; 55.9g Fat; 3.6g Carbs; 25.6g Protein; 0.3g Sugars

Ingredients

2 ounces cream cheese, room temperature
3 eggs, room temperature
1/2 teaspoon wheat gluten
1 stick butter
1 cup heavy cream
1 garlic clove, minced
2 cups Parmesan cheese, grated
1 teaspoon Italian seasoning

Directions

- Start by preheating your oven to 320 degrees F. Line a baking sheet with a Silpat mat.
- Blend the cream cheese, eggs, and gluten until uniform and creamy.
- Press the batter into the pan, keeping it nice and thin. Bake in the preheated oven for 5 to 6 minutes.
- Allow it to rest for 5 to 10 minutes before cutting into strips. Now, simmer the pasta in a lightly salted water for a couple of minutes or until it's done.
- Then, melt the butter in a skillet. Now, add the cream and garlic, and cook over a moderate heat, stirring with wire whisk.
- Stir in parmesan cheese and Italian seasonings; remove from heat. The sauce will thicken as it cools. Add warm pasta and serve immediately.

POULTRY

50. Creamy and Cheesy Chicken Salad 38

51. The Best Ever Chicken Stew..................................... 38

52. Rutabaga, Taro Leaf and Chicken Soup 39

53. Chicken Liver Pâté with Keto Flatbread................... 39

54. Chinese-Style Turkey Meatballs 40

55. Kid-Friendly Parmesan Chicken Meatballs............. 40

56. Tomato, Yogurt and Chicken Chowder.................... 41

57. Country Chicken Soup with Root Vegetables.......... 41

58. Chicken Drumsticks with
    Tangy Cauliflower Salad.. 42

59. Parmesan Breaded Chicken Breasts with Peppers... 42

60. Chicken Sausage with Spaghetti Squash 43

61. Prosciutto-Wrapped Chicken with Cottage Cheese 43

62. Sensational Chicken Wings with Broccoli............... 44

63. Zesty Chicken with Mayo-Avocado Sauce............... 44

64. Eggplant and Duck Quiche....................................... 45

65. Hungarian-Style Chicken Fillets 45

66. Roasted Chicken Wings with Cashew-Basil Pesto... 46

67. Mediterranean Chicken Breasts 46

68. Roasted Turkey Legs with Avocado Sauce 47

69. Chicken with Gorgonzola Panna Cotta 47

70. Mediterranean Chicken Legs in Sauce 48

71. Fried Chinese Cabbage with Ground Turkey 48

72. Smoked Turkey and Goat Cheese Spread 49

73. Chicken Fillets with Herby Sauce 49

74. Cheesy Turkey Meatballs with Basil Chutney 50

75. Crock Pot Turkey Legs 50

76. Grandma's Cauliflower and Turkey Soup 51

77. Leftover Chicken Chowder....................................... 51

78. Absolutely Incredible Turkey Kebabs...................... 52

79. Easy Grilled Chicken Salad 52

80. Spicy Chicken Strips with Hemp Seeds................... 53

81. Chicken Fillets with Cream-Mustard Sauce........... 53

82. Easy and Yummy Chicken Drumettes 54

83. Chicken Sausage with Salsa 54

84. Turkey Sausage with Bok Choy 55

85. Easy Herby Turkey Drumsticks 55

86. Mediterranean Chicken Drumsticks with Aioli..... 56

87. Ground Chicken with Peppers and Asiago Cheese.....56

88. The Best Chicken Tacos Ever.................................... 57

89. Turkey Soup with Baby Bok Choy 57

90. Mom's Turkey Soup.. 58

91. Vodka Duck Fillets... 58

92. Spicy Chicken with Brussels Sprouts...................... 59

93. Classic Tarragon Chicken Salad............................... 59

94. Chorizo with Asiago Cheese.................................... 60

95. Creamy Cauliflower and Chicken Soup.................. 60

96. Cheesy Turkey Dip with Fresno Chiles................... 61

97. Habanero and Turkey Bacon Balls 61

98. Oven Fried Crispy Chicken Legs 62

99. Holiday Turkey Wrapped in Prosciutto 62

100. Tomato Rum-Glazed Chicken Thighs..................... 63

50. Creamy and Cheesy Chicken Salad

Ready in about 20 minutes
Servings 6

Here's a super-easy and tasty lunch idea for all those who are on a keto diet! But also for everyone else!

Per serving: 183 Calories; 12.5g Fat; 1.7g Carbs; 16.3g Protein; 0.3g Sugars

Ingredients

2 chicken breasts
2 medium-sized cucumbers, sliced
1/2 teaspoon coarse salt
1/4 teaspoon ground black pepper
1/4 teaspoon chili pepper flakes
1/2 teaspoon dried oregano
1/3 teaspoon dried basil
2 romaine hearts, leaves separated
1/4 cup Parmesan, finely grated
For the dressing:
2 garlic cloves, minced
2 large egg yolks
1 tablespoon fresh lime juice
1 teaspoon mustard
1/4 cup olive oil

Directions

- Firstly, grill the chicken breast until done; cut them into cubes.
- Toss the cucumbers and chicken with the salt, black pepper, chili pepper, oregano, and basil. Place the romaine leaves in a salad bowl.
- Now, add the cucumber and chicken mixture. Prepare the dressing by whisking all the dressing ingredients.
- Dress the salad; scatter parmesan over the top, serve and enjoy!

51. The Best Ever Chicken Stew

Ready in about 1 hour
Servings 6

Winter is the perfect time of the year to enjoy a hearty and spicy chicken stew. These simply chicken drumsticks, gently cooked with beautiful vegetables and aromatics, are guaranteed to hit the spot!

Per serving: 239 Calories; 9.7g Fat; 11.5g Carbs; 25.6g Protein; 4.9g Sugars

Ingredients

2 tablespoons tallow, room temperature
2 medium-sized shallots, finely chopped
2 garlic cloves, sliced
1 quart chicken broth
1 sprig rosemary
1 teaspoon dried marjoram
1 pound chicken drumsticks
1 celery, chopped
1/2 pound carrots, chopped
1 bell pepper, chopped
1 poblano pepper, chopped
2 ripe tomatoes, chopped
1 teaspoon salt
1/2 teaspoon ground black pepper
1/2 teaspoon smoked paprika

Directions

- Melt the tallow in a large heavy pot that is preheated over a moderate flame. Sweat the shallots and garlic until aromatic and just tender.
- Now, turn the heat to medium-high. Stir in the chicken broth, rosemary, marjoram, and chicken drumsticks; bring to a boil.
- Add the remaining ingredients and reduce the heat to medium-low. Simmer, covered, for 50 minutes.
- Discard the bones and chop the chicken into small chunks. Serve hot!

52. Rutabaga, Taro Leaf and Chicken Soup

Ready in about 45 minutes
Servings 4

You can use a small knife to test your chicken for doneness. If the juices run clear, the chicken is ready.

Per serving: 256 Calories; 8.9g Fat; 7.2g Carbs; 35.1g Protein; 3.4g Sugars

Ingredients

1 pound chicken thighs
1/2 cup rutabaga, cubed
2 carrots, peeled
2 celery stalks
1/2 cup leek, chopped
1/4 teaspoon garlic, granulated
1/4 teaspoon ground cloves
1/2 cup taro leaves, roughly chopped
1 tablespoon fresh parsley, chopped
Salt and black pepper, to taste
1 cup chicken consommé, canned
3 cups water
1 teaspoon cayenne pepper

Directions

- Add all of the above ingredients, except for cayenne pepper, to a large-sized stock pot. Bring to a rapid boil over high heat.
- Now, turn the heat to medium-low. Let it simmer, partially covered, an additional 35 minutes or until the chicken is pinkish-brown.
- Next, discard the chicken and vegetables. Add cayenne pepper to the broth; allow it to simmer an additional 8 minutes.
- When the chicken thighs are cool enough to handle, cut off the meat from bones. Afterwards, add the meat back to the soup and serve warm.

53. Chicken Liver Pâté with Keto Flatbread

Ready in about 2 hours
Servings 4

Chicken liver and flatbread is a luxurious combination! In addition, eating liver can help you lose weight and fight fatigue.

Per serving: 395 Calories; 30.2g Fat; 11.6g Carbs; 17.9g Protein; 1.4g Sugars

Ingredients

10 ounces chicken livers
1/2 teaspoon Italian seasoning blend
4 tablespoons olive oil
1 white onion, finely chopped
1 teaspoon granulated garlic
For Flatbread:
1/2 cup flax meal
1 ¼ cups almond flour
1 ½ tablespoons psyllium husks
Salt, to taste
1 cup lukewarm water
1/2 stick butter
1/2 teaspoon turmeric powder
1/2 teaspoon fresh ginger, minced

Directions

- Blend the chicken livers, Italian seasoning, olive oil, onion and granulated garlic. Mix until everything is well combined and reserve.
- Then, prepare the flatbread by mixing all dry ingredients in a bowl. Then, mix all wet ingredients. After that, add the wet ingredients to the dry mixture. Mix well.
- Allow the dough to rest at room temperature for 1 to 2 hours. Now, divide the dough into 8 balls. Roll out each dough ball until it is very thin.
- Cook in a lightly greased skillet that is preheated over medium-high heat. Cook for 1 minute per side. Serve with chicken liver pâté. Enjoy!

54. Chinese-Style Turkey Meatballs

Ready in about 20 minutes
Servings 4

These tender and mouthwatering meatballs can be served on any occasion. Don't forget to add a pinch of Sichuan peppercorn for some extra oomph!

Per serving: 244 Calories; 13.7g Fat; 5g Carbs; 27.6g Protein; 3.2g Sugars

Ingredients

For the Meatballs:
3/4 pound ground turkey
1 egg
1/3 cup cheddar cheese, freshly grated
1/3 teaspoon black pepper
1/3 teaspoon Five-spice powder
For the Sauce:
1 1/3 cups water
1/3 cup red wine vinegar
2 tablespoons Worcestershire sauce
1/2 cup tomato puree, sugar-free
1/2 teaspoon cayenne pepper
3/4 cup erythritol
1/3 teaspoon guar gum

Directions

- Thoroughly combine ground turkey, the egg, cheese, black pepper and Five-spice powder in a mixing bowl. Now, form the mixture into balls (about 28 meatballs).
- Preheat a nonstick skillet over a medium heat. Brown your meatballs on all sides for 3 to 4 minutes; set them aside.
- Next, add the water, vinegar, Worcestershire sauce, tomato puree, cayenne pepper and erythritol to the skillet. Whisk until well mixed.
- After that, gradually add the guar gum. Whisk until the sauce is thickened. Decrease the temperature and bring the sauce to a simmer; make sure to stir periodically.
- Add the meatballs to the sauce; continue to simmer for 8 to 12 minutes on low or until your meatballs are thoroughly cooked. Serve with lettuce and enjoy!

55. Kid-Friendly Parmesan Chicken Meatballs

Ready in about 20 minutes
Servings 6

These meatballs are high in protein and low in carbs. It sounds like the perfect family lunch!

Per serving: 222 Calories; 6.7g Fat; 5.3g Carbs; 34.2g Protein; 2.7g Sugars

Ingredients

For the Meatballs:
3/4 cup Parmesan cheese, grated
2 eggs, lightly beaten
1 tablespoon fresh parsley leaves, chopped
1 tablespoon sage leaves, chopped
1 teaspoon onion powder
2 garlic cloves, finely minced
1/3 teaspoon dried rosemary
Salt and ground black pepper, to your liking
1/2 teaspoon red pepper flakes, crushed
1 ¼ pounds chicken, ground
For the sauce:
2 ½ tablespoons bacon fat
1 white onion, peeled and finely chopped
3 ripe tomatoes, chopped
1 cup chicken stock

Directions

- Thoroughly combine all ingredients for the meatballs. Now, shape your meatballs to the desired size.
- Warm 1 tablespoon of bacon fat in a nonstick skillet over a moderate heat. Now, cook the meatballs for 2 to 4 minutes or until they are cooked through; reserve, keeping them warm.
- Next, heat the remaining fat in the same skillet. Sauté the onions until translucent. Stir in tomatoes and chicken stock; cook 3 to 4 minutes more.
- Fold in reserved meatballs, reduce the heat to medium-low and let it simmer approximately 6 minutes. Enjoy!

56. Tomato, Yogurt and Chicken Chowder

Ready in about 35 minutes
Servings 6

A homemade tomato bisque soup is easy to prepare and it freezes and reheats well too. To serve, if you don't have a garden chervil on hand, use a fresh, roughly chopped cilantro.

Per serving: 238 Calories; 15.5g Fat; 9.1g Carbs; 36g Protein; 6.8g Sugars

Ingredients

2 tablespoons coconut oil
3 chicken drumsticks, deboned and chopped
1/2 teaspoon sea salt
1/2 teaspoon mixed peppercorns, freshly ground
2 shallots, chopped
1/2 cup celery, thinly sliced
1 fresh jalapeño, deveined and minced
2 cloves garlic, roughly chopped
2 cups tomato bisque, preferably homemade, sugar-free
2 cups water
1 bay leaf
1 tablespoon flax seed meal
1/2 cup Greek-style yogurt

Directions

- Melt the coconut oil in a large pot over a moderately high heat. Sear the meat, stirring periodically, for 6 minutes or until it is browned. Season with salt and peppercorns; then, reserve, keeping warm.
- Now, sauté the shallots, celery, jalapeño and garlic in pan drippings until they are tender and aromatic.
- Add a splash of tomato bisque to scrape and stir the browned bits from the pot. Next, pour in the remaining tomato bisque along with 2 cups of water.
- Throw in the bay leaf and let it simmer for 25 minutes over medium-low heat.
- Afterwards, add flax seed meal and yogurt; continue to cook over low heat until it is thoroughly heated. Serve in individual bowls garnished with fresh garden chervil. Bon appétit!

57. Country Chicken Soup with Root Vegetables

Ready in about 25 minutes
Servings 4

Cozy up to a bowl of a delicious chicken soup this autumn. This rustic soup can be blended to give a smooth texture, if desired.

Per serving: 342 Calories; 22.4g Fat; 10.3g Carbs; 25.2g Protein; 5.4g Sugars

Ingredients

1 tablespoon olive oil
1 teaspoon garlic, finely minced
1 parsnip, chopped
1/2 cup turnip, chopped
1 carrot, chopped
2 chicken breasts, boneless and cut into chunks
Salt and pepper, to taste
4 cups water
1 cup full-fat milk
1 cup heavy cream
2 bouillon cubes
1 whole egg
4 tablespoons fresh chives, roughly chopped

Directions

- Heat the oil in a heavy pot over a moderate heat; now, cook the garlic until aromatic. Add the parsnip, turnip and carrot. Cook until your vegetables are softened.
- Stir in the chicken; cook until it is no longer pink, for 3 to 4 minutes, stirring periodically. Season with salt and pepper.
- Pour in the water, milk, and heavy cream. Add the bouillon cubes and bring it to a boil.
- Reduce the heat to medium-low; let it simmer for 20 minutes longer. Add the beaten egg and stir an additional minute.
- Remove from the heat. Serve in individual bowls, garnished with chopped chives. Bon appétit!

58. Chicken Drumsticks with Tangy Cauliflower Salad

Ready in about 20 minutes
Servings 2

These chicken drumsticks are a cinch to make! They pair wonderfully with crispy and tangy low-carb cauliflower salad.

Per serving: 444 Calories; 36g Fat; 7.7g Carbs; 20.6g Protein; 3.2g Sugars

Ingredients

1/2 head of cauliflower
2 teaspoons butter
2 chicken drumsticks
1 teaspoon Hungarian paprika
Sea salt and ground black pepper, to taste
1/2 cup mayonnaise
1 teaspoon Dijon mustard
2 tablespoons dry white wine
1 red onion, finely minced
1/2 cup Colby cheese grated
2 tablespoons fresh Italian parsley, to serve

Directions

- Cook the cauliflower in a large pot of salted water until tender; cut into small florets and transfer to a salad bowl.
- Now, warm the butter in a pan over medium-high heat. Add the chicken, Hungarian paprika salt, and pepper.
- Cook for 7 to 8 minutes, turning periodically.
- Meanwhile, mix the mayonnaise with the mustard, wine, and minced red onion. Add to the bowl with cauliflower. Top with grated cheese.
- Serve with warm chicken drumsticks, garnished with Italian parsley. Bon appétit!

59. Parmesan Breaded Chicken Breasts with Peppers

Ready in about 30 minutes
Servings 4

A keto-style chicken tastes so good! Especially when served with roasted bell peppers. Just replace regular breadcrumbs with crushed pork rinds. Clever!

Per serving: 367 Calories; 16.9g Fat; 9g Carbs; 43g Protein; 6g Sugars

Ingredients

1 pound chicken breasts, butterflied
1 teaspoon salt
1/4 teaspoon ground black pepper, or more to taste
1 teaspoon fresh or dried dill, chopped
1/3 cup crushed pork rinds
1/3 cup Parmigiano-Reggiano, freshly grated
2 teaspoons vegetable oil
1 garlic clove, minced
3 bell peppers, quartered lengthwise

Directions

- Begin by preheating your oven to 420 degrees F. Cover the sides and bottom of a baking pan with a sheet of foil.
- Place butterflied chicken breast on the baking pan. Season with salt and pepper.
- Now, combine dill, pork rinds, Parmigiano-Reggiano, vegetable oil and garlic clove. Dip each chicken breast into this mixture.
- Arrange bell peppers around the prepared chicken breasts. Bake for 20 minutes or until juices run clear. Serve immediately and enjoy!

60. Chicken Sausage with Spaghetti Squash

Ready in about 15 minutes
Servings 4

This combination of chicken sausages and spaghetti squash is just wonderful! This is something worth trying!

Per serving: 447 Calories; 37.3g Fat; 5.8g Carbs; 21.3g Protein; 1.6g Sugars

Ingredients

2 teaspoons tallow
1 ½ pounds cheddar & bacon chicken sausages, sliced
1/2 cup yellow onions, finely chopped
1 banana pepper, deveined and finely minced
1 teaspoon garlic, minced
8 ounces spaghetti squash
1 teaspoon kosher salt
1/4 teaspoon black pepper, freshly ground
1 ¼ cups chicken broth
2/3 cup whipped cream

Directions

- Melt the tallow in a pan over a moderate heat. Then, cook the sausages about 8 minutes. Reserve.
- Cook the onions, pepper and garlic in pan drippings.
- Add the squash, salt, black pepper and chicken broth; bring to a boil until the sauce has thickened.
- Stir in the whipped cream and cook until thoroughly heated. Serve with reserved sausages. Bon appétit!

61. Prosciutto-Wrapped Chicken with Cottage Cheese

Ready in about 35 minutes
Servings 2

You don't need to be an expert chef to make this tasty, gourmet chicken dish. Your family will be delighted!

Per serving: 499 Calories; 18.9g Fat; 5.7g Carbs; 41.6g Protein; 3.2g Sugars

Ingredients

1 chicken breasts, boneless, skinless and flattened
1 teaspoon smoked paprika
Salt and ground black pepper, to taste pepper
1/2 cup Cottage cheese
1 tablespoon fresh cilantro, chopped
4 slices of prosciutto

Directions

- Start by preheating your oven to 390 degrees F. Line a baking pan with parchment paper.
- Season chicken breasts with smoked paprika, salt and pepper. Spread Cottage cheese over chicken breasts; scatter fresh cilantro over the top.
- Roll up and cut into 4 pieces. Now, wrap each piece with one slice of prosciutto; secure with a toothpick..
- Place the wrapped chicken in the baking pan; bake for 25 to 35 minutes. Serve warm.

62. Sensational Chicken Wings with Broccoli

Ready in about 50 minutes
Servings 4

Finger-licken' chicken wings can be made right at home with this surprisingly simple recipe. Cruciferous vegetable like broccoli pairs perfectly with crispy chicken wings.

Per serving: 450 Calories; 35.5g Fat; 9.6g Carbs; 25.1g Protein; 2.8g Sugars

Ingredients

1 pound chicken wings
1 pound broccoli, broken into florets
1 carrot, sliced
1 cup scallions, chopped
1 teaspoon garlic paste
1 teaspoon Italian seasoning mix (such as Old Sub Sailor)
3 tablespoons olive oil
2 cups Colby cheese, shredded

Directions

- Preheat your oven to 390 degrees F. Lightly grease a rimmed baking sheet.
- Roast the wings until cooked through and skin is crispy, about 35 minutes. Add broccoli, carrots, scallions, and garlic paste.
- Season the chicken and broccoli with Italian seasoning mix; drizzle them with olive oil.
- Roast an additional 13 to 15 minutes. Scatter shredded cheese over the top and serve warm. Bon appétit!

63. Zesty Chicken with Mayo-Avocado Sauce

Ready in about 20 minutes
Servings 4

If you are looking for clever ways to save the calories, bake lightly greased chicken thighs on a cookie sheet that is covered with foil.

Per serving: 370 Calories; 25g Fat; 4.1g Carbs; 31.4g Protein; 0.7g Sugars

Ingredients

1/3 cup almond meal
Sea salt and pepper, to your liking
1 teaspoon shallot powder
1 teaspoon lime zest
1 teaspoon cayenne pepper
1/3 teaspoon ground cumin
1/4 teaspoon chili flakes
2 eggs
8 chicken thighs, cut into bite-size chunks
2 tablespoons olive oil

For the Sauce:
1/2 cup mayonnaise
1/2 medium Hass avocado
1/2 teaspoon coarse salt
1 teaspoon garlic paste

Directions

- In a food processor, thoroughly combine the meal, salt, pepper, shallot powder, lime zest, cayenne pepper, cumin and chili flakes.
- Whisk the eggs in a separate shallow dish.
- Dry chicken thighs off with a paper towel. Dip chicken chunks in the whisked eggs, then in the almond meal mixture.
- Heat the oil in a skillet over medium heat; fry the chicken for 4 to 6 minutes; turn over and cook on the other side until thoroughly cooked.
- Place on paper towels to soak up excess oil.
- In the meantime, make the sauce by mixing all of the sauce ingredients. Serve warm chicken with sauce and enjoy!

64. Eggplant and Duck Quiche

Ready in about 45 minutes
Servings 4

Ground duck meat has a great texture like beef and an exceptional taste and nutritional benefits like chicken. Serve at room temperature.

Per serving: 562 Calories; 49.5g Fat; 6.7g Carbs; 22.5g Protein; 2.4g Sugars

Ingredients

1 ½ cups almond flour
1/2 teaspoon kosher salt
8 eggs
1 ½ tablespoons butter, melted
1 pound ground duck meat
1/4 teaspoon ground black pepper
1/2 teaspoon celery seeds
1/2 teaspoon basil, dried
1/3 cup whipping cream
1/2 pound eggplant, peeled and sliced

Directions

- Preheat your oven to 350 degrees F
- Mix almond flour with kosher salt. Fold in an egg and melted butter; mix to combine well.
- Now, press the crust into the bottom of a lightly-greased baking dish.
- Then, heat up a skillet and brown ground duck meat for 2 to 3 minutes, stirring continuously.
- In a mixing bowl, combine the remaining eggs with black pepper, celery seeds, basil, and whipping cream.
- Stir in browned meat; stir until everything is thoroughly combined. Pour the mixture into the prepared crust. Add the eggplant slices.
- Bake your quiche for 37 to 42 minutes. Transfer to a wire rack to cool slightly before slicing and serving.

65. Hungarian-Style Chicken Fillets

Ready in about 30 minutes
Servings 6

Hungarian cuisine is well known for its spices such as paprika, which give taste, color and heat to any traditional dish. In this recipe, caraway seeds and lemon rind work well too.

Per serving: 239 Calories; 8.6g Fat; 5.5g Carbs; 34.3g Protein; 3.3g Sugars

Ingredients

1 ½ pounds chicken fillets
1 teaspoon garlic paste
1 teaspoon Hungarian paprika
1/2 teaspoon marjoram
1 teaspoon dry thyme
1 teaspoon coarse salt
1/2 teaspoon freshly ground black pepper
1/2 cup tomato sauce, preferably homemade
1/4 cup low-sodium soy sauce
1 bell pepper, deveined and chopped
1 large-sized red onion, chopped
2 tablespoons curly parsley, for garnish

Directions

- Rub each chicken fillet with the garlic paste and seasonings. Place in a heavy pot that is preheated over medium flame.
- Cook for 4 to 5 minutes on each side.
- Pour in tomato sauce and soy sauce; bring it to a boil. Add bell pepper and onion.
- Reduce the heat to medium-low. Cook, partially covered, for 25 minutes more. Serve warm, garnished with fresh parsley. Bon appétit!

66. Roasted Chicken Wings with Cashew-Basil Pesto

Ready in about 35 minutes
Servings 4

Hot or cold, these chicken wings taste delicious! When it comes to the pesto, use roasted salted cashews for the best results.

Per serving: 580 Calories; 44.8g Fat; 8g Carbs; 38.7g Protein; 1.5g Sugars

Ingredients

1 pound chicken wings, skinless
Salt and ground black pepper, to taste
1 teaspoon cayenne pepper
1 cup scallions

For the Cashew-Basil Pesto:
1/2 cup fresh basil leaves
2 garlic cloves, minced
1/2 cup cashews
1/2 cup Romano cheese
1/2 cup olive oil

Directions

- Begin by preheating your oven to 392 degrees F. Rub the chicken wings with the salt, black pepper, and cayenne pepper.
- Arrange chicken wings in a lightly greased baking dish; scatter scallions around the chicken.
- Roast for 30 minutes, turning the baking dish once.
- In a food processor, pulse basil, garlic, cashews and Romano cheese. Add the oil in a constant tiny stream. Season with sea salt to taste.
- Serve the chicken wings on a platter, garnished with roasted scallions and cashew-basil pesto. Bon appétit!

67. Mediterranean Chicken Breasts

Ready in about 40 minutes
Servings 8

These chicken breasts are healthy and they taste so divine! Best of all, you only need 40 minutes to get your keto dinner ready!

Per serving: 306 Calories; 17.8g Fat; 3.1g Carbs; 31.7g Protein; 1.3g Sugars

Ingredients

4 chicken breasts, skinless and boneless
2 garlic cloves, pressed
1 teaspoon dried oregano
1/2 teaspoon dried basil
2 sprigs thyme
1 sprig rosemary
Salt and ground black pepper, to taste
2 tablespoons peanut oil
1 bell pepper, deveined and thinly sliced
10 Kalamata olives, pitted
1 ½ cups chicken stock

Directions

- Rub chicken breast with the garlic and seasonings. Heat the peanut oil in a pan that is preheated over a moderately high heat.
- Now, fry the chicken until it is browned on all sides, for 4 to 6 minutes.
- Add the remaining ingredients; bring it to boil. Reduce the heat to medium-low. Continue cooking, partially covered, for 30 minutes. Enjoy!

68. Roasted Turkey Legs with Avocado Sauce

Ready in about 1 hour 40 minutes
Servings 4

The meat is ready when the center reaches 180 degrees F on a meat thermometer. If you prefer a crispier skin, broil the turkey legs for 2 to 3 minutes on each side.

Per serving: 362 Calories; 22.3g Fat; 5.6g Carbs; 34.9g Protein; 0.3g Sugars

Ingredients

2 fat turkey legs
1 tablespoon poultry seasoning
1 ½ tablespoons olive oil
For the Sauce:
1 small-sized avocado, pitted and mashed
1 ounce full-fat sour cream
1 ounce mascarpone cheese
1 teaspoon fresh lemon juice
2 tablespoons fresh cilantro, finely chopped
1/3 teaspoon sea salt

Directions

- Preheat your oven to 345 degrees F. Sprinkle the turkey legs with poultry seasoning. Drizzle them with olive oil and lay on a baking sheet.
- Roast the turkey for about 45 minutes; turn over and roast another 50 minutes.
- Meanwhile, make the sauce by whisking all the sauce ingredients; keep in the refrigerator until ready to serve.
- To serve, slice the meat off the bones and serve with your avocado sauce.

69. Chicken with Gorgonzola Panna Cotta

Ready in about 20 minutes + chilling time
Servings 4

If you have never tried a savory panna cotta, here's the perfect chance to do it. Serve this royal meal for the next family dinner and watch it disappear at lightning speed!

Per serving: 483 Calories; 35.2g Fat; 1.5g Carbs; 38.5g Protein; 0.8g Sugars

Ingredients

1 tablespoon olive oil
2 chicken breasts, boneless and skinless
2 gelatin sheets
3/4 cup heavy cream
2 teaspoons granular Swerve
3 tablespoons water
1 cup gorgonzola dolce, crumbled
1/2 teaspoon ground bay leaf
1/2 teaspoon black peppercorns, whole
Salt and cayenne pepper, to your liking

Directions

- Heat olive oil in a heavy-bottomed skillet over moderately high heat; now, fry the chicken breasts for 5 to 6 minutes per side.
- Soak gelatin sheets in cold water for a few minutes to soften. Place in a pan; add the cream, Swerve, water and cheese.
- Add the spices. Simmer over a low flame, stirring for 2 to 4 minutes. Evenly divide the mixture between 4 ramekins.
- Place in your refrigerator overnight. To serve, run a thin knife around edge of panna cotta; now, flip ramekin onto a serving plate.
- Serve with fried chicken breasts. Bon appétit!

70. Mediterranean Chicken Legs in Sauce

Ready in about 50 minutes
Servings 6

Doubtless, with this recipe, you can bring Mediterranean aroma and flavor into your own kitchen. This chicken recipe might become a big hit in your home!

Per serving: 333 Calories; 20.2g Fat; 2g Carbs; 33.5g Protein; 0.3g Sugars

Ingredients

2 tablespoons ghee
1 ½ pounds chicken legs, skinless
1/2 cup scallions, chopped
2 garlic cloves, minced
1/2 cup dry sherry
1 rosemary sprig, chopped
2 thyme sprigs, chopped
1 tablespoon fresh oregano, chopped
1 tablespoon fresh basil, chopped
1 cup heavy cream
1/2 teaspoon salt
1/2 teaspoon mixed peppercorns, freshly crushed

Directions

- Preheat your oven to 400 degrees F.
- Melt the ghee in a pan that is preheated over a moderate flame; now, brown the chicken legs for 6 to 8 minutes.
- After that, stir in the scallions, garlic, sherry, and herbs. Transfer to a lightly greased casserole dish and cover it.
- Bake for 35 minutes or until a meat thermometer registers 165 degrees F; reserve.
- Mix cooking juices with heavy cream, salt and crushed peppercorns; simmer for a couple of minutes or until it is thickened and cooked through. Serve with reserved chicken. Bon appétit!

71. Fried Chinese Cabbage with Ground Turkey

Ready in about 45 minutes
Servings 4

You don't have to make a rock-solid plan to stay on your keto diet during the holidays. It will be easy with this amazing recipe. Make this unusual turkey recipe and delight your guests!

Per serving: 263 Calories; 22.8g Fat; 5.2g Carbs; 9.8g Protein; 2.7g Sugars

Ingredients

1 tablespoon canola oil
1/2 cup shallots, chopped
1 teaspoon fresh garlic, minced
1 pound Chinese cabbage, finely chopped
2 ripe tomatoes, chopped
1/2 teaspoon dried basil
1/2 teaspoon dried marjoram
1/2 teaspoon mustard seeds
1/3 teaspoon fennel seeds
Coarse salt and ground black pepper, to taste
1/2 pound turkey ground
2 slices smoked bacon, chopped

Directions

- Heat canola oil in a pan over a moderate flame. Now, cook the shallots and garlic until aromatic.
- Now, add the cabbage along with tomatoes and all seasonings. Cook an additional 5 minutes or until the leaves are wilted.
- Stir in ground turkey and chopped bacon. Turn the heat to medium-low and cook an additional 35 minutes, crumbling the meat with a wooden spatula.
- Serve warm in individual bowls. Bon appétit!

72. Smoked Turkey and Goat Cheese Spread

Ready in about 10 minutes
Servings 6

Nothing beats a cheesy, smoky spread on a luxury dinner party! A fresh flavor of cilantro will brighten the entire dish but you can substitute it with fresh chives or parsley.

Per serving: 212 Calories; 18.8g Fat; 2g Carbs; 10.6g Protein; 0.5g Sugars

Ingredients

4 ounces smoked turkey ham, chopped
4 ounces goat cheese, crumbled
2 tablespoons fresh cilantro, roughly chopped
2 tablespoons flaxseed meal
2 tablespoons sunflower seeds

Directions

- Combine all ingredients in your food processor until everything is well incorporated.
- Place in a serving bowl and scatter sunflower seeds over the top. Serve with veggie sticks and enjoy!

73. Chicken Fillets with Herby Sauce

Ready in about 15 minutes
Servings 6

These chicken fillets are definitely one of the best options to make your family meal a delicious pleasure. In this recipe, you can substitute chicken drumettes for fillets with the same result.

Per serving: 357 Calories; 26.2g Fat; 0.6g Carbs; 29.2g Protein; 0g Sugars

Ingredients

1 ½ tablespoons olive oil
1 ½ pounds chicken fillets
1 teaspoon kosher salt
1/2 teaspoon ground black pepper
1 stick butter
1 teaspoon garlic, finely minced
2 tablespoons shallots, finely minced
1/3 cup fresh cilantro, chopped
2 teaspoons apple cider vinegar

Directions

- Heat olive oil in a nonstick skillet that is preheated over a medium heat. Now, fry the chicken fillets on both sides for 10 minutes or until they're browned.
- In a mixing dish, thoroughly combine the remaining ingredients.
- Serve with fried chicken fillets and enjoy!

74. Cheesy Turkey Meatballs with Basil Chutney

Ready in about 30 minutes
Servings 6

A dish fit for the gods – it has a few layers of flavor that burst in your mouth! Be sure to choose a premium-quality turkey meat and you can't go wrong.

Per serving: 390 Calories; 27.2g Fat; 1.8g Carbs; 37.4g Protein; 0.5g Sugars

Ingredients

2 tablespoons olive oil

For the Meatballs:
1 ½ pounds ground turkey
1/2 teaspoon sea salt
1/4 teaspoon ground black pepper, or more to taste
3 tablespoons flax seed meal
1/2 cup Parmesan cheese, grated
1/2 teaspoon paprika
1/2 teaspoon garlic powder
1/2 teaspoon onion powder
1/4 teaspoon dried thyme
1/2 teaspoon celery seeds
2 small-sized eggs, lightly beaten

For the Basil Chutney:
2 tablespoons fresh lemon juice
1/2 cup fresh basil leaves
1/2 cup coriander leaves
1 teaspoon fresh ginger root, grated
2 tablespoons olive oil
2 tablespoons water
Salt and pepper, to taste
1 tablespoon green chili, minced

Directions

- Thoroughly combine all ingredients for the meatballs. Divide the mixture into 16 meatballs and reserve.
- Heat 2 tablespoons of olive oil in a cast-iron skillet that is preheated over a moderate heat. Brown the meatballs for 7 to 8 minutes on all sides.
- Then, prepare the chutney by mixing all the chutney ingredients in your food processor. Make sure to blend very well.
- Serve warm meatballs with basil chutney on the side.

75. Crock Pot Turkey Legs

Ready in about 6 hours
Servings 6

This mouthwatering recipe will take ordinary turkey legs from bland to outstanding! To serve, add a few sprinkles of paprika over warm gravy to enhance a visual impression.

Per serving: 280 Calories; 22.2g Fat; 4.3g Carbs; 15.8g Protein; 1.7g Sugars

Ingredients

2 turkey legs
1 tablespoon butter
1 tablespoon mustard
4 garlic cloves, sliced
1 leek, chopped
Salt and pepper, to taste
1 teaspoon dried rosemary
1/2 teaspoon smoked paprika
For the Gravy:
1/2 stick butter
1 cup heavy cream
3/4 teaspoon guar gum
Salt and pepper, to taste

Directions

- Rub turkey legs with 1 tablespoon of butter and mustard.
- Add turkey legs to a heavy-bottomed skillet that is preheated over moderately high heat. Brown the turkey legs for a couple of minutes on all sides.
- Transfer browned turkey to your crock pot; reserve the fat in the skillet. Now, add the garlic, leeks, salt, pepper, rosemary, and paprika.
- Cook on low for 6 hours; reserve.
- Warm 1/2 stick of the butter in the skillet with reserved fat over a moderate flame. Add heavy cream and whisk until heated through.
- Next, stir in guar gum, salt, and pepper. Allow the sauce to thicken, whisking continuously. Serve with warm turkey drumsticks and enjoy!

76. Grandma's Cauliflower and Turkey Soup

Ready in about 35 minutes
Servings 4

An old-fashioned, classic recipe that you have probably inherited from your grandma. This is something worth trying!

Per serving: 274 Calories; 14.4g Fat; 9.6g Carbs; 26.7g Protein; 4.1g Sugars

Ingredients

2 tablespoons sesame oil
2 shallots, chopped
2 garlic cloves, chopped
1 carrot, chopped
1 parsnip, chopped
4 ½ cups chicken stock
1/2 head cauliflower, broken into florets
1 pound turkey thighs
1 rosemary sprig
1/2 teaspoon celery seeds
2 bay leaves
Salt and ground black pepper, to your liking
1/2 teaspoon cayenne pepper
4 dollops of sour cream

Directions

- Heat sesame oil in a heavy pot that is preheated over a moderate flame. Now, sauté the shallots and garlic until they're aromatic.
- After that, stir in the carrots and parsnip; cook until they are softened, stirring constantly. Pour in the chicken stock, bringing to a boil.
- Add the cauliflower, turkey, rosemary, celery seeds, bay leaves, salt, black pepper and cayenne pepper.
- Reduce heat to medium-low; let it simmer for 25 to 30 minutes.
- Lastly, ladle the soup into four individual bowls. Serve with sour cream and enjoy!

77. Leftover Chicken Chowder

Ready in about 35 minutes
Servings 4

Use leftover chicken in this rich, rustic chowder and cheer yourself up during winter months. It will surprise you with its taste and aroma. Yummy!

Per serving: 350 Calories; 25.8g Fat; 9.5g Carbs; 20g Protein; 7.8g Sugars

Ingredients

2 tablespoons coconut oil
A bunch of scallions, chopped
2 cloves garlic, roughly chopped
1/2 pound leftover roast chicken, shredded and skin removed
2 rosemary sprigs
1 thyme sprigs
1 bay leaves
1 tablespoon chicken bouillon granules
3 cups water
1 ½ cups milk
1/2 cup whipped cream
1 whole egg, lightly beaten
2 tablespoons dry sherry

Directions

- Melt the coconut oil in a stockpot over a moderate flame. Now, sauté the scallions and garlic until they're just tender and aromatic.
- Add the chicken, seasonings, chicken bouillon granules and water; bring to a boil. Cook your chowder, partially covered, for 20 minutes.
- Lower the heat. Pour in the milk and whipped cream and cook until it has thickened. Add the egg and cook, stirring constantly, 1 to 2 minutes longer.
- Taste and adjust the seasonings. Afterwards, drizzle each serving with dry sherry and serve right away!

78. Absolutely Incredible Turkey Kebabs

Ready in about 30 minutes
Servings 6

Give this classic a full-on makeover with flavorful rub and colorful veggies. Party in your mouth!

Per serving: 293 Calories; 13.8g Fat; 8.7g Carbs; 34.5g Protein; 4.9g Sugars

Ingredients

1 ½ pounds British turkey diced thigh
2 tablespoons butter, at room temperature
1 tablespoon dry ranch seasoning
2 orange bell peppers, sliced
1 red bell peppers, sliced
1 green bell peppers, sliced
1 zucchini, cut into thick slices
1 red onion, cut into wedges
1 cucumber, sliced
1 cup radishes, sliced
2 tablespoons red wine vinegar
1 tablespoon fresh parsley, roughly chopped

Directions

- Rub the turkey with softened butter and toss with dry ranch seasoning. Thread the turkey pieces onto skewers.
- Alternate with bell peppers, zucchini, and onion until all the ingredients are used up. Now, place your skewers in the refrigerator while you're lighting the grill.
- Grill your kebabs, turning periodically, for 9 minutes or until they are cooked through.
- In the meantime, toss the cucumbers and radishes with red wine vinegar and fresh parsley.
- Serve kebabs immediately with the cucumber-radicchio salad on the side. Bon appétit!

79. Easy Grilled Chicken Salad

Ready in about 20 minutes
Servings 4

This chicken salad is healthy and it tastes so divine! Best of all, you only need 20 minutes to get your keto dinner ready!

Per serving: 408 Calories; 34.2g Fat; 4.8g Carbs; 22.7g Protein; 0.4g Sugars

Ingredients

2 chicken breasts
1/2 teaspoon sea salt
1/3 teaspoon red pepper flakes, crushed
1/4 teaspoon dried thyme, or more to taste
1 large-sized avocado, pitted and sliced
2 egg yolks
1 tablespoon lime juice
1/2 teaspoon mustard powder
1/3 teaspoon sea salt
1/3 cup olive oil
1 tablespoon Worcestershire sauce

Directions

- Preheat your grill on high. Season the chicken breasts with salt, pepper and thyme. Now, grill the chicken for 3 to 5 minutes on each side.
- Cut the grilled chicken into the strips.
- Divide avocado slices among four serving plates.
- Then, prepare the dressing. In a mixing dish or a measuring cup, thoroughly combine the remaining ingredients.
- Place the chicken strips on the serving plates and drizzle with the prepared dressing. Enjoy!

80. Spicy Chicken Strips with Hemp Seeds

Ready in about 55 minutes
Servings 6

When you run out of ideas, here is the perfect solution – roasted chicken with whatever vegetables you have on hand. Just make sure to use keto vegetables if possible.

Per serving: 420 Calories; 28.2g Fat; 5g Carbs; 35.3g Protein; 2.6g Sugars

Ingredients

3 chicken breasts, cut into strips
1/2 stick butter
Salt and pepper, to taste
2 tablespoons soy sauce
3 teaspoons apple cider vinegar
1/2 teaspoon hot chili sauce, sugar-free
2 tablespoons tomato paste
2 cloves garlic, minced
2 eggs
1/4 cup hemp seeds

Directions

- Preheat your oven to 410 degrees F. Lightly grease a baking dish with a nonstick cooking spray.
- Now, rub chicken wings with the butter, salt, and pepper.
- Drizzle with soy sauce, vinegar, chili sauce, tomato sauce and garlic. Let it marinate at least 30 minutes in your refrigerator.
- In a mixing dish, whisk the eggs with hemp seeds. Dip each chicken strip in the hemp mixture. Transfer your chicken to the baking dish.
- Bake for 20 to 25 minutes, turning once. You can broil these chicken strips to make them crispy, if desired.
- Serve garnished with fresh chives.

81. Chicken Fillets with Cream-Mustard Sauce

Ready in about 25 minutes
Servings 4

Tender, buttery chicken in a tangy and thick sauce! And the best is yet to come – You will have this 5-star meal done in no time!

Per serving: 311 Calories; 16.9g Fat; 2.1g Carbs; 33.6g Protein; 0.4g Sugars

Ingredients

1 pound chicken fillets
Salt and pepper, to taste
1 tablespoon butter, melted
1/2 cup scallions, chopped
1 teaspoon garlic paste
1/4 cup dry white wine
1/4 cup low-sodium chicken broth
1/2 cup double cream
2 tablespoons whole grain mustard
1/2 cup fresh cilantro, roughly chopped

Directions

- Rub the chicken fillets with salt and pepper to your liking.
- Melt the butter in a saucepan that is preheated over a moderate flame. Now, cook the chicken fillets until they are just barely done. Transfer the chicken to a plate and set it aside.
- Add the scallions and garlic paste to the saucepan; cook, stirring often, until it is aromatic or about 4 minutes.
- Raise the heat to medium-high; pour in wine and scrape the bits that may be stuck to the bottom of your saucepan.
- Next, pour in the broth; allow the liquid to reduce by about half. Stir in double cream and mustard.
- Pour the sauce over the reserved chicken fillets and serve garnished with fresh cilantro. Enjoy!

82. Easy and Yummy Chicken Drumettes

Ready in about 30 minutes
Servings 4

Give your chicken drumettes a simple but delicious make-over. Adding melted tallow and turkey stock makes all the difference.

Per serving: 165 Calories; 9.8g Fat; 7.7g Carbs; 12.4g Protein; 3.9g Sugars

Ingredients

2 tablespoons tallow
4 chicken drumettes
Salt, to taste
1/2 cup leeks, chopped
1 carrot, sliced
2 cloves garlic, minced
1 teaspoon cayenne pepper
1 teaspoon dried marjoram
1/2 teaspoon mustard seeds
1 cup turkey stock
2 tomatoes, crushed
1 tablespoon Worcestershire sauce
1 teaspoon mixed peppercorns
1 thyme sprig
1 rosemary sprig

Directions

- Melt the tallow in a saucepan over medium-high heat. Sprinkle the chicken drumettes with the salt.
- Then, fry the chicken drumettes until they are no longer pink and lightly browned on all sides; reserve.
- Now, cook the leeks, carrots and garlic in pan drippings over medium heat for 4 to 6 minutes.
- Reduce the heat to simmer, and add the remaining ingredients along with the reserved chicken. Simmer, partially covered, for 15 to 20 minutes. Serve warm.

83. Chicken Sausage with Salsa

Ready in about 15 minutes
Servings 4

If you prefer a more authentic Mexican flavor, make your own salsa sauce. It is also budget-friendly because you can freeze leftovers for later.

Per serving: 156 Calories; 4.2g Fat; 11.1g Carbs; 16.2g Protein; 5.4g Sugars

Ingredients

2 teaspoons lard, room temperature
4 chicken sausage, sliced
1/4 cup Sauvignon Blanc
1 cup pureed tomatoes
1 teaspoon granulated garlic
2 bell peppers, deveined and chopped
1 minced jalapeno, chopped
1 cup onion, diced
2 tablespoons fresh cilantro, minced
3 teaspoons lime juice

Directions

- Warm the lard in a heavy-bottomed skillet over moderately high heat.
- Sauté the sausage until well browned; pour in the wine and cook an additional 3 minutes. Reserve.
- Then, make the salsa by mixing pureed tomatoes, garlic, bell pepper, jalapeno pepper, onions, cilantro and lime juice.
- Serve the sausage with the salsa on the side. Bon appétit!

84. Turkey Sausage with Bok Choy

Ready in about 50 minutes
Servings 4

On the average, turkey sausages (mild breakfast links), have 4 grams of carbohydrates in 100 grams of product. Smoked sausage has about 8.4 grams of carbohydrates per serving size (2 ounces) while fresh raw sausages have 1.8 grams of carbohydrates per 100 grams of product.

Per serving: 189 Calories; 12g Fat; 12.6g Carbs; 9.4g Protein; 3g Sugars

Ingredients

1 tablespoon butter
4 mild turkey sausages, breakfast links, sliced
2 shallots, chopped
Coarse salt and ground black pepper, to taste
1 pound Bok choy, tough stem ends trimmed
1 cup chicken stock
1/2 cup full-fat milk
1/8 teaspoon freshly grated nutmeg
6 ounces Gruyère, coarsely grated

Directions

- Start by preheating an oven to 360 degrees F. Melt the butter in a pan; now, brown the sausage for a couple of minutes, stirring periodically; reserve.
- Add the shallots, salt, pepper, and Bok choy. Add the chicken stock and cook until just tender, 2 to 3 minutes.
- Spread the Bok choy mixture in a lightly greased baking dish. Top with reserved sausage.
- In a mixing bowl, thoroughly combine chicken stock, milk, and nutmeg. Pour the mixture over the sausage.
- Cover with a piece of foil and bake for 40 minutes. Remove the foil and scatter grated cheese over the top.
- Bake in upper third of oven an additional 4 minutes or until bubbly.

85. Easy Herby Turkey Drumsticks

Ready in about 1 hour
Servings 2

Turkey drumsticks are delicious and so fun to eat! A marinade will give a great flavor and keep turkey meat juicy, making it buttery tender on the grill.

Per serving: 488 Calories; 24.5g Fat; 2.1g Carbs; 33.6g Protein; 0.5g Sugars

Ingredients

2 tablespoons apple cider vinegar
2 thyme sprigs, chopped
2 rosemary sprigs, chopped
1 teaspoon dried marjoram
1 teaspoon dried basil
1 teaspoon granulated garlic
2 tablespoons olive oil
2 turkey drumsticks
Salt and black pepper, to taste
1/2 cup Taco bell sauce

Directions

- To make the marinade, thoroughly combine apple cider vinegar, thyme, rosemary, marjoram, basil, granulated garlic, and olive oil in a mixing bowl.
- Now, marinate the turkey at least 3 hours in the refrigerator.
- Cook turkey drumsticks on a preheated grill for 45 minutes to 1 hour or until a meat thermometer has reached the temperature of 180 degrees F. Season with salt and pepper to taste.
- Serve with Taco bell sauce on the side. Bon appétit!

86. Mediterranean Chicken Drumsticks with Aioli

Ready in about 35 minutes
Servings 4

This Mediterranean dish is a delightful combination of a crispy, flavorful chicken and savory, tangy dressing. Kalamata olives combine beautifully with Halloumi cheese in this recipe.

Per serving: 562 Calories; 43.8g Fat; 2.1g Carbs; 40.8g Protein; 1g Sugars

Ingredients

1 ½ tablespoons ghee
4 chicken drumsticks
Sea salt and crushed mixed peppercorns, to taste
1 tablespoon fresh parsley, chopped
6 Kalamata olives, pitted and halved
1 cup Halloumi cheese, cubed
1 hard-boiled egg yolk
1 tablespoon garlic, finely minced
1 tablespoon lemon juice
1/2 cup extra-virgin olive oil
1/4 teaspoon sea salt

Directions

- Preheat your oven to 395 degrees F.
- Melt the ghee in a nonstick skillet.
- Season chicken drumsticks with salt and crushed peppercorns; brown chicken drumsticks in hot skillet for 3 to 4 minutes.
- Arrange the fried chicken on a baking sheet; scatter fresh parsley and olives over the top.
- In the meantime, make Aioli by mixing the remaining ingredients, except for cheese, with an immersion blender. Mix until it comes together.
- Now, spread Aioli over fried chicken. Bake in the preheated oven approximately 25 minutes. Add Halloumi on top and bake an additional 3 to 4 minutes. Serve warm.

87. Ground Chicken with Peppers and Asiago Cheese

Ready in about 15 minutes
Servings 4

You'll be making this easy chicken dish on repeat all year long. Use the peppers of different colors to make an interesting and kid-friendly skillet.

Per serving: 301 Calories; 11.4g Fat; 10.2g Carbs; 37.9g Protein; 0.2g Sugars

Ingredients

1 tablespoon olive oil
1 teaspoon garlic, minced
1 cup shallots, chopped
1 chili pepper, deveined and chopped
4 bell peppers, deveined and chopped
1 pound chicken, ground
1/3 cup dry sherry
1 teaspoon Italian seasonings
Salt and black pepper, to taste
1/2 cup Asiago cheese, shredded

Directions

- Heat the oil in a pan that is preheated over a moderate flame. Now, sauté the garlic and shallots until they are aromatic.
- Now, stir in the peppers and ground chicken; cook until the chicken is no longer pink.
- Add sherry, Italian seasonings, salt and pepper. Cook an additional 5 minutes or until everything is thoroughly heated.
- Scatter Asiago cheese over the top, remove from heat and serve immediately. Bon appétit!

88. The Best Chicken Tacos Ever

Ready in about 20 minutes
Servings 4

Who said tacos can't be ketogenic? Use traditional Mexican Cotija cheese that's excellent for melting and try the easiest and yummiest tacos ever! You can add a few drizzles of lime juice to crispy lettuce leaves in order to complete your meal.

Per serving: 535 Calories; 33.3g Fat; 9.8g Carbs; 47.9g Protein; 3.5g Sugars

Ingredients

2 teaspoons lard, room temperature
2 small-sized white onions, peeled and finely chopped
1 clove garlic, minced
1 pound ground chicken
2 slices bacon, chopped
1 tablespoon Mexican seasoning
Coarse salt and freshly ground black pepper
2 ripe tomatoes, pureed
1 ½ cups Cotija cheese
1/2 cup Pico de gallo
1/2 cup sour cream
1 head lettuce

Directions

- Melt the lard in a pan over moderately high heat. Now, sweat the onions until translucent.
- Add the garlic, chicken, and bacon; continue sautéing until the chicken is no longer pink. Add Mexican seasoning, salt, and black pepper.
- After that, stir in tomatoes and cook for 5 minutes longer; reserve.
- Then, preheat your oven to 360 degrees F. Line a baking sheet with parchment paper. Make 4 piles of shredded cheese and gently press them down.
- Bake cheese piles for 6 minutes in the middle of the preheated oven.
- Let the tacos cool for 5 minutes and add chicken mixture. Serve garnished with Pico de gallo, sour cream, and fresh lettuce leaves.

89. Turkey Soup with Baby Bok Choy

Ready in about 40 minutes
Servings 8

For those who don't know, turkey carcass is leftover from carving a whole turkey. It is a practical way to use the whole turkey.

Per serving: 211 Calories; 11.8g Fat; 3.1g Carbs; 23.7g Protein; 1.5g Sugars

Ingredients

1 tablespoon olive oil
2 stalks celery with leaves, chopped
2 carrots, sliced
1/2 cup onion, halved water to cover salt and pepper to taste
1/2 pound baby Bok choy, sliced into quarters lengthwise
2 pounds turkey carcass
2 teaspoons bouillon granules
1 tablespoon chili garlic sauce
6 cups water

Directions

- Heat the oil in a large pot or Dutch oven over medium-high heat. Sauté the celery, carrots, onion and Bok choy until just tender, about 5 minutes.
- Add the remaining ingredients and bring to a rolling boil.
- Turn the heat to medium-low and cover the pot.
- Cook an additional 30 minutes or until everything is cooked through. Bon appétit!

90. Mom's Turkey Soup

Ready in about 30 minutes
Servings 4

Comforting and irresistible, this healthy turkey soup is loaded with protein and vitamins. Turkey and Greek yogurt are definitely a match made in heaven!

Per serving: 256 Calories; 18.8g Fat; 5.4g Carbs; 15.8g Protein; 3.2g Sugars

Ingredients

- 1/2 cup full fat Greek-style yogurt
- 1/2 stick butter
- 1/2 cup yellow squash, diced
- 2 garlic cloves, minced
- 4 ½ cups chicken broth
- 1/2 teaspoon sea salt
- 1/4 teaspoon ground black pepper
- 1/3 cup heavy cream
- 1 ½ cups leftover turkey, shredded

Directions

- Add Greek-style yogurt, butter, squash, and garlic to a stock pot; bring to a simmer over a medium-low heat.
- Cook until everything is thoroughly warmed. Add the remaining ingredients. Cook another 20 minutes, partially covered, and serve warm.

91. Vodka Duck Fillets

Ready in about 20 minutes
Servings 4

You will love this super-easy poultry lunch. It is extremely delicious and fulfilled, and it takes under 20 minutes to make.

Per serving: 351 Calories; 24.7g Fat; 9.6g Carbs; 22.1g Protein; 4.6g Sugars

Ingredients

- 1 tablespoon lard, room temperature
- 4 duck fillets
- 4 green onions, white and green parts, chopped
- Salt and cayenne pepper, to taste
- 1 teaspoon mixed peppercorns
- 1 ½ cups turkey stock
- 3 tablespoons Worcestershire sauce
- 2 ounces vodka
- 1/2 teaspoon ground bay leaf
- 1/2 cup sour cream

Directions

- Melt the lard in a skillet that is preheated over medium-high heat. Sear duck fillets, turning once, for 4 to 6 minutes.
- Now, add the remaining ingredients, except for the sour cream, to the skillet. Cook, partially covered, for a further 7 minutes.
- Serve warm, garnished with sour cream. Bon appétit!

92. Spicy Chicken with Brussels Sprouts

Ready in about 20 minutes
Servings 4

Have you missed spicy chicken breasts? Try this recipe and enjoy unexpected aromas and flavors! The star of this dish is chipotle chile powder that will give a smoky flavor and spiciness to the entire meal.

Per serving: 273 Calories; 15.4g Fat; 12.2g Carbs; 23g Protein; 3.1g Sugars

Ingredients

2 tablespoons sesame oil
1 ½ pounds Brussels sprouts, trimmed and cut into halves
1/4 teaspoon seasoned salt
2 cloves garlic, minced
3/4 pound chicken breasts, chopped into bite-sized pieces
1/2 cup white onions, chopped
1 cup bone broth, low-sodium
2 tablespoons Sauvignon wine
1/2 teaspoon chipotle chile powder
1/2 teaspoon whole black peppercorns
2 tablespoons fresh chives, chopped

Directions

- Heat 1 tablespoon of oil in a pan over a moderate heat. Now, sauté the Brussels sprouts for 2 to 4 minutes or until golden brown. Season with salt; reserve.
- Heat remaining 1 tablespoon of oil in the same pan that is preheated over moderately high heat Add the garlic and chicken; cook about 3 minutes.
- Add the onions, broth, wine, chipotle chile powder, and black peppercorns. Bring to a boil and reduce the heat to a simmer. Simmer for 4 minutes more.
- Add the reserved Brussels sprouts to the pan and serve warm garnished with fresh chopped chives. Bon appétit!

93. Classic Tarragon Chicken Salad

Ready in about 20 minutes
Servings 4

If you are following a ketogenic diet, then you should try this chicken salad for sure! Use white and dark chicken meat for the best results!

Per serving: 353 Calories; 23.5g Fat; 7.8g Carbs; 27.8g Protein; 2.2g Sugars

Ingredients

2 cups shredded skinless, boneless rotisserie chicken
2 avocados, pitted, peeled and diced
1 red onion, thinly sliced
1 tablespoon fresh tarragon, chopped
1/3 cup plain Greek yogurt
1/4 cup canola mayonnaise
1 tablespoon Dijon mustard
Salt and black pepper, to taste
3 hard-boiled eggs, cut into quarters

Directions

- Add shredded chicken and diced avocado to a mixing bowl. Toss with onion and tarragon.
- Stir in Greek yogurt, mayonnaise, and mustard; season with salt and pepper to taste and gently stir to combine well.
- Transfer to a nice salad bowl, garnish with hard-boiled eggs and serve well-chilled.

94. Chorizo with Asiago Cheese

Ready in about 20 minutes
Servings 4

This Italian spin on a classic sausage dish will blow your mind! Chorizo is an ultimate comfort food and it is sure to satisfy the whole family.

Per serving: 330 Calories; 17.2g Fat; 8.5g Carbs; 34.4g Protein; 1.5g Sugars

Ingredients

1 tablespoon extra-virgin olive oil
16 ounces smoked turkey and chicken chorizo, crumbled
4 spring onions, chopped
1 teaspoon garlic paste
Sea salt and ground black pepper, to taste
3/4 teaspoon ground ginger
1 teaspoon sage, dried
1 teaspoon basil
1 tomato, pureed
2 tablespoons ketchup
1 tablespoon dry sherry
1 teaspoon chili powder
2 tablespoons fresh parsley, roughly chopped
1 ½ cups Asiago cheese, grated

Directions

- Start by preheating an oven to 370 degrees F.
- Heat the oil in a heavy-bottomed over moderately high heat. Now, brown the ground turkey, along with onion for 5 to 6 minutes. Make sure to stir continuously, crumbling the meat.
- Add the garlic paste, salt, pepper, ginger, sage, basil, and tomato puree. Cook for a couple of minutes more or until everything is heated through.
- Add the remaining ingredients, ending with grated cheese; cook an additional 8 minutes or until cheese has completely melted.
- Garnish with avocado and cilantro. Serve with sour cream. Enjoy!

95. Creamy Cauliflower and Chicken Soup

Ready in about 30 minutes
Servings 6

Transform holiday leftovers into a completely new keto dish with this appetizing recipe. This soup freezes and reheats well.

Per serving: 231 Calories; 18.2g Fat; 5.9g Carbs; 11.9g Protein; 1.5g Sugars

Ingredients

1/2 stick butter
1/2 cup shallot, finely chopped
1 spring garlic, finely minced
1 celery, chopped
1/2 teaspoon kosher salt
1/4 teaspoon ground white pepper
1/4 teaspoon ground black pepper, or more to the taste
2 ½ cups water
3 cups chicken stock
1 cup leftover roast chicken, shredded
1 ¼ cups heavy cream
1 head cauliflower, broken into small-sized florets

Directions

- Melt the butter in a stock pot over a moderate heat. Now, sauté the shallot, spring garlic and celery for 4 minutes or until they're tender, stirring periodically.
- Then, stir in the salt, white pepper and black pepper, bringing to a boil. Add the remaining ingredients and lower the temperature; continue to simmer for 25 minutes.
- After that, blend the mixture with an immersion blender and serve immediately in individual bowls, garnished with dill pickles.

96. Cheesy Turkey Dip with Fresno Chiles

Ready in about 25 minutes
Servings 4

If you don't like spicy food, reduce the amount of heat in Fresno chiles by removing the white veins or simply omit the chiles.

Per serving: 284 Calories; 19g Fat; 3.2g Carbs; 26.7g Protein; 1g Sugars

Ingredients

Nonstick cooking spray
1 tablespoon olive oil
1 onion, chopped
1 garlic clove, minced
1 pound ground turkey
1 ½ cups Cottage cheese, creamed, 4% fat, softened
1/4 cup Greek-style yogurt
Salt and black pepper, to taste
1 Fresno chile, minced
1 teaspoon dried oregano
1/2 cup blue cheese, shredded
1 ½ cups Gruyère, shredded

Directions

- Preheat an oven to 360 degrees F. Lightly grease a baking pan with a nonstick cooking spray.
- Heat up a skillet over a moderately high flame. Heat the oil and sauté the onion and garlic until the onions are translucent.
- Now, brown the turkey until it is no longer pink; reserve.
- In a bowl, mix Cottage cheese and Greek yogurt until creamy and uniform. Add the salt, pepper, Fresno chiles and oregano along with the reserved turkey/onion mixture.
- Spoon into prepared baking dish; scatter shredded cheese on top. Bake approximately 18 minutes or until thoroughly heated. Serve with fresh veggie sticks.

97. Habanero and Turkey Bacon Balls

Ready in about 5 minutes
Servings 4

These fatty balls go perfectly with pickles or fresh veggie sticks. They are so delicious that you won't miss any bread or crackers.

Per serving: 195 Calories; 16.7g Fat; 2.2g Carbs; 8.8g Protein; 1.3g Sugars

Ingredients

4 ounces turkey bacon, chopped
4 ounces Cottage cheese
1 tablespoon butter, cold
1 habanero pepper, deveined and minced
1 teaspoon fresh sage, minced
2 tablespoons chives, finely chopped

Directions

- Thoroughly combine the bacon, cheese, butter, habanero pepper and fresh sage.
- Shape this mixture into 8 balls.
- Place finely chopped chives on a plate; roll your balls through to coat. Serve right away!

98. Oven Fried Crispy Chicken Legs

Ready in about 50 minutes
Servings 4

Here's a ridiculously simple trick to make crispy chicken legs that are tender and juicy on the inside. Just keep reading the recipe.

Per serving: 345 Calories; 14.1g Fat; 0.4g Carbs; 50.8g Protein; 0g Sugars

Ingredients

4 chicken legs
1 tablespoon butter
1 teaspoon bouillon powder
1/4 teaspoon ground black pepper, or more to the taste
Salt, to your liking
1 teaspoon paprika
1 teaspoon dried basil
1 teaspoon dried rosemary

Directions

- Start by preheating an oven to 420 degrees F. Line a rimmed baking sheet with a piece of parchment paper.
- Next, air-dry chicken legs and rub them with the butter. Then, sprinkle the chicken with all remaining ingredients.
- Arrange chicken legs out in a single layer on the prepared baking sheet.
- Bake chicken legs until skin is crispy, about 45 minutes. Serve with your favorite hot sauce.

99. Holiday Turkey Wrapped in Prosciutto

Ready in about 30 minutes
Servings 6

You don't need to be an expert chef to make this tasty, gourmet turkey dish. Your guests will be delighted!

Per serving: 286 Calories; 9.7g Fat; 7.9g Carbs; 39.9g Protein; 5.4g Sugars

Ingredients

2 pounds turkey breasts, marinated
1 ½ tablespoons coconut butter, room temperature
1 teaspoon cayenne pepper
1/2 teaspoon chili powder
1 sprig rosemary, finely chopped
2 sprigs fresh thyme, finely chopped
2 tablespoons Cabernet Sauvignon
1 teaspoon garlic, finely minced
1 teaspoon sea salt
1/2 teaspoon freshly ground black pepper
10 strips prosciutto

Directions

- Cut the turkey breasts into 10 even slices.
- Melt the coconut butter in a nonstick skillet over a moderate heat. Sear the turkey breasts for 2 to 3 minutes on each side.
- Sprinkle turkey breasts with all seasonings and minced garlic; drizzle with wine. Now, wrap each turkey piece into one prosciutto strip.
- Preheat your oven to 450 degrees F. Lay the wrapped turkey in a roasting pan; roast about 25 minutes.
- Serve garnished with fresh cilantro. Bon appétit!

100. Tomato Rum-Glazed Chicken Thighs

Ready in about 1 hour + marinating time
Servings 4

Is there anything better than glazed chicken thighs during autumn weeknights? Rum, tomato and chicken go hand in hand so you will love these boozy wings.

Per serving: 307 Calories; 12.1g Fat; 2.7g Carbs; 33.6g Protein; 1g Sugars

Ingredients

2 pounds chicken thighs
2 tablespoons olive oil
Sea salt and ground black pepper, to taste
1 teaspoon paprika
1 teaspoon dried oregano
1 teaspoon dried marjoram
2 ripe tomatoes, pureed
3/4 cup dark rum
3 tablespoons soy sauce
2 tablespoons Swerve
2 habanero chile peppers, minced
1 tablespoon minced fresh ginger
1 teaspoon ground allspice
2 tablespoons fresh lime juice, plus wedges for serving

Directions

- Start by preheating your oven to 420 degrees F.
- Now, toss chicken thighs with olive oil, salt, black pepper, paprika, oregano, and marjoram.
- In a separate mixing bowl, thoroughly combine pureed tomato puree, rum, soy sauce, Swerve, habanero peppers, ginger, allspice and fresh lime juice.
- Pour the rum/tomato mixture over chicken thighs and refrigerate, covered, for 2 hours.
- Discard the marinade and arrange chicken thighs on a rimmed baking pan. Bake for 50 minutes or until thoroughly cooked.
- In the meantime, cook the reserved marinade in a pan over a moderate heat; continue to cook until the liquid has reduced by half.
- Pour the sauce over the chicken thighs and place under the broiler for 4 minutes on high. Serve immediately.

PORK

101. The Easiest Meatballs Ever..........................65

102. Peppery Pork with Blue Cheese and Avocado.......65

103. Pork Belly with Homey Barbecue Sauce.................66

104. Oven-Roasted Pork Cutlets with Veggies..............66

105. Juicy Pork Medallions with Scallions.....................67

106. Crock Pot Peppery Pork Ribs.................67

107. Pork Stuffed Peppers with Yogurt-Chive Sauce.....68

108. Rolled Pork Loin with Leeks.................68

109. Grandma's Famous Pork Stew.................69

110. Pork Chops with Ancho Chile Sauce.....................69

111. Crock Pot Spare Ribs.................70

112. Bacon and Blue Cheese Balls.................70

113. Sage and Milk Pork Loin.................71

114. Fried Cabbage with Smoked Ham.................71

115. Grilled Creole-Style Pork Shoulder.................72

116. Pork and Mushroom Stuffed Zucchini.................72

117. Country Pork Goulash with Cauliflower Rice.......73

118. Timeless Pork Stew with Steamed Broccoli............73

119. Mom's Signature Pork Stew.................74

120. Pork Meatballs with Herby Tomato Sauce.............74

121. Spicy Pork Soup.................75

122. Bacon and Sausage Kraut.................75

123. Three-Cheese and Pork Sausage Balls.................76

124. Country Brie-Stuffed Meatballs.................76

125. North Carolina Pulled Pork.................77

126. Breakfast Muffins with Ground Pork.................77

127. Dinner Party Pork Gumbo.................78

128. Pork Meatloaf with Homemade Tomato Sauce......78

129. Pork Shoulder with Blue Cheese Sauce.................79

130. Carrot and Meat Loaf Muffins.................79

131. Hearty Pork Soup with Avocado.................80

132. Greek Souvlaki with Tzatziki Sauce.................80

133. Kansas City-Style Meatloaf.................81

134. Indian-Style Saucy Pork.................81

135. Pork Rib Chops with Spinach.................82

136. Breakfast Pork in a Mug.................82

137. Hot and Creamy Pork Chop Soup.................83

138. Pork Lettuce Wraps.................83

139. Pan-Seared Pork Steaks.................84

140. Grilled Pork and Vegetable Skewers.................84

141. Pork Loin with Cauliflower
and Bamboo Shoots.................85

142. Easy Aromatic Pork Chops.................85

143. Super Crispy Roasted Pork Shoulder.................86

144. Spicy Pork Sausage Frittata.................86

145. Chinese Pork Stir-Fry with Muenster Cheese........87

146. Crock Pot Hungarian Goulash.................87

147. Pork Quiche with Bell Peppers.................88

148. Summer Baby Back Ribs.................88

149. Ground Pork and Swiss Chard Skillet.................89

150. Pork Ribs with Roasted Peppers.................89

151. Holiday Pork and Bacon Meatloaf.................90

101. The Easiest Meatballs Ever

Ready in about 30 minutes
Servings 6

If you are a great believer in a combination of simplicity and tradition, this recipe will be perfect for you! It is important to place your meatball under the broiler. Otherwise, they turn mushy and pretty tasteless.

Per serving: 284 Calories; 14.8g Fat; 1.3g Carbs; 34.4g Protein; 0.3g Sugars

Ingredients

For the Meatballs:
1 pound ground pork
1/2 pound ground beef
1 tablespoon beef bouillon granules
2 small-sized eggs
2 cloves garlic, minced
1 tablespoon Montreal steak seasoning

For the Sauce:
3 teaspoons butter
1/2 teaspoon dried thyme
Salt and pepper to taste
1 cup bone broth
1 cup heavy whipping cream
Salt and pepper, to taste

Directions

- Begin by preheating an oven to 360 degrees F.
- Thoroughly combine all ingredients for the meatballs in a mixing bowl. Shape into 20 balls with oiled hands.
- Arrange the meatballs on a cookie sheet that is previously greased with a nonstick cooking spray.
- Bake for 18 to 22 minutes or until the meatballs are thoroughly cooked. Now, place your meatballs under the broiler for a couple of minutes to achieve a browned, crispy crust.
- Meanwhile, make the sauce in a pan. Firstly, melt the butter over a moderate heat. Slowly and gradually stir in the other ingredients for the sauce, whisking constantly.
- Bring to a boil and cook until the sauce is thickened. Serve the meatballs with the sauce on the side.

102. Peppery Pork with Blue Cheese and Avocado

Ready in about 20 minutes
Servings 2

Here's the perfect ketogenic lunch! A combo of ground pork, fresh vegetables, and full-fat dairy products will blow your mind!

Per serving: 431 Calories; 22.9g Fat; 15.2g Carbs; 42.2g Protein; 4g Sugars

Ingredients

1 tablespoon bacon grease
1/2 pound ground pork
1 bell pepper, deveined and chopped
1 jalapeno pepper, deveined and chopped
1/4 cup beef bone broth
Kosher salt and black pepper, to your liking
1/4 teaspoon marjoram
1 small head of Romaine lettuce, leaves separated
1/2 cup radicchio, trimmed and sliced
1 avocado, pitted, peeled and diced
2 teaspoons fresh lemon juice
2 shallots, chopped
2 tomatoes, diced
1/2 cup Greek yogurt
1/2 cup blue cheese, crumbled

Directions

- Warm the bacon grease in a saucepan over medium heat; now, brown ground pork for 8 minutes or so. Make sure to stir constantly, breaking the meat with a wooden spatula.
- Add the peppers and cook until they are tender and aromatic, approximately 3 minutes. Pour in bone broth; season with salt, pepper, and marjoram; cook an additional 4 to 5 minutes; reserve.
- Create a bed of lettuce leaves on two serving plates. Mound the meat-pepper mixture onto the plate.
- Arrange radicchio and avocado around the meat mixture; drizzle radicchio and avocado with fresh lemon juice.
- Top with shallots and tomatoes. Serve garnished with Greek yogurt and blue cheese. Bon appétit!

103. Pork Belly with Homey Barbecue Sauce

Ready in about 2 hours
Servings 8

Pork belly is the queen of low-carb foods. Serve with a selection of seasonal vegetables.

Per serving: 561 Calories; 34g Fat; 1.7g Carbs; 52.7g Protein; 0.8g Sugars

Ingredients

2 pounds pork belly
2 tablespoons vegetable oil
2 garlic cloves, halved
1 teaspoon salt
1/2 teaspoon freshly ground black pepper
For the Barbecue Sauce:
1/2 cup tomato puree
1 teaspoon hot sauce
1 teaspoon Dijon mustard
A few drops of liquid smoke
1/3 teaspoon ground cumin
1/3 teaspoon smoked paprika

Directions

- Preheat your oven to 420 degrees F.
- Now, rub the pork belly with vegetable oil and garlic. Sprinkle with salt and pepper.
- Roast the pork for 18 to 22 minutes. Now, decrease the heat to 330 degrees F. Roast for a further 1 hour 30 minutes.
- Meanwhile, whisk all ingredients for the barbecue sauce until everything is well blended.
- Remove the crackling and cut the pork belly into slices. Serve with the sauce on the side.

104. Oven-Roasted Pork Cutlets with Veggies

Ready in about 30 minutes + marinating time
Servings 4

On a bed of roasted veggies, pork cutlets are even more delicious! You can use another combo of low-carb vegetables if desired.

Per serving: 452 Calories; 34.8g Fat; 6.7g Carbs; 26.3g Protein; 2.5g Sugars

Ingredients

1 teaspoon garlic paste
1/2 teaspoon sea salt
1/2 teaspoon freshly ground black pepper
1 tablespoon yellow mustard
2 tablespoons cider vinegar
2 tablespoons lard, melted
4 pork cutlets
1 celery stalk, diced
2 carrots, sliced
1 cup leeks, sliced

Directions

- In a mixing bowl, combine the garlic paste, salt, black pepper, mustard and cider vinegar until well mixed. Add the pork cutlets and let them marinate for 2 hours.
- Now, melt the lard in an oven-safe pan over a moderate heat. Brown pork cutlets for 5 minutes on each side. Add the celery, carrots, and leeks.
- Cook an additional 5 minutes, stirring periodically.
- Transfer the pan to the oven; roast the pork with vegetables about 13 minutes. Serve the meat and vegetables along with pan juices. Bon appétit!

105. Juicy Pork Medallions with Scallions

Ready in about 20 minutes
Servings 4

Pan-seared pork medallions are perfect when served over fresh salad or a cauliflower rice. Add Mediterranean herbs and experience an unbelievable burst of flavor.

Per serving: 192 Calories; 6.9g Fat; 0.9g Carbs; 29.8g Protein; 0.4g Sugars

Ingredients

1 pound pork tenderloin, cut crosswise into 12 medallions
Coarse salt and ground black pepper, to taste
1/2 teaspoon garlic powder
1/2 teaspoon red pepper flakes, crushed
1 tablespoon butter
A bunch of scallions, roughly chopped
1 thyme sprig, minced
2 rosemary sprigs, minced
1 teaspoon dried sage, crushed

Directions

- Season each pork medallion with salt, black pepper, garlic powder and red pepper flakes.
- Then, melt the butter in a saucepan over medium-high heat. Cook pork tenderloin about 3 minutes per side.
- Add the scallions, thyme, and rosemary; cook until heated through, an additional 3 minutes. Serve sprinkled with dried sage. Bon appétit!

106. Crock Pot Peppery Pork Ribs

Ready in about 8 hours
Servings 4

The grandma's secret to the perfect pork chops – go nicely and slowly. Don't forget to add the driest red wine you can find like Merlo, Cabernet Sauvignon, Shiraz or Pinot Noir. Enjoy!

Per serving: 192 Calories; 6.9g Fat; 0.9g Carbs; 29.8g Protein; 0.4g Sugars

Ingredients

1 tablespoon lard
1 pound pork ribs
1 teaspoon Ancho chiles, minced
1 bell pepper, thinly sliced
1/4 cup Worcestershire sauce
1/4 cup dry red wine
1/2 teaspoon smoked cayenne pepper
1 garlic clove, crushed
1/2 teaspoon ground oregano
1/2 teaspoon ground cloves
1 teaspoon grated orange peel

Directions

- Treat the sides and bottom of your Crock pot with melted lard. Arrange pork chops and peppers on the bottom.
- Drizzle Worcestershire sauce and wine over everything. Sprinkle with cayenne pepper, garlic, oregano and ground cloves.
- Slow cook on Low setting approximately 8 hours. Serve on individual plates garnished with grated orange peel.

107. Pork Stuffed Peppers with Yogurt-Chive Sauce

Ready in about 40 minutes
Servings 4

Cooking stuffed peppers the same way all the time can get boring. You can use different type of meat and experiment with seasonings. A dollop of Greek yogurt sauce makes a huge difference.

Per serving: 330 Calories; 20.8g Fat; 8.6g Carbs; 27.1g Protein; 4.8g Sugars

Ingredients

6 bell peppers, deveined
1 tablespoon olive oil
1 small-sized yellow onion, chopped
1 garlic clove, minced
1/2 pound ground pork
1/3 pound ground veal
1 ripe tomato, chopped
1/2 teaspoon ground coriander
1/2 teaspoon sea salt
1/4 teaspoon ground black pepper, to taste
1 teaspoon paprika
1/2 cup Greek yogurt
2 tablespoon chives, chopped

Directions

- Parboil the peppers in salted water for 4 to 6 minutes.
- Heat the oil in a pan that is preheated over a moderate flame. Sauté the onions and garlic until tender and aromatic.
- Add the ground meat and cook, crumbling it with a spatula, for 5 to 6 minutes. Add chopped tomatoes and cook an additional 4 minutes or until thoroughly heated.
- Season with ground coriander, salt, black pepper, and paprika. Preheat the oven to 360 degrees F.
- Stuff the peppers and transfer them to a baking dish. Bake approximately 22 minutes.
- Meanwhile, combine Greek yogurt with chopped chives. Divide the peppers among individual serving plates; serve with a dollop of prepared yogurt-chive sauce and enjoy!

108. Rolled Pork Loin with Leeks

Ready in about 1 hour + marinating time
Servings 6

You can crush the thyme, rosemary and celery seeds in a mortar along with the garlic. Keep in mind that Burgundy wine has 1.6 grams of carbohydrates per serving size (4 ounces).

Per serving: 220 Calories; 6g Fat; 3g Carbs; 33.3g Protein; 0.8g Sugars

Ingredients

1 thyme sprig, chopped
1 rosemary sprig, chopped
1 teaspoon mustard seeds
1/2 teaspoon celery seeds
2 garlic cloves, pressed
1 tablespoon butter
1 ½ pounds boneless pork loin, butterflied
1/2 cup Burgundy wine
1 cup bone broth
1 leek, thinly sliced
1 teaspoon whole black peppercorns

Directions

- Pour a boiling water over your pork to ensure a crisp crackling; pat it dry. Spritz a roasting pan with a non-stick cooking spray.
- In a mixing dish, combine the thyme, rosemary, mustard seeds, celery seeds, garlic and butter.
- Unfold the pork loin; spread the herb/butter mixture all over the cut side; roll the pork loin. Secure with kitchen string and place in the roasting pan. Let it marinate at least 2 hours in the refrigerator.
- Preheat your oven to 400 degrees F.
- Add the wine, broth and leeks to the roasting pan; scatter whole peppercorns around the meat. Roast for 55 minutes to 1 hour, until juices run clear. Serve with fresh or pickled salad. Bon appétit!

109. Grandma's Famous Pork Stew

Ready in about 45 minutes
Servings 8

Nothing beats a hearty stew on a winter's night. A fresh flavor of cilantro will brighten the entire dish.

Per serving: 390 Calories; 27.8g Fat; 4.7g Carbs; 28.3g Protein; 2.3g Sugars

Ingredients

2 tablespoons lard, at room temperature
2 pounds pork shoulder, cut into 3/4-inch cubes
1 teaspoon sea salt
1 teaspoon mixed peppercorns, freshly cracked
1 large-sized red onion, chopped
1 chili pepper, minced
2 garlic cloves, finely minced
2 carrots, peeled and chopped
1 celery stalk, chopped
2 tablespoons dry red wine
3 cups beef stock, preferably homemade
2 ripe tomatoes, chopped
1 bay leaf
1/2 teaspoon dried basil
1 ½ teaspoons dried sage
1 teaspoon dried marjoram
1 cup fresh button mushrooms, sliced
1/2 cup fresh cilantro, chopped

Directions

- Melt the lard in a stockpot that is preheated over a moderate heat. Then, brown the meat for a few minutes; season with salt and peppercorns and reserve.
- Then, cook the onions, chili pepper, garlic, carrots and celery until they are tender. Add wine to deglaze the bottom of your pot.
- Add the remaining ingredients, except for fresh cilantro. Cook for 40 minutes, partially covered. Serve topped with fresh cilantro.

110. Pork Chops with Ancho Chile Sauce

Ready in about 30 minutes
Servings 6

Is there anything better than juicy pork chops with a hot, spicy sauce? This pork dish might earn a permanent spot in your keto meal plan.

Per serving: 347 Calories; 29.2g Fat; 0.2g Carbs; 20.2g Protein; 0.2g Sugars

Ingredients

1 tablespoon olive oil
6 pork chops
For the Sauce:
2 Ancho chiles, chopped
1/2 cup bone broth
2 garlic cloves, minced
1/2 teaspoon ground cumin
1 teaspoon dried basil
1/2 teaspoon red pepper flakes, crushed
Salt and ground black pepper, to taste
2 teaspoons olive oil

Directions

- Heat 1 tablespoon of olive oil in a saucepan that is preheated over a moderately high flame. Sear the pork chops until they're well browned and their juices run clear.
- To make the sauce, in a pot, boil Ancho chiles and bone broth for a couple of minutes. Now, remove your pot from the heat; allow the chiles to stand in the hot water for 15 to 25 minutes.
- Add the chiles along with the liquid to a blender or food processor; add the remaining ingredients for the sauce.
- Puree until creamy, smooth and uniform. Serve with warm pork chops and enjoy!

111. Crock Pot Spare Ribs

Ready in about 4 hours 30 minutes
Servings 4

You can totally rely on this foolproof pork recipe and make it for any family gathering! In addition, these spare ribs are surprisingly easy to make!

Per serving: 412 Calories; 22g Fat; 3g Carbs; 46.3g Protein; 1g Sugars

Ingredients

1 tablespoon lard, at room temperature
1 ½ pounds spare ribs
3/4 cup vegetable stock, preferably homemade
2 teaspoons Swerve
2 cloves garlic, chopped
1 Serrano pepper, chopped
A bunch of scallions, chopped
Salt, to taste
1/2 teaspoon ground cumin
1 teaspoon whole black peppercorns
2 bay leaves

Directions

- Melt the lard in a pan over a moderately high heat. Cook spare ribs for 8 minutes, turning occasionally.
- In the meantime, whisk the stock, Swerve, garlic, Serrano pepper, scallions, salt and cumin in a mixing dish.
- Transfer browned spare ribs to your crock pot; pour in the stock mixture. Add black peppercorns and bay leaves.
- Cook for 4 hours 30 minutes on Low heat setting. Serve on a bed of cauliflower rice. Bon appétit!

112. Bacon and Blue Cheese Balls

Ready in about 5 minutes
Servings 4

This recipe is not only rich in vitamin B complex, but it also has a smooth and amazing mouthfeel.

Per serving: 232 Calories; 17.6g Fat; 3.9g Carbs; 14.2g Protein; 1.1g Sugars

Ingredients

3 ounces blue cheese, crumbled
3 ounces Ricotta cheese
1 ½ tablespoons mayonnaise
2 teaspoons ketchup
1/2 cup bacon, chopped
2 tablespoons parsley, chopped

Directions

- Thoroughly combine all ingredients in a mixing dish.
- Shape the mixture into 8 equal balls. Serve well chilled.

113. Sage and Milk Pork Loin

Ready in about 1 hour 35 minutes
Servings 8

Looking for a delicious and satisfying family dish? Pork loin roast is one of the most convenient meat dishes that cooks perfectly in the oven. This time, we will add the milk for even juicier and more flavorful pork loin.

Per serving: 293 Calories; 15.4g Fat; 5.4g Carbs; 31.4g Protein; 4.4g Sugars

Ingredients

3 teaspoons olive oil
2 pounds pork loin
Salt and cayenne pepper, to taste
1 teaspoon dried thyme
1/2 cup shallots, sliced
2 bell peppers, deveined and thinly sliced
2 cup full-fat milk
1 tablespoon dried sage, crushed

Directions

- Start by preheating your oven to 330 degrees F.
- Heat the oil in a pan over a moderate flame. Sear the pork loin in a pan until just browned.
- Transfer the loin to a baking pan. Season with salt, pepper, and thyme. Scatter sliced shallot and peppers around the meat.
- Pour in the milk and cover the pan tightly with a piece of foil. Roast for 1 hour 30 minutes, turning the loin once or twice.
- Carve the pork loin and transfer to a serving plate along with roasted vegetables as well as cooking liquid. Serve garnished with sage leaves. Bon appétit!

114. Fried Cabbage with Smoked Ham

Ready in about 45 minutes
Servings 4

Fried cabbage is a classical low-carb side dish. With the addition of delicious smoked ham, it becomes a complete meal!

Per serving: 93 Calories; 2.6g Fat; 12.1g Carbs; 6.8g Protein; 3.6g Sugars

Ingredients

4 slices smoked ham, chopped
2 medium-sized shallots, diced
1 teaspoon garlic, minced
1 pound green cabbage, shredded
1/2 teaspoon kosher salt, or to taste
1/4 teaspoon cayenne pepper
1/2 teaspoon black peppercorns
1/4 teaspoon ground cumin

Directions

- Cook the ham in a pot over medium-high heat about 8 minutes.
- Add the shallots and garlic; sauté them for 5 to 7 minutes more. Stir in the cabbage and continue stirring for a couple of minutes more, adding a splash of stock if needed.
- Then, sprinkle with kosher salt, cayenne pepper, black peppercorns and ground cumin. Afterwards, turn the heat to low; let it simmer, covered, for 25 minutes longer. Enjoy!

115. Grilled Creole-Style Pork Shoulder

Ready in about 30 minutes + marinating time
Servings 6

Grilled meat become better with rubs! Rubs have an ability to stick to pork when grilled, which gives the meat the flavor and texture. Generally, rubs contain sugar, but we will skip it on a keto diet.

Per serving: 335 Calories; 24.3g Fat; 0.8g Carbs; 26.4g Protein; 0.8g Sugars

Ingredients

Salt and ground black pepper, to taste
1 teaspoon cayenne pepper
3 teaspoons extra-virgin olive oil
2 clove garlic, minced
A few drops of liquid smoke
1 tablespoon Creole seasoning
1 ½ tablespoons Worcestershire sauce
1 ½ pounds pork shoulder, cut into 6 serving portions

Directions

● Mix the salt, black pepper, cayenne pepper, olive oil, garlic, liquid smoke Creole seasoning, and Worcestershire sauce until you get a thick, creamy mixture.
● Rub the pork shoulder on all sides with the spice mixture, covering it completely. Allow it to stand for 1 hour 30 minutes at room temperature.
● Now lightly grease your grill and preheat it. Grill the pork about 18 minutes, turning occasionally.
● Serve with a cauliflower mash and salad of choice. Bon appétit!

116. Pork and Mushroom Stuffed Zucchini

Ready in about 50 minutes
Servings 8

The name says it all! Wonderful, fresh zucchini filled with the sauce of browned pork and fragrant mushrooms, topped with sinfully delicious Colby cheese. Lovely!

Per serving: 230 Calories; 11.8g Fat; 8.5g Carbs; 23.2g Protein; 3.2g Sugars

Ingredients

4 medium-sized zucchinis, cut into halves
2 tablespoons canola oil
2 shallots, chopped
1 garlic clove, pressed
1 pound ground pork
1 cup button mushrooms, chopped
Salt and ground black pepper, to taste
2 tomatoes, pureed
1/2 cup chicken stock
1 cup Colby cheese, freshly grated

Directions

● Scoop out zucchini flesh to create indentations.
● Preheat your oven to 360 degrees F. Then, spritz a baking pan with a nonstick cooking spray.
● Heat the oil in a saucepan over a moderate flame, Now, sweat the shallots for 2 to 3 minutes, stirring continuously.
● Now, add the garlic and cook an additional minute. Stir in ground pork and mushrooms; cook for a further 5 minutes.
● After that, add the pureed tomatoes and chicken stock. Season with salt and pepper.
● Reduce the heat to a medium-low; let it simmer, partially covered, for 10 minutes, stirring periodically.
● Divide the mixture between zucchini halves. Bake about 27 minutes in the preheated oven. Top with freshly grated cheese and serve immediately. Bon appétit!

117. Country Pork Goulash with Cauliflower Rice

Ready in about 25 minutes
Servings 6

Keto lovers claim that pork goulash is an ultimate comfort food. It is delicious and satisfying family lunch, isn't it?!

Per serving: 228 Calories; 8.7g Fat; 5.8g Carbs; 30.1g Protein; 2.6g Sugars

Ingredients

1 tablespoon lard, room temperature
2 white onions, chopped
1 heaping teaspoon garlic paste
1 ¼ pounds ground pork
2 slices bacon, chopped
Salt and red pepper, to taste
1 teaspoon capers
2 ripe Roma tomatoes, crushed
1 ½ cups bone broth
1/2 teaspoon fennel seeds
2 teaspoons smoked cayenne pepper
1 bay leaf
1/2 cup loosely packed fresh cilantro, roughly chopped
2 cups cauliflower rice, cooked

Directions

- Melt the lard in a pan that is preheated over a moderately high heat. Sauté the onions and garlic until just tender and fragrant.
- Stir in ground pork, and cook for 7 minutes, crumbling with a fork or spatula. Add the bacon, salt, red pepper, and capers and cook for 2 minutes more.
- Add the tomatoes, broth, fennel seeds, cayenne pepper, and bay leaf. Turn the heat to medium-low and simmer for 10 to 13 minutes or until everything is heated through.
- Garnish with fresh cilantro and serve with hot cauliflower rice.

118. Timeless Pork Stew with Steamed Broccoli

Ready in about 2 hours
Servings 6

This is a fantastic, classic-style pork stew recipe. Try this recipe next time you're in the mood to make something timeless and traditional.

Per serving: 336 Calories; 15.9g Fat; 8g Carbs; 35g Protein; 3.1g Sugars

Ingredients

1 ½ pounds pork stew meat, cubed
Ground black pepper to taste
1 teaspoon paprika
2 tablespoons lard, at room temperature
1 leek, chopped
1 teaspoon garlic, finely minced
1/4 cup dry red wine
2 bay leaves
1/2 teaspoon celery seeds
3 cups water
1 tablespoon beef bouillon granules
2 bell peppers, chopped
1 habanero pepper, chopped
1 stalk celery, chopped
1 tablespoon fresh coriander, chopped
1 tablespoon flax seed meal
1 cup broccoli, broken into florets

Directions

- Rub the pork stew meat with black pepper and paprika.
- Melt the lard in a stockpot that is preheated over a high flame. Brown the pork about 8 minutes, stirring periodically. Reserve, keeping warm.
- Now, sauté the leeks and garlic in pan drippings for 8 to 9 minutes or until they're tender. Add a splash of dry red wine to scrape up any browned bits from the bottom of your stockpot.
- Add the other ingredients, minus flax seed meal and broccoli. Turn the heat to medium-low and cover the pot; allow it to simmer for 1 hour 45 minutes.
- Now, stir in flax seed meal and continue cooking for 4 minutes more, stirring constantly.
- Meanwhile, fill a large pan with about 1-inch of water; bring to a rolling boil. Cook the broccoli in a steamer basket inside the pan. Steam about 9 minutes or until the broccoli is tender.
- Season with salt to taste and serve with warm pork stew.

119. Mom's Signature Pork Stew

Ready in about 25 minutes
Servings 4

Here is a foolproof pork recipe that is sure to please any crowd! It is worth the invested time, trust me.

Per serving: 295 Calories; 19.6g Fat; 10.7g Carbs; 20.3g Protein; 2.6g Sugars

Ingredients

1 tablespoon butter
2 shallots, chopped
1 carrot, chopped
1 teaspoon habanero pepper, deveined and minced
3/4 pound boneless pork shoulder, cubed
1/2 tablespoon garlic paste
1 ½ cups bone broth
1/2 teaspoon ground bay leaf
1/2 teaspoon ground cloves
Himalayan salt and ground black pepper, to taste
1 tablespoon fresh parsley, chopped
1 avocado, pitted, peeled and diced
1/2 cup sour cream, full-fat

Directions

- Melt the butter in a heavy-bottomed pot that is pre-heated over a moderate heat.
- Now, sauté the shallots, carrot, and habanero pepper for 3 minutes or until they are tender.
- After that, add cubed pork; cook an additional 5 minutes, stirring frequently.
- Then, add the garlic paste, broth, bay leaf powder ground cloves, salt, and pepper; turn the heat to a medium-high and bring it to a boil.
- Next, decrease the heat to a simmer. Cook an additional 15 minutes or until thoroughly heated.
- Serve in individual bowls, topped with fresh parsley and avocado and dolloped with well-chilled sour cream. Enjoy!

120. Pork Meatballs with Herby Tomato Sauce

Ready in about 50 minutes
Servings 6

Easy and delicious, these meatballs are a cinch to make. Low-carb, gluten-free and kid-friendly. Enjoy!

Per serving: 237 Calories; 12g Fat; 5.6g Carbs; 26.4g Protein; 2.7g Sugars

Ingredients

For the Meatballs:
1 pound beef, ground
1 egg, beaten
1/4 cup almond flour
3/4 cup grated parmesan cheese
2 ounces full-fat milk
Salt and ground black pepper, to taste
1 white onion, finely chopped
1 teaspoon garlic paste
1/2 tablespoon chili powder
1 teaspoon onion flakes
2 tablespoons fresh parsley, chopped
For the Sauce:
2 tablespoons olive oil
2 ripe tomatoes, chopped
Salt and ground black pepper, to taste
1 teaspoon red pepper flakes, crushed
1 teaspoon garlic powder
1 rosemary sprig
1 thyme sprig
1 tablespoon cider vinegar

Directions

- Start by preheating your oven to 360 degrees F. Now, spritz an oven safe dish with a nonstick cooking spray.
- In a mixing dish, thoroughly combine all ingredients for the meatballs. Next, shape the mixture into 2-inch balls; place them in a single layer in the greased baking dish. Spritz the meatballs with a cooking spray.
- In another mixing dish, thoroughly combine all ingredients for the sauce. Pour the sauce over the meatballs.
- Bake for 45 minutes or until everything is heated through. Bon appétit!

121. Spicy Pork Soup

Ready in about 1 hour
Servings 4

Anaheim chile adds a distinctive twist to this recipe. It is a mild hot pepper that can be replaced with poblano peppers or serrano pepper, which are tangier than Anaheim, with more earthy flavor.

Per serving: 341 Calories; 12.9g Fat; 8.8g Carbs; 45.4g Protein; 3.3g Sugars

Ingredients

2 tablespoons olive oil
1 ½ pounds pork stew meat, cubed
Salt and black pepper, to taste
1 onion, chopped
2 garlic cloves, crushed
1/2 cup dry white wine
2 carrots, thinly sliced
2 parsnips, thinly sliced
4 cups beef bone broth
1 ripe Roma tomato, crushed
1 Anaheim chile, seeded and cut into very thin strips with scissors
1/2 teaspoon dried basil
2 thyme sprigs
2 rosemary sprigs
Fresh cilantro, for garnish

Directions

- Heat olive oil in a heavy-bottomed pot that is preheated over a moderately high flame. Now, sear the pork cubes until they are just browned; reserve.
- Then, cook the onions and garlic in pan drippings for 3 to 4 minutes. Pour in wine to deglaze the bottom.
- Add the carrots, parsnip, and beef bone broth, bringing to a boil. Turn the heat to medium-low and simmer 6 to 7 more minutes.
- Add tomato, chile, basil, thyme, and rosemary; let it simmer an additional 50 minutes, partially covered. Serve hot garnished with chopped cilantro.

122. Bacon and Sausage Kraut

Ready in about 35 minutes
Servings 6

Sauerkraut with bacon is one of the most convenient and satisfying dishes. You can make a double batch and keep in your refrigerator ready to reheat throughout the week for an easy keto lunch.

Per serving: 309 Calories; 20.6g Fat; 9.2g Carbs; 19.3g Protein; 4.3g Sugars

Ingredients

4 slices bacon, chopped
2 pork sausages, sliced
1 onion, chopped
1 jalapeno pepper, finely minced
1 teaspoon garlic, finely minced
1/2 teaspoon celery seeds, ground
1/2 teaspoon ground cumin
1/4 teaspoon ground bay leaf
1 cup chicken stock
1/3 cup dry white wine
1 ½ pounds prepared sauerkraut, drained
1 tablespoon fresh parsley, for garnish
1 tablespoon Dijon mustard, for garnish

Directions

- Cook the bacon in a deep pan that is preheated over a moderate flame. Cook about 8 minutes, stirring periodically; reserve.
- Leave 1 tablespoon of the bacon grease in the pan. Now, add the sausage and cook until browned on all sides, about 5 minutes.
- Sauté the onions, jalapeno pepper and garlic in pan drippings until tender and aromatic, about 6 minutes.
- Add celery seeds, cumin, ground bay leaf, stock, wine and sauerkraut. Bring to a rolling boil and decrease the heat to low. Continue to cook an additional 15 minutes.
- Serve on individual plates garnished with parsley and Dijon mustard. Bon appétit!

123. Three-Cheese and Pork Sausage Balls

Ready in about 15 minutes + chilling time
Servings 6

These fatty balls are loaded with sausage, three kinds of cheese and aromatics. How could it be any better than this?

Per serving: 353 Calories; 30.7g Fat; 3g Carbs; 16.1g Protein; 1.4g Sugars

Ingredients

1 tablespoon olive oil
1/2 pound pork sausage, ground
1 tomato, pureed
1 teaspoon garlic paste
2 tablespoons onion, minced
4 ounces Neufchatel cheese, room temperature
1/4 teaspoon kosher salt
1/4 teaspoon ground black pepper
4 ounces chive & onion cream cheese
4 ounces fontina cheese, crumbled
2 tablespoons flaxseed meal

Directions

- Heat the oil in a skillet that is preheated over a moderate heat. Now, brown the sausage for 3 to 4 minutes, stirring periodically.
- Add tomatoes, garlic paste, and onion; cook for a further 5 minutes. Add the other ingredients and mix well to combine.
- Place the mixture in your refrigerator to harden. Shape the mixture into bite-sized balls. Serve well-chilled.

124. Country Brie-Stuffed Meatballs

Ready in about 25 minutes
Servings 5

This is another super-easy pork recipe, bursting with incredible flavor. Make these tender, gooey meatballs and amaze your family.

Per serving: 302 Calories; 17.3g Fat; 1.9g Carbs; 33.4g Protein; 0.3g Sugars

Ingredients

1 pound ground pork
1/3 cup heavy cream
2 eggs, beaten
1 tablespoon fresh cilantro
2 tablespoons shallots, minced
2 cloves garlic, minced
1 teaspoon kosher salt
1/2 teaspoon ground black pepper
1 teaspoon dried thyme
10 (1-inch) cubes of brie

Directions

- Combine all ingredients, except for cubes of brie, in a mixing bowl.
- Then, shape the mixture into 10 patties by using oiled hands. Now, place a piece of brie in the center of each patty and roll into a ball.
- Preheat your oven to 390 degrees F. Arrange the meatballs on a foil-lined baking pan. Bake for 20 to 22 minutes.
- Serve with mustard or low-carb salsa. Enjoy!

125. North Carolina Pulled Pork

Ready in about 4 hours 30 minutes + marinating time
Servings 4

A classic Carolina BBQ rub contains white and brown sugar. However, you can have a delicious North Carolina pulled pork without sugar!

Per serving: 350 Calories; 11g Fat; 5g Carbs; 53.6g Protein; 2.3g Sugars

Ingredients

1 teaspoon chipotle powder
1/2 tablespoon paprika
1 teaspoon garlic powder
1 teaspoon onion powder
Kosher salt and freshly ground black pepper, taste
1 teaspoon ground cumin
1 tablespoon liquid smoke sauce
1 ½ pounds pork butt
2 onions, cut into wedges
Water, enough to cover pork

Directions

- In a mixing bowl, thoroughly combine chipotle powder, paprika, garlic powder, onion powder, salt, black pepper, cumin and liquid smoke sauce.
- Spread this rub all over the pork butt. Cover the pork butt with a plastic wrap; let it marinate in your refrigerator for 3 hours.
- Then, preheat your oven to 325 degrees F. Wrap the pork tightly with aluminum foil. Roast the pork for 3 hours. Take the pork butt out of oven; turn the oven up to 375 degrees.
- Unwrap the pork and bake for a further 90 minutes or until internal temperature reaches 190 degrees F.
- Transfer the pork to a pot; add onion wedges and water. Continue to cook over a moderately high heat until thoroughly cooked.
- Afterwards, shred the pork with meat claws or two forks; taste and adjust the seasonings. Serve with your favorite ketogenic salad on the side.

126. Breakfast Muffins with Ground Pork

Ready in about 25 minutes
Servings 6

This breakfast is super-simple to make for a crowd! If your family like spicier food, add a teaspoon of minced chile pepper to the batter.

Per serving: 479 Calories; 42g Fat; 7.8g Carbs; 17.9g Protein; 0.5g Sugars

Ingredients

1 tablespoon canola oil
1 ½ cups ground pork
Salt and cayenne pepper, to your liking
1 stick butter
3 ½ cups almond flour
1/2 teaspoon baking powder
1/2 teaspoon baking soda
3 large eggs, lightly beaten
2 tablespoons full-fat milk
1/2 teaspoon ground cloves
1/2 teaspoon dried oregano

Directions

- Heat the oil in a frying pan over medium heat. Now, cook the ground pork until juices run clear, about 4 to 5 minutes.
- Then, preheat your oven to 360 degrees F.
- Add the remaining ingredients to a mixing dish, in the order listed above. Thoroughly combine until everything is well incorporated.
- Divide the mixture among 12 muffin cups. Bake in the preheated oven for 15 to 18 minutes.
- Allow your muffins to cool down before removing from the baking tin. Serve with a full-fat sour cream. Bon appétit!

127. Dinner Party Pork Gumbo

Ready in about 35 minutes
Servings 6

Everyone loves a good and rich gumbo! For the Keto version, just skip French cooking roux and use flaxseed meal instead.

Per serving: 427 Calories; 26.2g Fat; 13.6g Carbs; 35.2g Protein; 3.3g Sugars

Ingredients

2 tablespoons olive oil
1 pound pork shoulder, cubed
8 ounces pork sausage, sliced
2 shallots, toughly chopped
1 teaspoon beef bouillon granules
Sea salt and freshly cracked black pepper
1 teaspoon gumbo file
1 teaspoon crushed red pepper
1 tablespoon Cajun spice
4 cups bone broth
1 cup water
2 bell peppers, deveined and thinly sliced
2 celery stalks, chopped
1/4 cup flaxseed meal
3/4 pound okra

Directions

● Heat the oil in a heavy-bottomed pot that is preheated over a moderately high flame. Now, cook the pork until it is just browned; reserve.
● Add the sausage and cook in pan drippings approximately 5 minutes; reserve.
● Stir in the shallots and cook until they are softened. Add beef bouillon granules, salt, pepper, gumbo file, red pepper, Cajun spice and bone broth. Bring it to a boil.
● Add the water, bell pepper and celery, and reduce the heat to medium-low. Cook an additional 15 to 23 minutes.
● Afterwards, stir in the flax seed meal and okra; cook for a further 5 minutes or until heated through.

128. Pork Meatloaf with Homemade Tomato Sauce

Ready in about 45 minutes
Servings 6

If you haven't eaten a meatloaf in ages, here's some great news– this is among the most popular Keto staples! If you like a spicy food, add a dash or 2 of hot sauce.

Per serving: 251 Calories; 7.9g Fat; 6.5g Carbs; 34.6g Protein; 3g Sugars

Ingredients

Nonstick cooking spray
1 ½ pounds ground pork
1/4 cup pork rinds, crushed
1/3 cup flaxseed meal
2 shallots, chopped
3 cloves garlic, finely minced
1 large egg
Sea salt and ground black pepper
1 teaspoon mustard powder

For the Sauce:
2 ripe plum tomatoes, pureed
2 tablespoons ketchup
1 ½ tablespoons Swerve
1 tablespoon cider vinegar
1/2 teaspoon dried thyme
1 teaspoon fresh parsley

Directions

● Start by preheating your oven to 360 degrees F. Lightly spray a loaf pan with a nonstick cooking oil or line with foil.
● Add the pork mince, pork rinds, flaxseed meal, shallot, garlic, egg, salt, pepper, and mustard powder to a mixing dish. Thoroughly combine the ingredients until everything is well mixed.
● Press the meatloaf mixture into the pan.
● Next, cook the sauce ingredients over moderate heat. Pour the sauce evenly over the meatloaf. Bake for 40 minutes or until meat thermometer registers 165 degrees F.
● Allow it to cool down for a couple of minutes before slicing. Cut into 3/4-inch thick slices and serve immediately.

129. Pork Shoulder with Blue Cheese Sauce

Ready in about 30 minutes
Servings 6

This pork shoulder with a tangy and rich blue cheese sauce will make a stunning main course for the next family dinner.

Per serving: 495 Calories; 36.9g Fat; 3.6g Carbs; 33.4g Protein; 1.1g Sugars

Ingredients

1 ½ pounds pork shoulder, boneless and cut into 6 pieces
Salt and freshly cracked black peppercorns, to taste
1 teaspoon dried thyme
1 tablespoon butter
1 onion, chopped
2 garlic cloves, chopped
1/3 cup dry sherry wine
1/3 cup broth, preferably homemade
1 teaspoon dried hot chile flakes
1 tablespoon soy sauce
6 ounces blue cheese
1/3 cup double cream

Directions

- Rub each piece of pork shoulder with salt, black peppercorns, and thyme.
- Now, warn the butter in a sauté pan over a moderately high heat. Then, brown the pork on all sides about 18 minutes; reserve.
- Next, sauté the onions and garlic until onions are caramelized. Add the wine and broth and stir, scraping up any brown bits from the bottom.
- Turn the heat to medium and add the other ingredients; continue to simmer until the desired thickness is reached by evaporation.
- Serve reserved pork with the sauce on the side. Bon appétit!

130. Carrot and Meat Loaf Muffins

Ready in about 35 minutes
Servings 6

Meatloaf muffins are super cute and incredibly delicious. It's a great idea for a kid's birthday party!

Per serving: 220 Calories; 6.3g Fat; 5.4g Carbs; 33.8g Protein; 2.9g Sugars

Ingredients

1 pound pork, ground
1/2 pound turkey, ground
1 cup carrots, shredded
2 ripe tomatoes, pureed
1 ounce envelope onion soup mix
1 tablespoon Worcestershire sauce
1 tablespoon Dijon mustard
1/2 teaspoon dry basil
1 teaspoon dry oregano
Kosher salt and ground black pepper, to taste
2 cloves of garlic, minced
1 eggs, whisked
1 cup mozzarella cheese, shredded

Directions

- Start by preheating your oven to 350 degrees F.
- Then, thoroughly combine all ingredients until everything is blended.
- Spoon the mixture into a muffin tin that is previously coated with a nonstick cooking spray.
- Bake for 30 minutes; allow them to cool slightly before removing from the tin. Bon appétit!

131. Hearty Pork Soup with Avocado

Ready in about 20 minutes
Servings 6

Here's a hearty soup that is not just delicious! It's keto and healthy as well! Mezzeta peppers have less amount of carbohydrates in comparison with other chili peppers. For example, 5 pieces contain only 1 gram of carbs.

Per serving: 423 Calories; 31.8g Fat; 8g Carbs; 25.9g Protein; 2.9g Sugars

Ingredients

2 tablespoons lard
1 medium-sized yellow onion, peeled and chopped
2 cloves garlic, peeled and minced
1 teaspoon Mezzeta pepper, seeded and minced
1 celery, chopped
1 ¼ pounds pork shoulder, cut into chunks
3 cups beef broth, less-sodium
Sea salt and ground black pepper, to taste
A pinch of dried basil
2 ripe tomatoes, undrained
1/4 cup fresh parsley, roughly chopped
1 medium-sized avocado, pitted and sliced

Directions

- Melt the lard in a large-sized stock pot over a moderate flame. Next, sauté the onion, garlic, Mezzeta pepper and celery for 2 to 3 minutes or until the onion is translucent.
- Stir in the pork chunks and continue cooking for 4 minutes more, stirring continuously. Add the other ingredients.
- Now, lower the heat and simmer for 10 minutes, partially covered; make sure to stir periodically.
- Serve topped with fresh parsley leaves and sliced avocado.

132. Greek Souvlaki with Tzatziki Sauce

Ready in about 20 minutes + marinating time
Servings 6

This traditional Greek dish is easy to make in your own kitchen. And it is Keto as well. Perfect!

Per serving: 147 Calories; 4.8g Fat; 7.8g Carbs; 17.3g Protein; 5.5g Sugars

Ingredients

1/3 cup red wine vinegar
2 tablespoons cilantro, chopped
2 tablespoons fresh lemon juice
3 cloves garlic, smashed
Sea salt and ground black pepper, to taste
1 teaspoon Greek oregano
2 pounds pork loin, trimmed of silver skin and excess fat, cut into 1-inch cubes
Wooden skewers, soaked in cold water for 30 minutes before use

For Tzatziki Sauce:
1 small-sized cucumber, shredded and drained
1 cup full-fat Greek yogurt
1 teaspoon garlic, smashed
3 teaspoons olive oil
Sea salt, to taste
2 teaspoons fresh dill, finely minced

Directions

- To make the marinade, thoroughly combine the vinegar, cilantro, lemon juice, garlic, salt, black pepper and Greek oregano.
- Add the pork loin to the marinade. Let it marinate in your refrigerator for 3 hours. Now, thread the pork cubes onto the skewers.
- Grill your souvlaki until they browned on all sides, about 8 to 12 minutes in total.
- Mix all ingredients for Tzatziki sauce. Serve with souvlaki skewers. Bon appétit!

133. Kansas City-Style Meatloaf

Ready in about 1 hour 10 minutes
Servings 8

A chipotle salsa will give a kick of spice and delicate smoky notes to your meatloaf. It's best when nestled into the hot cauliflower rice.

Per serving: 318 Calories; 14.7g Fat; 6.2g Carbs; 39.3g Protein; 2.4g Sugars

Ingredients

2 pounds ground pork
2 eggs, beaten
1/2 cup shallots, chopped
1/2 cup chipotle salsa, bottled
8 ounces sharp Cheddar cheese, shredded
1 teaspoon garlic powder
1 teaspoon paprika
Sea salt and freshly ground black pepper, to taste
1 teaspoon lime zest
1 tablespoon whole grain mustard
1/2 cup tomato paste
1 tablespoon Swerve

Directions

- Start by preheating your oven to 360 degrees F.
- In a mixing bowl, thoroughly combine the ground pork with eggs, shallots, chipotle salsa, cheddar cheese, garlic powder, paprika, salt, pepper, lime zest, and mustard.
- Mix until everything is well incorporated. Press the mixture into a loaf pan that is previously greased with a nonstick cooking spray.
- Then, whisk the tomato paste with Swerve; pour the mixture over the top of your meatloaf.
- Bake about 65 minutes, rotating the pan once or twice. Place under the broiler during the last 5 minutes if desired.
- Let your meatloaf stand 5 to 10 minutes before slicing and serving.

134. Indian-Style Saucy Pork

Ready in about 1 hour 15 minutes
Servings 8

Curry powder is the king of spices in South India. It can help you reduce the risk of heart disease as well as protect the immune system.

Per serving: 369 Calories; 20.2g Fat; 2.9g Carbs; 41.3g Protein; 1.5g Sugars

Ingredients

1 tablespoon olive oil
2 pounds pork belly, cubed
Salt and freshly ground pepper
1/2 teaspoon ground coriander
A bunch of scallions, chopped
2 garlic cloves, minced
1/2 tablespoon curry powder
1/2 tablespoon ground cloves
2 tomatoes, pureed
1 bell pepper, deveined and chopped
1 Thai chile, deveined and minced
1/2 teaspoon fennel seeds
1/2 cup unsweetened coconut milk
2 cups bone broth

Directions

- Heat the oil in a saucepan over a moderate heat. Sprinkle the pork belly with salt, pepper and ground coriander.
- Cook the pork about 10 minutes, stirring frequently.
- Next, cook the scallions, garlic, curry, and cloves in pan drippings. Scrape the mixture into the slow cooker. Add the remaining ingredients. Cook, covered, for 1 hour over low heat. Serve warm.

135. Pork Rib Chops with Spinach

Ready in about 25 minutes + marinating time
Servings 6

Cooking pork rib chops can be a daunting task, but if you marinate them for 2 hours, it won't be a problem. These pork rib chops go wonderfully with celery, peppers, and spinach. Yummy!

Per serving: 234 Calories; 11g Fat; 2g Carbs; 29.8g Protein; 0.6g Sugars

Ingredients

1 ½ pounds pork rib chops
Sea salt and ground black pepper, to taste
2 tablespoons oyster sauce
1 tablespoon cider vinegar
1 tablespoon fresh lime juice
1/4 cup Champagne wine
1 tablespoon garlic paste
2 teaspoons olive oil
1 red onion, sliced
1 celery stalk, sliced
1 bell pepper, chopped
2 cups spinach

Directions

- Season pork rib chops with salt and pepper. In another small dish, make the marinade by whisking the oyster sauce, vinegar, lime juice, Champagne and garlic paste.
- Add the pork to the marinade; let it stand for at least 2 hours.
- Next, heat 1 teaspoon of olive oil in a large-sized pan that is preheated over a moderate flame; cook the onion, celery and bell pepper about 5 minutes, stirring frequently; reserve.
- Heat another teaspoon of olive oil in the same pan. Add the pork, along with marinade, to the pan. Now, brown the pork for 3 to 5 minutes per side.
- Add the reserved vegetables to the pan along with spinach. Cook until the spinach leaves are wilted, about 6 minutes. Serve warm. Bon appétit!

136. Breakfast Pork in a Mug

Ready in about 10 minutes
Servings 2

Need some easy breakfast ideas? Here's the recipe that is affordable and satisfying. Be inspired and serve it with fresh lettuce, tomato or sliced bell peppers.

Per serving: 327 Calories; 16.6g Fat; 5.8g Carbs; 40g Protein; 2.6g Sugars

Ingredients

1/2 pound ground pork
1/2 cup Asiago cheese, shredded
1/2 cup tomato sauce
Salt and ground black pepper, to taste
1 teaspoon garlic paste
1/2 teaspoon onion powder
1/2 teaspoon cayenne pepper

Directions

- Thoroughly combine all ingredients in a mixing bowl.
- Divide the mixture among 2 microwave-safe mugs.
- Microwave for 7 minutes and serve warm with pickles. Bon appétit!

137. Hot and Creamy Pork Chop Soup

Ready in about 25 minutes
Servings 4

This hearty soup is inexpensive but tasty lunch for the whole family. Nothing can compete with a homey, old-fashioned pork soup!

Per serving: 490 Calories; 44g Fat; 8.1g Carbs; 24.3g Protein; 2.6g Sugars

Ingredients

2 tablespoons olive oil
1 shallot, chopped
1 small-sized carrot, chopped
1 celery stalk, chopped
3/4 pound bone-in pork chops
3 cups water
1 tablespoon chicken bouillon granules
1/2 teaspoon red pepper flakes
Seasoned salt and freshly cracked black pepper, to taste
2 tomatoes, pureed
1 cup double cream
1/2 teaspoon Tabasco sauce
1/2 cup avocado, pitted, peeled and diced

Directions

● Heat 1 tablespoon of olive oil in a pot that is preheated over medium-high heat. Now, sauté the shallots until they are just softened.
● Then, stir in the carrots and celery. Cook until they are slightly softened; reserve.
● Heat the remaining tablespoon of olive oil; brown pork chops for 4 minutes, stirring periodically.
● When the pork chops are cool enough to handle, discard any bones and chop them into bite-size chunks. Add to the pot along with reserved vegetables.
● Add water, bouillon granules, red paper flakes, salt, pepper and pureed tomatoes. Continue to simmer, partially covered, for 10 minutes more.
● Stir in double cream and cook until heated through, stirring continuously. Serve drizzled with Tabasco sauce and garnished with avocado. Bon appétit!

138. Pork Lettuce Wraps

Ready in about 15 minutes
Servings 4

Who said that buns are the best choice for ground pork? Try these sinfully delicious wraps and you'll probably change your mind!

Per serving: 110 Calories; 2.7g Fat; 5.1g Carbs; 15.8g Protein; 2.1g Sugars

Ingredients

2 tablespoons apple cider vinegar
1/4 teaspoon kosher salt
1 celery, grated
2 spring onions, sliced
1 teaspoon capers
1/2 pound ground pork
2 garlic cloves, finely minced
1 jalapeno pepper, deveined and finely minced
1 tablespoon Worcestershire sauce
1/2 teaspoon salt
1/3 teaspoon freshly cracked mixed peppercorns
1 ½ teaspoons Dijon mustard
1 head lettuce
1 tablespoon sunflower seeds

Directions

● In a mixing dish or a measuring cup, thoroughly whisk the vinegar with the kosher salt, celery, spring onions and capers.
● In a pan, brown the ground pork with garlic and jalapeno for 7 minutes over a moderate flame.
● Now, add Worcestershire sauce, salt, peppercorns, and mustard to the pan; stir to combine.
● Then, assemble your wraps. Divide pork mixture among lettuce leaves; top with reserved celery mixture. Afterwards, sprinkle with raw sunflower seeds and serve.

139. Pan-Seared Pork Steaks

Ready in about 30 minutes
Servings 4

Pork steak, also known as Boston butt or pork blade steak, is a pork cut that is high in protein and low in carbs. Serve as an easy family lunch or a protein-packed dinner.

Per serving: 305 Calories; 20.6g Fat; 3.7g Carbs; 22.5g Protein; 1.3g Sugars

Ingredients

2 tablespoons lard, room temperature
4 pork butt steaks
1/4 cup dry red wine
1 teaspoon celery seeds
1/2 teaspoon cayenne pepper
1/2 teaspoon salt
1/2 teaspoon freshly ground black pepper
1 red onion, peeled and chopped
1 garlic clove, minced

Directions

- Melt 1 tablespoon of lard in a cast-iron skillet that is preheated over a moderate heat. Cover the skillet and sear the butt steaks for 10 minutes on each side.
- Add a splash of red wine to deglaze the pot. Season with celery seeds, cayenne pepper, salt and black pepper; cook an additional 8 to 12 minutes; reserve.
- Warm remaining 1 tablespoon of lard in the same skillet; cook the onions and garlic until tender and aromatic. Serve with seared pork butt steaks. Bon appétit!

140. Grilled Pork and Vegetable Skewers

Ready in about 20 minutes + marinating time
Servings 6

As one of the favorite family dishes, this recipe makes the meat very tender. With a fresh salad, it is a complete meal!

Per serving: 428 Calories; 31.6g Fat; 7.7g Carbs; 28.9g Protein; 4.2g Sugars

Ingredients

2 tablespoons fresh lime juice
3 tablespoons olive oil
3 tablespoons tamari sauce
1 tablespoon Italian spice mix
2 cloves garlic, crushed
1 ½ pounds pork shoulder, cubed
1 pound small button mushrooms
1 onion, cut into wedges
1 zucchini, cubed
1 green bell pepper, cut into thick slices
1 red bell pepper, cut into thick slices
Wooden skewers, soaked in cold water for 30 minutes

Directions

- To make the marinade, thoroughly combine fresh lime juice, olive oil, tamari sauce, Italian spice mix and crushed garlic.
- Now, marinate the pork for a couple of hours. Thread the pork cubes, mushrooms, onion, zucchini and peppers onto skewers.
- Cook on the preheated grill approximately 13 to minutes, or to the desired doneness, turning skewers frequently for even cooking. Enjoy!

141. Pork Loin with Cauliflower and Bamboo Shoots

Ready in about 20 minutes
Servings 6

Here's an amazing low-carb dinner recipe that might become a family favorite! Can you imagine a better way to end your day on a keto diet?

Per serving: 356 Calories; 19.5g Fat; 6.4g Carbs; 33.1g Protein; 3g Sugars

Ingredients

1 ½ pounds pork loin, boneless
Celery salt and ground black pepper, to taste
1/4 teaspoon dried thyme
1/2 teaspoon dried marjoram
1/2 teaspoon garlic powder
2 tablespoons oyster sauce
1/4 cup vodka
1 ½ tablespoons olive oil
1 yellow onion, chopped
1 head cauliflower, broken into florets
1 (8-ounce) can bamboo shoots

Directions

- Add pork loin to a mixing dish. Add celery salt, black pepper, thyme, marjoram, garlic powder, oyster sauce, vodka and olive oil to the mixing dish; toss to combine well.
- Now, heat 1 tablespoon of olive oil in a nonstick skillet over medium-high heat; sauté the onions until translucent.
- Add cauliflower and cook an additional 3 to 4 minutes or until just tender; reserve.
- Heat another tablespoon of olive oil in the same skillet over high heat. Discard the marinade and brown the pork for 3 minutes on each side.
- Pour in reserved marinade; add reserved cauliflower mixture and canned bamboo shoots.
- Continue to cook an additional 3 to 4 minutes or until the liquid has thickened. Serve immediately. Enjoy!

142. Easy Aromatic Pork Chops

Ready in about 30 minutes
Servings 4

For this delicious pork recipe, use a decent quality drinking wine like Pinot gris, Sauvignon blanc or Semillons. You can skip the wine by substituting it with chicken broth and water (in the same proportion) + Dijon mustard to taste.

Per serving: 335 Calories; 26.3g Fat; 2.5g Carbs; 18.3g Protein; 0.8g Sugars

Ingredients

2 tablespoons lard, melted
1/2 cup red onion, thinly sliced
3 cloves garlic, minced
4 pork chops
1/4 cup dry white wine
2 tablespoons Worcestershire sauce
1 teaspoon dried thyme
4 allspice berries, lightly crushed
1/2 teaspoon fresh ginger root, grated

Directions

- Melt the lard in a saucepan over medium heat. Sauté the onions and garlic until aromatic and just browned.
- Add the pork and cook 15 to 20 minutes, turning once or twice. Add dry white wine, Worcestershire sauce, thyme, crushed allspice berries and fresh ginger.
- Cook an additional 8 minutes or until everything is thoroughly heated. Bon appétit!

143. Super Crispy Roasted Pork Shoulder

Ready in about 25 minutes
Servings 4

Pork shoulder is probably one of the most convenient and versatile foods to cook under the broiler. Adding a freshly grated Asiago cheese will complete your meal.

Per serving: 476 Calories; 35.3g Fat; 6.2g Carbs; 31.1g Protein; 1.2g Sugars

Ingredients

1 pound pork shoulder, cut into 1-inch-thick pieces
Salt and cayenne pepper, to taste
2 tablespoons lard
2 shallots, sliced
2 cloves garlic, smashed
1 thyme sprig
1 rosemary sprig
1 tablespoon tamarind paste
1 tablespoon fish sauce
2 tablespoons Kalamata olives, pitted and sliced
2 tablespoons rice vinegar
1 cup bone broth
1/2 cup Asiago cheese, freshly grated

Directions

- Start by preheating your broiler. Sprinkle your pork with salt and cayenne pepper on all sides.
- Melt the lard in a pan that is preheated over a moderately high flame. Sweat the shallots and garlic for about 5 minutes; reserve.
- Warm the remaining 1 tablespoon of lard. Sear the pork for 7 to 8 minutes, turning once; reserve.
- Now, cook the garlic, thyme, rosemary, tamarind paste, fish sauce, olives, vinegar, and bone broth in pan drippings. Cook until the sauce is reduced by about half. Transfer to an oven-safe dish.
- Add the reserved pork along with the shallot mixture; sprinkle with grated Asiago cheese. Lastly, broil until everything is thoroughly heated, about 5 minutes.

144. Spicy Pork Sausage Frittata

Ready in about 35 minutes
Servings 4

This recipe is so versatile so you can try a different keto breakfast every morning! Combine the eggs with a pork sausage, ham, bacon, prosciutto or ground meat.

Per serving: 423 Calories; 35.4g Fat; 4.1g Carbs; 22.6g Protein; 2g Sugars

Ingredients

3 tablespoons olive oil
1 cup onion, chopped
1 teaspoon jalapeno pepper, finely minced
2 garlic cloves, minced
1 teaspoon salt
1/2 teaspoon ground black pepper
1/4 teaspoon cayenne pepper
1/2 pound pork sausages, thinly sliced
8 eggs, beaten
1 teaspoon dried sage, crushed

Directions

- Heat the oil in a nonstick skillet over a medium-high heat. Now, sauté the onions, peppers and garlic until the onion becomes translucent, about 4 minutes.
- Season with salt, black pepper, and cayenne pepper. Then, stir in the sausage and cook, stirring often, until they're no longer pink.
- Transfer the mixture to a lightly greased baking dish. Pour the eggs over the top and sprinkle with dried sage.
- Bake in the preheated oven at 420 degrees F for 25 minutes. Bon appétit!

145. Chinese Pork Stir-Fry with Muenster Cheese

Ready in about 20 minutes
Servings 6

Muenster cheese is lower in fat than other commonly used cheeses on a ketogenic diet like Monterey Jack and Cheddar. It is also smoother in texture. This buttery, mild cheese pairs perfectly with Beaujolais wine.

Per serving: 320 Calories; 15.4g Fat; 2.7g Carbs; 39.8g Protein; 1.3g Sugars

Ingredients

1 tablespoon lard, softened
1 ½ pounds pork butt, cut into strips
Celery salt and freshly ground black pepper, to taste
1/2 teaspoon red pepper flakes
A bunch of scallions, roughly chopped
2 bell peppers, sliced
1/4 cup bone broth
1/2 teaspoon Chinese hot sauce
1 tablespoon peanut butter
1 tablespoon soy sauce
2 tablespoons Sauvignon
3 ounces Muenster cheese, cut into small pieces

Directions

- Melt the lard in an oven-safe skillet that is preheated over a moderately high heat. Toss pork strips with salt, black pepper, and red pepper flakes.
- Stir-fry pork strips approximately 4 minutes. Add scallions and bell peppers; cook an additional 3 minutes.
- Now, add bone broth, hot sauce, peanut butter, soy sauce, and Sauvignon; stir-fry for a couple of minutes more.
- Scatter small pieces of Muenster cheese on top of pork mixture, cover and continue to cook until cheese has just melted. Bon appétit!

146. Crock Pot Hungarian Goulash

Ready in about 10 hours
Servings 4

Traditional Hungarian goulash is the perfect for keto lunch! If you used to serve hot cooked rice on the side, just swap it for a cauliflower rice. It will surprise you with its taste!

Per serving: 517 Calories; 35.7g Fat; 10.7g Carbs; 38.2g Protein; 4g Sugars

Ingredients

1 ½ tablespoons butter
1 pound pork shoulder off the bone, chopped
1 cup yellow onions, chopped
3 garlic cloves, crushed
2 teaspoons cayenne pepper
1 teaspoon sweet Hungarian paprika
1 teaspoon caraway seeds, ground
4 cups chicken stock
2 ½ cups tomato puree
2 chili peppers, deveined and finely chopped
For the Sour Cream Sauce:
1 cup sour cream
1 bunch parsley, chopped
1 teaspoon lemon zest

Directions

- Melt the butter in a sauté pan that is preheated over a moderate heat. Now, cook the pork until just browned; reserve.
- Add the onions and garlic and continue to sauté until they are just tender and fragrant.
- Transfer reserved pork along with the onions and garlic to your crock pot. Add the cayenne pepper, paprika, caraway seeds, stock, tomato puree and chili peppers.
- Cover and cook for 8 to 10 hours on low heat setting.
- In the meantime, make the sour cream sauce by whisking all the sauce ingredients. Serve warm goulash in individual bowls, dolloped with the sour cream sauce. Enjoy!

147. Pork Quiche with Bell Peppers

Ready in about 50 minutes
Servings 6

Sometimes a true comfort food such pork quiche and a cup of yoghurt is all you really need. Whether it is a family lunch or celebratory dinner, pork quiche is always a great idea!

Per serving: 478 Calories; 36g Fat; 4.9g Carbs; 33.5g Protein; 1.4g Sugars

Ingredients

6 eggs, lightly beaten
2 ½ cups almond flour
1 stick butter, melted
1 ¼ pounds ground pork
Salt and pepper, to the taste
1 green bell pepper, thinly sliced
1 red bell pepper, thinly sliced
1 cup heavy cream
1/2 teaspoon mustard seeds
1/2 teaspoon dried dill weed

Directions

- Start by preheating your oven to 350 degrees F
- Add an egg, flour, and butter to a mixing dish; mix to combine well.
- Press the batter dough in a baking pan that is previously greased with a nonstick cooking spray.
- Next, brown ground pork for 3 to 5 minutes, crumbling with a wide spatula; season with salt and pepper.
- In another mixing bowl, thoroughly combine the remaining ingredients; add browned pork.
- Spread this mixture over the crust and bake for 35 to 43 minutes in the preheated oven. Eat warm and enjoy!

148. Summer Baby Back Ribs

Ready in about 1 hour 40 minutes + marinating time
Servings 6

Summer is better with a barbecue! It's the perfect time to get back in shape while eating your favorite food!

Per serving: 255 Calories; 13.9g Fat; 0.8g Carbs; 29.9g Protein; 0.1g Sugars

Ingredients

1 ½ pounds baby back ribs
Salt and ground black pepper, to taste
1 teaspoon dried marjoram
1 lime, halved
1 garlic clove, minced

Directions

- Season the baby back ribs with the salt, pepper and marjoram. Now, rub your ribs with the cut sides of lime.
- Cover and transfer to your refrigerator for 6 hours. Place the minced garlic on top of the ribs.
- Grill for about 1 hour 30 minutes, turning twice to ensure even cooking. Serve with mustard and salads on the side.

149. Ground Pork and Swiss Chard Skillet

Ready in about 25 minutes
Servings 4

Are you craving a burger? Try this homey dish with ground pork and you won't miss a burger bun!

Per serving: 349 Calories; 13g Fat; 8.4g Carbs; 45.3g Protein; 3.5g Sugars

Ingredients

2 tablespoons vegetable oil
2 cloves garlic, pressed
1 cup leeks, sliced
1 Serrano pepper, sliced
1 bell pepper, chopped
1 ½ pounds ground pork
1 teaspoon sea salt
1/4 teaspoon lemon pepper, or more to taste
1/4 cup tomato puree
1/4 cup dry sherry wine
1 bunch Swiss chard, trimmed and roughly chopped
1 cup beef bone broth

Directions

- Heat 1 tablespoon of vegetable oil in a pan over a moderately high heat. Now, sauté the garlic, leeks, and peppers until they are just softened; reserve.
- Heat the remaining tablespoon of vegetable oil; add the ground pork and cook, stirring frequently, for 3 to 4 minutes more.
- Add the remaining ingredients along with sautéed vegetables. Cook, covered, an additional 10 minutes or until everything is thoroughly cooked.
- Uncover and cook for a further 5 minute or until the liquid has evaporated. Serve warm!

150. Pork Ribs with Roasted Peppers

Ready in about 2 hours
Servings 4

The perfect mix of flavors and textures in this oven-roasted pork dish will amaze your family and friends. Don't be shy about seasonings and enjoy experimenting with them.

Per serving: 370 Calories; 21.3g Fat; 8.3g Carbs; 33.7g Protein; 3.7g Sugars

Ingredients

2 tablespoons olive oil
1 pound baby back ribs
Salt and pepper, to your liking
1 tablespoon garlic paste
1 red onion, chopped
2 rosemary sprigs
1 tablespoon crushed sage
1 tablespoon tamarind paste
1 cup beef broth
1/2 cup dry sherry
1/2 cup soy sauce
2 roasted red bell peppers, chopped
2 roasted chile peppers, chopped

Directions

- Start by preheating your oven to 340 degrees F. Spritz a roasting pan with a nonstick cooking spray.
- Heat the oil in an ovenproof pan over a moderately high heat. Now, brown the meat on all sides for 10 minutes; sprinkle with salt and pepper.
- Add the garlic paste, onion, rosemary and sage. Cook an additional 4 minutes or until heated through. Stir in the remaining ingredients.
- Bake for 1 hour 30 minutes in the middle of the pre-heated oven and serve immediately.

151. Holiday Pork and Bacon Meatloaf

Ready in about 1 hour 10 minutes
Servings 6

You don't have to make a rock-solid plan to stay on your keto diet during the holidays. It will be easy with this amazing recipe. Make this meatloaf and you'll be just fine.

Per serving: 405 Calories; 24.6g Fat; 2.8g Carbs; 40.6g Protein; 0.9g Sugars

Ingredients

1 teaspoon lard, melted
1 yellow onion, chopped
1 teaspoon garlic, finely minced
1 ¼ pounds ground pork
1 egg, beaten
2 ounces half-and-half
1 teaspoon celery seeds
Salt and ground black pepper, to taste
1/4 teaspoon cayenne pepper
1/2 pound pork sausage, broken up
1 bunch cilantro, roughly chopped
6 strips bacon

Directions

- Preheat your oven to 395 degrees F. Lightly grease a baking dish and set it aside.
- Heat the lard in a cast-iron skillet over a medium heat. Next, sauté the onions and garlic until they are tender and fragrant, for 2 to 4 minutes.
- Stir in the pork and cook until it is no longer pink, about 2 minutes.
- In a mixing bowl, thoroughly combine the egg, half-and-half, celery seeds, salt, black pepper, cayenne pepper, pork sausage and cilantro.
- Add the reserved pork mixture; stir to combine well. Lastly, shape the mixture into a loaf.
- Place the bacon on the top of your meatloaf. Bake about 1 hour. Allow it to cool on a wire rack before serving. Bon appétit!

BEEF

152. Spicy Habanero and Ground Beef Dinner.............. 92

153. Meatballs with Roasted Peppers and Manchego.... 92

154. The Best Sloppy Joes Ever 93

155. Grilled Rib Eye Steak 93

156. Beef Sausage with Mayo Sauce 94

157. Slow Cooker Beef Chuck Roast 94

158. Finger-Lickin' Good Beef Brisket............................ 95

159. Winter Guinness Beef Stew....................................... 95

160. Greek Prosciutto-Wrapped Meatloaf...................... 96

161. Greek-Style Cold Beef Salad 96

162. Slow Cooker Cajun Beef Brisket and Veggies 97

163. Colorful Beef Skewers with Spicy Relish 97

164. Oven Roasted Rib-Eye Steak 98

165. Stuffed Tomatoes with Cotija Cheese 98

166. Juicy Grilled Steak Medallions 99

167. Smoked Beef Sausage Bake with Broccoli.............. 99

168. Keto Tacos with Bacon Sauce 100

169. Broccoli and Ground Beef Delight 100

170. Burgundy Beef Soup with Pancetta 101

171. Smoky and Yummy Beef Medley 101

172. Beef Soup with Chili Drizzle 102

173. Rich Beef Mishmash 102

174. Cheeseburger Soup with Ume Plum Vinegar....... 103

175. Marsala Beef Ribs... 103

176. Beef Sausage and Colby Dip 104

177. Bacon-Wrapped Meatballs with Parsley Sauce 104

178. Sunday Flank Steak 105

179. Father's Day Stuffed Avocado 105

180. Beef Sausage and Vegetable Skillet........................ 106

181. Spicy Sausage and Vegetable Casserole 106

182. Hamburger Soup with Cabbage 107

183. Ultimate Thai Beef Salad 107

184. Hungarian Beef Stew 108

185. Za'atar Strip Steaks with Cabbage 108

186. Spicy Winter Sauerkraut with Ground Beef......... 109

187. Winter Cheeseburger Soup..................................... 109

188. Zucchini Spaghetti with Bolognese Sauce 110

189. Filet Mignon with Sour Cream-Mustard Sauce ... 110

190. Saucy Beef Short Loin.. 111

191. Old-Fashioned Beef Stew 111

192. Filet Mignon Steaks with Wine Sauce 112

193. Mini Meatloaf Muffins with

      Cremini Mushrooms 112

194. Crock Pot Beef Brisket with Blue Cheese 113

195. Sriracha and Scallion Chuck 113

196. Beef Casserole with Sour Cream Sauce................. 114

197. Buttery Roasted Chuck with Horseradish Sauce 114

198. Italian-Style Holiday Meatloaf............................... 115

199. Royal Keto Lasagna.. 115

200. Cabbage, Beef and Cheese Casserole..................... 116

201. Top Round Steak with Marsala Sauce 116

202. Skirt Steak and Eggs Skillet.................................... 117

152. Spicy Habanero and Ground Beef Dinner

Ready in about 40 minutes
Servings 6

This beef dish is easy to make and easy to eat! How could it be any better than this?!

Per serving: 361 Calories; 21.9g Fat; 8.4g Carbs; 29g Protein; 1.5g Sugars

Ingredients

2 tablespoons tallow, at room temperature
1 ½ pounds ground chuck
1/4 teaspoon caraway seeds, ground
1/2 teaspoon dried basil
1/2 teaspoon dried thyme
1/2 teaspoon paprika
1/2 teaspoon ground bay leaf
1 teaspoon fennel seeds
1/2 teaspoon salt
1/2 teaspoon ground black pepper
2 shallots, chopped
2 garlic cloves, minced
1 teaspoon habanero pepper, minced
2 ripe Roma tomatoes, crushed
1/2 cup dry sherry wine

For Ketogenic Tortillas:
4 egg whites
1/4 cup coconut flour
1/3 teaspoon baking powder
6 tablespoons water
A pinch of table salt
A pinch of Swerve

Directions

- Melt the tallow in a wok that is preheated over a moderately high heat.
- Now, brown the ground chuck for 4 minutes, crumbling it with a fork. Add all seasonings along with shallots, garlic, and habanero pepper. Continue to cook 9 minutes longer.
- Now, stir in the tomatoes and sherry. Now, turn the heat to medium-low, cover, and let it simmer an additional 20 minutes.
- Meanwhile, make the tortillas by mixing the eggs, coconut flour and baking powder in a bowl. Add the water, salt and Swerve and mix until everything is well incorporated.
- Preheat a nonstick skillet over a moderate flame. Bake tortillas for a couple of minutes on each side. Repeat until you run out of batter.
- Serve ground beef mixture with warm tortillas. Enjoy!

153. Meatballs with Roasted Peppers and Manchego

Ready in about 1 hour
Servings 4

Inspired by the classic Mexican cuisine, this comfort dish uses freshly grated cheese, flavorful tomato sauce, and roasted peppers.

Per serving: 348 Calories; 13.7g Fat; 11.9g Carbs; 42.8g Protein; 4.7g Sugars

Ingredients

4 bell peppers, deveined and chopped
2 chipotle peppers, deveined and minced
2 leeks, chopped
3 garlic cloves
3 tablespoons parmesan cheese, grated
1 egg
Salt and freshly ground black pepper
1 pound ground beef
2 ripe tomatoes, crushed
1 ½ cups chicken broth
1/2 teaspoon fresh ginger, ground
1 teaspoon lemon thyme
1/2 cup Manchego cheese, crumbled

Directions

- Broil the peppers for approximately 20 minutes, turning once or twice. Allow them to stand at least 30 minutes to loosen skin.
- Peel the peppers; remove stems and seeds; slice chipotle peppers into halves and reserve.
- In a mixing dish, combine the leeks, garlic, parmesan, egg, salt, pepper, and ground beef. Heat a heavy-bottomed skillet over a moderately high heat.
- Brown meatballs on all sides about 10 minutes.
- Now, make the tomato sauce. Heat the tomatoes, chicken broth, ginger and lemon thyme in a pan that is preheated over medium-high heat; season with salt and pepper to taste.
- Bring to a boil and then, decrease the heat to medium. Add meatballs and let them simmer until they are thoroughly cooked, gently stirring.
- Serve meatballs with the tomato sauce and roasted peppers. Garnish with crumbled Manchego and enjoy!

154. The Best Sloppy Joes Ever

Ready in about 30 minutes
Servings 6

Make sure to choose a chuck with a good fat content; otherwise, your Sloppy Joes will come out dry.

Per serving: 313 Calories; 20.6g Fat; 3.5g Carbs; 26.6g Protein; 0.3g Sugars

Ingredients

2 teaspoons tallow, room temperature
2 shallots, finely chopped
1 teaspoon garlic, minced
1 ½ pounds ground chuck
1/2 cup pureed tomatoes
1 teaspoon deli mustard
1 teaspoon celery seeds
1 tablespoon coconut vinegar
Salt and ground pepper, to taste
1 teaspoon cayenne pepper
1 teaspoon chipotle powder

Directions

- Melt 1 tablespoons of tallow in a heavy-bottomed skillet over a moderately high flame.
- Now, sauté the shallots and garlic until tender and aromatic; reserve.
- In the same skillet, melt another tablespoon of tallow. Now, brown ground chuck, crumbling with a spatula.
- Add the vegetables back to the skillet; stir in the remaining ingredients. Turn the heat to medium-low; simmer for 20 minutes; stirring periodically.
- Serve over keto buns. Bon appétit!

155. Grilled Rib Eye Steak

Ready in about 20 minutes
Servings 6

Use a meat thermometer to determine the level of doneness of the meat. Here are the temperatures: Rare = 120 degrees F; Medium rare = 130 degrees F; Medium = 140 degrees F; Well-done = 160 degrees F.

Per serving: 314 Calories; 11.4g Fat; 1g Carbs; 48.2g Protein; 0.6g Sugars

Ingredients

1 tablespoon oyster sauce
1 tablespoon Worcestershire sauce
2 tablespoons Swerve sweetener
2 garlic cloves, smashed
1 thyme sprig, chopped
2 rosemary sprigs, chopped
1 teaspoon dried sage, crushed
1/2 teaspoon chipotle powder
Celery salt and ground black pepper, to taste
2 tablespoons dry red wine
2 tablespoons olive oil
2 pounds rib eye steaks

Directions

- In a mixing bowl, thoroughly combine oyster sauce, Worcestershire sauce, Swerve, garlic, thyme, rosemary, sage, chipotle powder, salt, pepper, wine and olive oil.
- Now, marinate the rib eye steaks in your refrigerator overnight.
- Preheat your grill that is previously lightly greased. Grill rib eye steaks over direct heat for 4 to 5 minutes on each side for medium-rare. Bon appétit!

156. Beef Sausage with Mayo Sauce

Ready in about 15 minutes
Servings 4

Enjoy this "good-for-you" meal that is chock-full of gourmet sausage, great aromatics, and amazing sauce. This is the perfect idea for those short on time.

Per serving: 549 Calories; 49.3g Fat; 9.7g Carbs; 16.2g Protein; 2.3g Sugars

Ingredients

1 tablespoon lard, at room temperature
1 red onion, chopped
1 garlic clove, finely minced
1 pound beef sausage, crumbled
1/2 teaspoon salt
1/3 teaspoon red pepper flakes
1/2 teaspoon dried marjoram
2 tablespoons cilantro, minced
For the Sauce:
1/4 cup mayonnaise
1 tablespoon tomato puree
1 ½ teaspoon mustard
1 teaspoon cayenne pepper
A pinch of salt

Directions

- Melt the lard over medium-high heat. Add the onion and garlic and cook for 2 minutes or until tender and fragrant.
- Stir in the beef and continue to cook for about 3 minutes more. Stir in the salt, red pepper, marjoram and cilantro; cook for 1 more minute.
- Then, make the sauce by whisking all the sauce ingredients. Serve over low-carb flat bread. Enjoy!

157. Slow Cooker Beef Chuck Roast

Ready in about 6 hours
Servings 8

This super tender beef chuck roast will win your table! Serve with horseradish sauce.

Per serving: 519 Calories; 39.6g Fat; 2.7g Carbs; 34.4g Protein; 1.4g Sugars

Ingredients

2 pounds beef chuck roast
2 tablespoons olive oil
1 large-sized white onion, cut into wedges
3 garlic cloves, minced
2 rosemary springs
1 thyme sprig
1/3 cup dry red wine
Salt and pepper to taste
2 tablespoons Worcestershire sauce
1/2 cup beef broth
2 tablespoons fresh parsley, chopped
1 cup Provolone, sliced

Directions

- Add the beef, olive oil, onion, garlic, rosemary and thyme to your Crock pot.
- Now, add dry red wine, salt, pepper, Worcestershire sauce, beef broth.
- Cover and cook on High settings until meat is tender, about 6 hours.
- Serve garnished with fresh parsley and sliced Provolone cheese. Bon appétit!

158. Finger-Lickin' Good Beef Brisket

Ready in about 3 hours 30 minutes
Servings 8

Delight your family with this beef brisket that's rubbed with tangy mustard, pungent garlic, and a mix of dried aromatics.

Per serving: 219 Calories; 7.2g Fat; 0.6g Carbs; 34.6g Protein; 0.1g Sugars

Ingredients

2 pounds beef brisket, trimmed
1 tablespoon Dijon mustard
2 garlic cloves, halved
1 teaspoon sea salt
1/2 teaspoon freshly ground black pepper
1 teaspoon shallot powder
1 teaspoon dried rosemary
1 teaspoon dried marjoram
1/4 cup dry red wine

Directions

- Start by preheating an oven to 375 degrees F. Rub the raw brisket with garlic and Dijon mustard.
- Then, make a dry rub by mixing the remaining ingredients. Season the brisket on both sides with the rub. Pour the wine into the pan.
- Lay beef brisket in a baking pan. Roast in the oven for 1 hour.
- Decrease the oven temperature to 300 degrees F; roast an additional 2 hours 30 minutes.
- Afterwards, slice the meat and serve with juice from the baking pan. Bon appétit!

159. Winter Guinness Beef Stew

Ready in about 1 hour
Servings 6

This Irish-style stew will blow your mind! Don't forget about browning meat, it will add an excellent flavor to this stew. You can add a hot pepper sauce if your family likes spicy food!

Per serving: 444 Calories; 14.2g Fat; 7.1g Carbs; 66.3g Protein; 2.7g Sugars

Ingredients

1 ½ tablespoons canola oil
1 ½ pounds chuck shoulder, cut into bite-size cubes
1 cup leeks, chopped
1 celery stalk, chopped
1 parsnip, chopped
2 carrots, chopped
1 ½ cups tomato puree
3 cups boiling water
1 cup Guinness beer
1 tablespoon beef bouillon granules
1 bay leaf
1/2 teaspoon caraway seeds
1/4 cup mint leaves, chopped, to serve

Directions

- Heat the oil in a stockpot over medium-high heat. Now, sauté chuck shoulder cubes until they are browned; reserve.
- Then, sauté the vegetables in pan drippings for 8 minutes, stirring periodically.
- Throw in the remaining ingredients, except for mint leaves, and bring to a rapid boil. Now, turn the heat to medium-low; let it simmer about 50 minutes.
- Ladle into individual serving bowls and serve garnished with mint leaves. Bon appétit!

160. Greek Prosciutto-Wrapped Meatloaf

Ready in about 55 minutes
Servings 8

You can serve this meatloaf as a wonderful everyday dish or a holiday main course. The key ingredient is the Greek seasoning blend with its rich and pungent flavor.

Per serving: 442 Calories; 20.6g Fat; 4.9g Carbs; 56.3g Protein; 1g Sugars

Ingredients

3 teaspoons sesame oil
2 shallots, finely chopped
2 pounds ground beef
1/2 pound ground lamb
1/4 cup half-and-half
6 ounces feta cheese, crumbled
2 eggs, beaten
2 teaspoons Greek seasoning blend
1 tablespoon brown mustard
1 tablespoon Worcester sauce
1/2 cup chopped Kalamata olives
8 slices of prosciutto

Directions

- Preheat your oven to 390 degrees F.
- Heat the oil in a cast-iron skillet that is preheated over a medium flame. Sauté the shallot until it becomes soft and lightly browned.
- In a large mixing bowl, thoroughly combine the remaining ingredients, except for prosciutto. Add sautéed onion and mix well.
- Shape the mixture into a meatloaf. Wrap the meatloaf in the slices of prosciutto and transfer it to a baking pan.
- Cover with a piece of aluminum foil. Bake for 40 minutes. Remove the foil and bake an additional 10 to 13 minutes. Bon appétit!

161. Greek-Style Cold Beef Salad

Ready in about 20 minutes
Servings 6

Full of Mediterranean vegetables and crowd-pleasing beef, and tossed with a tangy dressing, you'll have dinner ready for your family in less than 20 minutes. Top with Kalamata olives if desired.

Per serving: 315 Calories; 13.8g Fat; 8.4g Carbs; 37.5g Protein; 4.4g Sugars

Ingredients

2 cucumbers, thinly sliced
1 orange bell pepper, thinly sliced
1 green bell pepper, thinly sliced
1 red onion, peeled and thinly sliced
1 cup grape tomatoes, halved
1 head of butter lettuce, leaves separated
1 ½ pounds beef rump steak
Salt and ground black pepper, to your liking
1/2 teaspoon dried oregano
1 tablespoon fresh lemon juice
1/4 cup extra-virgin olive oil
1 tablespoon soy sauce

Directions

- In a salad bowl, toss the cucumbers, bell pepper, onions, tomato, and butter lettuce leaves.
- Preheat a barbecue grill; cook the steak for 3 minutes per side. Then, thinly slice steak across the grain.
- Add the slices of meat to the salad.
- Make the dressing by whisking the salt, pepper, oregano, lemon juice, olive oil and soy sauce.
- Dress the salad and serve well-chilled. Enjoy!

162. Slow Cooker Cajun Beef Brisket and Veggies

Ready in about 6 hours + marinating time
Servings 6

Marinated and seasoned beef brisket goes wonderfully with slow-cooked vegetables. Trim the fat off beef brisket before slow cooking.

Per serving: 296 Calories; 12g Fat; 7g Carbs; 35.2g Protein; 3.8g Sugars

Ingredients

1 ½ pounds beef brisket
1 teaspoon garlic, smashed
Ground black pepper, to taste
1 tablespoon Cajun seasonings
2 tablespoons dry red wine
2 tablespoons Worcestershire sauce
2 tablespoons vegetable oil
2 yellow onions, sliced into half moons
2 carrots, sliced
2 celery stalks, chopped
1 cup stock

Directions

- Rub beef brisket with garlic, black pepper and Cajun seasonings. Add the wine, Worcestershire sauce and 1 tablespoon of vegetable oil.
- Wrap with foil and place in the refrigerator for 3 hours.
- Heat 1 tablespoon of vegetable oil in your slow cooker. Now, sauté the onions until just tender.
- In a pan, sear the brisket until it has a golden brown crust. Transfer to your slow cooker. Add the carrots, celery and stock
- Cover and cook on Low heat setting for 6 hours or until the beef brisket is as soft as you want it. Bon appétit!

163. Colorful Beef Skewers with Spicy Relish

Ready in about 20 minutes
Servings 6

For the best results, use the grilling method to cook these colorful skewers. They might become one of your favorite low-carb dinner hacks!

Per serving: 413 Calories; 21.1g Fat; 9.7g Carbs; 45.3g Protein; 5.8g Sugars

Ingredients

2 teaspoons yellow mustard
2 garlic cloves, minced
1 small red chile pepper, finely chopped
3 tablespoons olive oil
2 ½ tablespoons sherry vinegar
Salt and ground black pepper, to taste
2 pounds beef tenderloin, cut into cubes
1 cup onions, cut into wedges
2 zucchinis, cut into thick slices
1 green bell peppers, diced
1 red bell pepper, diced
1/2 medium-sized pineapple, peeled and diced
12 bamboo skewers, soaked in cold water (for 30 minutes)

Directions

- Preheat your grill on medium-high.
- Prepare the relish by mixing yellow mustard, garlic, chile pepper, olive oil and sherry vinegar.
- Season the meat and vegetables with the salt and pepper. Spritz the ingredients with a nonstick cooking spray.
- Thread meat cubes onto skewers, alternating with vegetables and pineapple. Season to taste and grill about 10 minutes, turning periodically. Serve with the relish.

164. Oven Roasted Rib-Eye Steak

Ready in about 25 minutes
Servings 6

Keep in mind that thinner steak actually shortens the cooking time. Therefore, try to purchase the steak that is about one-inch thick.

Per serving: 343 Calories; 27.3g Fat; 3g Carbs; 20.1g Protein; 0g Sugars

Ingredients

1 tablespoon vegetable oil
1 ½ pounds rib-eye steak
1 teaspoon sea salt
1/2 teaspoon ground black pepper
2 garlic cloves, minced
1/2 cup Worcester sauce
2 tablespoons apple cider vinegar

Directions

- Preheat your oven to 350 degrees F. Grease a roasting pan with a nonstick cooking spray.
- Heat vegetable oil in a skillet that is preheated over a medium-high heat. Season the steak with salt and black pepper; sear the steak until just browned or about 3 minutes.
- Place the steak in the prepared roasting pan. In a mixing bowl, combine the garlic, Worcester sauce and apple cider vinegar. Pour this mixture over the steak.
- Afterwards, cover tightly with a piece of foil. Roast the steak about 20 minutes or until it is tender and well browned. Enjoy!

165. Stuffed Tomatoes with Cotija Cheese

Ready in about 35 minutes
Servings 4

Make these amazing stuffed tomatoes and you won't miss a bun. All the comfort without any guilt.

Per serving: 244 Calories; 9.6g Fat; 11g Carbs; 28.9g Protein; 7g Sugars

Ingredients

1 tablespoon olive oil
1 cup scallions, chopped
2 cloves garlic, minced
1 pound ground beef
2 tablespoons tomato paste, sugar-free
Salt and pepper, to your liking
1/2 teaspoon cumin seeds
8 tomatoes, scoop out the pulp and chop it
1 teaspoon mild paprika
1 teaspoon dried coriander leaves
1/2 cup beef broth
3/4 cup Cotija cheese, shredded

Directions

- Start by preheating your oven to 350 degrees F. Lightly grease a casserole dish with a cooking spray.
- Heat the oil in a saucepan over a moderately high heat. Sauté the scallions and garlic until aromatic.
- Stir in ground meat; cook for 5 minutes, crumbling with a spatula. Add tomato paste and cook until heated through. Season with salt, pepper and cumin seeds.
- Fill the tomatoes with beef mixture and transfer them to the prepared casserole dish.
- In a mixing bowl, whisk tomato pulp with paprika, coriander and broth. Pour the mixture over the stuffed tomatoes.
- Bake until tomatoes are tender, about 20 minutes. Top with Cotija cheese and bake an additional 5 minutes. Bon appétit!

166. Juicy Grilled Steak Medallions

Ready in about 50 minutes
Servings 4

You won't believe how fast this beef dish will be done! This is excellent served over grilled vegetables.

Per serving: 326 Calories; 11.1g Fat; 1.6g Carbs; 52g Protein; 0.2g Sugars

Ingredients

4 steak medallions, 1 1/2 inches thick
1 teaspoon sea salt
1/2 teaspoon ground black pepper
1 tablespoon cayenne pepper
1 teaspoon fennel seeds
1 teaspoon celery seeds
1/2 teaspoon chipotle powder
2 tablespoons fresh lime juice
1 tablespoon ginger root, freshly grated

Directions

- Place steak medallions in a large-sized resealable bag. Then, thoroughly combine the remaining ingredients to make the marinade.
- Marinate steak medallions for 40 minutes at room temperature.
- Preheat your grill to medium-high. Remove medallions from marinade and grill on each side to desired doneness, about 5 to 6 minutes. Serve warm.

167. Smoked Beef Sausage Bake with Broccoli

Ready in about 45 minutes
Servings 4

This recipe will take the most important meal of the day from "Blah" to "Wow". It's a great way to kick-start your day!

Per serving: 289 Calories; 19.7g Fat; 9.3g Carbs; 19.8g Protein; 3.4g Sugars

Ingredients

4 smoked beef sausages, sliced
1 red bell pepper, thinly sliced
1 green bell pepper, thinly sliced
2 shallots, chopped
1 cup broccoli, broken into florets
2 garlic cloves, minced
Salt and black pepper, to taste
1 teaspoon marjoram
1/2 teaspoon ground bay leaf
6 eggs, whisked
2 tablespoons fresh parsley, roughly chopped

Directions

- Start by preheating your oven to 370 degrees F.
- Heat up a nonstick skillet over a moderate flame; now, cook the sausage for 3 minutes, stirring periodically.
- Add the peppers, shallots, broccoli, and garlic; continue cooking for 5 minutes. Season with salt, pepper, marjoram, and ground bay leaf.
- Transfer the sausage mixture to a previously greased baking dish. Pour the whisked eggs over it. Bake for 35 minutes. Serve garnished with fresh parsley.

168. Keto Tacos with Bacon Sauce

Ready in about 30 minutes
Servings 4

Try these flavorful keto tacos with crunchy mozzarella shells and homemade taco filling. They get a serious flavor boost from a rich bacon sauce.

Per serving: 258 Calories; 19.3g Fat; 5g Carbs; 16.3g Protein; 2.9g Sugars

Ingredients

1 ½ cups Cotija cheese, shredded
1 ½ cups ground beef
2 Campari tomatoes, crushed
Salt and ground black pepper, to taste
1/2 teaspoon onion powder
1/2 teaspoon celery salt
1/2 teaspoon ground cumin
6 slices bacon, chopped
1/2 cup bone broth
3 tablespoons tomato paste
2 teaspoon champagne vinegar
2 jalapeno peppers, minced

Directions

- Start by preheating your oven to 390 degrees F. Spritz a baking pan with a nonstick cooking spray.
- Spread 6 piles of Cotija cheese on the baking pan; bake for 15 minutes; leave taco shells to cool down for a couple of minutes.
- In a nonstick skillet, brown the beef for 4 to 5 minutes, crumbling with a spatula. Add crushed tomatoes, salt, pepper, onion powder, celery salt, and ground cumin.
- Cook until everything is cooked through.
- Then, make the sauce by cooking the bacon for 2 to 3 minutes, stirring constantly. Add the remaining ingredients and cook until everything comes together.
- Afterwards, assemble your tacos. Divide the meat mixture among 6 taco shells; top with the bacon sauce. Bon appétit!

169. Broccoli and Ground Beef Delight

Ready in about 20 minutes
Servings 4

Treat your family and guests to a plate chock-full of lovely meat, vegetable and aromatics. Serve with a homemade low-carb bread.

Per serving: 241 Calories; 7.6g Fat; 6g Carbs; 36g Protein; 1.9g Sugars

Ingredients

2 teaspoons avocado oil
1 head broccoli, cut into small florets
1 teaspoon garlic, minced
1 cup red onion, sliced
1 pound ground beef
1/2 teaspoon salt
1/2 ground black pepper
1/4 teaspoon cayenne pepper
1/2 cup beef bone broth
2 tablespoons Marsala wine
1/2 teaspoon dill weed
1/2 teaspoon turmeric

Directions

- Heat 1 teaspoon of avocado oil in a pan that is pre-heated over a moderate flame. Then, cook the broccoli for 3 to 4 minutes, stirring often.
- Now, stir in the garlic and onion; cook until aromatic and just tender, or about 2 minutes. Reserve.
- Heat another teaspoon of avocado oil. Stir in the beef and cook until it is well browned.
- Add the reserved broccoli mixture, lower the heat and add the remaining ingredients. Cook, covered, until everything is heated through, or about 10 minutes.
- Serve with a dollop of sour cream. Enjoy!

170. Burgundy Beef Soup with Pancetta

Ready in about 2 hours 10 minutes
Servings 4

This soup is so yummy and satisfying, you won't even miss the noodles! When it comes to the meat, opt for oxtails, brisket or even veal shanks.

Per serving: 340 Calories; 19.6g Fat; 8.5g Carbs; 30.2g Protein; 1.2g Sugars

Ingredients

2 tablespoons olive oil
4 ounces pancetta, chopped
1 shallot, chopped
2 cloves garlic, minced
1/2 cup carrots, thinly sliced
1 celery rib, chopped
1 pound beef, cubed
2 bay leaves
2 sprigs thyme
1 sprig rosemary
1 small-sized ripe tomato, crushed
1 tablespoon soy sauce
2 tablespoons dry red wine
1/2 tablespoon bouillon granules
4 cups water
1 tablespoon flaxseed meal
2 tablespoons fresh parsley, roughly chopped

Directions

- Start by preheating your oven to 320 degrees F.
- Heat 1 tablespoon of oil in a stock pot that is preheated over a moderate flame. Now, fry the pancetta for 3 to 4 minutes, crumbling it with a fork; reserve.
- Now, heat another tablespoon of olive oil; sauté the shallots and garlic for 3 minutes or until they are softened. Stir in beef and cook until it browns.
- Add the remaining ingredients, except for flaxseed and parsley, bringing to a rolling boil. Decrease the heat, cover the pot, and let your soup simmer for a further 2 hours.
- Uncover and stir in 1 tablespoon of flax seed meal that has been dissolved in 2 tablespoons of cold water.
- Stir to combine well and cook an additional 3 minutes or until thoroughly warmed. Serve garnished with fresh parsley and crumbled pancetta. Bon appétit!

171. Smoky and Yummy Beef Medley

Ready in about 1 hour 40 minutes
Servings 6

Cook beef sirloin steak until meltingly tender in spicy juices. Serve with a dollop of full-fat sour cream.

Per serving: 375 Calories; 13.3g Fat; 5.6g Carbs; 55.1g Protein; 2.9g Sugars

Ingredients

3 teaspoons tallow, room temperature
2 pounds boneless beef sirloin steak, cubed
Seasoned salt and cayenne pepper, to taste
1/2 teaspoon black peppercorns, crushed
1 cup yellow onions, chopped
2 cloves garlic, minced
1 tablespoon smoked paprika
1 teaspoon caraway seeds, crushed
1/2 teaspoon mustard seeds
2 thyme sprigs
1 rosemary sprig
6 cups bone broth
1 tablespoon fish sauce
2 ripe Roma tomatoes, pureed
1 tablespoon dry white wine
2 bay leaves

Directions

- Heat 1 teaspoon of tallow in a heavy-bottomed pot over a moderate heat. Now, brown the beef until it is no longer pink.
- Season with salt, cayenne pepper, and black peppercorns; reserve.
- In the same pot, heat remaining 2 teaspoons of tallow over a moderate heat. Cook the onions and garlic until they're softened, stirring continuously.
- Now, add the paprika, caraway seeds, mustard seeds, thyme, and rosemary; cook an additional minute or until they are fragrant.
- Add the remaining ingredients. Cook, partially covered, for 1 hour 30 minutes more. Discard bay leaves and serve in individual bowls. Bon appétit!

172. Beef Soup with Chili Drizzle

Ready in about 1 hour 10 minutes
Servings 6

This rich and flavorful soup highlights the sweet flavor of green peas as well as the spiciness of chili drizzle. Chopped fresh cilantro works well too.

Per serving: 375 Calories; 14.4g Fat; 11.8g Carbs; 47.6g Protein; 4.7g Sugars

Ingredients

1 tablespoon canola oil
2 pounds beef chuck (well-marbled), boneless and cubed
2 onions, peeled and chopped
1 parsnip, chopped
1 celery with leaves, chopped
2 carrots, chopped
1/2 cup ripe olives, pitted and halved
1 ripe tomato, pureed
6 cups water
2 tablespoons instant bouillon granules
1/2 teaspoon ground bay leaf
1/2 teaspoon ground cumin
1/2 cup frozen green peas
For the chili drizzle:
2 red chilies
1 tablespoon extra-virgin olive oil
2 tablespoons lemon juice
Salt, to taste

Directions

- Heat the oil in a stockpot over a moderately high heat. Now, brown the beef cubes for 3 to 5 minutes, stirring often; reserve.
- Next, in pan drippings, cook the onions, parsnip, celery and carrots until just tender. Add the olives, tomato, water, bouillon granules, ground bay leaf and cumin.
- Stir in reserved beef and bring the soup to a boil.
- Turn the heat to medium-low; let it simmer, partially covered, about 50 minutes. Add green peas and cook for a further 15 minutes.
- Meanwhile, make the chili drizzle by blending all ingredients in your food processor.
- Afterwards, top with chili drizzle and serve.

173. Rich Beef Mishmash

Ready in about 2 hours
Servings 4

Cozy up with a warming bowl of the beef mishmash, which is slow-cooked and generously spiced. Just like a grandma used to make.

Per serving: 467 Calories; 18.7g Fat; 13.7g Carbs; 58g Protein; 6.2g Sugars

Ingredients

2 tablespoons lard
1 ½ pounds ground beef
2 garlic cloves, minced
2 leeks, chopped
1 carrot, chopped
2 bell peppers, chopped
1 jalapeno, pepper, finely minced
1 celery with leaves, chopped
4 cups beef broth
Salt and pepper, to taste
1 teaspoon dried marjoram
1 teaspoon fennel seeds
1/4 teaspoon freshly grated nutmeg
1 tablespoon flaxseed meal

Directions

- Melt 1 tablespoon of lard in a pan (Dutch oven). Then, brown the beef, crumbling with a spatula; reserve.
- In the same pan (Dutch oven), melt the remaining tablespoon of lard. Cook the vegetables until they are softened.
- Add the beef back to the pan (Dutch oven) and pour in beef broth. Add the seasonings and bring to a boil.
- Reduce the heat to medium-low. Let it simmer approximately 1 hour 50 minutes.
- Afterwards, stir in the flaxseed meal. Let it boil for 1 to 2 minutes, stirring frequently. Serve warm in individual bowls.

174. Cheeseburger Soup with Ume Plum Vinegar

Ready in about 30 minutes
Servings 6

Adding sour and fruity ume plum vinegar is a great way to layer and intensify the flavors of your burger soup. This hearty soup is fast-to-fix thanks to Colby cheese, ripe tomatoes, and ground chuck.

Per serving: 238 Calories; 12.6g Fat; 5.6g Carbs; 25.1g Protein; 2.5g Sugars

Ingredients

1 tablespoon olive oil
1 ½ pounds ground chuck
2 onions, chopped
2 garlic cloves, chopped
2 cups bone broth
1 cup ripe tomatoes, pureed
Salt and ground black peppercorns, to your liking
2 bay leaves
1 teaspoon dried oregano
1 cup Colby cheese, shredded
2 tablespoons ume plum vinegar

Directions

- Heat the oil in a pot over a moderately high heat. Now, cook the beef until it is well browned, crumbling with a fork. Drain and reserve.
- Cook the onion and garlic in pan drippings. Cook until they are tender, about 5 minutes.
- Add the other ingredients, minus cheese and ume plum vinegar, and bring to a rapid boiling. Cook an additional 20 minutes.
- Stir in Colby cheese and continue to cook until cheese melts.
- Ladle into individual soup bowls. Drizzle each serving with ume plum vinegar and serve right away. Bon appétit!

175. Marsala Beef Ribs

Ready in about 2 hours 30 minutes
Servings 8

If you are looking for something really special for the next family gathering, these beef ribs will fit the bill. If you don't have Marsala wine on hand, a good substitute would be dry white wine.

Per serving: 231 Calories; 8.9g Fat; 1.3g Carbs; 34.7g Protein; 0.7g Sugars

Ingredients

2 pounds beef ribs
1 teaspoon kosher salt
1/4 teaspoon ground black pepper, or more to taste
1/2 teaspoon chili powder
1 tablespoon coconut oil
1/2 cup Marsala wine
3/4 cup pureed fresh ripe tomatoes
2 garlic cloves, minced

Directions

- Start by preheating your oven to 325 degrees F.
- Season beef ribs with salt, black pepper and chili powder on all sides.
- Preheat the coconut oil in a large-sized skillet over a medium-high flame. Sear the ribs until browned on all sides.
- Transfer beef ribs to a baking dish. In a mixing bowl, combine the remaining ingredients; pour this mixture over beef ribs.
- Cover with a piece of foil. Let it roast for 2 hours in the preheated oven. Remove the foil and roast for a further 20 to 30 minutes.

176. Beef Sausage and Colby Dip

Ready in about 20 minutes
Servings 8

Looking for a surprisingly sensational and rich dipping sauce to amaze your guests? Give this recipe a try! To make it budget-friendly, you can use leftover smoked beef.

Per serving: 333 Calories; 29.2g Fat; 2.9g Carbs; 14.7g Protein; 0.8g Sugars

Ingredients

1 tablespoon lard, at room temperature
1 onion, finely chopped
2 garlic cloves, minced
1 ½ cups smoked beef sausages, crumbled
1 cup cream cheese, at room temperature
1 ½ cups Colby cheese, shredded
2 tablespoons fresh chives, roughly chopped

Directions

- Start by preheating an oven to 330 degrees F.
- Melt the lard in a pan over a moderately high heat. Then, sweat the onion for 3 to 4 minutes. Stir in the garlic and continue sautéing until aromatic.
- Add the sautéed onion and garlic to a mixing dish. Add the sausage, cream cheese, Colby cheese; mix to combine well.
- Transfer the mixture to a baking dish; bake for 15 minutes. Garnish with fresh chives and serve with veggie sticks. Bon appétit!

177. Bacon-Wrapped Meatballs with Parsley Sauce

Ready in about 30 minutes
Servings 6

You should be prepared to expect unexpected on a ketogenic diet. In this recipe, crushed pork rinds can become a great replacement for breadcrumbs.

Per serving: 399 Calories; 27g Fat; 1.8g Carbs; 37.7g Protein; 0.2g Sugars

Ingredients

1 pound ground beef
1 egg, beaten
1 ½ tablespoons olive oil
1/2 cup crushed pork rinds
1/4 cup fresh cilantro, chopped
2 cloves garlic, smashed
Sea salt and ground black pepper, to your liking
1/2 teaspoon cayenne pepper
1/2 pound bacon slices
Toothpicks

For the Parsley Sauce:
1 cup fresh parsley
1 tablespoon almonds, toasted
1 tablespoon sunflower seeds, soaked
1/2 tablespoon olive oil
Sea salt and black pepper, to taste

Directions

- Preheat your oven to 390 degrees F.
- Then, in a mixing bowl, thoroughly combine the ground beef, egg, olive oil, crushed pork rinds, cilantro, garlic, salt, black pepper, and cayenne pepper.
- Shape the mixture into 1.5-inch meatballs. Wrap each ball with a slice of bacon; secure with a toothpick.
- Arrange the meatballs on a baking sheet; bake in the preheated oven for 25 to 30 minutes.
- In the meantime, make the parsley sauce. Pulse all ingredients in a food processor until uniform and smooth.
- Serve warm meatballs with parsley sauce on the side and enjoy!

178. Sunday Flank Steak

Ready in about 20 minutes + marinating time
Servings 6

Extremely tender, mouth-watering juicy, these steaks sound like a great idea for Sunday family lunch. Serve with fresh or pickled salad.

Per serving: 350 Calories; 17.3g Fat; 2.1g Carbs; 42.7g Protein; 0.6g Sugars

Ingredients

2 tablespoons olive oil
2 tablespoons soy sauce
1 teaspoon garlic paste
A bunch of scallions, chopped
1 tablespoon lime lemon juice
1/4 cup dry red wine
2 pounds flank steak
Salt and cayenne pepper, to taste
1/2 teaspoon black peppercorns, crushed

Directions

- In a mixing bowl, thoroughly combine the oil, soy sauce, garlic paste, scallions, lemon juice, and red wine.
- Now, season the flank steak with salt, cayenne pepper and black peppercorns. Place the meat in a marinade; cover and refrigerate for 6 hours.
- Preheat a nonstick skillet over a moderately high flame. Fry your steaks about 10 minutes, turning once. Bon appétit!

179. Father's Day Stuffed Avocado

Ready in about 20 minutes
Servings 6

These avocado "boats" are healthy and oh-so-delicious! Serve as a starter or a complete dinner with mayo and sour cream. Enjoy!

Per serving: 407 Calories; 28.8g Fat; 16.4g Carbs; 23.4g Protein; 2.4g Sugars

Ingredients

1 tablespoon avocado oil
3/4 pound beef, ground
1/3 cup beef broth
1/2 cup shallots, sliced
Salt and black pepper, to taste
3 ripe avocados, pitted and halved
2 small-sized tomatoes, chopped
3/4 cup Colby cheese, shredded
3 tablespoons Kalamata olives, pitted and sliced
1/2 cup mayonnaise

Directions

- Preheat an oven to 340 degrees F.
- Het avocado oil in a pan over a moderate heat; now, brown the ground beef for 2 to 3 minutes, crumbling it with a wooden spatula.
- Add the broth and shallots. Cook until the shallots turn translucent. Season with salt and pepper.
- Then, scoop out some of the middle of each avocado. Mash the avocado flash that you scooped out along with chopped tomatoes.
- Add the reserved beef mixture and stuff your avocado. Afterward, top with shredded cheese and sliced olives.
- Place stuffed avocado on a roasting pan. Bake for 8 to 10 minutes in the preheated oven. Serve with mayonnaise and enjoy!

180. Beef Sausage and Vegetable Skillet

Ready in about 40 minutes
Servings 4

Beef sausage is an all-time favorite, isn't it? This recipe is very economical and practical, so go for it!

Per serving: 250 Calories; 17.5g Fat; 15.4g Carbs; 6.8g Protein; 5.7g Sugars

Ingredients

2 tablespoons canola oil
4 beef sausages, sliced
2 shallots, chopped
2 spring garlic, minced
2 bell peppers, deveined and chopped
1 parsnip, chopped
Salt and pepper, to taste
2 ripe tomatoes, pureed
2 tablespoons ketchup, sugar-free
1 ½ cups beef bone broth
1/4 cup dry red wine
2 thyme sprigs
2 rosemary sprigs

Directions

- Heat the oil in a deep skillet over a moderate heat. Cook the sausage for 2 to 3 minutes, stirring periodically.
- Stir in the shallots, garlic, bell peppers, and parsnip; season with salt and pepper. Cook approximately 7 minutes.
- Add the remaining ingredients and bring it to a boil. Reduce the heat to medium-low. Let it simmer for 25 minutes. Serve warm.

181. Spicy Sausage and Vegetable Casserole

Ready in about 30 minutes
Servings 4

A rich, homey casserole is one of the best ways to amaze your family for another gathering! In addition, this recipe is easy to follow and fun to eat.

Per serving: 424 Calories; 32.4g Fat; 9g Carbs; 23.7g Protein; 1.8g Sugars

Ingredients

1 tablespoon tallow, softened
4 beef sausages
1 banana shallot, sliced
1 cup broccoli, broken into small florets
1 carrot, sliced
1 celery stalk, chopped
1 bell pepper, sliced
1 dried Poblano pepper, crushed
2 garlic cloves, finely chopped
Salt, to taste
1 teaspoon black peppercorns, freshly crushed
1/2 teaspoon smoked cayenne pepper
1 ¼ cups beef stock, preferably homemade

Directions

- Melt the tallow in a nonstick skillet over a moderately high heat. Cook sausages until they are browned on all sides; reserve.
- Now, cook the shallot, broccoli, carrots, celery, peppers, and garlic in the same skillet; cook for 6 to 9 minutes or until the vegetables are tender.
- Season with salt, peppercorns and smoked cayenne pepper. Transfer the sautéed vegetables to a lightly greased casserole dish. Nestle the reserved sausages within the sautéed vegetables.
- Pour in the stock and bake in the preheated oven at 350 degrees F for about 10 minutes. Serve warm garnished with fresh chives if desired.

182. Hamburger Soup with Cabbage

Ready in about 35 minutes
Servings 4

If you feel like simplifying things, this recipe will be your next favorite. This soup freezes and reheats well so you can make a double batch.

Per serving: 307 Calories; 23.6g Fat; 8.4g Carbs; 14.8g Protein; 3.2g Sugars

Ingredients

2 tablespoons lard, melted
3/4 pound ground chuck
1/2 cup scallions, chopped
2 cloves garlic, minced
1 carrot, diced
1 cup cabbage, shredded
1 celery with leaves, diced
1 tomato, pureed
6 cups chicken broth
1 bay leaf
Seasoned salt and ground black pepper, to taste
1 cup sour cream

Directions

- Melt the lard in a stockpot. Cook the chuck until it is no longer pink; reserve.
- Then, cook the scallions, garlic, carrot, cabbage, and celery in the pan drippings, stirring constantly.
- Stir in the other ingredients along with reserved chuck, bringing to a rapid boil. Turn the heat to a simmer. Cook another 27 minutes, partially covered.
- Taste and adjust the seasonings. Ladle into individual bowls; serve dolloped with full-fat sour cream.

183. Ultimate Thai Beef Salad

Ready in about 15 minutes
Servings 4

If you are craving a spicy, refreshing and healthy meal, dig into this wonderful lunch salad! Thai chili (also known as Bird's eye chili) is famous for its antibacterial properties.

Per serving: 404 Calories; 32.9g Fat; 18.3g Carbs; 12.8g Protein; 4.3g Sugars

Ingredients

1/2 pound beef rump steak, cut into strips
1/2 teaspoon sea salt
1/3 teaspoon freshly cracked black pepper
1 teaspoon soy sauce
2 tablespoons sesame oil
1 red onion, peeled and sliced
1 garlic clove, minced
1 bunch fresh mint
2 avocados, pitted, peeled and sliced
2 cucumbers, sliced
1 bunch fresh Thai basil, leaves picked
1 teaspoon minced Thai chili
2 tablespoons rice vinegar
1 tablespoon fresh lime juice
1/4 cup pumpkin seeds

Directions

- Combine the beef with the salt, pepper and soy sauce.
- Preheat the oil in a nonstick skillet over medium-low heat. Then, sauté the onion and garlic until tender and aromatic, about 4 minutes.
- Cook the beef on a grill pan for 5 minutes or until cooked to your liking.
- Arrange fresh mint, avocado slices, cucumber, Thai basil, and Thai chili in a nice salad bowl. Top with the beef slices. Add the onion-garlic mixture.
- Drizzle with rice vinegar and lime juice. Sprinkle with pumpkin seeds and serve.

184. Hungarian Beef Stew

Ready in about 1 hour 25 minutes
Servings 4

Here is an ideal recipe for cheap cuts! A traditional Hungarian stew highlights the best of their amazingly rich and delicious cuisine.

Per serving: 357 Calories; 15.8g Fat; 10g Carbs; 40.2g Protein; 4.2g Sugars

Ingredients

2 tablespoons olive oil
1 ¼ pounds chuck-eye roast, diced
Celery salt and ground black pepper, to taste
1 tablespoon Hungarian paprika
1 tablespoon pear cider vinegar
1/2 cup Cabernet Sauvignon
4 cups water
2 tablespoons beef bouillon granules
1/4 teaspoon ground bay leaf
2 onions, peeled and chopped
1 celery with leaves, chopped
2 carrots, peeled and cut into 1/4-inch rounds
1 tablespoon flaxseed meal

Directions

- Heat the oil in a heavy-bottomed pot. Then, cook the meat until no longer pink, for 3 to 4 minutes; work in batches and set aside. Season with celery salt, pepper, and Hungarian paprika.
- Now, pour the vinegar and Cabernet Sauvignon to deglaze the bottom of the pot. Add the water, beef bouillon granules and reserved beef to the pot.
- Stir in the ground bay leaf, onions, celery and carrots and cook an additional 1 hour 15 minutes over medium-low heat.
- Add the flaxseed meal to thicken the liquid; stir constantly for 3 minutes. Serve in individual bowls and enjoy!

185. Za'atar Strip Steaks with Cabbage

Ready in about 20 minutes +marinating time
Servings 4

New York strip steak is actually a strip steak without the bones. It is incredibly tender cut of beef that goes perfectly with sautéed vegetables like cabbage and peppers.

Per serving: 321 Calories; 14g Fat; 8.3g Carbs; 36.7g Protein; 3.3g Sugars

Ingredients

1 pound New York strip steaks, cut into bite-sized pieces
1 tablespoon hoisin sauce
1 tablespoon fresh lemon juice
Sea salt and ground black pepper, to taste
1 teaspoon Za'atar
2 tablespoons sesame oil
1 yellow onion, chopped
2 garlic cloves, chopped
1 cup cabbage, shredded
1 bell pepper, chopped

Directions

- Toss strip steaks with hoisin sauce, fresh lemon juice, salt, black pepper and Za'atar seasoning. Marinate in the refrigerator for at least 3 hours.
- Heat the oil in a skillet that is preheated over a moderately high heat. Now, brown strip steaks for 3 to 4 minutes, stirring occasionally.
- Add the onions to the same skillet and cook until it is translucent. Add the garlic, cabbage and bell pepper and turn the heat to medium-low.
- Simmer an additional 10 minutes and serve warm. Bon appétit!

186. Spicy Winter Sauerkraut with Ground Beef

Ready in about 20 minutes
Servings 4

Sauerkraut is loaded with dietary fiber, vitamin C, vitamin A, and vitamin K. In addition, it contains a significant amount of magnesium, iron, manganese, copper, and calcium.

Per serving: 330 Calories; 12.2g Fat; 8.7g Carbs; 44.4g Protein; 3.6g Sugars

Ingredients

1 tablespoon tallow, melted
2 onions, chopped
2 garlic cloves, smashed
1 ¼ pounds ground beef
18 ounces sauerkraut, rinsed and well drained
1 teaspoon chili pepper flakes
1 teaspoon mustard powder
1 bay leaf
Sea salt and ground black pepper, to taste

Directions

* Heat a saucepan over a moderately high heat. Now, warm the tallow and cook the onions and garlic until aromatic.
* Stir in ground beef and cook until it is slightly browned.
* Add the remaining ingredients. Reduce the heat to medium. Cook about 6 minutes or until everything is thoroughly cooked. Bon appétit!

187. Winter Cheeseburger Soup

Ready in about 20 minutes
Servings 4

The best cheeseburger soup you could taste is now available to you! Plus, it is low-carb and healthy!

Per serving: 326 Calories; 20.5g Fat; 8.5g Carbs; 26.8g Protein; 1.6g Sugars

Ingredients

2 tablespoons coconut oil
1/2 pound ground beef
1 cup shallots, chopped
1 celery stalk, chopped
1 tablespoon celery leaves, chopped
1 tablespoon fresh cilantro, chopped
4 cups beef bone broth
1/2 cup full-fat milk
1 cup pepper jack cheese, shredded
1 tablespoon rice vinegar

Directions

* Melt the coconut oil in a stock pot that is preheated over a moderate heat. Now, cook the ground beef until it is no longer pink; reserve.
* Add the shallots and chopped celery stalk; cook an additional 2 minutes, stirring continuously. Add a splash of broth if needed.
* Add celery leaves, cilantro and broth and bring to a boil; cook another 10 minutes, partially covered.
* Gradually add the milk to the soup, stirring often. Reduce the heat and let it simmer an additional 5 minutes. Fold in the cheese and remove from the heat.
* Add the vinegar and stir until cheese is completely melted. Bon appétit!

188. Zucchini Spaghetti with Bolognese Sauce

Ready in about 1 hour 35 minutes
Servings 4

For a keto and light version of the world-famous pasta recipe, try these flavorful zucchini spaghetti. You won't miss whole wheat pasta, trust me!

Per serving: 477 Calories; 25.6g Fat; 16.3g Carbs; 41.8g Protein; 8.3g Sugars

Ingredients

For Bolognese:
2 tablespoons olive oil
1 onion, finely chopped
2 garlic cloves, thinly sliced
1 celery with leaves, finely chopped
1 carrot, finely chopped
2 slices bacon, chopped
1 pound ground beef
2 tomatoes, pureed
2 tablespoons tomato paste
1/2 cup dry white wine
1/2 cup water
2 rosemary sprigs
1 teaspoon dried oregano
1 teaspoon dried basil
1 teaspoon fresh thyme leaves
Salt and ground black pepper, to taste

For Zucchini Spaghetti:
4 zucchinis, peeled
2 tablespoons olive oil
1/4 cup water
Salt, to taste

Directions

- Heat the oil in a sauté pan that is preheated over a moderate flame. Now, sauté the onions, garlic, celery and carrots until they are tender.
- Now, stir in the bacon and ground beef. Cook for 7 more minutes, breaking up lumps with a spatula.
- Stir in the other ingredients for the sauce and simmer for 1 hour 15 minutes over medium-low heat. Taste and adjust the seasonings.
- Meanwhile, make your zucchini spaghetti. Slice the zucchinis into long strips i.e. noodle-shape strands.
- Heat the oil in a pan over medium heat; cook zucchini for 1 minute or so, stirring continuously. Pour in water and cook 6 more minutes.
- Sprinkle with salt to taste and serve with prepared Bolognese sauce. Enjoy!

189. Filet Mignon with Sour Cream-Mustard Sauce

Ready in about 20 minutes
Servings 4

Saucy filet mignon topped with sour cream-mustard sauce is sure to satisfy. Mediterranean herbs create depth of flavors.

Per serving: 321 Calories; 13.7g Fat; 1g Carbs; 45g Protein; 0g Sugars

Ingredients

1/3 cup sour cream
1 tablespoon stone-ground mustard
1 ½ tablespoons flat-leaf parsley, finely chopped
4 (1 ½-inch) thick filet mignon steaks
1/2 teaspoon seasoned salt
1/4 teaspoon ground black pepper
2 sprigs thyme, chopped
1 sprig rosemary, chopped
1 tablespoon vegetable oil

Directions

- In a mixing bowl, whisk together the sour cream, mustard, and parsley. Keep in your refrigerator until ready to serve.
- Then, season filet mignon steaks with salt, pepper, thyme, and rosemary.
- Heat the oil in a pan that is preheated over a moderately high heat for 4 minutes on each side. Serve with prepared mustard sauce and enjoy!

190. Saucy Beef Short Loin

Ready in about 2 hours
Servings 4

This fabulous beef dish is low in carbs but high in protein. It's made with thinly sliced beef short loin, vegetables and Worcestershire-wine sauce.

Per serving: 238 Calories; 9.2g Fat; 6.3g Carbs; 27.4g Protein; 2.7g Sugars

Ingredients

1 tablespoon olive oil
1 pound beef short loin, thinly sliced
1 leek, sliced
1 parsnip, chopped
3 garlic cloves, thinly sliced
1/2 teaspoon grated nutmeg
1 teaspoon lemon zest
1/2 teaspoon red pepper flakes, crushed
1/3 cup red wine
2 tablespoons Worcestershire sauce
1 ½ cups beef stock

Directions

- Heat the oil in a heavy-bottomed skillet that is pre-heated over a moderate heat. Sear beef short loin for 10 to 13 minutes; reserve.
- Then, in the same skillet, cook the leeks, parsnip and garlic for 3 to 4 minutes, stirring constantly.
- Add the remaining ingredients and bring to a rapid boil. Then, turn the heat to a simmer. Cook for 1 ½ to 2 hours. Bon appétit!

191. Old-Fashioned Beef Stew

Ready in about 40 minutes
Servings 6

For this soup, use old-time favorites: good-quality beef, fresh mushrooms, and the best aromatics. Just like grandma used to make!

Per serving: 259 Calories; 10.1g Fat; 4.1g Carbs; 35.7g Protein; 1.4g Sugars

Ingredients

1 tablespoon tallow, at room temperature
1 ½ pounds beef stew meat, cubed
1 cup leeks, thinly sliced
2 garlic cloves, chopped
1 tablespoon cremini mushrooms, thinly sliced
Salt and black pepper, to taste
1 teaspoon dried marjoram
1 teaspoon cayenne pepper
1/4 teaspoon smoked paprika
1 bay leaf
4 cubes beef bouillon, crumbled
4 cups water
1 egg, lightly whisked

Directions

- Melt the tallow in your pot that is preheated over a moderate flame.
- Now, sear the beef until it's just browned; make sure to stir periodically. Set aside.
- In pan drippings, cook the leeks and garlic for 1 to 1 minute 30 seconds or until aromatic. Stir in the mushrooms; cook until they're tender and fragrant.
- Add the remaining ingredients, cover and cook for 30 to 40 minutes. Add the whisked egg in hot soup and stir for 1 minute. Serve in individual bowls and enjoy!

192. Filet Mignon Steaks with Wine Sauce

Ready in about 30 minutes
Servings 4

Need more ideas for what to make with beef steaks? Try these filet mignon steaks for an easy mid-week meal.

Per serving: 451 Calories; 34.4g Fat; 3.6g Carbs; 29.7g Protein; 1.2g Sugars

Ingredients

4 (6-ounce) filet mignon steaks
1 tablespoon deli mustard
Celery salt and freshly ground pepper, to taste
2 rosemary sprigs
1 thyme sprigs
2 tablespoons lard, room temperature
1 cup scallions, chopped
2 garlic cloves, minced
1 red bell pepper, deveined and chopped
1/2 cup dry red wine

Directions

- Rub filet mignon steaks with mustard. Sprinkle filet mignon steaks with the salt, pepper, rosemary and thyme.
- Heat the lard in a heavy-bottomed skillet over a moderate heat. Cook filet mignon steaks for 10 minutes on each side or until a thermometer registers 120 degrees F.
- Now, cook the scallions, garlic, and pepper in pan drippings about 3 minutes. Pour in the wine to scrape up any browned bits from the bottom of the skillet.
- Now, cook until the liquid is reduced by half. Serve immediately.

193. Mini Meatloaf Muffins with Cremini Mushrooms

Ready in about 40 minutes
Servings 6

Full of amazing flavors of mushrooms, pine nuts, and crushed chicharrones, these mini meatloaves are sure to please. The most perfect ketogenic bites you can imagine!

Per serving: 404 Calories; 22.8g Fat; 6.2g Carbs; 44g Protein; 2.8g Sugars

Ingredients

1 tablespoon olive oil
1 yellow onion, chopped
1/2 pound Cremini mushrooms, chopped
3/4 cup Romano cheese, grated
1/2 cup crushed chicharrones
1/2 teaspoon granulated garlic
2 eggs, lightly beaten
1/4 cup pine nuts, ground
1 ¼ pounds ground beef
1/2 cup tomato puree
Salt and ground black pepper, to taste
1 teaspoon cayenne pepper

Directions

- Begin by preheating your oven to 390 degrees F.
- Heat the oil in a pan that is preheated over a moderately high heat. Now, sauté the onion until it is translucent and aromatic.
- Stir in the mushrooms and cook an additional 4 minutes or until almost all of the liquid has evaporated.
- Add the cheese, crushed chicharrones, granulated garlic, eggs, pine nuts and ground beef. Now, mix until everything is well incorporated.
- Divide the meatloaf mixture among lightly greased muffin cups. Bake for 25 minutes.
- Meanwhile, mix tomato puree with salt, black pepper and cayenne pepper. Spread the tomato mixture over meatloaves.
- Bake until a thermometer registers 165 degrees F, 5 to 10 minutes more. Allow your meatloaves to cool for a couple of minutes before removing from the pan. Bon appétit!

194. Crock Pot Beef Brisket with Blue Cheese

Ready in about 8 hours
Servings 6

Beef brisket is an amazing dish because it turns great every time! Additionally, you can use leftovers, cold or warm, for sandwiches, dips, and salads.

Per serving: 397 Calories; 31.4g Fat; 3.9g Carbs; 23.5g Protein; 2.3g Sugars

Ingredients

2 tablespoons olive oil
1 shallot, chopped
1/2 tablespoon garlic paste
1 ½ pounds corned beef brisket
1/4 teaspoon cloves, ground
1/3 teaspoon ground coriander
1/4 cup soy sauce
1 cup water
6 ounces blue cheese, crumbled

Directions

- Heat a sauté pan with the olive oil over medium heat. Cook the shallot until it is softened.
- Add garlic paste and cook an additional minute; transfer to your Crock pot that is previously greased with a nonstick cooking spray.
- Sear the brisket until it has a golden-brown crust. Transfer to the Crock pot. Add the remaining ingredient, except for blue cheese.
- Cover and cook on Low heat setting for 6 to 8 hours or until the meat is very tender. Serve topped with blue cheese. Enjoy!

195. Sriracha and Scallion Chuck

Ready in about 50 minutes
Servings 4

This isn't an average recipe for chuck pot roast. This chuck is marinated in Sriracha-scallion sauce and then, cooked to perfection in hot tallow.

Per serving: 292 Calories; 14.3g Fat; 3.9g Carbs; 36.9g Protein; 1.7g Sugars

Ingredients

2 tablespoons soy sauce
1 teaspoon Sriracha sauce
1 tablespoon garlic paste
Salt and crushed mixed peppercorns, to taste
1 teaspoon mustard seeds
1/2 teaspoon dried marjoram
1 bunch scallions, chopped
1/2 tablespoon tallow
1 ½ pounds chuck pot roast, cubed
1/4 teaspoon cumin
1/4 teaspoon celery seeds
1 tablespoon fresh parsley, roughly chopped

Directions

- Whisk the soy sauce, Sriracha sauce and garlic paste in a mixing bowl. Add the salt, crushed peppercorns, mustard seeds, marjoram, and scallions.
- Add the cubed beef and let it marinate for 40 minutes in your refrigerator.
- Melt the tallow a frying pan over a moderately high heat. Cook marinated beef for 5 to 6 minutes, stirring frequently; work in batches to cook beef cubes through evenly.
- Season with cumin and celery seeds. Serve garnished with fresh parsley. Enjoy!

196. Beef Casserole with Sour Cream Sauce

Ready in about 25 minutes
Servings 4

Everyone loves a good casserole! This keto version is the ultimate comfort food.

Per serving: 509 Calories; 29.6g Fat; 16.1g Carbs; 45.2g Protein; 6.4g Sugars

Ingredients

1 tablespoon olive oil
1 pound ground beef
2 ripe tomatoes, chopped
2 ounces sun-dried tomatoes, chopped
1/2 tablespoon dill relish
1/2 teaspoon salt
1/4 teaspoon ground black pepper
1/2 teaspoon chili powder
1 teaspoon Italian seasoning
1 cup cheddar cheese
3/4 cup sour cream
1 teaspoon minced garlic
1/2 cup shallots, finely chopped

Directions

- Preheat the oven to 400 degrees F.
- Then, heat the oil in a nonstick skillet that is preheated over a moderate flame.
- Brown the ground beef in butter, crumbling it with a large spatula. Add the tomatoes, dill relish and seasonings.
- Place the beef mixture in a baking dish. Top with cheese and bake for about 18 minutes.
- Meanwhile, thoroughly combine the sour cream with the garlic and shallots. Serve with your casserole dish.

197. Buttery Roasted Chuck with Horseradish Sauce

Ready in about 2 hours
Servings 6

Check out this buttery-tender chuck that is marinated with dry red wine, mustard, and fragrant Italian seasoning mix.

Per serving: 493 Calories; 39.4g Fat; 2.9g Carbs; 27.9g Protein; 0.8g Sugars

Ingredients

1 ½ pounds chuck
2 bay leaves
1/4 cup vegetable oil
1 garlic clove, minced
1 tablespoon Italian seasoning mix
1 ½ tablespoons whole grain mustard
1/3 cup dry red wine
1 teaspoon sea salt
1/4 teaspoon black pepper, to taste
1/2 teaspoon cayenne pepper, or more to taste

For the Sauce:
2 tablespoons prepared horseradish
1/4 cup sour cream
2 tablespoons mayonnaise

Directions

- Toss the chuck with bay leaves, vegetable oil, garlic, Italian seasoning, mustard, red wine, salt, black pepper and cayenne pepper.
- Let it marinate overnight in the refrigerator. Place your chuck in a baking dish that is lined with a piece of foil; pour the marinade over it.
- Wrap with the foil. Then, bake at 375 degrees F for 2 hours or until a thermometer registers 125 degrees F.
- In the meantime, mix all ingredients for the sauce. Slice your chuck across the grain and serve with the sauce on the side.

198. Italian-Style Holiday Meatloaf

Ready in about 50 minutes
Servings 6

Making a festive meatloaf has never been easier! Try this holiday classic with a keto twist.

Per serving: 163 Calories; 8.4g Fat; 9.6g Carbs; 12.2g Protein; 2.1g Sugars

Ingredients

Nonstick cooking spray
2 pounds ground chuck
1 egg, slightly beaten
2 shallots, chopped
1 tablespoon garlic paste
1 tablespoon mustard
1 ½ teaspoons coconut aminos
2 tablespoons fresh pureed tomato
1/3 cup full-fat milk
1/3 cup almond flour
2 tablespoons flaxseed meal
1 teaspoon Italian seasonings
Seasoned salt and ground black pepper
1/4 teaspoon ground sage

For the Tomato Sauce:
2 ripe tomatoes, crushed
Salt and black pepper, to taste
1 tablespoon cilantro, minced

Directions

● Start by preheating your oven 360 degrees F. Lightly grease a loaf pan with a nonstick cooking spray.
● In a mixing bowl, thoroughly combine all the meatloaf ingredients.
● Now, press the meatloaf mixture into the prepared meatloaf.
● Add all ingredients for the sauce to a pan that is preheated over medium-low heat. Simmer for 2 to 3 minutes, stirring periodically.
● Spread the sauce over the top of your meatloaf. Bake for 45 minutes. Let it cool down for a couple of minutes before slicing and serving. Bon appétit!

199. Royal Keto Lasagna

Ready in about 1 hour 30 minutes
Servings 6

This keto lasagna is the ultimate comfort food. It might become your weeknight favorite. Make it tonight and enjoy!

Per serving: 494 Calories; 41g Fat; 8.8g Carbs; 24.1g Protein; 2.2g Sugars

Ingredients

For the Lasagna Sheets:
3 eggs, whisked
6 ounces mascarpone cheese, at room temperature
1/2 cup Parmesan cheese, grated
1 cup Colby cheese, shredded
1/2 teaspoon dried oregano
1/2 teaspoon onion powder
1/2 teaspoon cumin powder

For the Filling:
1 tablespoon olive oil
1 ½ pounds ground chuck
1 onion, chopped
2 garlic cloves, minced
2 slices bacon, chopped
1 cup tomato sauce
1/2 teaspoon oregano
1/2 teaspoon dried basil
2 cups sour cream
1 cup mascarpone cheese
1/4 cup fresh parsley, finely chopped

Directions

● Start by preheating your oven to 370 degrees F. Now, coat a baking pan with a sheet of parchment paper or Silpat mat.
● Then, thoroughly combine the eggs and 6 ounces of mascarpone cheese with a hand mixer.
● Add the other ingredients for the lasagna sheets; mix to combine well.
● Press the mixture onto the baking pan, creating an even layer. Bake approximately 20 minutes.
● Now, refrigerate the "sheet" for 30 minutes. Cut into lasagna sheets and set aside.
● Next, heat the oil in a pan that is preheated over a moderate heat. Brown ground beef for 3 to 4 minutes.
● Add the onion, garlic and bacon and cook an additional 3 minutes, stirring constantly. Now, stir in tomato sauce, oregano and basil; cook an additional 13 minutes.
● Pour 1/4 cup of the sauce into the bottom of a previously greased casserole dish. Top with the first lasagna sheet. Repeat these steps 3 times.
● Top with sour cream and 1 cup of mascarpone cheese. Sprinkle fresh parsley over the top. Bake for 15 to 22 minutes longer. Serve warm and enjoy!

200. Cabbage, Beef and Cheese Casserole

Ready in about 55 minutes
Servings 6

This 5-layer casserole uses basic ingredients but they are combined in a great way! It has all the flavors your family loves, but it's adapted for a keto diet.

Per serving: 467 Calories; 37g Fat; 8.8g Carbs; 27.1g Protein; 4.3g Sugars

Ingredients

1 head of cabbage, cut into quarters
1/2 pound ground chuck
1/2 pound ground turkey
1 leek, chopped
2 slices bacon, chopped
1 teaspoon dried basil
1 teaspoon dried oregano
1/2 teaspoon dried marjoram
Salt and black pepper, to taste
1 cup salsa, preferably homemade
1 ½ cups cream cheese, crumbled
8 slices American cheese
2 eggs

Directions

- Firstly, boil cabbage approximately 5 minutes; drain. Preheat your oven to 400 degrees F.
- Preheat a pan over a moderately high heat; cook ground beef and turkey, breaking with a spatula, for 4 to 5 minutes.
- Now, add the leeks and bacon; cook for a further 3 minutes, stirring frequently.
- Stir in the basil, oregano, marjoram, salt, pepper and salsa; bring it to a boil. Turn the heat to medium-low; cook an additional 6 minutes.
- Add 1/2 of this mixture to the bottom of a lightly greased baking dish. Add a layer of boiled cabbage leaves. Repeat layers one more time.
- In a mixing bowl, combine cream cheese, American cheese, and eggs. Top your casserole with the cheese layer and bake for 30 minutes or until everything is thoroughly cooked.
- Allow your casserole to cool down for a couple of minutes before slicing and serving.

201. Top Round Steak with Marsala Sauce

Ready in about 1 hour 40 minutes
Servings 6

You can substitute top round steak with top sirloin in this recipe. Bear in mind that top round contains less fat than top sirloin which means you should use a liquid throughout the cooking process.

Per serving: 339 Calories; 21.7g Fat; 9.2g Carbs; 35g Protein; 1.2g Sugars

Ingredients

1 ½ pounds top round steak, cut into 4 serving-size pieces
2 tablespoons olive oil
1 shallot, chopped
1 garlic clove, pressed
1 ½ cups Brussels sprouts, quartered
1 teaspoon ground bay leaf
1/2 teaspoon dried basil
1 tablespoon dried sage, crushed
1/2 teaspoon sea salt
1/4 teaspoon freshly ground black pepper
1 cup broth

For the Sauce:
1/2 cup Marsala wine
1/2 cup chicken broth
1/4 teaspoon freshly grated nutmeg
3/4 teaspoon Dijon mustard
1 cup double cream

Directions

- Begin by preheating your oven to 340 degrees F. Flatten each top round steak with a meat tenderizer.
- Heat olive oil in an oven-safe pan over medium-high heat. Now, cook the steak until just browned; reserve.
- Next, cook the shallots and garlic in pan drippings in the same pan until they're softened. After that, cook Brussels sprouts until tender and smell good.
- Add the round steak back to the pan. Season with ground bay leaf, basil, sage, salt, and pepper. Pour in 1 cup of broth. Wrap with foil and roast for 1 hour 10 minutes.
- Add the wine, 1/2 cup chicken cup of broth and nutmeg to the same roasting pan. Let it simmer for 15 to 18 minutes or until the sauce is reduced to half.
- Now, stir in the mustard and double cream; cook an additional 15 minutes or until everything is heated through.
- Divide top round steak among four serving plates; ladle the sauce over them and serve warm.

202. Skirt Steak and Eggs Skillet

Ready in about 30 minutes
Servings 6

You can't go wrong with a combo of skirt steak, peppers, and eggs! Serve as an energy-boosting breakfast or a mid-week special lunch.

Per serving: 429 Calories; 27.8g Fat; 3.2g Carbs; 39.1g Protein; 1.6g Sugars

Ingredients

2 tablespoons olive oil
1 ½ pounds skirt steak, cut into cubes
Celery salt and ground black pepper, to taste
1/2 teaspoon red pepper flakes
1/2 cup spring onions onion, chopped
1 teaspoon garlic, minced
1 bell pepper, chopped
1 serrano pepper, chopped
6 eggs

Directions

- Heat the oil in a nonstick skillet over a moderately high flame. Cook beef cubes for 10 minutes or until no longer pink, stirring periodically. Season with salt, black pepper and red pepper flakes and set aside.
- In the same skillet, cook spring onion and garlic until aromatic, 3 to 4 minutes. Stir in the peppers and cook for 3 minutes more.
- Now, create six holes in the mixture to reveal the bottom of your pan. Crack an egg into each hole. Now, cook, covered, for 4 to 6 minutes or until the eggs are set. Serve right away!

FISH & SEAFOOD

203. Breakfast Avocado and Tuna Balls......................... 119

204. Hot and Spicy Fish Stew..................................... 119

205. Easy Oven-Baked Cod Fillets............................... 120

206. Ricotta and Tuna Spread 120

207. Colorful Scallop Dinner..................................... 121

208. Tuna and Cottage Cheese Stuffed Peppers 121

209. Halibut Steaks with Cheesy Cauliflower 122

210. Smoked Tilapia Pie 122

211. Spring Shrimp Salad 123

212. Salmon with Pine Nuts Sauce
     and Sautéed Brussels Sprouts............................. 123

213. Aromatic Red Snapper Soup 124

214. Easy Fried Tiger Prawns.................................... 124

215. Saucy Chilean Sea Bass with Dijon Sauce............. 125

216. Two-Cheese and Smoked Salmon Dip.................. 125

217. Halibut Steaks for Two 126

218. Tuna and Avocado Salad with Mayo Dressing..... 126

219. Pan-Seared Fish Fillets with Mesclun Salad 127

220. Mediterranean-Style Snapper Salad..................... 127

221. Cod and Cauliflower Patties 128

222. Boozy Prawns with Mignonette Sauce 128

223. Creole Salmon Fillets..................................... 129

224. Fish Cutlets with Parsley Mashed Cauliflower..... 129

225. Prawn Cocktail Salad.................................... 130

226. Halibut en Persillade 130

227. Hearty Pollock Chowder.................................... 131

228. Summer Fish Cakes 131

229. Sardine Salad Pickled Pepper Boats...................... 132

230. Asian-Inspired Tilapia Chowder............................ 132

231. Smoked Salmon and Cheese Stuffed Tomatoes ... 133

232. Chilean Sea Bass with Cauliflower and Chutney. 133

233. Grilled Halloumi and Tuna Salad 134

234. Colorful Tuna Salad with Bocconcini 134

235. Tuna Fillets with Greens............................... 135

236. One-Pot Seafood Stew 135

237. Seafood and Andouille Medley 136

238. Quatre Épices Salmon Fillets with Cheese............ 136

239. Easy Parmesan Crusted Tilapia 137

240. Creamy Anchovy Salad 137

241. Moms' Aromatic Fish Curry................................ 138

242. Pan-Seared Trout Fillets with Chimichurri 138

243. Sunday Amberjack Fillets with Parmesan Sauce 139

244. Crabmeat, Prosciutto and Vegetable Delight........ 139

245. Fish with Cremini Mushrooms
     and Sour Cream Sauce.............................. 140

246. Spring Salad with Harissa Crab Mayo.................. 140

247. Grilled Clams with Tomato Sauce 141

248. Prawn and Avocado Cocktail Salad...................... 141

249. Chinese-Style Milkfish with
     Mushroom-Pepper Coulis 142

250. Tuna and Vegetable Kebabs 142

251. Mackerel Steak Casserole with Cheese and Veggies 143

252. Classic Seafood Chowder.................................... 143

253. Smoky Cholula Seafood Dip 144

203. Breakfast Avocado and Tuna Balls

Ready in about 5 minutes
Servings 4

How to tell if your avocado is ripe and ready to eat? If the avocado doesn't yield to gentle pressure it is under-ripe but you can still buy it if it doesn't have any brown spots, dark blemishes or bruises. A ripe avocado is soft to the touch and it yields to the gentle pressure.

Per serving: 316 Calories; 24.4g Fat; 8.9g Carbs; 17.4g Protein; 1.4g Sugars

Ingredients

3 ounces sunflower seeds
1 avocado, pitted and peeled
1 can tuna
Salt, to taste
1/2 teaspoon freshly ground black pepper
1/2 teaspoon smoked paprika
1/2 cup onion, chopped
1/2 teaspoon dried dill

Directions

- Thoroughly mix all ingredients in a mixing dish. Shape the mixture into 8 balls.
- Serve well chilled and enjoy!

204. Hot and Spicy Fish Stew

Ready in about 25 minutes
Servings 4

This is an easy and versatile fish stew recipe. You can experiment with ingredients, from fish and seafood to seasonings and wine. Shrimp, scallops, and salmon work well too.

Per serving: 296 Calories; 8.6g Fat; 5.5g Carbs; 41.4g Protein; 2.7g Sugars

Ingredients

1 tablespoon sesame oil
1 cup onions, chopped
1 teaspoon garlic, smashed
Sea salt, to taste
4 cups water
1 cup fresh tomato, pureed
1 tablespoon chicken bouillon granules
1/2 pound sea bass, cut into 2-inch pieces
1/3 pound halibut, cut into 2-inch pieces
2 rosemary sprigs, chopped
1/2 cup Sauvignon blanc
1/8 teaspoon Tabasco sauce, or more to taste

Directions

- Heat the oil in a large stockpot that is preheated over medium heat. Now, sauté the onions and garlic until they're softened and aromatic.
- Add the salt, water, tomato and chicken bouillon granules; cook an additional 13 minutes.
- Stir in the remaining ingredients and bring to a rolling boil.
- After that, turn the heat to medium-low and let it simmer until the fish easily flakes apart, about 4 minutes.
- Taste and adjust the seasonings. Ladle the soup into individual bowls and serve hot.

205. Easy Oven-Baked Cod Fillets

Ready in about 30 minutes
Servings 4

Cod is a great source of protein, omega-3 fatty acids, and vitamin B12. Did you know that cod liver oil can lower your blood pressure, prevent heart disease, and protect eyesight?

Per serving: 195 Calories; 8.2g Fat; 0.5g Carbs; 28.7g Protein; 0.1g Sugars

Ingredients

2 tablespoons olive oil
1/2 tablespoon yellow mustard
1 teaspoon garlic paste
1/2 tablespoon fresh lemon juice
1/2 teaspoon shallot powder
Salt and ground black pepper, to taste
1/2 teaspoon red pepper flakes, crushed
4 cod fillets
1/4 cup fresh cilantro, chopped

Directions

- Start by preheating your oven to 420 degrees F. Lightly grease a baking dish with a nonstick cooking spray.
- In a small mixing dish, thoroughly combine the oil, mustard, garlic paste, lemon juice, shallot powder, salt, black pepper and red pepper.
- Rub this mixture on all sides of your fish.
- Bake 15 to 22 minutes in the middle of the preheated oven. Serve sprinkled with fresh cilantro.

206. Ricotta and Tuna Spread

Ready in about 10 minutes
Servings 6

This tuna spread has a perfect nutritional profile. It will provide you and your family with a well-balanced and flavorful meal.

Per serving: 384 Calories; 20.4g Fat; 2.5g Carbs; 45.9g Protein; 0.4g Sugars

Ingredients

1 (6-ounce) can tuna in oil, drained
1/2 cup Ricotta cheese
1/2 teaspoon turmeric
2 ounces pecans, ground
1 tablespoon fresh cilantro, chopped

Directions

- Blend tuna, Ricotta cheese, turmeric powder and pecans in your blender.
- Transfer to a serving bowl and serve garnished with fresh cilantro.
- Serve with veggie sticks. Bon appétit!

207. Colorful Scallop Dinner

Ready in about 10 minutes
Servings 4

With their subtle flavors, scallops are perfect for family lunch or a luxurious party dinner. One of the best ways to eat scallops is to make this fresh and easy salad.

Per serving: 260 Calories; 13.6g Fat; 7.9g Carbs; 28.1g Protein; 4.5g Sugars

Ingredients

1 pound sea scallops, halved horizontally
4 spring garlic, roughly chopped
2 plum tomatoes, sliced
1 cucumber, sliced
1 head of Iceberg lettuce, torn into bite-sized pieces
1/2 tablespoon deli mustard
1/4 cup extra-virgin olive oil
2 tablespoons fresh lemon juice
Sea salt and freshly ground pepper, to your liking
1/2 teaspoon dried dill weed
1/2 cup ripe olives, pitted and sliced

Directions

- Add the scallops to a pot of a lightly salted water; cook for 1 to 3 minutes or until opaque; rinse under running water and transfer to a salad bowl.
- Stir in spring garlic, tomatoes, cucumber, and lettuce; gently toss to combine.
- In a mixing dish, thoroughly combine the mustard, olive oil, lemon, salt, pepper and dill. Drizzle this mixture over the vegetables in the salad bowl.
- Serve topped with ripe olives and enjoy!

208. Tuna and Cottage Cheese Stuffed Peppers

Ready in about 25 minutes
Servings 4

Are you excited to have another recipe to add to your keto meal plan?! These peppers are perfect for busy weeknights!

Per serving: 273 Calories; 13.9g Fat; 7.1g Carbs; 28.9g Protein; 4.1g Sugars

Ingredients

4 bell peppers
10 ounces canned tuna, drained
1 yellow onion, finely chopped
1 garlic clove, smashed
1/3 cup mayonnaise
1/3 cup Kalamata olives, pitted and chopped
Sea salt and cayenne pepper, to taste
1/2 teaspoon dried parsley
1/2 teaspoon dried oregano
1 cup Cottage cheese

Directions

- Start by preheating your oven to broil. Arrange bell peppers on a baking sheet; broil for 6 minutes, turning the peppers once; make sure to rotate the baking sheet once or twice.
- Once the peppers are cool enough to handle, cut them in half; remove seeds and membranes.
- In a mixing bowl, thoroughly combine tuna, onion, garlic, mayonnaise, olives, salt, cayenne pepper, dried parsley, oregano and Cottage cheese.
- Now, fill the peppers with the tuna mixture. Bake stuffed peppers in the oven for 10 minutes or until thoroughly heated. Serve warm or at room temperature. Enjoy!

209. Halibut Steaks with Cheesy Cauliflower

Ready in about 25 minutes
Servings 4

Cheesy cauliflower casserole with crispy pan-fried fish steaks might become your keto staple. It is guaranteed to make your meals so much better.

Per serving: 508 Calories; 22.9g Fat; 4.7g Carbs; 68.6g Protein; 1.8g Sugars

Ingredients

1 head of cauliflower, broken into florets
2 tablespoons olive oil
Sea salt and ground black pepper, to taste
1 cup Colby cheese, shredded
4 halibut steaks
1/2 teaspoon dried sage
1/2 teaspoon dried basil
1 ½ tablespoons fresh parsley, chopped
1 lemon, cut into wedges

Directions

- Begin by preheating your oven to 390 degrees F.
- Cook the cauliflower in a pot of lightly salted water until just tender.
- Transfer to a well-greased casserole dish. Drizzle with 1 tablespoon of olive oil. Season with salt and pepper to taste.
- Scatter shredded cheese on top of the cauliflower; bake approximately 17 minutes.
- In the meantime, heat the remaining tablespoon of olive oil in a pan that is preheated over a moderately high flame. Fry the halibut steaks until golden and crisp.
- Season with sage, basil, salt, and pepper. Serve garnished with fresh parsley and lemon wedges. Bon appétit!

210. Smoked Tilapia Pie

Ready in about 45 minutes
Servings 6

Here's a million-dollar fish pie you will crave during winter days! Serve with coleslaw, tomatillo salsa verde or pickled onions.

Per serving: 416 Calories; 34.2g Fat; 8.5g Carbs; 19.5g Protein; 1.7g Sugars

Ingredients

For the Crust:
1 cup almond flour
3 tablespoons flaxseed meal
2 teaspoons ground psyllium husk powder
1/2 teaspoon baking powder
1/2 teaspoon baking soda
1/2 teaspoon kosher salt
1/2 stick butter
2 eggs
2 tablespoons water

For the Filling:
10 ounces smoked tilapia, chopped
1 teaspoon Dijon mustard
1/2 cup sour cream
1/2 cup mayonnaise
2 eggs
1 teaspoon dried rosemary
1/2 teaspoon dried basil
Salt and ground black pepper, to taste
1 ½ cups Cheddar cheese, shredded

Directions

- Preheat your oven to 360 degrees F.
- Mix all the crust ingredients in your food processor. Press into a baking pan that is lined with parchment paper.
- Bake the crust in the middle of the preheated oven approximately 13 minutes.
- Then, thoroughly combine all the ingredients for the filling. Spread the mixture over the pie crust. Bake an additional 30 minutes or until the pie is golden at the edges. Bon appétit!

211. Spring Shrimp Salad

Ready in about 10 minutes + chilling time
Servings 6

Just a touch of hot sauce gives this recipe a different twist on the usual shrimp salad. This salad tastes better the next day!

Per serving: 209 Calories; 9.5g Fat; 12.8g Carbs; 20.2g Protein; 3.1g Sugars

Ingredients

1 medium-sized lime, cut into wedges
2 pounds shrimp
1/2 cup mayonnaise
1/2 cup sour cream
1/2 teaspoon yellow mustard
1 tablespoon Marsala wine
1 tablespoon wine vinegar
1/2 teaspoon freshly ground black pepper
4 spring onions, chopped
2 cucumbers, sliced
1 ½ cups radishes, sliced
1 tablespoon hot sauce

Directions

- Add the salt and lime wedges to a large pot; bring to a boil over high heat. Then, peel and devein the shrimp.
- Add the shrimp and cook for 2 to 3 minutes, until they are opaque.
- Drain and rinse your shrimp under running water. After that, peel your shrimp.
- In a mixing dish, thoroughly combine the remaining ingredients. Add the shrimp and gently stir to combine well.
- Place in the refrigerator until ready to serve. Enjoy!

212. Salmon with Pine Nuts Sauce and Sautéed Brussels Sprouts

Ready in about 25 minutes
Servings 4

Prepare to become addicted to this surprisingly delicious fish dish. Bear in mind that cooking salmon too long can dry it out so it will lose its natural texture and flavors.

Per serving: 372 Calories; 27.8g Fat; 8.6g Carbs; 26.5g Protein; 2.6g Sugars

Ingredients

1 pound salmon
Sea salt and freshly ground black pepper, to taste
1 teaspoon dried marjoram
1/3 cup fresh cilantro
2 garlic cloves, crushed
1/3 cup pine nuts, chopped
1 tablespoon lime juice
1/4 cup olive oil
1/2 cup chicken broth
1/2 pounds Brussels sprouts
1 medium-sized tomato, cut into slices

Directions

- Sprinkle salmon with salt, black pepper and marjoram on all sides; set aside.
- Now, pulse cilantro, garlic, pine nuts, lemon juice, and olive oil in your food processor until it reaches a paste consistency.
- Heat up a nonstick skillet over medium-high heat. Spritz the bottom of the skillet with a nonstick cooking spray and fry the salmon for 2 to 4 minutes on each side; reserve.
- In the same skillet, place chicken broth and Brussels sprouts; sauté for 4 to 6 minutes or until Brussels sprouts are as tender as you want; reserve.
- Now, sear tomato slices in the same skillet for 2 minutes on each side.
- Serve warm salmon topped with cilantro sauce and tomato slice, garnished with sautéed Brussels sprouts. Bon appétit!

213. Aromatic Red Snapper Soup

Ready in about 20 minutes
Servings 4

Looking for a last-minute soup recipe for a family lunch? This stunning fish soup will fit the bill! And the best of all – it is ready in 20 minutes!

Per serving: 316 Calories; 14.3g Fat; 10g Carbs; 32.7g Protein; 5.1g Sugars

Ingredients

1/2 stick butter, melted
2 onions, finely chopped
2 garlic cloves, minced
1/4 cup fresh cilantro, chopped
2 tomatoes, pureed
2 cups shellfish stock
1 cup water
1/4 cup dry white wine
1 pound red snapper, chopped
2 rosemary sprigs, chopped
2 thyme sprigs, chopped
1/2 teaspoon dried dill weed
Sea salt and ground black pepper, to taste

Directions

- Melt the butter in a stockpot that is preheated over a moderate heat. Sauté the onions and garlic for 3 minutes or until aromatic.
- Stir in fresh cilantro and cook 1 to 2 minutes more. Add pureed tomatoes, stock, water, wine, and fish; bring to a boil.
- Reduce the heat and let it simmer until the fish is thoroughly cooked, about 15 minutes. Add the remaining seasonings and serve warm.

214. Easy Fried Tiger Prawns

Ready in about 10 minutes + marinating time
Servings 4

Juicy, marinated tiger prawns quickly seared in a skillet with aromatics. Crisp dry sherry and fresh lime juice will add just the right amount of tanginess to this amazing seafood dish.

Per serving: 294 Calories; 14.3g Fat; 3.6g Carbs; 34.6g Protein; 0.1g Sugars

Ingredients

1 teaspoon red pepper flakes, crushed
1 tablespoon garlic paste
1 teaspoon dried rosemary
1/2 teaspoon mustard seeds
1 ½ tablespoons fresh lime juice
2 tablespoons dry sherry
1 ½ pounds tiger prawns, peeled and deveined
1/2 stick butter, at room temperature
Salt and ground black pepper, to taste

Directions

- Thoroughly combine red pepper, flakes, garlic paste, rosemary, mustard seeds, lime juice and dry sherry in a mixing bowl.
- Add the prawns to the mixing dish and let them marinate for 1 hour in the refrigerator.
- Melt the butter in a skillet that is preheated over medium-high heat. Now, discard marinade and fry prawns for 3 to 5 minutes, turning once or twice.
- Season with salt and pepper to taste. Serve warm and enjoy!

215. Saucy Chilean Sea Bass with Dijon Sauce

Ready in about 15 minutes + marinating time
Servings 4

A fantastic fish dinner with Dijon creamy sauce – all made in one skillet! This tangy fish dish is quick, easy and addictive.

Per serving: 228 Calories; 13g Fat; 6.5g Carbs; 13.7g Protein; 2.1g Sugars

Ingredients

1 pound wild Chilean sea bass, cubed
Sea salt, to taste
1/2 teaspoon paprika
1 cup scallions, chopped
2 cloves garlic, minced
2 Poblano pepper, chopped
1/2 cup dry sherry wine
1 tablespoon avocado oil
1 cup double cream
1 teaspoon Dijon mustard
1/4 teaspoon ground black pepper

Directions

- Toss the fish, salt, paprika, scallions, garlic, peppers and wine in a mixing bowl. Let it marinate in your refrigerator for 2 hours.
- Warm avocado oil in a cast-iron skillet over a moderate heat. Cook the fish along with marinade until it is thoroughly cooked, about 5 minutes; reserve cooked fish.
- In the same skillet, place double cream, Dijon mustard, and ground black pepper. Bring to a boil, and then, lower the heat.
- Continue to cook until everything is heated through, approximately 3 minutes.
- Add the fish back to the skillet, remove from heat and serve immediately.

216. Two-Cheese and Smoked Salmon Dip

Ready in about 10 minutes
Servings 10

This fish dip is terrific in so many ways. It is loaded with two kinds of cheese, mouth-watering smoked salmon, and seasonings. It takes 10 minutes to prepare and tastes wonderfully.

Per serving: 109 Calories; 6.3g Fat; 1.3g Carbs; 11.4g Protein; 0.8g Sugars

Ingredients

10 ounces smoked salmon, chopped
5 ounces Cottage cheese
5 ounces Feta cheese
4 hard-boiled egg yolks, finely chopped
Salt and freshly ground black pepper, to your liking
1/2 teaspoon smoked paprika
1/4 cup fresh chives, chopped

Directions

- Add all ingredients, except for chopped chives, to a mixing dish. Stir until everything is well combined.
- Put in a mound on a serving plate. Garnish with fresh chopped chives and serve well-chilled. Bon appétit!

217. Halibut Steaks for Two

Ready in about 35 minutes
Servings 2

Any day with seafood is a great day! This is the perfect recipe for a romantic dinner with wine and candles.

Per serving: 308 Calories; 10.9g Fat; 2g Carbs; 46.5g Protein; 0.2g Sugars

Ingredients

1/3 cup fresh lime juice
2 teaspoons olive oil
1/3 teaspoon salt
1/3 teaspoon pepper
1 teaspoon dry dill weed
1 teaspoon dry thyme
1 teaspoon garlic, finely minced
2 halibut steaks
1/3 cup fresh cilantro, chopped

Directions

- In a mixing bowl, combine fresh lime juice with olive oil, salt, pepper, dill, thyme and garlic. Add halibut steak and let it marinate about 20 minutes.
- Now, grill your fish steaks approximately 13 minutes, turning once or twice; make sure to baste them with the reserved marinade.
- Garnish with fresh cilantro leaves. Serve warm with your favorite salad. Enjoy!

218. Tuna and Avocado Salad with Mayo Dressing

Ready in about 5 minutes
Servings 4

Tuna in spring water is low in calories and carbs but high in protein and omega 3. Serve with crisp, white wine like Pinot Blanc, Muscadet or Viognier.

Per serving: 244 Calories; 12.7g Fat; 12.3g Carbs; 23.4g Protein; 4.8g Sugars

Ingredients

2 cans tuna chunks in spring water
1 avocado, pitted, peeled and diced
2 bell peppers, deveined and sliced
1 cup cherry tomatoes, halved or quartered
1 head arugula
1 red onion, chopped
1/4 cup mayonnaise
1 teaspoon deli mustard
Salt and ground black pepper, to taste
2 tablespoons fresh lime juice
1/2 cup Kalamata olives, pitted and sliced

Directions

- Combine tuna, avocado, bell peppers, cherry tomato, arugula and onion in a salad bowl.
- In a small mixing bowl, whisk the mayonnaise with mustard, salt, pepper and lime juice. Dress the salad and gently toss to combine.
- Top with Kalamata olives and serve well-chilled. Bon appétit!

219. Pan-Seared Fish Fillets with Mesclun Salad

Ready in about 15 minutes + marinating time
Servings 4

White fish fillets are always a big hit in the summertime! Serve with delicate Mesclun salad and enjoy!

Per serving: 425 Calories; 27.2g Fat; 6.1g Carbs; 38.3g Protein; 4.1g Sugars

Ingredients

4 white fish fillets
Salt and ground black pepper, to taste
2 tablespoons fresh lime juice
2 garlic cloves, minced
2 tablespoons fresh chives, chopped
2 tablespoons fresh coriander, chopped
1 tablespoon butter, softened

For Mesclun Salad:
1 head Romaine lettuce
1 cup chicory
1 cup frissee
1 cup arugula
2 tablespoons basil, chiffonade
2 tablespoons dandelion
1/2 cup apple cider
Salt and ground black pepper, to your liking
1/4 cup extra-virgin olive oil

Directions

- Toss white fish fillets with salt, pepper, lime juice, garlic, chives, and coriander; allow it to marinate at least 1 hour in the refrigerator.
- Melt the butter in a pan over a moderate heat; sear the fish fillets on each side for 4 minutes. Use the marinade as a basting sauce.
- In the meantime, place Romaine lettuce, chicory, frissee, arugula, basil and dandelion in a salad bowl.
- Make a dressing for your salad by whisking the remaining ingredients. Dress the salad and serve with warm fish fillets. Bon appétit!

220. Mediterranean-Style Snapper Salad

Ready in about 15 minutes
Servings 4

Treat your family to a refreshing bowl of something fabulous like this rich snapper salad. This salad will nourish your appetite and delight your taste buds!

Per serving: 507 Calories; 42.8g Fat; 9g Carbs; 24.4g Protein; 2.2g Sugars

Ingredients

4 snapper fillets
Sea salt and ground black pepper, to taste
1 teaspoon ground sumac
2 tablespoons butter, melted
4 cups baby spinach
12 grape tomatoes, halved
1 carrot, thinly sliced
2 shallots, thinly sliced
6 ounces Halloumi cheese, crumbled
1/2 cup ripe olives, pitted and sliced

For the Vinaigrette:
1 lemon, juiced and zested
1/3 cup extra-virgin olive oil
1/2 tablespoon brown mustard
1 clove garlic, smashed
1 teaspoon dried oregano
2 tablespoons fresh mint, finely chopped
Sea salt and ground black pepper, to taste
1 teaspoon red pepper flakes, crushed

Directions

- Lay the fish fillets on a clean board and sprinkle both sides with salt, pepper and sumac.
- Warm the butter in a pan that is preheated over a moderate flame. Fry the fish for 5 minutes on each side.
- In a nice salad bowl, toss baby spinach, tomatoes, carrots, shallots, cheese and olives. Top with chopped fish.
- Now, thoroughly combine all ingredients for the vinaigrette in your blender. Dress the salad and serve well-chilled. Bon appétit!

221. Cod and Cauliflower Patties

Ready in about 20 minutes
Servings 5

This keto version of a family favorite dish means you can eat better and healthier without sacrificing flavor. Lovely!

Per serving: 326 Calories; 21.7g Fat; 9g Carbs; 25.6g Protein; 1.8g Sugars

Ingredients

1 teaspoon ghee
3 cups cauliflower rice
2 ½ cups cod fish, cooked
Sea salt and freshly cracked black peppercorns, to taste
1 teaspoon dried basil
1/2 teaspoon dried oregano
1/2 teaspoon dried rosemary
1/4 cup shallots, chopped
2 eggs, whisked
1/2 cup almond flour
1/2 cup Parmesan cheese
3 tablespoons olive oil

Directions

- Melt the ghee in a pan over a medium heat. Then, cook the cauli-rice for 6 minutes, until crisp-tender; allow it to cool to room temperature.
- Then, mix the cooked and chilled cauli-rice with cooked fish, salt, pepper, basil, oregano, and rosemary.
- After that, stir in the shallots, eggs, almond flour, and parmesan cheese; mix to combine well.
- Shape the mixture into 10 patties. Heat the oil in a nonstick skillet that is previously preheated over a moderate flame.
- Cook for 5 minutes on each side. Serve with mayo and enjoy!

222. Boozy Prawns with Mignonette Sauce

Ready in about 15 minutes
Servings 4

Looking for easy ways to ditch the carbs? Look no further because this recipe is everything you want for a ketogenic dinner – saucy seafood with veggies and tangy sauce.

Per serving: 252 Calories; 7.3g Fat; 9.3g Carbs; 36.6g Protein; 2.1g Sugars

Ingredients

1 ½ tablespoons olive oil
1 leek, chopped
2 garlic cloves, minced
1 Roma tomato, chopped
1/2 teaspoon seasoned salt
1 ½ pounds prawns, shelled and deveined
2 tablespoons vodka

For Mignonette Sauce:
1/2 cup shallots, chopped
1 teaspoon black pepper, coarsely ground
1/2 cup white wine vinegar

Directions

- Heat the oil in a pan over a moderately high heat. Now, sauté the leeks and garlic for 3 minutes or until they are tender and aromatic.
- Add Roma tomato and salt; turn the heat to medium-low and cook prawns until thoroughly cooked.
- Stir in vodka and remove from heat.
- Meanwhile, in a mixing dish, thoroughly combine the shallots, black pepper, and white wine vinegar. Let it stand in the refrigerator until ready to serve.
- Serve warm prawns with Mignonette sauce on the side. Bon appétit!

223. Creole Salmon Fillets

Ready in about 40 minutes
Servings 4

Looking for a last-minute recipe for a family gathering? Richly flavored with seasonings and marinated in a blend of Worcestershire sauce, lime juice and avocado oil, this gourmet dish will amaze your family!

Per serving: 266 Calories; 11.5g Fat; 5.6g Carbs; 34.9g Protein; 4.2g Sugars

Ingredients

1/3 cup fresh lime juice
1/3 cup Worcestershire sauce
3 teaspoons avocado oil
1/4 cup fresh chives, chopped
2 garlic cloves, minced
1/4 teaspoon onion powder
1 teaspoon lemon thyme
1/4 teaspoon ground black pepper
1/4 teaspoon white pepper
1 teaspoon dried oregano
4 salmon fillets

Directions

- To make the marinade, thoroughly mix the lime juice, Worcestershire sauce, avocado oil, fresh chives, garlic, and onion powder.
- Place the salmon fillets in the marinade; place in the refrigerator for 20 to 25 minutes. Season the salmon fillets with lemon thyme, black pepper, white pepper and oregano.
- Place the salmon fillets on the preheated grill and reserve the marinade.
- Cook your salmon for 10 to 12 minutes, turning once and brushing with the reserved marinade.

224. Fish Cutlets with Parsley Mashed Cauliflower

Ready in about 35 minutes
Servings 4

These grilled fish cutlets with cauliflower puree are definitely one of the best options to make you luncheon a delicious pleasure. In this recipe, you can substitute swordfish for halibut, tuna or salmon.

Per serving: 404 Calories; 22.2g Fat; 6.7g Carbs; 43.5g Protein; 2.9g Sugars

Ingredients

1 pound swordfish cutlets, about 3/4 inch thick
1/2 teaspoon celery salt
1/2 teaspoon mixed peppercorns, freshly ground
1/2 teaspoon dried marjoram
1/2 teaspoon dried basil
1/2 teaspoon dried sage, crushed
1 ½ tablespoons butter, at room temperature
1 tablespoon fresh lime juice
1/2 cup fresh chives, roughly chopped
1 pound cauliflower, broken into florets
1/4 cup heavy cream
2 tablespoons butter
1/4 cup Colby cheese, freshly grated
Salt and pepper, to your liking
1 tablespoon fresh parsley, finely chopped

Directions

- Preheat your grill to high. Rub your fish with salt, peppercorns, marjoram, basil, and sage. Whisk butter with fresh lime juice and reserve.
- Grill fish cutlets for 8 minutes, coating with butter/lime mixture. Turn the fish cutlet over and brush another side with butter/lime mixture.
- Grill another 8 minutes. Transfer to a serving platter and sprinkle with fresh chives.
- Next, cook the cauliflower in a microwave-safe bowl with cream and butter. Microwave on high for 10 to 12 minutes, stirring once.
- Then, stir in Colby cheese, and pulse in your food processor until the mixture is creamy and smooth. Season with salt, pepper and parsley. Serve with grilled fish cutlets.

225. Prawn Cocktail Salad

Ready in about 10 minutes
Servings 6

For parties, romantic dinner or family brunch, a light and refreshing seafood cocktail salad is always a good idea!

Per serving: 196 Calories; 8.3g Fat; 9.5g Carbs; 21.4g Protein; 2.3g Sugars

Ingredients

2 pounds prawns, peeled leaving tails intact
Sea salt and freshly ground black pepper, to taste
1 carrot, sliced
1 cup scallions, chopped
1/2 cup cucumber, chopped
1/2 head Romaine lettuce, torn into pieces
1/4 cup chopped fresh dill
Juice from 1 fresh lemon
1/4 cup capers, drained
1 teaspoon deli mustard
1/2 cup mayonnaise

Directions

- Bring a pot of salted water to a boil; cook the prawns for 3 minutes. Drain and transfer to a mixing bowl; allow them to cool completely.
- Toss gently with the remaining ingredients. Place in the refrigerator until ready to serve. Bon appétit!

226. Halibut en Persillade

Ready in about 20 minutes
Servings 4

It is extremely important to heat the oil in a cast-iron skillet so the halibut steaks won't stick to the bottom. Seared halibut steaks go perfectly with a simple Persillade sauce. It pairs with white Burgundy and dry rosé Chardonnay.

Per serving: 273 Calories; 19.2g Fat; 4.3g Carbs; 22.6g Protein; 1.6g Sugars

Ingredients

2 tablespoons coconut oil, at room temperature
4 halibut steaks
1/2 cup scallions, sliced
2 cloves garlic, finely minced
1 tablespoon fresh lime juice
1/2 teaspoon fresh ginger, grated
Salt and ground black pepper, to taste
2 tablespoons fresh cilantro, chopped
1 tablespoon oyster sauce
1 tablespoon Worcestershire sauce
3 tablespoons clam juice
1/2 fresh lemon, zested and juiced
1/4 cup fresh parsley, finely chopped
1 teaspoon garlic
1 ½ tablespoons olive oil

Directions

- Heat the oil in a cast-iron skillet over high flame until it begins to smoke.
- Fry halibut until golden brown, approximately 7 minutes. Turn and fry on the other side 4 minutes more. Reserve.
- Cook the scallions and garlic in pan drippings until tender. Add the remaining ingredients along with reserved halibut steaks; cover and cook for 5 minutes more.
- Divide among four serving plates.
- Then, whisk the remaining ingredients to make Persillade sauce. Spoon over halibut steaks on the serving plates and serve.

227. Hearty Pollock Chowder

Ready in about 30 minutes
Servings 4

The best of vegetable and fish chowders come together in one super-healthy dish! It would be great if you could find hickory smoke salt for this recipe.

Per serving: 170 Calories; 5.8g Fat; 8.7g Carbs; 20g Protein; 4.2g Sugars

Ingredients

1 ¼ pounds pollock fillets, skin removed
3 teaspoons butter
2 shallots, chopped
1 celery with leaves, chopped
1 parsnip, chopped
2 carrots, chopped
Sea salt and ground black pepper, to taste
1 teaspoon Old Bay seasonings
3 cups boiling water
1/2 cup clam juice
1/4 cup dry white wine
1/2 cup full-fat milk

Directions

- Chop pollock fillets into bite-sized pieces.
- Warm the butter in a pan over a moderately high flame. Cook the vegetables until they're softened. Season with salt, pepper and Old Bay seasonings.
- Stir in chopped fish and cook for 12 to 15 minutes more. Add the boiling water and clam juice. Afterwards, pour in the white wine and milk.
- Bring to a boil. Reduce the heat and cook for 15 minutes longer. Bon appétit!

228. Summer Fish Cakes

Ready in about 30 minutes
Servings 6

These fish patties are loaded with soft cheese, eggs and herbs. Afterwards, they are baked for a lighter, healthier version of an all-time favorite.

Per serving: 234 Calories; 10.6g Fat; 2.5g Carbs; 31.2g Protein; 0.2g Sugars

Ingredients

1 ½ pounds cod, boned and flaked
2 eggs, lightly beaten
1/3 cup almond flour
2 tablespoons flax meal
1/2 cup Ricotta cheese, at room temperature
2 teaspoons Dijon mustard
Sea salt and freshly ground black pepper, to taste
1 tablespoon fresh chives, chopped
1 tablespoon fresh cilantro, chopped
2 tablespoons peanut oil

Directions

- Preheat your oven to 390 degrees F. Pat the fish dry and transfer to a mixing bowl.
- Add the eggs; gradually add the flour and flax meal and mix to combine well. Add the remaining ingredients and mix to combine well.
- Now, shape the mixture into 120patties and arrange them on a lightly greased baking pan.
- Bake for 20 to 25 minutes, turning once. Enjoy!

229. Sardine Salad Pickled Pepper Boats

Ready in about 10 minutes
Servings 4

These avocado "boats" are healthy and oh-so-delicious! Serve as a starter or a complete keto dinner. Enjoy!

Per serving: 120 Calories; 5.4g Fat; 5.8g Carbs; 12.3g Protein; 2.4g Sugars

Ingredients

2 (3.75-ounce) cans sardines, drained
1 teaspoon deli mustard
1 carrot, chopped
1 cup scallions, chopped
2 tablespoons fresh lemon
Salt and freshly ground black pepper, to taste
4 pickled peppers, slice into halves
1 tablespoon fresh parsley, chopped

Directions

- In a mixing bowl, thoroughly combine sardines, mustard, carrot, scallions, lemon juice, salt and black pepper.
- Mix until everything is well incorporated.
- Fill pickle boats with sardine salad. Serve well-chilled garnished with fresh parsley.

230. Asian-Inspired Tilapia Chowder

Ready in about 30 minutes
Servings 6

A touch of banana chili pepper adds a heat to this flavorful chowder while a full-fat milk successfully balances the flavors of fish and vegetables. Enjoy!

Per serving: 165 Calories; 5.5g Fat; 4g Carbs; 25.4g Protein; 2.7g Sugars

Ingredients

3 teaspoons sesame oil
1/2 cup scallions, sliced
1 garlic clove, smashed
1 celery stalk, diced
1 bell pepper, deveined and sliced
1 banana chili pepper, deveined and sliced
1 tablespoon fish sauce
2 ½ cups hot water
1 teaspoon Five-spice powder
1 ¼ pounds tilapia fish fillets, cut into small chunks
3/4 cup full-fat milk
1/2 teaspoon paprika
1/4 cup fresh mint, chopped

Directions

- Heat sesame oil in a stockpot that is preheated over a moderately high heat. Cook the scallions and garlic until they are softened.
- Now, add celery, peppers, fish sauce, water, and Five-spice powder. Cover with the lid, turn the heat to medium-low and simmer for 13 minutes longer.
- Now, stir in fish chunks and cook an additional 12 minutes or until the fish is cooked through. Add milk, stir well, and remove from heat.
- Ladle into individual serving plates. Sprinkle with paprika and serve garnished with fresh mint. Bon appétit!

231. Smoked Salmon and Cheese Stuffed Tomatoes

Ready in about 30 minutes
Servings 6

Making stuffed vegetables doesn't involve hours spent in the kitchen. This is the perfect idea for those short on time.

Per serving: 303 Calories; 22.9g Fat; 7.8g Carbs; 17g Protein; 4.2g Sugars

Ingredients

10 ounces smoked salmon, flaked
1 red onion, finely chopped
2 garlic cloves, minced
2 tablespoons cilantro, chopped
1/2 cup aioli
1 teaspoon yellow mustard
1 tablespoon white vinegar
Sea salt and ground black pepper, to taste
1 ½ cups Monterey Jack cheese, shredded
6 medium-sized tomatoes

Directions

- Preheat an oven to 400 degrees F.
- In a mixing bowl, thoroughly combine the salmon, onion, garlic, cilantro, aioli, mustard, vinegar, salt, and pepper.
- Slice your tomatoes in half horizontally; then, scoop out pulp and seeds.
- Stuff tomatoes with the filling, and bake until they are thoroughly cooked and tops are golden, about 20 minutes.
- Add the shredded cheese and place in the oven for a further 5 minutes. Bon appétit!

232. Chilean Sea Bass with Cauliflower and Chutney

Ready in about 30 minutes
Servings 4

Enjoy this "good-for-you" meal that is chock-full of gourmet fish, sauteed vegetables, tangy tomato chutney and aromatics!

Per serving: 291 Calories; 9.5g Fat; 8.5g Carbs; 42.5g Protein; 4.4g Sugars

Ingredients

2 tablespoons olive oil, for drizzling
1 pound cauliflower, cut into florets
2 bell peppers, thinly sliced
1 onion, thinly sliced
Sea salt and freshly ground black pepper, to taste
1 teaspoon cayenne pepper
1 ½ pounds wild Chilean sea bass

For Tomato Chutney:
1 teaspoon vegetable oil
2 garlic cloves, sliced
1 cup ripe on-the-vine plum tomatoes
1 tablespoon small capers
1/2 teaspoon kosher salt
1/4 teaspoon black pepper

Directions

- Heat 1 tablespoon of olive oil in a pan that is preheated over a moderate flame.
- Now, cook the cauliflower florets, bell peppers, and onion until they are slightly tender; season with salt, black pepper, and cayenne pepper; set aside.
- Preheat another tablespoon of olive oil. Sear sea bass on each side for 5 minutes.
- To make chutney, heat 1 teaspoon of vegetable oil in a pan over a moderately high heat. Sauté the garlic until just browned and aromatic.
- Add the plum tomatoes and cook, stirring occasionally, until heated through, or 10 minutes. Season with capers, salt, and pepper.
- Divide seared fish among 4 serving plates. Serve garnished with sautéed cauliflower mixture and tomato chutney. Enjoy!

233. Grilled Halloumi and Tuna Salad

Ready in about 15 minutes
Servings 4

Tuna fish and fresh vegetables are tossed with a high-quality grilled cheese for a quick and protein-packed salad. You can use a spiral vegetable slicer for a better food presentation.

Per serving: 199 Calories; 10.6g Fat; 13.1g Carbs; 14.2g Protein; 6.2g Sugars

Ingredients

1 cup halloumi cheese
2 cucumbers, thinly sliced
1/2 cup radishes, thinly sliced
2 tablespoons sunflower seeds
1 ½ tablespoons extra-virgin olive oil
1 can light tuna fish in water, rinsed
1/2 head Romaine lettuce
2 medium-sized Roma tomatoes, sliced
1 red onion, thinly sliced
1 tablespoon lime juice
Sea salt and black pepper, to taste
Dried rosemary, to taste

Directions

- Grill halloumi cheese over medium high heat. Cut into cubes.
- Toss grilled halloumi cheese with the remaining ingredients. Bon appétit!

234. Colorful Tuna Salad with Bocconcini

Ready in about 10 minutes
Servings 4

You just have to try this wonderful fish salad. Actually, variations are endless, but the idea is to use low-carb vegetables in a certain amount. Fast, easy and super fresh!

Per serving: 273 Calories; 11.7g Fat; 7.7g Carbs; 34.2g Protein; 2.5g Sugars

Ingredients

1 head Iceberg lettuce
1/2 cup yellow onion, thinly sliced
2 cans tuna in brine, drained
1 teaspoon Pasilla chili pepper, finely chopped
1 green bell pepper, sliced
1 yellow bell pepper, sliced
1 cucumber, sliced
1/2 cup radishes, sliced
1 tomato, diced
1/2 cup Kalamata olives, pitted and sliced
2 teaspoons peanut butter
1 teaspoon olive oil
1 teaspoon champagne vinegar
1 tablespoon oyster sauce
1/4 teaspoon black peppercorns, preferably freshly ground
2 garlic cloves, minced
8 ounces bocconcini

Directions

- Mix Iceberg lettuce, onion, tuna, peppers, cucumbers, radishes, tomatoes and Kalamata olives in a salad bowl.
- In a small mixing dish, thoroughly combine peanut butter, olive oil, champagne vinegar, oyster sauce black peppercorns, and garlic.
- Add this vinaigrette to the salad bowl; toss until everything is well coated.
- Top with bocconcini and serve well-chilled. Bon appétit!

235. Tuna Fillets with Greens

Ready in about 20 minutes
Servings 6

If you cook tuna fillets for 8 minutes, they will be juicy and pink in the center. If you cook them for 10 to 12 minutes they will be cooked through and will flake easily with a fork. Therefore, bake these tuna fillets according to your personal preferences.

Per serving: 444 Calories; 38.2g Fat; 4.7g Carbs; 21.9g Protein; 1.5g Sugars

Ingredients

6 tuna fillets
3 tablespoons olive oil, plus more for drizzling
Salt and ground black pepper, to your liking
1 fresh lime, sliced
1 tablespoons apple cider vinegar
2 teaspoons yellow mustard
Salt and red pepper flakes, to taste
2 cups baby spinach
1 cup rocket lettuce
1 yellow onion, thinly sliced
1/2 cup radishes, thinly sliced

Directions

- Start by preheating your oven to 450 degrees F. Then, coat a baking dish with parchment paper or Silpat mat.
- Now, drizzle each tuna fillet with olive oil; season with salt and pepper.
- Transfer tuna fillets to the baking dish. Top with lime slices and bake 8 to 12 minutes.
- In a mixing dish, whisk the vinegar, mustard, salt and red pepper flakes.
- Arrange baby spinach, rocket lettuce, onion and radishes on 6 serving plates. Drizzle with vinegar/mustard mixture. Top with tuna fillets. Bon appétit!

236. One-Pot Seafood Stew

Ready in about 20 minutes
Servings 4

This seafood stew might become one of your favorite family recipes of all time! This amazing stew reheats well.

Per serving: 209 Calories; 12.6g Fat; 7.6g Carbs; 15.2g Protein; 3.1g Sugars

Ingredients

1/2 stick butter, at room temperature
2 onions, chopped
2 garlic cloves, pressed
2 tomatoes, pureed
1 celery stalk, chopped
2 cups shellfish stock
1 cup hot water
2 tablespoons dry white wine
1/2 teaspoon lemon zest
1/2 pound shrimp
1/2 pound mussels
1 teaspoon Italian seasonings
1 teaspoon saffron threads
Salt and ground black pepper, to taste

Directions

- Melt the butter in a stockpot over a moderate heat. Cook the onion and garlic until aromatic.
- Now, stir in pureed tomatoes; cook for 8 minutes or until heated through.
- Add the remaining ingredients and bring to a rapid boil. Reduce the heat to a simmer and cook an additional 4 minutes.
- Ladle into individual bowls and serve warm.

237. Seafood and Andouille Medley

Ready in about 25 minutes
Servings 4

Is there anything better than rich, warm medley during winter weekdays? Serve with a sour cream on the side for a full keto experience.

Per serving: 481 Calories; 26.9g Fat; 10g Carbs; 46.6g Protein; 1.1g Sugars

Ingredients

1/2 stick butter, melted
2 andouille sausages, cut crosswise into 1/2-inch-thick slices
2 garlic cloves, finely minced
1 shallot, chopped
2 tomatoes, pureed
1 tablespoon oyster sauce
3/4 cup clam juice
1/3 cup dry white wine
1/2 pound skinned sole, cut into chunks
20 sea scallops
2 tablespoons fresh cilantro, chopped

Directions

- Melt the butter in a heavy-bottomed pot over medium-high heat. Cook the sausages until no longer pink; reserve.
- Now, sauté the garlic and shallots in pan drippings until they are softened; reserve.
- Add the pureed tomatoes, oyster sauce, clam juice and wine; simmer for another 12 minutes.
- Add the skinned sole, scallops and reserved sausages. Let it simmer, partially covered, for 6 minutes.
- Serve garnished with fresh cilantro. Bon appétit!

238. Quatre Épices Salmon Fillets with Cheese

Ready in about 20 minutes
Servings 6

Salmon fillets go so well with quatre épices. Quatre épices is a spice mix that contains pepper, ginger, nutmeg and cloves. It is widely used in French and Middle Eastern cuisines.

Per serving: 354 Calories; 20.2g Fat; 4.5g Carbs; 39.6g Protein; 1.4g Sugars

Ingredients

6 salmon fillets
1 teaspoon seasoned salt
1 teaspoon Quatre épices
1 cup cauliflower
1/2 red onion, thinly sliced
1 garlic clove, finely minced
1 cup Colby cheese, grated
3 tablespoons mayonnaise
1 teaspoon whole grain mustard
1 tablespoon fresh lemon juice
2 tablespoons avocado oil

Directions

- Preheat your oven to 400 degrees F. Line a baking dish with aluminum foil.
- Sprinkle salmon fillets with salt and Quatre épices on all sides and place on a piece of foil. Arrange cauliflower and onions around them.
- Wrap the fish and vegetable with foil. Bake for 10 minutes or until salmon fillets flake easily with a fork.
- In a mixing bowl, thoroughly combine garlic, cheese, mayo, mustard, lemon juice, and avocado oil.
- Pour this mixture over the fish and veggies. Bake for a further 5 to 6 minutes or until the top is golden. Serve warm garnished with fresh chives.

239. Easy Parmesan Crusted Tilapia

Ready in about 15 minutes
Servings 4

Use aluminum foil to make clean-up easier and keep your fish moist and evenly cooked. This is perfect served with a cauliflower rice.

Per serving: 222 Calories; 12.6g Fat; 0.9g Carbs; 27.9g Protein; 0g Sugars

Ingredients

1 pound tilapia fillets, cut into 4 servings
1/3 teaspoon salt
1/3 teaspoon ground black pepper
1/4 teaspoon red pepper flakes, crushed
2 tablespoons olive oil
3/4 cup grated Parmesan cheese

Directions

- Season the fish fillets with salt, black pepper and red pepper flakes.
- Brush tilapia fillets with olive oil; now, press them into the Parmesan cheese.
- Place fish fillets on a foil-lined baking sheet. Bake approximately 10 minutes or until fish fillets are opaque.

240. Creamy Anchovy Salad

Ready in about 10 minutes
Servings 4

Anchovy salad is a must-have during the summer season. You can turn this evergreen recipe into a keto favorite.

Per serving: 195 Calories; 14.7g Fat; 9g Carbs; 7.8g Protein; 4.5g Sugars

Ingredients

1 head of Romaine lettuce
2 cans anchovies, chopped
1 cup red onions, chopped
1 carrot, thinly sliced
1 cucumber, thinly sliced
Sea salt and ground black pepper, to taste
3/4 cup mayonnaise
1 teaspoon yellow mustard
1/2 teaspoon smoked cayenne pepper
1/4 cup fresh chives, roughly chopped

Directions

- Arrange lettuce leaves in a salad bowl. Add anchovies, onions, carrot, and cucumber. Season with salt and pepper.
- Now, stir in mayonnaise and mustard. Sprinkle with cayenne pepper and toss until everything is well combined.
- Serve well-chilled and garnished with fresh chives. Bon appétit!

241. Moms' Aromatic Fish Curry

Ready in about 25 minutes
Servings 6

This amazing curry combines fresh fish with curry leaves, cardamom pods, garlic and coconut milk, plus flavor-building ingredients like coriander and ginger.

Per serving: 270 Calories; 16.9g Fat; 8.6g Carbs; 22.3g Protein; 2.2g Sugars

Ingredients

2 tablespoons fresh lime juice
2 pounds blue grenadier, cut into large pieces
2 tablespoons olive oil
8 fresh curry leaves
1 cup shallots, chopped
2 green chilies, minced
1/2 tablespoon fresh ginger, grated
2 garlic cloves, finely chopped
2 green cardamom pods
1 teaspoon dried basil
Salt and black pepper, to taste
4 Roma tomatoes, pureed
1 tablespoon ground coriander
1 cup coconut milk

Directions

- Drizzle blue grenadier with lime juice.
- Heat the oil in a nonstick skillet over a moderate flame. Cook curry leaves and shallots until the shallot is softened, about 4 minutes.
- After that, add the chilies, ginger and garlic and cook an additional minute or until fragrant. Add the remaining ingredients, except for coconut milk, and simmer for 10 minutes or until heated through.
- Now, stir in the fish; pour in 1 cup of coconut milk and cook, covered, for 6 minutes longer. Serve warm and enjoy!

242. Pan-Seared Trout Fillets with Chimichurri

Ready in about 15 minutes
Servings 6

If you are craving a spicy food, use hot Madras curry powder instead of turmeric powder. Eventually, you'll become totally addicted to this fish dish.

Per serving: 265 Calories; 20.9g Fat; 4g Carbs; 17.1g Protein; 0.2g Sugars

Ingredients

2 tablespoons ghee
6 trout fillets
Celery salt and ground black pepper, to taste
1/2 teaspoon turmeric powder
1/2 tablespoon yellow mustard

For Chimichurri Sauce:
1/3 cup wine vinegar
1/2 teaspoon salt
3 garlic cloves, minced
1/2 shallot, finely chopped
1 Fresno chili pepper, finely chopped
1/2 cup fresh flat-leaf parsley, minced
1 tablespoon fresh oregano leaves, finely chopped
1/3 cup extra-virgin olive oil

Directions

- Heat ghee in a large stainless skillet that is preheated over a moderately high heat. Season trout fillets with salt, pepper and turmeric powder; brush with yellow mustard.
- Sear the trout fillet for 4 to 5 minutes on each side.
- Meanwhile, pulse wine vinegar, salt, garlic, shallot, Fresno chili pepper, parsley, and oregano in your food processor.
- With the food processor running slowly, gradually add olive oil and blend until uniform and smooth. You can keep Chimichurri in the refrigerator for up to 2 days.
- Serve warm fish fillets with Chimichurri sauce on the side. Bon appétit!

243. Sunday Amberjack Fillets with Parmesan Sauce

Ready in about 20 minutes
Servings 6

These fish fillets with sauce are definitely one of the best options to make you luncheon a delicious pleasure. In this recipe, you can substitute amberjack for any type of white fish you like.

Per serving: 285 Calories; 20.4g Fat; 1.2g Carbs; 23.8g Protein; 0.1g Sugars

Ingredients

2 tablespoons ghee, at room temperature
6 amberjack fillets
1 teaspoon sea salt
1/2 teaspoon ground black pepper
1/4 teaspoon cayenne pepper, or more to taste
1/4 cup fresh tarragon chopped
1 lemon, cut into wedges
For the Sauce:
3 teaspoons ghee, at room temperature
1 teaspoon garlic, finely minced
1/3 cup beef bone broth
3/4 cup heavy cream
1/3 cup Parmesan cheese, grated
Salt and ground black pepper, to taste

Directions

- Melt the ghee in a large bottomed non-stick frying pan.
- Then, coat both sides of your fish with the salt, black pepper, cayenne pepper and chopped tarragon.
- Fry the fish fillets for about 10 minutes or until the edges are turning opaque and segments flake apart.
- To make the sauce, melt 3 teaspoons of ghee in a pan over a moderate heat. Then, sauté the garlic until aromatic, about 3 minutes.
- Add the broth and cream; continue to cook stirring constantly, about 6 minutes.
- Stir in Parmesan cheese and continue stirring until everything is thoroughly cooked. Season with salt and pepper to taste.
- Serve fish fillets with the sauce garnished with fresh lemon wedges.

244. Crabmeat, Prosciutto and Vegetable Delight

Ready in about 10 minutes
Servings 4

This salad is so simple and quick to make and contains great flavors of canned crabmeat, prosciutto, tahini, olives and fresh vegetables. Enjoy!

Per serving: 232 Calories; 15.6g Fat; 6g Carbs; 18.9g Protein; 1g Sugars

Ingredients

3 tablespoons olive oil
1 tablespoon tahini
1/2 lemon, zested and juiced
Coarse salt and ground black pepper, to your liking
2 (6-ounce) cans lump crabmeat, drained
2 ounces thinly sliced prosciutto, chopped
4 cups baby spinach
10 cherry tomato, halved
10 ripe olives, pitted and halved
1/2 cup fresh Italian parsley, chopped

Directions

- In a small-sized mixing dish, whisk the oil, tahini, lemon zest, lemon juice, salt, and pepper.
- In a salad bowl, gently toss crabmeat with prosciutto, spinach, cherry tomatoes, and olives. Drizzle with the prepared dressing and toss to combine.
- Serve garnished with fresh parsley in individual salad bowls.

245. Fish with Cremini Mushrooms and Sour Cream Sauce

Ready in about 20 minutes
Servings 4

Halibut fillets are really, really versatile. This time, we will cook them with cremini mushrooms. Kick it up a notch with a garlicky sour cream sauce.

Per serving: 585 Calories; 30.5g Fat; 8.5g Carbs; 66.8g Protein; 2.8g Sugars

Ingredients

2 tablespoons vegetable oil
1 onion, chopped
1/2 pound cremini mushrooms, thinly sliced
Coarse salt and freshly ground black pepper, to taste
4 skinless halibut fillets
1 tablespoon ghee
2 garlic cloves, chopped
1 ½ cups clam juice
1 cup sour cream
1/2 cup fresh parsley, chopped

Directions

● Heat 1 tablespoon of vegetable oil in a pan over a moderately high heat. Sauté the onion until it's softened.
● Now, stir in the mushrooms, salt, and black pepper; cook for 5 minutes.
● Wipe out your pan, and heat the remaining tablespoon of vegetable oil. Now, sear fish fillets over medium-high heat approximately 4 minutes per side. Transfer to a plate with mushroom mixture.
● Melt ghee over a moderately high flame. Cook the garlic until slightly browned.
● Pour in clam juice and work it back and forth, stirring continuously over high heat until reduced by half.
● Remove sauce from heat; let it cool slightly before quickly whisking in the sour cream. Serve with cremini mushrooms and fish, garnished with fresh parsley. Bon appétit!

246. Spring Salad with Harissa Crab Mayo

Ready in about 15 minutes
Servings 4

Here is an easy seafood-inspired mayo to prepare! It pairs perfectly with spring vegetables like radishes, lettuce, cucumbers and so on.

Per serving: 293 Calories; 27.1g Fat; 7.3g Carbs; 9.3g Protein; 3.2g Sugars

Ingredients

For the Crab Mayo:
2 egg yolks
1/2 tablespoon whole grain mustard
1/2 teaspoon harissa
3/4 cup olive oil
2 tablespoons fresh lemon juice
A pinch of salt
A pinch of freshly ground black pepper
1 clove garlic, crushed
1/2 teaspoon dried dill weed
1 pound white crabmeat
For the Salad:
1 head Iceberg lettuce
1/2 cup chervil
A bunch of scallions, chopped
1 cup radishes, sliced
1 bell pepper, julienned

Directions

● Whisk the egg yolks and mustard; slowly pour in the oil, in a tiny stream, until you have a thick mixture.
● Now, add the lemon juice, salt, black pepper, garlic, dill and crabmeat. Place in your refrigerator until ready to serve.
● In a salad bowl, place all salad ingredients. Toss with prepared crab mayo and serve well-chilled. Bon appétit!

247. Grilled Clams with Tomato Sauce

Ready in about 25 minutes
Servings 4

Clams are plentiful, flavorful and easy to cook. Tangy tomato sauce is classic with clams. Enjoy!

Per serving: 134 Calories; 7.8g Fat; 7.9g Carbs; 8.3g Protein; 3.2g Sugars

Ingredients

40 littleneck clams
For the Sauce:
2 tablespoons olive oil
1 onion, chopped
1 teaspoon crushed garlic
2 tomatoes, pureed
Sea salt and freshly ground black pepper, to taste
1/2 teaspoon cayenne pepper
1/3 cup dry sherry
1 lemon, cut into wedges

Directions

- Heat grill to medium-high. Cook until clams open, about 6 minutes.
- Heat the oil in sauté pan over a moderate heat. Cook the onion and garlic until aromatic.
- Add pureed tomatoes, salt, black pepper and cayenne pepper and cook an additional 10 minutes or until everything is thoroughly cooked.
- Remove from heat and add dry sherry; stir to combine. Serve with grilled clams, garnished with fresh lemon wedges.

248. Prawn and Avocado Cocktail Salad

Ready in about 10 minutes + chilling time
Servings 6

Looking for a really glamorous cocktail starter? Try this refreshing seafood cocktail salad! Drizzle the slices of avocado with some extra lime juice to keep them from turning brown.

Per serving: 236 Calories; 14.3g Fat; 11.3g Carbs; 16.3g Protein; 2.7g Sugars

Ingredients

1 pound large king prawns, peeled leaving tails intact
1/2 cup Lebanese cucumber, chopped
1 small-sized red onion, thinly sliced
1/2 cup mayonnaise
1 tablespoon Worcestershire sauce
2 teaspoons fresh lime juice
A few drops red Tabasco pepper sauce
1/2 head iceberg lettuce leaves
1 avocado, pitted and sliced

Directions

- Bring a pot of salted water to a boil; cook the prawns for 3 minutes. Drain and transfer to a mixing bowl.
- In the mixing bowl, combine the prawns with chopped cucumber and red onion. In another bowl, thoroughly combine mayonnaise with Worcestershire sauce, lime juice and Tabasco pepper sauce.
- Add the mayo mixture to the prawn mixture. Place in your refrigerator until serving time.
- To serve, arrange lettuce leaves and avocado slices on a serving platter. Mound the salad onto lettuce leaves and serve well chilled. Enjoy!

249. Chinese-Style Milkfish with Mushroom-Pepper Coulis

Ready in about 35 minutes
Servings 4

Milkfish is a great source of omega-3 fatty acids, which are linked to reduced blood pressure and enhanced immune function.

Per serving: 415 Calories; 28g Fat; 4.4g Carbs; 34.5g Protein; 2.3g Sugars

Ingredients

For the Fish:
2 tablespoons sesame oil
2 milkfishes, scaled
1/2 teaspoon salt
1/4 teaspoon ground black pepper
1/2 teaspoon red pepper flakes, crushed
1/3 cup Rosé wine
2 tablespoons Chinese dark soy sauce

For the Mushroom/Pepper Coulis:
1 ½ ounces olive oil
1/2 onion, peeled and chopped
1 bell pepper, deveined and chopped
2 ounces Cremini mushrooms, chopped
3 tablespoons consommé
1/2 tablespoon champagne vinegar
1/2 teaspoon kosher
1/4 teaspoon ground black pepper
1/8 teaspoon freshly grated nutmeg

Directions

- Heat sesame oil in a pan over medium-high heat. Season milkfish with salt, black pepper, and red pepper flakes.
- Fry milkfish in batches about 5 minutes per side or until golden brown; reserve, keeping warm.
- Add Rosé wine and Chinese dark soy sauce to the same pan. Bring to a rolling boil; reduce heat to medium-low and let it simmer an additional 5 minutes.
- Add milkfish back to the pan, and continue to cook, basting with wine sauce, about 3 minutes.
- To make your coulis, heat olive oil in a skillet that is preheated over a moderate heat. Now, cook the onions until translucent.
- After that, turn the heat to medium-low and add the peppers and mushrooms along with a splash of consommé; cook, stirring frequently, another 13 minutes or until they are softened.
- Now, process the sautéed mixture in your blender until creamy and uniform.
- Add the remaining ingredients, stir to combine well and serve with prepared fish.

250. Tuna and Vegetable Kebabs

Ready in about 15 minutes
Servings 4

Fish kebabs are a cinch to make on the grill. With an addition of vegetables, this is amazing, belly-filling recipe.

Per serving: 257 Calories; 12.5g Fat; 7g Carbs; 27.5g Protein; 5.1g Sugars

Ingredients

1 pound 1 1/4 -inch-thick tuna, cut into bite-sized cubes
Salt and crushed black peppercorns
1/2 teaspoon rosemary
1/2 teaspoon thyme
2 tablespoons sesame oil
2 tablespoons soy sauce
1 onion, cut into wedges
1 zucchini, diced
1 cup grape tomatoes

Directions

- Preheat your grill on high. Season tuna cubes and vegetables with salt, peppercorns, rosemary, and thyme. Drizzle with sesame oil and soy sauce.
- Alternate seasoned tuna cubes, onion, zucchini and tomatoes on each of 8 metal skewers.
- Grill 5 minutes for medium-rare, turning frequently. Bon appétit!

251. Mackerel Steak Casserole with Cheese and Veggies

Ready in about 30 minutes
Servings 4

Fresh-from-the-sea fish steaks are a great family meal for any occasion. This rich and flavorful casserole is simply delicious and it is ready in 30 minutes.

Per serving: 301 Calories; 14g Fat; 10g Carbs; 33.3g Protein; 3.3g Sugars

Ingredients

1/2 stick butter
1 cup carrots, thinly sliced
1 cup parsnip, thinly sliced
2 cloves garlic, thinly sliced
2 onions, thinly sliced
1/4 cup clam juice
3 tomatoes, thinly sliced
1 pound mackerel steaks
1 tablespoon Old Bay seasoning
Salt and black pepper, to your liking
1 cup mozzarella, shredded
1/2 cup fresh chives, chopped

Directions

- Preheat your oven to 450 degrees F.
- Melt the butter in a pan that is previously preheated over a moderate flame. Cook the carrots, parsnip, garlic, and onions until they are tender.
- Add clam juice and tomatoes and cook 4 minutes more. Transfer this vegetable mixture to a casserole dish.
- Lay the fish steaks on top of the vegetable layer. Sprinkle with seasonings. Cover with foil and roast for 10 minutes, until the fish is opaque in the center.
- Top with shredded cheese and bake another 5 minutes. Serve warm garnished with fresh chopped chives. Bon appétit!

252. Classic Seafood Chowder

Ready in about 15 minutes
Servings 5

If you like smooth, velvety chowder, use an immersion blender to process the chowder after cooking. This simple step will give your dish a special, sophisticated touch.

Per serving: 404 Calories; 30g Fat; 5.3g Carbs; 23.9g Protein; 1.1g Sugars

Ingredients

1/2 stick butter
2 tablespoons green onion, chopped
1 teaspoon minced garlic
3/4 pound shrimp, peeled and deveined
1/2 pound crab meat
1/3 cup dry white wine
3 bouillon cubes
1 quart water
2 cups heavy cream
1 tablespoon tomato paste
1 teaspoon dried rosemary
Salt and ground black pepper, to taste
1 egg, lightly beaten

Directions

- Melt the butter in a large pot that is preheated over medium-high heat.
- Now, cook the onion and garlic until they are tender and aromatic.
- Add the shrimp, crab meat, wine, bouillon cubes and water. Now, cook until the seafood is thoroughly warmed, about 5 minutes.
- Reduce the heat to low and add the remaining ingredients. Simmer, stirring occasionally, for an additional 2 to 3 minutes. Bon appétit!

253. Smoky Cholula Seafood Dip

Ready in about 10 minutes + chilling time
Servings 8

Cholula is a chili-based hot sauce, made from chile pepin and arbol peppers, used mainly in Mexican cuisine. It will give a tart but not too spicy flavor to your dip.

Per serving: 108 Calories; 5.4g Fat; 5g Carbs; 8.2g Protein; 1g Sugars

Ingredients

1/2 cup mayonnaise
2 cloves garlic, finely minced
12 ounces seafood, canned and drained
Sea salt and ground black pepper, to taste
1/4 teaspoon white pepper
1 teaspoon smoked paprika
1/2 teaspoon dried dill weed
1 tablespoon Cholula
A few drops of liquid smoke

Directions

- In a mixing bowl, gently stir mayo, garlic, and canned seafood.
- Now, add the remaining ingredients and stir with a wide spatula until everything is well incorporated.
- Cover and place in your refrigerator until it is thoroughly chilled. Serve well-chilled with fresh or pickled veggies. Bon appétit!

FAST SNACKS & APPETIZERS

254. Smoked Bacon Fries....................................... 146

255. Caramelized Garlic Mushrooms 146

256. Cilantro and Ricotta Balls 147

257. Cocktail Meatballs with Romano Cheese 147

258. Chicken Wings with Tomato Dip 148

259. Spicy Tuna Deviled Eggs 148

260. Broccoli and Goat Cheese Dip 149

261. Cheese, Mortadella and Salami Roll-Ups 149

262. Paprika and Mustard Bacon Chips 150

263. Easy Rutabaga Fries 150

264. Dilled Chicken Wingettes with Goat Cheese Dip 151

265. Cheese, Ham and Greek Yogurt Dip 151

266. Cocktail Salad on a Stick 152

267. Greek-Style Meat and Cheese Dip 152

268. Celery Root French Fries with Pine Nuts 153

269. Cheese-Stuffed Cocktail Meatballs 153

270. Chorizo and Ricotta Balls 154

271. Pork Rinds with Mangold-Ricotta Dip 154

272. Cheese Greasy Cucumber Bites 155

273. Italian-Style Egg and Mortadella Bites 155

274. Sriracha and Parm Chicken Wings...................... 156

275. Crispy Cheesy Cauliflower Bites 156

276. Chicharrones with Homemade Guacamole 157

277. Classic Bacon Deviled Eggs 157

278. Cheesy Peppery Bites with Pancetta..................... 158

279. Mediterranean Cheese Ball...................................... 158

280. Two-Cheese and Artichoke Dip........................... 159

281. Shrimp-Stuffed Celery Sticks................................ 159

282. Oven-Baked Zucchini Bites................................... 160

283. Cheese and Crab Stuffed Mushrooms.................. 160

284. Prawns on Sticks... 161

285. Easy and Spicy Shrimp Appetizer......................... 161

286. Hot and Spicy Cocktail Meatballs........................ 162

287. Paprika Provolone Crisps...................................... 162

288. Pepperoni and Cheese Bites................................... 163

289. Roasted Cherry Tomatoes with
Cheese-Chive Sauce... 163

290. Mini Salami Pizza Cups.. 164

291. Turkey Tenders with Spicy and Tangy Sauce........ 164

292. Muffin Appetizer with Herbes de Provence 165

293. Mexican-Style Keto Rolls 165

294. Crock Pot Little Smokies...................................... 166

295. Adobo Cheese Snack 166

296. Tortilla Chips with Guacamole 167

297. Saucy Cheesy Baby Carrots................................... 167

298. Two-Cheese and Ground Meat Dip...................... 168

299. Dippable Cheese Crisps... 168

300. Cauliflower Balls with Greek Yoghurt Sauce........ 169

301. Paprika and Rosemary Crackers............................ 169

302. Prosciutto-Broccoli Muffins with Tomato Dip..... 170

254. Smoked Bacon Fries

Ready in about 15 minutes
Servings 6

Once you make these bacon fries, you won't need potato chips! Serve with salsa, ketchup or barbecue dip.

Per serving: 409 Calories; 31.6g Fat; 1.1g Carbs; 28g Protein; 0g Sugars

Ingredients

1 pound smoked bacon, cut into small squares
1 teaspoon mustard seeds
1 tablespoon paprika

Directions

- Preheat an oven to 360 degrees F.
- Bake smoked bacon for 12 to 15 minutes. Season with mustard seeds and paprika. Enjoy!

255. Caramelized Garlic Mushrooms

Ready in about 10 minutes
Servings 4

These caramelized mushrooms bring the flavors of summer days to your kitchen. Serve with sour cream and mayo for a full keto experience!

Per serving: 75 Calories; 5.2g Fat; 3.3g Carbs; 2.9g Protein; 0.1g Sugars

Ingredients

2 teaspoons olive oil
1 tablespoon butter
2 cloves garlic, minced
1 pound Portobello mushrooms, sliced
1 tablespoon soy sauce
Salt and pepper, to taste

Directions

- Heat the oil and butter in a large skillet that is preheated over a moderate heat. Add garlic and cook until aromatic, 30 seconds or so.
- Stir in the mushrooms and cook them for 3 minutes, allowing them to caramelize.
- Now, add soy sauce, salt and pepper; cook for 4 minutes more or to desired doneness. Enjoy!

256. Cilantro and Ricotta Balls

Ready in about 10 minutes + chilling time
Servings 6

Fun, easy and delicious, cheese balls are perfect for a party! In addition, these balls look spectacular on a serving platter.

Per serving: 108 Calories; 9g Fat; 2.2g Carbs; 4.8g Protein; 0.1g Sugars

Ingredients

1 cup Ricotta cheese
3 tablespoons butter
1/4 teaspoon red wine vinegar
Salt and pepper, to taste
1/2 cup fresh cilantro, finely chopped

Directions

- Blend all ingredients, except for cilantro, in a food processor.
- Place the mixture in the refrigerator for 3 hours.
- Shape the mixture into 10 to 12 balls; roll them in chopped cilantro until evenly coated. Serve with cocktail sticks and enjoy your party!

257. Cocktail Meatballs with Romano Cheese

Ready in about 40 minutes
Servings 5

These meatballs are so amazing on their own, you won't need to serve them with anything else. Toothpicks and napkins would be just fine.

Per serving: 244 Calories; 13.3g Fat; 3.7g Carbs; 28.1g Protein; 1.2g Sugars

Ingredients

1/3 pound ground turkey
1/3 pound ground pork
1/3 pound ground beef
2 ounces Romano cheese, grated
2 tablespoons buttermilk
2 eggs, whisked
1/2 yellow onion, chopped
2 cloves garlic, minced
1 tablespoon Dijon mustard
1 teaspoon ancho chili powder
Salt and ground black pepper, to taste
1/2 cup ground almonds

Directions

- Thoroughly combine all of the above ingredients, except for ground almonds, in a mixing dish.
- Grease your hands with oil and roll the mixture into 20 meatballs. Place ground almond in a shallow bowl.
- Toss your meatballs in ground almond until they're completely coated.
- Heat up a nonstick skillet over a moderately high heat. Now, spritz the bottom and sides of the skillet with a nonstick cooking spray.
- Cook your meatballs about 13 minutes, until they're golden brown all around. Serve with toothpicks on a large serving platter. Bon appétit!

258. Chicken Wings with Tomato Dip

Ready in about 50 minutes
Servings 6

This is the classic recipe for chicken wings with a little keto twist. Crispy and flavorful, chicken wings go wonderfully with fresh tomato dip.

Per serving: 236 Calories; 13.5g Fat; 9g Carbs; 19.4g Protein; 6.8g Sugars

Ingredients

12 chicken wings
Salt and pepper, to taste
For the Tomato Dip:
4 ripe tomatoes, crushed
1 onion, finely chopped
1 cup mango, peeled and chopped
1 teaspoon chili pepper, deveined and finely minced
2 heaping tablespoons cilantro, finely chopped
2 tablespoons lime juice

Directions

● Start by preheating your oven to 400 degrees F. Set a wire rack inside a rimmed baking sheet.
● Season chicken wings with salt and pepper. Bake wings approximately 45 minutes or until skin is crispy.
● Then, thoroughly combine all ingredients for the tomato dip. Place in your refrigerator until ready to serve.

259. Spicy Tuna Deviled Eggs

Ready in about 20 minutes
Servings 6

Can you imagine a cocktail party without charming deviled eggs? They are mouth-watering, appetizing and so easy to make.

Per serving: 203 Calories; 13.3g Fat; 3.8g Carbs; 17.2g Protein; 1.5g Sugars

Ingredients

12 eggs
1/3 cup mayonnaise
1 can tuna in spring water, drained
1/2 teaspoon smoked cayenne pepper
1/4 teaspoon fresh or dried dill weed
2 pickled jalapenos, minced
Salt and black pepper, to taste

Directions

● Place the eggs in a wide pot; cover with cold water by 1 inch. Bring to a rapid boil.
● Decrease the heat to medium-low; let them simmer an additional 10 minutes.
● Peel the eggs and rinse them under running water.
● Slice each egg in half lengthwise and remove the yolks. Thoroughly combine the yolks with the remaining ingredients.
● Divide the mixture among egg whites and arrange deviled eggs on a nice serving platter. Enjoy!

260. Broccoli and Goat Cheese Dip

Ready in about 10 minutes
Servings 8

If it has broccoli in it, it's automatically healthy. Broccoli is a great source of vitamins C, K, and E as well as dietary fiber and minerals. Serve this fantastic dipping sauce with an assortment of crudités.

Per serving: 134 Calories; 10.2g Fat; 6.5g Carbs; 5.1g Protein; 1.7g Sugars

Ingredients

1 pound broccoli, broken into florets
1/2 cup sour cream
1/2 cup goat cheese
1 teaspoon shallot powder
1 teaspoon Italian seasoning mix
1 teaspoon garlic powder
1/3 cup mayonnaise

Directions

● Steam the broccoli for 4 to 5 minutes or until crisp-tender. Transfer to a food processor.
● Add the remaining ingredients, except for mayonnaise. Puree in the food processor until well blended.
● Stir in mayonnaise and puree until creamy, uniform and smooth. Serve well-chilled and enjoy!

261. Cheese, Mortadella and Salami Roll-Ups

Ready in about 10 minutes
Servings 5

It's not a party without these mellow roll-ups. This is an utterly addicting snack so consider preparing a double batch.

Per serving: 381 Calories; 31.2g Fat; 7.8g Carbs; 17.6g Protein; 1.7g Sugars

Ingredients

10 slices Provolone cheese
4 ounces mayonnaise
10 slices Mortadella
10 slices Genoa salami
10 olives, pitted

Directions

● Spread a thin layer of mayo onto each slice of cheese. Add a slice of Mortadella on top of the mayo.
● Top with a slice of Genoa salami. Roll them up; place olives on the top and secure with toothpicks.
● Serve immediately.

262. Paprika and Mustard Bacon Chips

Ready in about 20 minutes
Servings 4

You won't miss potato chips, not at all, trust us! Serve with salsa, guacamole or barbecue dip.

Per serving: 118 Calories; 10g Fat; 1.9g Carbs; 5g Protein; 0.4g Sugars

Ingredients

12 bacon strips, cut into small squares
1 tablespoon smoked paprika
1 tablespoon mustard

Directions

● Preheat your oven to 360 degrees F
● Toss the bacon strips with paprika and mustard.
● Arrange bacon squares on a parchment lined baking sheet. Bake for 10 to 15 minutes. Enjoy!

263. Easy Rutabaga Fries

Ready in about 35 minutes
Servings 4

Make this grab-and-go quick snack and delight your family especially kids! It's good to know that you can make fries out of almost any type of veggies.

Per serving: 134 Calories; 10.8g Fat; 9.9g Carbs; 1.5g Protein; 6.8g Sugars

Ingredients

1 ½ pounds rutabaga, cut into sticks 1/4-inch wide
3 tablespoons olive oil
Salt and ground black pepper, to taste
1/2 teaspoon cayenne pepper
1/2 teaspoon mustard seeds

Directions

● Add rutabaga sticks to a mixing dish. In another small-sized mixing dish, whisk the other ingredients.
● Add the oil mixture to the rutabaga sticks and toss to coat well.
● Preheat your oven to 440 degrees F. Line a baking sheet with parchment paper.
● Place seasoned rutabaga sticks on the baking sheet. Roast them approximately 30 minutes, turning baking sheet occasionally. Serve warm and enjoy!

264. Dilled Chicken Wingettes with Goat Cheese Dip

Ready in about 1 hour 15 minutes
Servings 10

Here's an ultimate comfort food perfect for any occasion, from a cocktail party and Super Bowl party to kid's birthday parties!

Per serving: 227 Calories; 10.2g Fat; 0.4g Carbs; 31.5g Protein; 0.2g Sugars

Ingredients

Nonstick cooking spray
3 pounds chicken wingettes
Salt and black pepper, to taste
1/4 teaspoon smoked paprika
1 teaspoon dried dill weed

For Goat Cheese Dip:
1 cup goat cheese, crumbled
1/3 cup mayonnaise
2 tablespoons Greek-style yogurt
1 teaspoon Dijon mustard
2 cloves garlic, smashed
1 teaspoon onion powder
1/2 teaspoon ground cumin
1/4 cup fresh coriander leaves, finely chopped

Directions

- Preheat your oven to 390 degrees F. Set a wire rack inside a rimmed baking sheet. Spritz the rack with a nonstick cooking oil.
- Toss chicken wingettes with salt, pepper, paprika, and dill.
- Place the chicken wingettes skin side up on the rack. Bake in the lower quarter of the oven for 30 to 35 minutes.
- Turn the oven up to 420 degrees F. Bake for a further 40 minutes on the higher shelf, rotating the baking sheet once.
- In the meantime, combine goat cheese, mayo, yogurt, mustard, garlic, onion powder and ground cumin. Serve with warm wingettes, garnished with fresh cilantro.

265. Cheese, Ham and Greek Yogurt Dip

Ready in about 5 minutes
Servings 6

Looking for creative ways to eat cheese on a keto diet? This silky dip is both healthy and gourmet. Enjoy!

Per serving: 147 Calories; 10.6g Fat; 2.7g Carbs; 10.2g Protein; 0.2g Sugars

Ingredients

5 ounces Greek yogurt
5 ounces Ricotta cheese, at room temperature
1 cup Colby cheese, shredded
1/2 cup ham, crumbled
2 tablespoons fresh parsley, chopped

Directions

- Thoroughly combine all of the above ingredients, except for parsley, in a mixing dish.
- Garnish with fresh parsley. Serve with veggie sticks. Bon appétit!

266. Cocktail Salad on a Stick

Ready in about 10 minutes
Servings 6

Your favorite salad on a stick! Is it possible? Keep reading and delight your guests for the next cocktail party.

Per serving: 249 Calories; 19.3g Fat; 10g Carbs; 9.7g Protein; 2.1g Sugars

Ingredients

2 cans of tiny pickled beets, drained and rinsed
2 bell peppers, sliced
4 ounces blue cheese, cubed
1 cup prosciutto, sliced
1/2 cup olives, pitted
1/3 cup champagne vinegar
1/3 cup olive oil
1/2 teaspoon cumin seeds

Directions

- Tread pickled beets, bell peppers, blue cheese, prosciutto, and olives onto cocktail sticks.
- Drizzle with champagne vinegar and olive oil; sprinkle with cumin seeds. Bon appétit!

267. Greek-Style Meat and Cheese Dip

Ready in about 10 minutes
Servings 24

This dipping sauce brings the flavors of a sunny day in Greece to your kitchen. Serve with veggie sticks for a full keto experience!

Per serving: 153 Calories; 11.2g Fat; 2.2g Carbs; 10.8g Protein; 0.6g Sugars

Ingredients

1 pound ground beef
1/2 pound ground lamb
2 cups sour cream
1 cup cream cheese
1 cup feta cheese
1/2 cup tomato puree
2 garlic cloves, minced
1 sprig dried rosemary, crushed
1 sprig dried thyme, crushed
1 cup Kalamata olives, pitted and sliced

Directions

- Brown ground meat in a pan that is preheated over a medium-high heat. Crumble with a wide spatula and set aside.
- In a large bowl, thoroughly combine the remaining ingredients, except for olives.
- Layer the cheese mixture with meat mixture. Top with sliced Kalamata olives and serve with your favorite dippers.

268. Celery Root French Fries with Pine Nuts

Ready in about 35 minutes
Servings 6

Here's an amazing low-carb alternative to potato fries. Even if you don't follow a ketogenic diet, you will surely enjoy roasted vegetable sticks.

Per serving: 96 Calories; 8.5g Fat; 4.1g Carbs; 1.5g Protein; 1.7g Sugars

Ingredients

1 ½ pounds celery root, cut into sticks
Salt and ground black pepper, to taste
1/2 teaspoon cayenne pepper
2 tablespoons olive oil
1 tablespoon Cajun seasoning
1/4 cup pine nuts, coarsely ground

Directions

- Preheat your oven to 390 degrees F. Line a baking sheet with a parchment paper or Silpat mat.
- Mix celery root, salt, black pepper, cayenne pepper, olive oil and Cajun seasoning in a mixing dish.
- Arrange celery stick on the prepared baking sheet and bake for 30 minutes, flipping every 10 minutes to promote even cooking.
- Arrange on a serving platter and sprinkle with pine nuts. Serve hot with a homemade mayo or seafood dipping sauce. Bon appétit!

269. Cheese-Stuffed Cocktail Meatballs

Ready in about 25 minutes
Servings 10

Here is a keto twist on an old party favorite! Monterey Jack cheese tucked inside each meatball creates a burst of flavor.

Per serving: 186 Calories; 9.6g Fat; 1.2g Carbs; 23.9g Protein; 0.4g Sugars

Ingredients

1/2 pound ground turkey
1 pound ground pork
1/3 cup Parmesan cheese, freshly grated
Sea salt and ground black pepper, to taste
1 teaspoon red pepper flakes, crushed
1 teaspoon oyster sauce
1/2 cup onion, finely chopped
2 cloves garlic, minced
2 eggs
1 cup Monterey Jack cheese, cubed

Directions

- Start by preheating your oven to 390 degrees F. Coat a baking pan with parchment paper.
- Thoroughly combine all ingredients, except for Monterey Jack cheese, in a mixing bowl.
- Shape this meat mixture into 40 meatballs. Press 1 cheese cube into the middle of each meatball; be sure to seal it inside.
- Gently place the meatballs on the prepared baking pan.
- Bake about 20 minutes until they are browned and slightly crisp on top. Serve on a serving platter with toothpicks.

270. Chorizo and Ricotta Balls

Ready in about 15 minutes + chilling time
Servings 5

These easy and yummy balls made even heartier with cooked chorizo! Kalamata olives give the right amount of tanginess to the whole thing.

Per serving: 327 Calories; 25.7g Fat; 6.4g Carbs; 17g Protein; 1g Sugars

Ingredients

10 ounces chorizo, chopped
10 ounces Ricotta cheese, softened
1/4 cup mayonnaise
1/2 teaspoon deli mustard
2 teaspoons tomato paste
8 Kalamata olives, pitted

Directions

- Heat up the skillet over a moderate flame. Now, cook chorizo until well browned. Transfer it to a mixing bowl.
- Add the remaining ingredients and transfer to your refrigerator until it is well chilled. Bon appétit!

271. Pork Rinds with Mangold-Ricotta Dip

Ready in about 2 hours
Servings 8

Pork rinds, also called cracklings, are an oven-roasted pork skin. It pairs perfectly with a cheesy dip made of fresh greens and aromatic herbs.

Per serving: 163 Calories; 12.8g Fat; 3.9g Carbs; 7.9g Protein; 0.1g Sugars

Ingredients

Pork skin
Salt
1 tablespoon butter
2 cups mangold, torn into pieces and steamed
1 rosemary sprig, chopped
1 thyme sprig, chopped
1 teaspoon shallot powder
1 teaspoon garlic powder
1/4 teaspoon cumin powder
Sea salt and ground black pepper, to taste
12 ounces Ricotta cheese
1/2 cup aioli

Directions

- Start by preheating your oven to 340 degrees F. Salt pork skin according to your personal preferences.
- Arrange pork skin on a cookie sheet that is lined with a parchment paper.
- Bake for 2 hours and then, allow it to cool for a couple of minutes before serving.
- In the meantime, steam mangold leaves until just tender, about 8 minutes. Combine with the remaining ingredients in a large serving bowl.
- Serve with prepared pork rinds and enjoy!

272. Cheese Greasy Cucumber Bites

Ready in about 10 minutes
Servings 10

If you can't find bacon bits, simply chop the bacon strips into small crumbs. You can refrigerate this snack for up to 3 days.

Per serving: 63 Calories; 4.3g Fat; 2.7g Carbs; 4g Protein; 1.1g Sugars

Ingredients

1 cup blue cheese
2 tablespoons real bacon bits
1/4 cup parsley, chopped
1 teaspoon chili powder
2 cucumbers, cut into thick slices

Directions

- Blend the cheese, real bacon bits, parsley and chili powder until everything is well combined.
- Spoon the cheese mixture onto the cucumber slices and serve right away!

273. Italian-Style Egg and Mortadella Bites

Ready in about 5 minutes + chilling time
Servings 6

You will love this super-easy recipe. It features a few basic ingredients and takes under 5 minutes to make.

Per serving: 327 Calories; 25.7g Fat; 6.4g Carbs; 17g Protein; 1g Sugars

Ingredients

6 hard-boiled eggs, peeled and chopped
1/2 teaspoon Italian seasonings
1/3 cup mayonnaise
Sea salt and ground black pepper, to taste
1/2 teaspoon cayenne pepper
1/2 cup cream cheese, softened
6 slices Mortadella, chopped

Directions

- Combine all of the above ingredients in a mixing dish.
- Shape the mixture into balls.
- Transfer the balls to the refrigerator for 1 hour. Keep in the refrigerator up to 4 days. Bon appétit!

274. Sriracha and Parm Chicken Wings

Ready in about 1 hour 10 minutes
Servings 6

The next-level wings your guests will love! These wings carry some of the flavors of Mexican cuisine, so you can increase or reduce the spiciness by controlling the amount of Sriracha chili sauce.

Per serving: 312 Calories; 23g Fat; 0.9g Carbs; 24.6g Protein; 0.1g Sugars

Ingredients

2 pounds chicken wings
Coarse salt and freshly ground black pepper, to taste
1/2 teaspoon smoked cayenne pepper
1 tablespoon balsamic vinegar
2 teaspoons Sriracha chili sauce
2 cloves garlic, smashed
1 stick butter
1 cup Parmesan cheese
2 tablespoons oyster sauce
1/2 cup fresh chives, chopped

Directions

- Preheat an oven to 420 degrees F. Set a metal rack on top of a baking sheet.
- Season chicken wings with salt, black pepper, cayenne pepper. Now, roast the wings until the skin is crisp, about 45 minutes.
- In the meantime, simmer the vinegar, Sriracha, and garlic until the mixture has reduced slightly, about 12 minutes.
- In a shallow bowl, combine softened butter with parmesan cheese and oyster sauce.
- Next, toss chicken wings with Sriracha mixture. After that, dredge chicken wings in parmesan mixture until fully coated; then place on the baking sheet.
- Bake an additional 10 minutes. Garnish with fresh chopped chives and enjoy!

275. Crispy Cheesy Cauliflower Bites

Ready in about 40 minutes
Servings 6

Jazz up any dinner party with these crispy bites! Harissa paste is a type of a hot chili pepper paste. It is made of chiles, garlic, olive oil, and aromatic spices.

Per serving: 167 Calories; 13.4g Fat; 2.4g Carbs; 7.5g Protein; 1.1g Sugars

Ingredients

1 head of cauliflower, broken into small florets
1/4 cup olive oil
Sea salt and ground black pepper, to your liking
1 teaspoon lemongrass, grated
1 teaspoon harissa paste
1 cup Romano cheese, freshly grated

Directions

- Start by preheating your oven to 450 degrees F. Spritz a baking sheet with a nonstick cooking spray.
- Toss cauliflower florets with olive oil, salt black pepper, grated lemongrass and harissa paste.
- Arrange cauliflower florets on the prepared baking sheet.
- Roast, tossing once or twice, until cauliflower is tender, about 40 minutes. Serve with aioli or any other ketogenic dip and enjoy!

276. Chicharrones with Homemade Guacamole

Ready in about 2 hours
Servings 6

Try this crunchy pork snack with a homemade Guacamole for the next dinner party! As a matter of fact, the crispness of the pork skin is a great complement to the creaminess of the sauce so the flavors and textures are balanced perfectly!

Per serving: 199 Calories; 16.1g Fat; 8g Carbs; 7.5g Protein; 1.5g Sugars

Ingredients

1 whole pork skin from a pork belly
Salt, to taste

For Guacamole:
2 avocados, seeded, peeled and chopped
1/2 fresh lime, juiced
Coarse salt and pepper, to taste
1/4 teaspoon ground cumin
1 small-sized yellow onion, finely chopped
1 teaspoon chili pepper, deveined and finely minced
1 cup tomatoes, chopped
2 tablespoons cilantro, chopped
2 cloves garlic, crushed

Directions

● Preheat your oven to 330 degrees F. Line a large baking sheet with parchment paper.
● Cut the skin into pieces and bake them for 2 hours.
● Meanwhile, make your guacamole by mixing all of the guacamole ingredients in the order listed above.
● Serve chicharrones with fresh guacamole and enjoy!

277. Classic Bacon Deviled Eggs

Ready in about 20 minutes
Servings 10

This is the classic recipe for deviled eggs with a little twist. Spicy, flavorful and mouthwatering, these bites are simply wonderful.

Per serving: 128 Calories; 9.7g Fat; 3.3g Carbs; 6.8g Protein; 1.1g Sugars

Ingredients

10 eggs
1/2 cup mayonnaise
1/4 cup cooked bacon, chopped
2 teaspoons lemon juice
1 tablespoon Marsala wine
2 teaspoons country-style Dijon mustard
1/4 teaspoon hot pepper sauce
Salt and red pepper flakes, to taste
Fresh dill weed sprigs, to serve

Directions

● Place the eggs in a single layer in a pan; cover with 2 inches of water.
● Bring to a boil over a high heat; now, reduce the heat and cook, covered, for 1 minute.
● Remove from heat and wait for 15 minutes; rinse.
● After that, peel the eggs and halve them lengthwise. Remove the yolks and mash them with a fork. Add mayonnaise, bacon, lemon juice, wine, mustard, and hot pepper sauce.
● Season with salt and crushed red pepper; mix until everything is well combined.
● Divide the mayonnaise-bacon mixture among egg whites. Afterwards, serve garnished with fresh dill weed.

278. Cheesy Peppery Bites with Pancetta

Ready in about 20 minutes
Servings 4

Here's your foolproof, basic party recipe you'll never want to be without. In this recipe, you can freely use prosciutto or speck instead of pancetta.

Per serving: 252 Calories; 13.7g Fat; 5.6g Carbs; 26g Protein; 1g Sugars

Ingredients

2 tablespoons butter, softened
1 small shallot, peeled and minced
1/2 pound ground beef
6 ounces Cottage cheese, softened
1 teaspoon garlic, smashed
1 tablespoon fresh parsley, finely chopped
Salt and pepper, to taste
4 bell peppers, deveined and quartered
5 slices pancetta, chopped

Directions

- Preheat an oven to 380 degrees F.
- Melt the butter in a heavy-bottomed skillet that is preheated over a moderately high flame. Now, sauté the shallot until it is slightly tender.
- Add ground beef and cook an additional 4 minutes or until slightly browned.
- Then, beat Cottage cheese with hand mixer until softened. Add the meat mixture along with the garlic and parsley; gently stir until everything is well combined; add salt and pepper to taste.
- Stuff each pepper slice with the meat/cheese mixture. Scatter chopped pancetta over the top of each pepper.
- Bake about 13 minutes or until the stuffing is well browned and the peppers are tender. Bon appétit!

279. Mediterranean Cheese Ball

Ready in about 10 minutes
Servings 6

This is the cheese ball you can serve at any party. Like mini cheese balls but way more fun!

Per serving: 182 Calories; 15.5g Fat; 3g Carbs; 7.6g Protein; 1.2g Sugars

Ingredients

6 ounces Neufchatel cheese
1/4 cup aioli
1 tablespoon tomato paste
6 slices of Iberian ham, chopped
6 Kalamata olives, pitted and chopped
1 teaspoon dried basil
1 teaspoon dried oregano
1 teaspoon dried rosemary

Directions

- Thoroughly combine Neufchatel cheese, aioli, tomato paste, chopped ham and olives in a mixing bowl; mix until everything is homogeneous.
- In a shallow dish, combine dried basil, oregano, and rosemary.
- Shape the mixture into a ball. Roll the ball in the herb mixture. Refrigerate until ready to serve. Serve with veggie sticks. Bon appétit!

280. Two-Cheese and Artichoke Dip

Ready in about 5 minutes
Servings 8

This easy and elegant dipping sauce makes a delicious appetizer that suits almost any diet. Serve with sliced bell peppers, celery sticks, or pickled onions. So good, right?

Per serving: 157 Calories; 11g Fat; 9g Carbs; 6.5g Protein; 1.5g Sugars

Ingredients

12 ounces canned artichoke hearts, drained
1/2 pound mascarpone cheese
1/2 cup Colby cheese, shredded
1/2 cup mayonnaise
2 garlic cloves, minced
2 tablespoons coriander
2 tablespoons spring onions
Celery salt and ground black pepper, to taste
1 teaspoon dried rosemary
1 teaspoon paprika

Directions

- Thoroughly combine all ingredients in a mixing bowl.
- Transfer the dipping mixture to a nice serving dish.
- Serve and enjoy!

281. Shrimp-Stuffed Celery Sticks

Ready in about 10 minutes
Servings 16

It's not a party without these crispy and tasty sticks. This is an utterly addicting snack so consider preparing a double batch.

Per serving: 29 Calories; 1.9g Fat; 0.7g Carbs; 2.5g Protein; 0.2g Sugars

Ingredients

6 ounces fully cooked deveined shrimp, chopped
2 tablespoons soy sauce
1/3 cup cream cheese
Salt and crushed red pepper, to your liking
1/2 teaspoon oregano
1 teaspoon yellow mustard
8 celery sticks, cut in halves

Directions

- Thoroughly combine the shrimp, soy sauce, cream cheese, salt, pepper, oregano and mustard.
- Then, place celery sticks on a serving plate; divide the shrimp mixture among celery sticks and serve immediately.

282. Oven-Baked Zucchini Bites

Ready in about 40 minutes
Servings 4

A buttery-like texture of zucchini and its mild flavor, when prepared in this manner, pair so well with seasonings and egg whites.

Per serving: 91 Calories; 6.1g Fat; 6g Carbs; 4.2g Protein; 3.5g Sugars

Ingredients

4 zucchinis, cut into thick slices
2 tablespoons butter, melted
2 egg whites
Coarse salt and crushed black peppercorns, to taste
1/2 teaspoon red pepper flakes, crushed
1/2 teaspoon dried dill weed

Directions

- Begin by preheating an oven to 420 degrees F. Coat a rimmed baking sheet with parchment paper or Silpat mat.
- In a mixing bowl, whisk the butter with two egg whites. Add the seasonings.
- Now, toss the zucchini slices with this mixture.
- Arrange coated zucchini slices on the baking sheet; bake for 35 minutes until the slices are golden, turning once.
- Check for doneness and bake another 5 minutes if needed. Serve at room temperature and enjoy!

283. Cheese and Crab Stuffed Mushrooms

Ready in about 25 minutes
Servings 4

Fragrant and tender mushroom caps loaded with seafood, cheese, and mayo! Even those who don't like keto food may have a change of heart when they try this recipe!

Per serving: 221 Calories; 13.5g Fat; 6g Carbs; 19.8g Protein; 3.7g Sugars

Ingredients

1 pound medium-sized white mushrooms, stems removed
Salt and pepper, to taste
1/2 teaspoon celery seeds
1/2 teaspoon dried basil
1/2 pound crab meat
1 cup cream cheese
1/4 cup mayonnaise
2 garlic cloves, smashed
1 heaping tablespoon cilantro, minced

Directions

- Begin by preheating your oven to 390 degrees F. Spritz a rimmed baking sheet with a nonstick cooking spray.
- Season mushroom caps with salt, pepper, celery seeds and dried basil.
- In a mixing dish, thoroughly combine the remaining ingredients. Stuff the mushroom caps and transfer them to the prepared baking sheet.
- Bake for 17 to 22 minutes or until tops are golden. Enjoy!

284. Prawns on Sticks

Ready in about 15 minutes
Servings 4

If you are in a seafood mood, give this recipe a try! This is one of the easiest ways to serve this sophisticated but low-carb appetizer.

Per serving: 218 Calories; 11g Fat; 7.1g Carbs; 23.5g Protein; 5.4g Sugars

Ingredients

3 tablespoons vegetable oil
1 pound king prawns, peeled and deveined
3 garlic cloves, minced
1 tablespoon fresh sage, minced
1 teaspoon fresh rosemary
Salt and cayenne pepper, to taste
1 tablespoon fresh lime juice
2 tablespoons cilantro, chopped
1 red bell pepper, diced
1 green bell pepper, diced
1 cup cherry tomatoes
Bamboo skewers

Directions

- Heat vegetable oil in a wok over a moderately high heat.
- Now, cook the prawns with garlic until they are fragrant. Stir in the sage, rosemary, salt and cayenne pepper. Cook an additional minute, stirring frequently.
- Remove from heat and toss with lime juice and fresh cilantro. Tread the prawns onto skewers, alternating them with peppers and cherry tomatoes.
- Serve on a serving platter. Bon appétit!

285. Easy and Spicy Shrimp Appetizer

Ready in about 15 minutes
Servings 6

Shrimp is a real crowd pleaser. Toss with whatever spices you have on hand and sear quickly in the preheated pan. Serve with a classic Marinara sauce.

Per serving: 107 Calories; 4.9g Fat; 1g Carbs; 15.3g Protein; 0.2g Sugars

Ingredients

2 tablespoons coconut oil, room temperature
1 pound shrimp, deveined and shelled, tail on
1 teaspoon garlic, minced
1/2 cup scallions, chopped
1 teaspoon ancho chili powder
2 tablespoons apple cider vinegar
1/4 cup chicken stock
1 teaspoon paprika
Salt and ground black pepper, to taste
Some coriander springs, for garnish

Directions

- Heat coconut oil in a frying pan over a moderately high flame. Now, cook shrimp together with garlic and scallions.
- Add chili powder, vinegar, and chicken stock and continue to cook 3 minutes more. Season with paprika, salt, and pepper to taste.
- Serve with toothpicks, garnished with coriander sprigs.

286. Hot and Spicy Cocktail Meatballs

Ready in about 15 minutes
Servings 10

Loaded with cheese and aromatics, these meatballs will liven up any gathering. Serve with low-carb Marinara Sauce.

Per serving: 158 Calories; 7.9g Fat; 0.4g Carbs; 20.4g Protein; 0.1g Sugars

Ingredients

3/4 pound ground lamb
1/2 pound ground pork
1/4 cup crushed pork rinds
1 large-sized egg, beaten
1/3 cup heavy cream
1/3 cup Parmesan cheese, grated
Sea salt and ground black pepper, to taste
1 teaspoon fresh rosemary, minced
2 garlic cloves, finely minced
1 teaspoon onion powder
1/2 teaspoon cumin, ground
1 teaspoon hot sauce

Directions

- Thoroughly combine all ingredients in a bowl by using oiled hands. Shape the mixture into balls.
- In a preheated pan, brown the meatballs on one side for 4 minutes; then flip them over and cook another 3 to 5 minutes.
- Turn down the heat to low, cover the pan and let them cook an additional 3 minutes or until heated through.
- Serve with cocktail sticks.

287. Paprika Provolone Crisps

Ready in about 15 minutes
Servings 6

Homemade keto snacks are a cinch to make. In addition, they are healthy and so delicious. Here's an amazing low carb snack that takes only 15 minutes to make.

Per serving: 268 Calories; 20.4g Fat; 3.4g Carbs; 18.1g Protein; 0.4g Sugars

Ingredients

3 cups provolone cheese, shredded
4 tablespoons ground flaxseed meal
1 teaspoon paprika powder

Directions

- Begin by preheating your oven to 420 degrees F.
- Then, drop a tablespoon of shredded cheese into 12 separate piles. Sprinkle ground flaxseed meal and paprika powder over the top.
- Bake in the middle of your oven for roughly 10 to 12 minutes. Store in airtight container. Bon appétit!

288. Pepperoni and Cheese Bites

Ready in about 10 minutes
Servings 5

This is another keto snack recipe, bursting with amazing flavor. You can add any deli cheese such as provolone or mozzarella.

Per serving: 341 Calories; 30.6g Fat; 3.4g Carbs; 12.8g Protein; 0.5g Sugars

Ingredients

5 ounces Pepperoni, chopped
5 ounces cream cheese
4 large egg yolks, hard-boiled
2 tablespoons mayonnaise
1 teaspoon deli mustard
1/2 teaspoon paprika
2 tablespoons hemp hearts

Directions

- Add Pepperoni, cheese and egg yolks to a mixing dish; stir to combine well.
- Now, stir in mayonnaise, mustard, and paprika; stir again.
- Shape the mixture into 10 balls.
- Place hemp hearts on a medium plate; roll each ball through to coat. Arrange these balls on a nice serving platter and serve.

289. Roasted Cherry Tomatoes with Cheese-Chive Sauce

Ready in about 25 minutes
Servings 6

Seasoned with the best, hand-picked Mediterranean herbs and drizzled with high-quality olive oil, these bite-sized tomatoes will burst and release their juices for an extra layer of flavor.

Per serving: 230 Calories; 21g Fat; 6g Carbs; 5.1g Protein; 4.5g Sugars

Ingredients

Nonstick cooking spray
1 ½ pounds cherry tomatoes
1 rosemary sprig, chopped
1 teaspoon dried oregano
1 teaspoon dried sage, crushed
1/4 cup extra-virgin olive oil
Celery salt, to taste

For the Sauce:
1 cup cream cheese
1/2 cup homemade mayonnaise
1/2 cup fresh chives, chopped

Directions

- Preheat your oven to 425 degrees F. Spritz a baking sheet with a nonstick cooking spray.
- Toss cherry tomatoes with rosemary, oregano, sage, oil, and celery salt and arrange on the prepared baking sheet.
- Bake about 23 minutes, rotating the baking sheet once or twice.
- Meanwhile, make the dipping sauce by whisking all the sauce ingredients in a mixing dish. Serve with warm roasted tomatoes and enjoy!

290. Mini Salami Pizza Cups

Ready in about 20 minutes
Servings 6

A mild flavor of Cheddar cheese combines beautifully with the tanginess of marinara sauce and olives in this recipe.

Per serving: 162 Calories; 13.1g Fat; 2.5g Carbs; 8.7g Protein; 1.1g Sugars

Ingredients

1 cup Cheddar cheese, shredded
1/2 cup marinara
1 teaspoon dried oregano
1/2 teaspoon dried basil
1/2 cup green olives, pitted and chopped
12 Genoa salami slices

Directions

- Preheat an oven to 360 degrees F; spritz a muffin pan with a nonstick cooking spray.
- Divide 1/2 cup of cheddar cheese among muffin cups. Divide marinara sauce among muffin cups.
- Sprinkle each cup with oregano, basil, and chopped olives. Add a salami slice to each muffin cup. Top with the remaining 1/2 cup of cheese.
- Bake approximately 17 minutes. Allow them to cool slightly before removing from the muffin pan.

291. Turkey Tenders with Spicy and Tangy Sauce

Ready in about 30 minutes
Servings 8

If you have never tried a low-carb "breading", give this recipe a try. These turkey tenders are crispy and mouthwatering.

Per serving: 153 Calories; 6.7g Fat; 4.6g Carbs; 21.8g Protein; 0.7g Sugars

Ingredients

1 ¼ pounds turkey tenderloin, cut into 20 pieces
1 teaspoon kosher salt
1/2 teaspoon ground black pepper
1 teaspoon smoked paprika
1/3 cup flax meal
3/4 cup almond flour
2 eggs
For the Sauce:
1/3 cup tomato puree
1/2 tablespoon Louisiana hot sauce
1 teaspoon Dijon mustard
1 ½ teaspoons soy sauce
1 teaspoon garlic powder
1 teaspoon paprika
1/3 teaspoon cumin
1/2 teaspoon red pepper flakes, crushed

Directions

- Preheat an oven to 370 degrees F. Then, spritz a baking pan with a nonstick cooking spray.
- Season turkey pieces with salt, pepper and paprika. Thoroughly combine flax meal with almond flour.
- Dip each piece of turkey in the beaten egg. Then, coat them with the almond flour mixture.
- Arrange the turkey pieces on the prepared baking pan. Bake approximately 25 minutes.
- Meanwhile, make the sauce by whisking all the sauce ingredients. Serve with hot turkey tenders.

292. Muffin Appetizer with Herbes de Provence

Ready in about 20 minutes
Servings 6

Are you craving the flavors of Southern France? Herbes de Provence is a spice that features rosemary, marjoram, thyme and savory as main ingredients. This mix may include citrus zest, fennel seeds, and tarragon too.

Per serving: 269 Calories; 20.7g Fat; 7g Carbs; 15.5g Protein; 1.3g Sugars

Ingredients

Nonstick cooking spray
1/3 cup flaxseed meal
2/3 cup almond flour
2 tablespoons xylitol
2 teaspoons psyllium
1/8 teaspoon kosher salt
1/8 teaspoon grated nutmeg
1 teaspoon herbes de Provence
1/2 teaspoon baking powder
2 eggs
1/2 cup yogurt
10 slices salami, chopped

Directions

- Start by preheating your oven to 360 degrees F. Lightly grease a muffin pan with a nonstick cooking spray.
- Thoroughly combine flaxseed meal with almond flour, xylitol, psyllium, salt, nutmeg, herbes de Provence and baking powder; stir until well combined.
- Now, stir in the eggs, yogurt, and salami. Press the mixture into prepared muffin cups.
- Bake about 15 minutes and transfer to a wire rack to cool slightly before removing from the muffin pan. Bon appétit!

293. Mexican-Style Keto Rolls

Ready in about 25 minutes
Servings 6

This recipe takes the best Mexican flavors and magically transforms them into an ultimate keto snack. Whenever the urge for tacos hits you, reach for these bites instead.

Per serving: 261 Calories; 18.6g Fat; 6.7g Carbs; 17.3g Protein; 6.7g Sugars

Ingredients

3 cups Mexican mix cheese, shredded
1 yellow onion, chopped
2 garlic cloves, crushed
1 ½ cups ground beef
Salt and freshly ground black peppercorns, to your liking
1/2 teaspoon ground cumin
2 tomatoes, crushed
1/4 cup sour cream
1/4 cup mayonnaise

Directions

- Begin by preheating an oven to 390 degrees F. Line a baking pan with parchment paper or Silpat mat.
- Place shredded cheese to cover the bottom of your baking pan. Bake approximately 13 minutes, or until the cheese is slightly browned on top.
- In the meantime, heat up a nonstick skillet over a moderately high flame. Sweat the onion until just tender and fragrant.
- Now, cook the garlic until it is slightly browned, about 1 minutes. Stir in ground beef; cook until it is no longer pink and season with salt, peppercorns and ground cumin.
- Top cheese "crust" with meat mixture and bake for a further 7 minutes. Top with tomatoes, sour cream, and mayonnaise.
- Cut into 12 slices. Afterwards, roll each slice and serve warm. Bon appétit!

294. Crock Pot Little Smokies

Ready in about 2 hours 30 minutes
Servings 6

When you're looking for just the right thing to serve for an easy and effective appetizer, this recipe will fit the bill. You can come up with your favorite combination of aromatics.

Per serving: 271 Calories; 22.2g Fat; 4.5g Carbs; 12.3g Protein; 0.6g Sugars

Ingredients

1 ½ pounds cocktail franks
3 tablespoons wholegrain mustard
1 bottle barbecue sauce
1 tablespoon Swerve
1 teaspoon onion powder

Directions

- Heat up a pan over a moderately high heat; now, brown the sausage about 3 minutes.
- Treat your Crock pot with a nonstick cooking spray. Add all of the above ingredients and stir well.
- Cook on Low heat setting for 2 ½ hours. Serve little smokies with toothpicks. Bon appétit!

295. Adobo Cheese Snack

Ready in about 15 minutes
Servings 5

This is a great snack for your next dinner party because you can prepare a whole bunch in advance. Keep the cheese sticks in your freezer and fry them just before serving time. Easy peasy lemon squeezy!

Per serving: 338 Calories; 26.5g Fat; 3.4g Carbs; 21g Protein; 1.2g Sugars

Ingredients

10 pieces string cheese
Cooking oil
1/2 cup almond flour
1/3 cup Parmesan cheese powder
1 teaspoon Adobo spice mix
2 eggs
2 tablespoons whole milk

Directions

- Cut string cheese in half lengthwise.
- Heat cooking oil in a deep frying pan that is preheated over a moderately high heat.
- Mix almond flour, parmesan, Adobo spice mix, eggs and milk until everything is well incorporated.
- Dip cheese sticks into the batter and cover on all sides.
- Fry cheese sticks for 4 to 5 minutes, until golden brown; work in batches. Transfer to paper towels to soak up excess fat. Serve with hot sauce.

296. Tortilla Chips with Guacamole

Ready in about 20 minutes
Servings 10

The key ingredients for the perfect guacamole are a good, ripe avocado and a certain amount of chili peppers. These bites are so flavorful and delicious!

Per serving: 109 Calories; 8.4g Fat; 8.3g Carbs; 2.2g Protein; 1.4g Sugars

Ingredients

For the chips:
1 tablespoon coconut oil
3/4 cup almond flour
2 tablespoons coconut flour
1/4 teaspoon baking powder
1/4 cup psyllium husk powder
1/3 teaspoon xanthan gum
1/3 teaspoon turmeric powder
3/4 cup hot water
2 tablespoons avocado oil

For the Guacamole:
2 ripe avocados, seeded and peeled
Fresh juice of 1 fresh lemon
Salt and pepper, to taste
1/3 teaspoon cayenne pepper
1 small-sized onion, chopped
1 serrano chili pepper, stems and seeds removed, minced
1 cup ripe plum tomatoes, seeded and chopped
2 tablespoons fresh cilantro, chopped
2 garlic cloves, finely minced

Directions

- Thoroughly combine the coconut oil, almond flour, coconut flour, baking powder, psyllium powder, xanthan gum, and turmeric. Pour in water and knead into a dough.
- Spread coconut flour on a working surface.
- Then, roll out your dough very thin, about 1.2-inch thick. Drizzle with avocado oil.
- Cut the dough into triangles; bake tortilla triangles in the preheated oven at 350 degrees F, on a parchment lined baking sheet for 10 minutes.
- Your chips will crisp up as they cool.
- Meanwhile, prepare your guacamole by mixing scooped avocado pulp and fresh lemon juice. Add the remaining ingredients and stir until everything is well blended.

297. Saucy Cheesy Baby Carrots

Ready in about 35 minutes
Servings 6

Here is a keto snack worth trying for the next dinner party! A great way to eat baby carrots!

Per serving: 216 Calories; 18.7g Fat; 9.4g Carbs; 3.5g Protein; 5.4g Sugars

Ingredients

1 ½ pounds baby carrots, florets separated
1 stick butter, melted
1/2 teaspoon coarse salt
1/4 teaspoon ground black pepper
1/4 teaspoon ground cumin
1/4 teaspoon dried dill weed
1/2 cup Asiago cheese, grated

Directions

- Begin by preheating your oven to 400 degrees F.
- Coat baby carrots with melted butter, salt, pepper, cumin and dill weed.
- Bake for 30 minutes in the middle of the preheated oven, stirring once or twice.
- Top with shredded Asiago cheese and bake an additional 5 minutes or until cheese is slightly browned. Bon appétit!

298. Two-Cheese and Ground Meat Dip

Ready in about 15 minutes
Servings 10

Bring this simple, cheesy meat dip to the next potluck and you're sure to get invited back! It will literally melt in your mouth!

Per serving: 195 Calories; 12g Fat; 1.5g Carbs; 19.5g Protein; 0.3g Sugars

Ingredients

1 tablespoon olive oil
1/2 pound ground beef
1/2 pound ground pork
Salt and ground black pepper, to taste
1 teaspoon onion powder
1/2 teaspoon garlic powder
1/2 teaspoon red pepper flakes, crushed
8 ounces mascarpone cheese, at room temperature
6 ounces Colby cheese, shredded

Directions

- Heat the oil in a large-sized skillet that is preheated over a moderate flame. Now, cook the ground meat until it is well browned, crumbling with a spatula as it cooks.
- Add the seasonings and mascarpone cheese. Top with shredded Colby cheese. Cover and allow cheese to melt, about 5 minutes.
- Serve with veggie sticks and enjoy!

299. Dippable Cheese Crisps

Ready in about 20 minutes
Servings 6

Healthy, low-carb and guilt-free, these spicy crisps might become your favorite snack for movie night at home.

Per serving: 225 Calories; 19.3g Fat; 0.6g Carbs; 12.1g Protein; 0.3g Sugars

Ingredients

1 cup Romano cheese, finely shredded
1 cup Pepper Jack cheese, shredded
4 slices bacon, cooked and crumbled
1 jalapeño, finely chopped
1/4 teaspoon red pepper flakes
1/2 teaspoon ground cumin
1/4 teaspoon cardamom
Salt and pepper, to taste

Directions

- Begin by preheating your oven to 400 degrees F. Line a baking sheet with a sheet of parchment paper.
- Spoon 1 tablespoon of Romano cheese into a small mound on the parchment paper. Top with about 1 tablespoon of shredded Pepper Jack cheese.
- Add bacon and chopped jalapeño. Sprinkle with red pepper, cumin, cardamom, salt, and pepper; gently flatten each mound.
- Bake approximately 12 minutes. Transfer the baking sheet to a wire rack to cool before serving. Serve with marinara sauce. Bon appétit!

300. Cauliflower Balls with Greek Yoghurt Sauce

Ready in about 30 minutes
Servings 6

These cauliflower balls can truly be a life-saver on the ketogenic diet! They're shockingly tasty and go wonderfully with a tangy Greek yogurt sauce.

Per serving: 182 Calories; 13.1g Fat; 5.9g Carbs; 11.5g Protein; 2.2g Sugars

Ingredients

1 head cauliflower
1/2 cup Parmesan cheese, grated
3 eggs
1 cup Asiago cheese, shredded
1 onion, finely chopped
1 garlic clove, minced
Salt and black pepper, to taste

For Greek Yoghurt Sauce:
1 cup Greek yogurt
1 teaspoon lemon juice
1 garlic clove, minced
1 tablespoon mayonnaise
1 tablespoon olive oil
1/2 teaspoon dried dill weed

Directions

- Cook the cauliflower in a large pot of salted water until tender, about 6 minutes; cut into florets.
- Preheat your oven to 400 degrees F. Coat a baking pan with parchment paper.
- Mash the cauliflower with Parmesan, eggs, cheese, onion, garlic, salt and black pepper; shape the mixture into balls.
- Bake for 22 minutes or until they are slightly crisp.
- To make the sauce, whisk all remaining ingredients. Serve cauliflower balls with Greek yogurt sauce on the side.

301. Paprika and Rosemary Crackers

Ready in about 30 minutes
Servings 12

Go nuts for these amazing, crunchy crackers! They go perfectly with different kinds of cheese dips.

Per serving: 119 Calories; 8g Fat; 14.7g Carbs; 2.6g Protein; 0.2g Sugars

Ingredients

3/4 cup sesame seeds
2 tablespoons sunflower seeds
2 tablespoons flax seeds
1 tablespoon pecans, ground
1/3 cup sunflower seeds
1/4 cup psyllium husks
Coarse sea salt, to taste
1 teaspoon paprika
1 teaspoon dried rosemary
Warm water

Directions

- In a mixing bowl, thoroughly combine all the dry ingredients.
- Pour in the warm water and stir to form a dough.
- Place the dough in between two large pieces of parchment pepper; roll it out as thin as possible.
- Cut the cracker dough into rectangles. Prick with a fork and transfer to a lined baking sheet.
- Bake in the preheated oven at 360 degrees F for 8 to 13 minutes or until golden. Flip them over and bake another 10 minutes. Bon appétit!

302. Prosciutto-Broccoli Muffins with Tomato Dip

Ready in about 30 minutes
Servings 6

Who said there's no such thing as ketogenic muffins? Moreover, these muffins will really make you feel full for a couple of hours!

Per serving: 375 Calories; 27.6g Fat; 7g Carbs; 24.8g Protein; 2.9g Sugars

Ingredients

1 head broccoli, grated
1 cup scallions, chopped
5 ounces prosciutto, chopped
6 eggs, whisked
1 ½ cups Colby cheese, freshly grated
Sea salt and ground black pepper, to taste
1/2 teaspoon black mustard seeds
1/2 teaspoon marjoram
1/2 teaspoon coriander

For the Dipping Sauce:
2 ripe tomatoes, chopped
1 garlic clove, chopped
1 roasted pepper, chopped
1 small onion, chopped
2 tablespoons olive oil
1/2 teaspoon oregano
1 teaspoon basil
1 teaspoon rosemary

Directions

- Begin by preheating your oven to 390 degrees F. Lightly butter a muffin pan.
- Combine broccoli, scallions and chopped prosciutto in a mixing dish. Now, stir in the eggs and cheese; stir to combine well.
- After that, sprinkle with salt, black pepper, black mustard seeds, marjoram, and coriander; stir again to combine thoroughly.
- Next, divide the mixture among prepared muffin cups and bake approximately 30 minutes, or until thoroughly cooked.
- In the meantime, make tomato sauce by whisking the remaining ingredients. Serve with warm broccoli muffins and enjoy!

VEGAN

303. Spicy Tofu with Vegan Tzatziki 172

304. Mushroom Stuffed Avocado 172

305. Fried Tofu with Peppers 173

306. Flavorful Tofu Cubes with Pecans 173

307. Easy Kale Dip with Crudités............................... 174

308. Crave-Worthy Stuffed Mushrooms........................ 174

309. Creamy Avocado and Zucchini Soup.................. 175

310. Sunday Stuffed Mushrooms................................. 175

311. Rich Dark Chocolate Smoothie........................... 176

312. Winter Chanterelle and Leek Stew........................ 176

313. Parmesan Tomato Chips 177

314. Roasted Asparagus with Baba Ghanoush 177

315. Creamy Broccoli Soup...................................... 178

316. Stuffed Avocado with Pecans................................ 178

317. Roasted Curried Cauliflower with Peppers 179

318. Tofu Stuffed Zucchini with Cashew Nuts 179

319. Spinach Chips with Garlic-Avocado Dip 180

320. Brussels Sprouts with Tempeh.............................. 180

321. Garam Masala Broccoli Delight 181

322. Zoodles with Cashew Parmesan 181

323. Summer Salad with Sunflower Seed Dressing...... 182

324. Rainbow Vegan Soup.. 182

325. Morning Protein Smoothie.................................. 183

326. African-Style Carrot Salad 183

327. Roasted Cabbage with Sesame 184

328. Winter Mushroom Stew.. 184

329. Garlicky Savoy Cabbage 185

330. Voodles with Avocado Sauce................................. 185

331. Creamy Cauliflower Soup 186

332. Ethiopian Stuffed Peppers with Cauliflower Rice 186

333. Cream of Almond and Cauliflower Soup 187

334. Vegan Tofu Skillet 187

335. Chocolate and Blackberry Smoothie.................... 188

336. Rich Breakfast Granola..................................... 188

337. Nutty and Yummy Cauliflower Salad 189

338. Overnight "Oats" with Strawberries...................... 189

339. Coconut and Hazelnut "Cereals" 190

340. The Best Guacamole Ever..................................... 190

341. Rich and Easy Granola 191

342. Smoked Tofu with Asian Tomato Sauce............... 191

343. Chia Breakfast Pudding with Plums..................... 192

344. Sautéed Fennel with Basil-Tomato Sauce............. 192

345. Autumn Oven-Roasted Vegetables........................ 193

346. Creamed Eggplant and Cashew Soup 193

347. Chocolate and Butternut Squash Smoothie.......... 194

348. Raspberry and Peanut Butter Smoothie............... 194

349. Cremini Mushroom and Broccoli Delight........... 195

350. Crunchy-Topped Vegetable Bake........................ 195

351. Artichoke and Tofu Stir Fry................................. 196

303. Spicy Tofu with Vegan Tzatziki

Ready in about 40 minutes
Servings 4

Cucumber is an extremely watery ingredient so be careful with it because your vegan tzatziki might become soggy and not so easy on the eyes. Pulse the cucumbers in your blender until pulpy; then, you must salt them to drain and eliminate as much water as possible. Place the cucumbers on a paper towel. The longer they sit, the more liquid will be drawn out.

Per serving: 162 Calories; 10.9g Fat; 8g Carbs; 9.5g Protein; 4.3g Sugars

Ingredients

12 ounces tofu, pressed and cut into 1/4-inch thick slices
1 cup scallions, chopped
1 garlic clove, minced
2 tablespoons champagne vinegar
1 tablespoon Sriracha sauce
2 tablespoons sesame oil

For Vegan Tzatziki:
2 cloves garlic, pressed
2 tablespoons fresh lemon juice
Sea salt and ground black pepper, to taste
1 teaspoon fresh or dried dill weed
1 cup non-dairy yogurt
1 cucumber, shredded

Directions

- Place tofu slices, scallions, garlic, vinegar, and Sriracha sauce in a bowl; let it stand for 30 minutes.
- Heat the oil in a nonstick skillet over medium-high heat. Cook tofu until it is golden brown, about 5 minutes.
- To make vegan tzatziki, thoroughly combine garlic, lemon juice, salt, black pepper, dill and yogurt in a mixing bowl.
- Stir in shredded cucumber; stir until everything is well incorporated.
- Place the tzatziki in the refrigerator until ready to serve. Divide tofu among serving plates and serve with a dollop of tzatziki. Enjoy!

304. Mushroom Stuffed Avocado

Ready in about 10 minutes
Servings 8

These stuffed avocados are filled with delicious sautéed mushrooms and fresh tomato. It's perfect for lunch or a healthy snack.

Per serving: 245 Calories; 23.2g Fat; 10g Carbs; 2.4g Protein; 1.5g Sugars

Ingredients

4 avocados, pitted and halved
2 tablespoons olive oil
2 cups button mushrooms, chopped
1 onion, chopped
1 teaspoon garlic, crushed
Salt and black pepper, to taste
1 teaspoon deli mustard
1 tomato, chopped

Directions

- Scoop out about 2 teaspoons of avocado flesh from each half; reserve scooped avocado flash.
- Heat the oil in a sauté pan that is preheated over a moderately high flame. Now, cook the mushrooms, onion, and garlic until the mushrooms are tender and the onion is translucent.
- Add the reserved avocado flash to the mushroom mixture and mix to combine. Now, add the salt, black pepper, mustard, and tomato.
- Divide the mushroom mixture among avocado halves and serve immediately.

305. Fried Tofu with Peppers

Ready in about 40 minutes
Servings 2

Check out this creative recipe to turn any tofu block into something amazing! Be inspired and experiment with seasonings.

Per serving: 223 Calories; 15.9g Fat; 8.1g Carbs; 15.6g Protein; 2g Sugars

Ingredients

12 ounces extra firm tofu, pressed and cubed
1 ½ tablespoons flaxseed meal
Salt and ground black pepper, to taste
1 teaspoon garlic paste
1/2 teaspoon paprika
1 teaspoon shallot powder
1/2 teaspoon ground bay leaf
1 tablespoon olive oil
1 red bell pepper, deveined and sliced
1 green bell pepper, deveined and sliced
1 serrano pepper, deveined and sliced

Directions

- Place the tofu, flaxseed meal, salt, black pepper, garlic paste, paprika, shallot powder, and ground bay leaf in a container.
- Cover, toss to coat, and let it marinate at least 30 minutes.
- Heat olive oil in a saucepan over a moderate heat. Cook your tofu along with peppers for 5 to 7 minutes, gently stirring.
- Serve immediately and enjoy!

306. Flavorful Tofu Cubes with Pecans

Ready in about 13 minutes
Servings 4

Here's a great, luscious combo of firm tofu, nuts and seasonings. Serve with a glass of dry white wine.

Per serving: 232 Calories; 21.6g Fat; 5.3g Carbs; 8.3g Protein; 1.4g Sugars

Ingredients

3 teaspoons olive oil
1 cup extra firm tofu, pressed and cubed
1/4 cup pecans, coarsely chopped
1 ½ tablespoons soy sauce
3 tablespoons vegetable broth
1/2 teaspoon granulated garlic
1 teaspoon cayenne pepper
1/2 teaspoon turmeric powder
Sea salt and ground black pepper, to taste
2 teaspoons sunflower seeds

Directions

- Heat the oil in a frying pan that is preheated over a moderate heat. Once hot, fry the tofu cubes until golden brown, stirring periodically.
- Stir in the pecans; increase the temperature and cook on high for 2 minutes or until fragrant.
- Add the remaining ingredients, reduce the heat to medium-low and cook an additional 5 minutes.
- Serve drizzled with hot sauce and enjoy!

307. Easy Kale Dip with Crudités

Ready in about 25 minutes
Servings 6

This double-dip worthy vegan dip is the best served with an assortment of crudités. It is perfect when you need a snack in a hurry.

Per serving: 75 Calories; 3g Fat; 9g Carbs; 2.9g Protein; 1.7g Sugars

Ingredients

2 cups kale
1 cup tofu, pressed, drained and crumbled
1/2 cup soy milk
2 teaspoons nutritional yeast
2 garlic cloves, minced
2 teaspoons olive oil
1 teaspoon sea salt
1/4 teaspoon ground black pepper, or more to taste
1/2 teaspoon paprika
1 teaspoon dried basil
1/2 teaspoon dried dill weed

Directions

- Start by preheating your oven to 400 degrees F. Lightly oil a casserole dish with a nonstick cooking spray.
- Now, parboil the kale leaves until it is just wilted.
- Puree the remaining ingredients in your food processor or blender. Stir in the kale; stir until the mixture is homogeneous.
- Bake approximately 13 minutes. Now, serve with a crudités platter. Bon appétit!

308. Crave-Worthy Stuffed Mushrooms

Ready in about 35 minutes
Servings 4

Who said you can't have the best of both – keto and vegan? Make this surprisingly delicious recipe and break that myth.

Per serving: 206 Calories; 13.4g Fat; 10g Carbs; 12.7g Protein; 4.6g Sugars

Ingredients

1/2 head cauliflower
1 pound medium-sized brown cremini mushrooms, cleaned and stems removed
2 tablespoons vegetable oil
1 onion, finely chopped
1 teaspoon garlic, minced
1 bell pepper, chopped
1 teaspoon Italian seasoning mix
Salt and black pepper, to taste
1 cup vegan parmesan

Directions

- Cook the cauliflower in a large pot of salted water until tender, about 6 minutes; cut into florets.
- Then, pulse cauliflower florets in your food processor until they resemble small rice-like granules.
- Preheat an oven to 360 degrees F. Now, bake mushroom caps for 8 to 12 minutes or until they are just tender.
- Heat the oil in a heavy-bottomed skillet; sauté the onion, garlic and bell pepper until they are softened.
- Add Italian seasoning mix along with salt and pepper; taste and adjust seasonings. Fold in cauliflower rice.
- Next, divide the filling mixture among mushroom caps. Top with vegan parmesan and bake 17 minutes longer. Serve warm.

309. Creamy Avocado and Zucchini Soup

Ready in about 45 minutes
Servings 4

Grab a large pot and prepare a double batch of this amazing, thick and rich soup! It can be stored for up to three days in the refrigerator or in the freezer for up to one month.

Per serving: 165 Calories; 13.4g Fat; 11g Carbs; 2.2g Protein; 3.3g Sugars

Ingredients

3 teaspoons vegetable oil
1 yellow onion, chopped
1 carrot, sliced
1 parsnip, sliced
3 cups zucchini, peeled and chopped
1/4 teaspoon ground black pepper
4 cups water
1 tablespoon vegetable bouillon powder
1 tomato, pureed
1 avocado pitted, peeled and diced

Directions

- Heat the oil in a heavy-bottomed pot that is preheated over a moderate heat. Now, sweat the onions until they are softened.
- Add the carrot, parsnip, and zucchini and cook for 7 more minutes; season with black pepper. Reserve vegetables.
- After that, add the water, vegetable bouillon powder, and pureed tomato; bring it to a rapid boil. Turn the heat to medium-low and let it simmer for 18 minutes.
- Add reserved vegetables and simmer for a further 18 minutes. Remove from heat and stir in the avocado.
- Blend the soup in batches until smooth and creamy.

310. Sunday Stuffed Mushrooms

Ready in about 30 minutes
Servings 4

If you crave stuffed vegetables, nothing could be easier than filling mushroom caps with a tasty nutty stuffing and bake them in the preheated oven.

Per serving: 139 Calories; 11.2g Fat; 7.4g Carbs; 4.8g Protein; 3.6g Sugars

Ingredients

2 tablespoons sesame oil
1 cup onions, chopped
1 garlic clove, minced
1 pound white mushrooms, stems removed
Salt and black pepper, to taste
1/4 cup raw walnuts, crushed
2 tablespoons cilantro, chopped

Directions

- Begin by preheating an oven to 360 degrees F. Lightly grease a large baking sheet with a nonstick cooking spray.
- Heat sesame oil in a frying pan that is preheated over medium-high heat. Now, sauté the onions and garlic until aromatic.
- Then, chop the mushroom stems and cook until they are tender. Heat off, season with salt and pepper; stir in walnuts.
- Stuff the mushroom caps with walnut/mushroom mixture and arrange them on the prepared baking sheet.
- Bake for 25 minutes and transfer to a wire rack to cool slightly. Garnish with fresh cilantro and serve. Bon appétit!

311. Rich Dark Chocolate Smoothie

Ready in about 10 minutes
Servings 2

The incredible combination of nuts, cocoa and seeds is fitting for breakfast or a snack. Once you taste how good this smoothie is, it will become your ketogenic breakfast staple.

Per serving: 335 Calories; 31.7g Fat; 12.7g Carbs; 7g Protein; 4.9g Sugars

Ingredients

8 walnuts
3/4 cup almond milk
1/4 cup water
1 ½ cups lettuce
2 teaspoons vegan protein powder, zero carbs
1 tablespoon chia seeds
1 tablespoon unsweetened cocoa powder
4 fresh dates, pitted

Directions

- Process all ingredients in your blender until everything is uniform and creamy.
- Divide between two glasses and serve well-chilled.

312. Winter Chanterelle and Leek Stew

Ready in about 25 minutes
Servings 4

Chanterelle, also known as "egg mushroom", is a fleshy wild mushroom with many health benefits. They are loaded with vitamin B, protein, selenium, zinc, and potassium. Enjoy!

Per serving: 114 Calories; 7.3g Fat; 10g Carbs; 2.1g Protein; 4.3g Sugars

Ingredients

2 tablespoons olive oil
1 cup leeks, chopped
2 garlic cloves, pressed
1/2 cup celery with leaves, chopped
2 carrots, chopped
1 cup fresh Chanterelle, sliced
2 tablespoons dry red wine
2 rosemary sprigs, chopped
1 thyme sprig, chopped
3 ½ cups roasted vegetable stock
1/2 teaspoon cayenne pepper
1 teaspoon Hungarian paprika
2 ripe tomatoes, pureed
1 tablespoon flaxseed meal

Directions

- Heat the oil in a stockpot over a moderate flame. Now, cook the leeks until they are tender.
- Add garlic, celery, and carrots and cook for a further 4 minutes or until they are softened.
- Now, stir in Chanterelle mushrooms; cook until they lose their liquid; reserve the vegetables.
- Pour in the wine to deglaze the bottom of the stockpot. Now, add rosemary and thyme.
- Add roasted vegetable stock, cayenne pepper, Hungarian paprika, and tomatoes; stir in reserved vegetables and bring to a boil.
- Reduce heat to a simmer. Let it simmer, covered, an additional 15 minutes. Add flaxseed meal to thicken the soup. Serve in individual soup bowls with a few sprinkles of Hungarian paprika.

313. Parmesan Tomato Chips

Ready in about 5 hours
Servings 6

This simple but endlessly crave-worthy vegan snack is both sophisticated and rustic. It contains Italian seasonings but you can also try sprinkling in a pinch of dill weed or chili powder.

Per serving: 161 Calories; 14g Fat; 7.2g Carbs; 4.6g Protein; 3g Sugars

Ingredients

1 ½ pounds tomatoes, sliced
1/4 cup extra-virgin olive oil
1 tablespoon Italian seasoning mix

For Vegan Parmesan:
1/2 cup pumpkin seeds
1 tablespoon nutritional yeast
Salt and black pepper, to taste
1 teaspoon garlic powder

Directions

- Drizzle sliced tomatoes with olive oil.
- Now, preheat your oven to 200 degrees F. Coat a baking pan with Silpat mat.
- Pulse all the parmesan ingredients in your food processor until you reach a Parmesan cheese consistency.
- Mix parmesan with Italian seasoning mix. Then, toss seasoned tomato slices with parmesan mixture until they are well coated.
- Arrange tomato slices on the baking pan and bake for 5 hours. Store in an airtight container.

314. Roasted Asparagus with Baba Ghanoush

Ready in about 45 minutes
Servings 6

The eggplant season is a great time to try out this classic Middle Eastern dip! Ultimately, you need something creamy, soft and delicious to serve with timeless roasted asparagus spears.

Per serving: 149 Calories; 12.1g Fat; 9g Carbs; 3.6g Protein; 4.3g Sugars

Ingredients

1 ½ pounds asparagus spears, trim and cut off the woody ends
1/4 cup olive oil
1 teaspoon sea salt
1/2 teaspoon ground black pepper, to taste
1/2 teaspoon paprika

For Baba Ghanoush:
3/4 pound eggplant
2 teaspoons olive oil
1/2 cup scallions, chopped
2 cloves garlic, minced
1 tablespoon tahini
2 tablespoons fresh lemon juice
1/2 teaspoon cayenne pepper
Salt and ground black pepper, to taste
1/4 cup fresh parsley leaves, chopped

Directions

- Begin by preheating your oven to 390 degrees F. Line a baking sheet with parchment paper.
- Place the asparagus spears on the baking sheet.
- Toss asparagus spears with the oil, salt, pepper, and paprika. Bake about 9 minutes or until thoroughly cooked.
- Then, make Baba Ghanoush. Preheat your oven to 425 degrees F.
- Place the eggplants on a lined cookie sheet. Set under the broiler approximately 30 minutes; allow eggplants to cool. Now, peel the eggplants and remove the stems.
- Heat 2 teaspoons of olive oil in a frying pan over a moderately high flame. Now, sauté the scallions and garlic until tender and aromatic.
- Add the roasted eggplant, scallion mixture, tahini, lemon juice, cayenne pepper, salt and black pepper to your food processor. Pulse until ingredients are evenly mixed.
- Garnish with parsley and serve with roasted asparagus spears. Bon appétit!

315. Creamy Broccoli Soup

Ready in about 15 minutes
Servings 4

This is an amazing recipe not only for vegans but also for all health-conscious people. Coconut milk works well too.

Per serving: 252 Calories; 20.3g Fat; 11.8g Carbs; 8.1g Protein; 2.4g Sugars

Ingredients

2 tablespoons coconut oil, at room temperature
2 shallots, finely chopped
1 teaspoon garlic, minced
1 pound broccoli, cut into small florets
8 ounces kale leaves, torn into small pieces
4 cups vegetable broth
1/2 cup almond milk
1/2 teaspoon kosher salt
1/2 teaspoon crushed red pepper flakes
2 tablespoons chives, coarsely chopped

Directions

- Heat the coconut oil in a pot that is preheated over a moderate flame. Then, sauté the shallots and garlic until they're fragrant and slightly browned.
- Now, add the broccoli, kale and vegetable broth; bring to a boil for 5 minutes.
- Pour in the almond milk, salt and pepper; cover and let your soup simmer over a moderate flame.
- Afterwards, blend the soup with an immersion blender; serve right away garnished with fresh chopped chives!

316. Stuffed Avocado with Pecans

Ready in about 10 minutes
Servings 4

With its mild flavor and great, creamy texture, avocado is the perfect fruit for this raw meal. If you'd like a little kick of fire, just add a few sprinkles of chili pepper flakes.

Per serving: 263 Calories; 24.8g Fat; 10g Carbs; 3.5g Protein; 2.5g Sugars

Ingredients

2 avocados, peeled and pitted
5 ounces pecans, ground
2 carrots, chopped
1 garlic clove
1 teaspoon lemon juice
1 tablespoon soy sauce
Salt and freshly ground black pepper, to taste

Directions

- In a mixing bowl, thoroughly combine avocado pulp with pecans, carrots, garlic, lemon juice, and soy sauce.
- Season with salt and black pepper to taste. Divide the mixture among avocado halves.
- You can add some extra pecans for garnish. Bon appétit!

317. Roasted Curried Cauliflower with Peppers

Ready in about 35 minutes
Servings 4

Roasted vegetables are a must-have for Sunday lunch or Christmas dinner. In addition, this recipe is super-easy and extremely addictive, high in fiber and vitamins but low in carbs!

Per serving: 166 Calories; 13.9g Fat; 9.4g Carbs; 3g Protein; 4.4g Sugars

Ingredients

1 pound cauliflower, broken into florets
2 bell peppers, halved
2 pasilla peppers, halved
1/4 cup extra-virgin olive oil
1/2 teaspoon sea salt
1/4 teaspoon freshly ground black pepper, or more to taste
1/2 teaspoon cayenne pepper
1 teaspoon curry powder
1/2 teaspoon nigella seeds

Directions

- Preheat your oven to 425 degrees F. Line a large baking sheet with a piece of parchment paper.
- Drizzle cauliflower and peppers with extra-virgin olive oil. Sprinkle with salt, black pepper, cayenne pepper, curry powder and nigella seeds
- Next, arrange the vegetables on the prepared baking sheet.
- Roast the vegetables, tossing periodically, until they are slightly browned, about 30 minutes.
- Serve with a homemade tomato dip or mushroom pate. Bon appétit!

318. Tofu Stuffed Zucchini with Cashew Nuts

Ready in about 50 minutes
Servings 4

This is another recipe for stuffed vegetables, bursting with amazing flavors! These ultra delicious stuffed zucchini boats are rich, spicy, and comforting!

Per serving: 148 Calories; 10g Fat; 9.8g Carbs; 7.5g Protein; 5.5g Sugars

Ingredients

1 tablespoon olive oil
2 (12-ounce) packages firm tofu, drained and crumbled
2 garlic cloves, pressed
1/2 cup scallions, chopped
2 cups tomato puree
1/4 teaspoon turmeric
1/4 teaspoon chili powder
Sea salt and cayenne pepper, to taste
4 zucchinis, cut into halves lengthwise and scoop out the insides
1 tablespoon nutritional yeast
2 ounces cashew nuts, lightly salted and chopped

Directions

- Heat the oil in a pan that is preheated over a moderate heat; now, cook the tofu, garlic, and scallions for 4 to 6 minutes.
- Stir in 1 cup of tomato puree and scooped zucchini flesh; add all seasonings and cook an additional 6 minutes, until tofu is slightly browned.
- Next, preheat your oven to 360 degrees F.
- Divide the tofu mixture among zucchini shells. Place stuffed zucchini shells in a baking dish that is previously greased with a cooking spray. Pour in the remaining 1 cup of tomato puree.
- Bake approximately 30 minutes. Sprinkle with nutritional yeast and cashew nuts; bake an additional 5 to 6 minutes. Enjoy!

319. Spinach Chips with Garlic-Avocado Dip

Ready in about 20 minutes
Servings 6

This avocado dip works very well with any type of vegetable crisps like beetroot chips or zucchini chips. This time, we tossed fresh spinach leaves with a high-quality olive oil, salt, and garlic powder to achieve your keto requirements.

Per serving: 269 Calories; 26.7g Fat; 9.4g Carbs; 2.3g Protein; 0.6g Sugars

Ingredients

3 ripe avocados, pitted
2 teaspoons lime juice
Salt and black pepper, to taste
2 garlic cloves, finely minced
2 tablespoons extra-virgin olive oil
1/2 teaspoon red pepper flakes

For Spinach Chips:
2 cups baby spinach, washed and dried
1 tablespoon olive oil
Sea salt and garlic powder, to taste

Directions

- Mash avocado pulp with a fork. Add fresh lime juice, salt, pepper, garlic, and 2 tablespoons of olive oil.
- Mix until everything is well incorporated. Transfer to a serving bowl and sprinkle with red pepper flakes.
- Then, preheat your oven to 300 degrees F. Line a baking sheet with a Silpat mat.
- Arrange spinach leaves on the baking sheet; toss with 1 tablespoon of olive oil, salt, and garlic powder.
- Bake for 8 to 12 minutes so the leaves have dried up. Serve with well-chilled avocado dip. Bon appétit!

320. Brussels Sprouts with Tempeh

Ready in about 20 minutes
Servings 4

An amazingly quick dish that features vegetables and vegan protein. Add another combo of spices if desired. Enjoy!

Per serving: 179 Calories; 11.7g Fat; 12.1g Carbs; 10.5g Protein; 2g Sugars

Ingredients

2 tablespoons olive oil
2 garlic cloves, minced
1/2 cup leeks, chopped
10 ounces tempeh, crumbled
2 tablespoons water
2 tablespoons soy sauce
1 tablespoon tomato puree
1/2 pound Brussels sprouts, quartered
Sea salt and ground black pepper, to taste

Directions

- Heat the oil in a saucepan that is preheated over a moderate heat. Now, cook the garlic and leeks until tender and aromatic.
- Now, add the tempeh, water and soy sauce. Cook until the tempeh just beginning to brown, about 5 minutes.
- Stir in shredded cabbage; season with salt and pepper; turn the heat to low and cook, stirring often, for about 13 minutes. Serve warm.

321. Garam Masala Broccoli Delight

Ready in about 15 minutes
Servings 4

Don't let this short list of ingredients fool you! They make a perfect match, trust me. Broccoli is a powerhouse of amazing nutrients like Vitamin C and K, as well as minerals and fiber.

Per serving: 100 Calories; 8.2g Fat; 4.7g Carbs; 3.7g Protein; 0.9g Sugars

Ingredients

3/4 pound broccoli, broken into florets
1/4 cup extra-virgin olive oil
Seasoned salt and ground black pepper, to taste
1 garlic clove, smashed
1 tablespoon sesame paste
1 tablespoon fresh lime juice
1/2 teaspoon Garam Masala

Directions

- Steam broccoli for 7 minutes, until it is crisp-tender but still vibrant green. Pulse in your blender or a food processor until rice-like consistency is achieved.
- Now, add the oil, salt, black paper, garlic, sesame paste, fresh lime juice and Garam Masala.
- Blend until everything is well incorporated.
- Drizzle with some extra olive oil and serve immediately. Otherwise, keep in your refrigerator until ready to serve.

322. Zoodles with Cashew Parmesan

Ready in about 15 minutes
Servings 4

This vegan parmesan can be used on salads, roasted vegetables, and sandwiches. Its rich flavor is a nice complement to almost any food. It can be stored in an airtight container in the refrigerator for up to 2 months.

Per serving: 145 Calories; 10.6g Fat; 9g Carbs; 5.5g Protein; 3.3g Sugars

Ingredients

For Zoodles:
4 zucchinis, peeled
2 tablespoons olive oil
1/2 cup water
Salt and cayenne pepper, to taste

For Cashew Parmesan:
1/2 cup raw cashews
2 tablespoons nutritional yeast
Sea salt and black pepper, to taste
1/4 teaspoon shallot powder
1/2 teaspoon garlic powder

Directions

- Slice the zucchinis into long strips i.e. noodle-shape strands.
- Heat the oil in a pan over medium heat; cook zucchini for 1 minute or so, stirring continuously. Pour in water and cook 6 more minutes. Season with salt and cayenne pepper to taste.
- Then, pulse all parmesan ingredients in your food processor until you reach a Parmesan cheese consistency.
- Top cooked zoodles with cashew parmesan and enjoy!

323. Summer Salad with Sunflower Seed Dressing

Ready in about 3 hours 15 minutes
Servings 4

To pre-soak the sunflower seeds, just leave it out on the counter overnight in lukewarm water and they will be ready to use in the morning.

Per serving: 208 Calories; 15.6g Fat; 10g Carbs; 7.6g Protein; 4.2g Sugars

Ingredients

For Sunflower Seed Dressing:
1 cup sunflower seeds, raw and hulled
2 cups water
2 tablespoons scallions, chopped
1 garlic clove, chopped
1 lime, freshly squeezed
Salt and black pepper, to taste
1/2 teaspoon red pepper flakes crushed
1/4 teaspoon rosemary, minced
2 tablespoons coconut milk

For the salad:
1 head fresh lettuce, separated into leaves
3 tomatoes, diced
3 cucumbers, sliced
2 tablespoons Kalamata olives, pitted

Directions

- Soak the sunflower seeds in water at least 3 hours. Drain the sunflower seeds; transfer them to your blender and add the remaining ingredients for the dressing.
- Puree until creamy, smooth and uniform.
- Put all the salad ingredients into four serving bowls. Toss with dressing and serve immediately. Bon appétit!

324. Rainbow Vegan Soup

Ready in about 25 minutes
Servings 6

Eat a rainbow! With colorful veggies, fragrant herbs, and a rich texture, you'll never miss the meat or noodles in this amazing vegan soup.

Per serving: 142 Calories; 11.4g Fat; 9g Carbs; 2.9g Protein; 3.3g Sugars

Ingredients

2 teaspoons olive oil
1 shallot, chopped
2 cloves garlic, minced
1 celery stalk, chopped
1 zucchini, chopped
1 carrot, sliced
1 cup kale, torn into pieces
1 cup mustard greens, torn into pieces
Sea salt and ground black pepper, to taste
2 thyme sprigs, chopped
1 rosemary sprig, chopped
2 bay leaves
6 cups vegetable stock
2 ripe tomatoes, chopped
1 cup almond milk, unflavored
1 tablespoon white miso paste
1/2 cup watercress

Directions

- Heat olive oil in a large pot that is preheated over a moderately high heat. Now, sauté the shallots, garlic, celery, zucchini, and carrots until they're softened.
- Now, add the kale, mustard greens, salt, ground black pepper, thyme, rosemary, bay leaves, vegetable stock and tomatoes.
- Reduce the heat to simmer. Let it simmer another 15 minutes, leaving the lid slightly ajar.
- After that, add almond milk, white miso paste, and watercress. Cook an additional 5 minutes, stirring periodically. Bon appétit!

325. Morning Protein Smoothie

Ready in about 5 minutes
Servings 4

Breakfast in less than 5 minutes! This smoothie has a beautiful color and amazing taste, a true feast for the eyes and belly.

Per serving: 247 Calories; 21.7g Fat; 14.9g Carbs; 2.6g Protein; 9g Sugars

Ingredients

1/2 cup water
1 ½ cups almond milk
1 banana, peeled and sliced
1/3 cup frozen cherries
1/3 cup fresh blueberries
1/4 teaspoon vanilla extract
1 tablespoon vegan protein powder, zero carbs

Directions

● Mix all ingredients in your blender or a smoothie maker until creamy and uniform.
● Serve in individual glasses and enjoy!

326. African-Style Carrot Salad

Ready in about 10 minutes
Servings 4

Harissa, a flavor-packed condiment, is Northwest African chili paste that can be found ready-made in jars or cans. It is a unique mix of hot chili peppers, tomatoes, olive oil, garlic, and spices.

Per serving: 196 Calories; 17.2g Fat; 11g Carbs; 1.2g Protein; 5.3g Sugars

Ingredients

1 pound carrots, coarsely shredded
1/4 cup fresh cilantro, chopped

For the Vinaigrette:
3 garlic cloves, smashed
Sea salt and ground black pepper, to taste
1/3 cup extra-virgin olive oil
1 lime, freshly squeezed
2 tablespoons balsamic vinegar
1/2 teaspoon ground cumin
1/2 teaspoon harissa

Directions

● Place shredded carrots and fresh, chopped cilantro in a salad bowl.
● Combine all ingredients for the vinaigrette; mix until everything is well incorporated.
● Add the vinaigrette to the carrot salad and toss to coat well. Bon appétit!

327. Roasted Cabbage with Sesame

Ready in about 45 minutes
Servings 6

Roast cabbage wedges with sesame seeds for a simple holiday side dish. Add a pinch of chili paper flakes for some extra oomph!

Per serving: 186 Calories; 17g Fat; 8g Carbs; 2.1g Protein; 4.9g Sugars

Ingredients

Nonstick cooking spray
2 pounds green cabbage, cut into wedges
1/4 cup olive oil
Coarsely salt and freshly ground black pepper, to taste
1 teaspoon sesame seeds
2 tablespoons fresh chives, chopped

Directions

- Begin by preheating your oven to 390 degrees F. Brush a rimmed baking sheet with a nonstick cooking spray.
- Add the cabbage wedges to the baking sheet. Toss with olive oil, salt, black pepper and sesame seeds.
- Roast for 40 to 45 minutes, until cabbage is softened. Serve garnished with fresh chopped chives. Bon appétit!

328. Winter Mushroom Stew

Ready in about 50 minutes
Servings 4

What could be better than a hearty warm stew during chilly winter days?! Chanterelle mushrooms are a wild species with many health benefits. They are loaded with Vitamin B1, B6, and B9, dietary fiber, zinc and potassium.

Per serving: 65 Calories; 2.7g Fat; 9g Carbs; 2.7g Protein; 4.9g Sugars

Ingredients

2 teaspoons olive oil
1 yellow onion, chopped
1 garlic clove, finely minced
1/2 cup celery, chopped
1/2 cup carrot, chopped
1 green bell pepper, chopped
1 jalapeno pepper, chopped
2 ½ cups Chanterelle mushrooms, thinly sliced
1 ½ cups vegetable stock
2 ripe tomatoes, chopped
2 thyme sprigs, chopped
1 rosemary sprig, chopped
2 bay leaves
1/2 teaspoon salt
1/4 teaspoon ground black pepper, or more to taste
1/4 teaspoon grated nutmeg
2 tablespoons apple cider vinegar

Directions

- Heat the oil in a pot that is preheated over a moderately high heat. Now, sauté the onions and garlic until tender and fragrant.
- Stir in the celery, carrots, pepper, and mushrooms. Cook for 12 minutes more, stirring periodically; add a splash of vegetable stock to prevent sticking.
- Add the remaining ingredients, except for apple cider vinegar.
- Turn the heat to medium-low; let it simmer for 25 to 35 minutes or until everything is thoroughly cooked.
- Ladle into individual bowls, drizzle each serving with apple cider vinegar and eat warm.

329. Garlicky Savoy Cabbage

Ready in about 25 minutes
Servings 4

Once you ditch animal products, it opens a whole new perspective on nutrition and dieting. You will soon realize that a plant-based diet is a shortcut to successful weight loss.

Per serving: 118 Calories; 7g Fat; 13.4g Carbs; 2.9g Protein; 7.3g Sugars

Ingredients

2 pounds Savoy cabbage, torn into pieces
2 tablespoons almond oil
1 teaspoon garlic, minced
1/2 teaspoon dried basil
1/2 teaspoon red pepper flakes, crushed
Salt and ground black pepper, to the taste

Directions

- Cook Savoy cabbage in a pot of a lightly salted water approximately 20 minutes over a moderate heat. Drain and reserve.
- Now, heat the oil in a sauté pan over a medium-high heat. Now, cook the garlic until just aromatic.
- Add reserved Savoy cabbage, basil, red pepper, salt and black pepper; stir until everything is heated through.
- Taste, adjust the seasonings and serve warm over a cauliflower rice.

330. Voodles with Avocado Sauce

Ready in about 15 minutes
Servings 4

Voodles (spiralized vegetables) make a great substitute for a classic whole grain pasta. You can roast them in the preheated oven or cook in a boiling water.

Per serving: 233 Calories; 20.2g Fat; 11g Carbs; 1.9g Protein; 3g Sugars

Ingredients

1/2 pound carrots
1/2 pound bell peppers
1 tablespoon olive oil
1 avocado, peeled and pitted
1 lemon, juiced and zested
2 tablespoons sesame oil
2 tablespoons cilantro, chopped
1 shallot, chopped
1 jalapeno pepper, deveined and minced
Salt and black pepper, to taste

Directions

- Spiralize carrots and bell peppers by using a spiralizer or a julienne peeler.
- Heat olive oil in a wok or a large nonstick skillet. Sauté carrots and peppers in hot olive oil for about 8 minutes.
- Then, mix all remaining ingredients until creamy. Pour avocado sauce over voodles and serve immediately.

331. Creamy Cauliflower Soup

Ready in about 20 minutes
Servings 4

Comforting and irresistible, this healthy plant-based soup is loaded with protein and vitamins. Cauliflower is definitely a vegetable made in heaven!

Per serving: 94 Calories; 7.2g Fat; 7g Carbs; 2.7g Protein; 3.2g Sugars

Ingredients

4 cups water
2 heads of cauliflower, broken into florets
1 ½ tablespoons vegetable bouillon granules
1/4 teaspoon ground bay leaves
1/4 teaspoon ground cloves
2 tablespoons extra-virgin olive oil
1/2 teaspoon red pepper flakes

Directions

- In a heavy-bottomed pot, bring the water to a boil over a moderately high heat.
- Stir in the cauliflower florets; cook for 10 minutes.
- Add the bouillon granules, ground bay leaves, and ground cloves. Now, reduce the heat to medium-low; continue to cook for 5 minutes longer.
- Puree this mixture by using a food processor or an immersion blender.
- Divide among four soup bowl; drizzle each serving with olive oil and sprinkle with red pepper. Eat warm.

332. Ethiopian Stuffed Peppers with Cauliflower Rice

Ready in about 40 minutes
Servings 4

Cauliflower rice is a staple you should have in your kitchen during a ketogenic diet. Every vegan dish is fast and cheap to pull together once you make a batch of cauliflower rice.

Per serving: 77 Calories; 4.8g Fat; 8.4g Carbs; 1.6g Protein; 3.2g Sugars

Ingredients

1 small head cauliflower
4 bell peppers
1 ½ tablespoons oil
1 onion, chopped
1 garlic cloves, minced
1 teaspoon chipotle powder
1 teaspoon Berbere
2 ripe tomatoes, pureed
Sea salt and pepper, to taste

Directions

- To make cauliflower rice, grate the cauliflower into the size of rice. Place on a kitchen towel to soak up any excess moisture.
- Next, preheat your oven to 360 degrees F. Lightly grease a casserole dish.
- Cut off the top of the bell peppers. Now, discard the seeds and core.
- Roast the peppers in a parchment lined baking pan for 18 minutes until the skin is slightly browned.
- In the meantime, heat the oil over medium-high heat. Sauté the onion and garlic until tender and fragrant.
- Add cauliflower rice, chipotle powder, and Berbere spice. Cook until the cauliflower rice is tender, about 6 minutes.
- Divide the cauliflower mixture among bell peppers. Place in the casserole dish.
- Mix the tomatoes, salt, and pepper. Pour the tomato mixture over the peppers. Bake about 10 minutes, depending on desired tenderness. Serve immediately.

333. Cream of Almond and Cauliflower Soup

Ready in about 25 minutes
Servings 4

With its nutty, rich and spectacular flavor, this soup will amaze you and your family! Make sure to use blanched i.e. skinless, white almonds.

Per serving: 114 Calories; 6.5g Fat; 12.4g Carbs; 3.8g Protein; 2g Sugars

Ingredients

1 tablespoon almond oil
1 cup shallots, chopped
1 celery with leaves, chopped
2 cloves garlic, minced
1 head cauliflower, broken into florets
4 cups water
Salt and white pepper, to taste
1/4 cup ground almonds
1 tablespoon fresh parsley, chopped

Directions

● Heat the oil in a stockpot that is preheated over a moderate heat. Now, sauté the shallots, celery and garlic until tender, about 6 minutes.
● Add the cauliflower, water, salt, and white pepper. Add the ground almonds.
● Bring to a boil; then, reduce the heat to low; continue to simmer for about 17 minutes.
● Next, puree the soup with an immersion blender. Serve garnished with fresh parsley. Bon appétit!

334. Vegan Tofu Skillet

Ready in about 25 minutes
Servings 4

This vegan meal is incredibly tasty and easy to make for dinner or brunch. Use another combo of vegetables if desired – just make sure to use low-carb veggies.

Per serving: 128 Calories; 8.3g Fat; 10g Carbs; 5.1g Protein; 4g Sugars

Ingredients

2 tablespoons olive oil
1 (14-ounce) block tofu, pressed and cubed
1 celery stalk, chopped
1 bunch scallions, chopped
1 teaspoon cayenne pepper
1 teaspoon garlic powder
2 tablespoons Worcestershire sauce
Salt and black pepper, to taste
1 pound Brussels sprouts, trimmed and quartered
1/2 teaspoon turmeric powder
1/2 teaspoon dried sill weed
1/4 teaspoon dried basil

Directions

● Heat 1 tablespoon of olive oil in a large-sized skillet over a moderately high flame. Add tofu cubes and cook, gently stirring, for 8 minutes.
● Now, add the celery and scallions; cook until they are softened, about 5 minutes
● Add cayenne pepper, garlic powder, Worcestershire sauce, salt, and pepper; continue to cook for 3 more minutes; reserve.
● Heat the remaining 1 tablespoon of oil in the same pan. Cook Brussels sprouts along with the remaining seasonings for 4 minutes.
● Add tofu mixture to Brussels sprouts and serve warm. Enjoy!

335. Chocolate and Blackberry Smoothie

Ready in about 5 minutes
Servings 2

Serve this smoothie as a well-balanced breakfast or an energy-boosting afternoon snack. You can skip cocoa powder, if desired, and have a completely new taste.

Per serving: 103 Calories; 5.9g Fat; 11g Carbs; 4.1g Protein; 4.4g Sugars

Ingredients

1 cup blackberries
1 cup water
1 tablespoon chia seeds
1 tablespoon cocoa
1/4 teaspoon ground nutmeg
1 tablespoon peanut butter
Liquid Stevia, to taste

Directions

- Add all ingredients to your blender or a food processor.
- Mix until creamy and uniform. Pour into two tall glasses and serve immediately. Enjoy!

336. Rich Breakfast Granola

Ready in about 1 hour
Servings 8

Cereal for breakfast? Yes please! If you think granola isn't ketogenic food, think twice. This rich but fairly simple breakfast is sure to satisfy your cereal cravings.

Per serving: 262 Calories; 24.3g Fat; 9.2g Carbs; 5.1g Protein; 5.1g Sugars

Ingredients

2 tablespoons coconut oil
1/3 cup coconut flakes
1 ½ cups coconut milk
2 tablespoons sugar
1/8 teaspoon Himalayan salt
1 teaspoon orange zest
1/8 teaspoon nutmeg, freshly grated
1/2 teaspoon ground cinnamon
1/2 cup walnuts, chopped
1/2 cup almonds, slivered
2 tablespoons pepitas
2 tablespoons sunflower seeds
1/4 cup flax seed

Directions

- Warm coconut oil in a deep pan that is preheated over a moderately high flame. Toast coconut flakes for 1 to 2 minutes.
- Add the remaining ingredients; stir to combine.
- Preheat your oven to 300 degrees F. Spread mixture out in an even layer onto a parchment lined baking sheet.
- Bake for 1 hour, gently tossing every 15 minutes. Serve with some extra coconut milk. Bon appétit!

337. Nutty and Yummy Cauliflower Salad

Ready in about 15 minutes + chilling time
Servings 4

Make this fantastic salad a day ahead to let flavors blend. Generally speaking, pecans are pretty low in carbs but the amount matters too.

Per serving: 281 Calories; 26.8g Fat; 15.6g Carbs; 4.2g Protein; 4.3g Sugars

Ingredients

1 head fresh cauliflower, cut into florets
1 cup spring onions, chopped
4 ounces bottled roasted peppers, chopped
1/4 cup extra-virgin olive oil
1 tablespoon wine vinegar
1 teaspoon yellow mustard
Coarse salt and black pepper, to your liking
1/2 cup green olives, pitted and chopped
1/2 cup pecans, coarsely chopped

Directions

- Steam the cauliflower florets for 4 to 6 minutes; set aside to cool.
- In a salad bowl, place spring onions and roasted peppers.
- In a mixing dish, whisk olive oil, vinegar, mustard, salt and pepper. Drizzle over the veggies in the salad bowl.
- Now, add the reserved cauliflower and toss to combine well. Scatter green olives and pecans over the top and serve.

338. Overnight "Oats" with Strawberries

Ready in about 5 minutes + chilling time
Servings 4

It's so easy to make a tasty vegan breakfast! The other topping ideas include macadamia nuts, walnuts, raspberries or quince.

Per serving: 176 Calories; 12.7g Fat; 6g Carbs; 9.7g Protein; 1.8g Sugars

Ingredients

1/2 cup water
1/2 cup unsweetened almond milk
3/4 cup hemp hearts
6 drops of liquid stevia
1/4 teaspoon ground cloves
1/4 teaspoon ground cinnamon
1 cup strawberries, halved

Directions

- Combine all ingredients, except for strawberries, in an airtight container.
- Cover and place in your refrigerator overnight.
- In the morning, top with fresh strawberries and serve immediately.

339. Coconut and Hazelnut "Cereals"

Ready in about 10 minutes
Servings 4

Quick and easy breakfast cereals without grains make a great vegan kick-start to your busy day. Enjoy!

Per serving: 279 Calories; 23.6g Fat; 11g Carbs; 7.2g Protein; 6g Sugars

Ingredients

2 tablespoons coconut oil
1/3 cup coconut shreds
2 ½ cups coconut milk, full-fat
1/2 cup water
2 tablespoons confectioners' erythritol
1/8 teaspoon salt
1/2 teaspoon vanilla paste
1/2 cup flax seed
16 hazelnuts, roughly chopped

Directions

- Melt coconut oil in a pan over a moderate heat. Then, add coconut shreds, coconut milk, water, confectioners' erythritol, salt, vanilla paste, and flax seed.
- Simmer for 5 minutes, stirring periodically. Allow it to cool down slightly.
- Then, ladle into four individual bowls. Serve topped with chopped hazelnuts. Bon appétit!

340. The Best Guacamole Ever

Ready in about 10 minutes + chilling time
Servings 8

Choose ripe avocados and fresh tomatoes for this guacamole and you cannot go wrong. Don't over mash your avocados because you want a chunky sauce not smooth and squashy.

Per serving: 112 Calories; 9.9g Fat; 6.5g Carbs; 1.3g Protein; 1.4g Sugars

Ingredients

2 Haas avocados, peeled, pitted, and mashed
2 tablespoons fresh lime juice
Sea salt and ground black pepper, to taste
1/2 teaspoon cumin, ground
1 yellow onion, chopped
2 tablespoons coriander leaves, chopped
1 cup fresh tomatoes, chopped
2 garlic cloves, minced
1 red chili, deseeded and finely chopped

Directions

- In a bowl, thoroughly combine the avocados, lime juice, salt and black pepper.
- Stir in the onion, cilantro, tomatoes, and garlic; sprinkle with paprika.
- Keep in your refrigerator until ready to serve. Bon appétit!

341. Rich and Easy Granola

Ready in about 1 hour
Servings 6

A keto granola? Seriously? Try this recipe and you will see – a keto granola is just as good as any type of granola you tried before.

Per serving: 449 Calories; 44.9g Fat; 11g Carbs; 9.3g Protein; 1.4g Sugars

Ingredients

1/2 cup pecans, chopped
1 cup walnuts, chopped
1/3 cup flax meal
1/3 cup coconut milk
1/3 cup sesame seeds
1/3 cup pumpkin seeds
8 drops stevia
1/3 cup coconut oil, melted
1 ½ teaspoons vanilla paste
1 teaspoon ground cloves
1 teaspoon freshly grated nutmeg
1 teaspoon orange zest
1/3 cup water

Directions

- Begin by preheating your oven to 300 degrees F. Line a baking sheet with parchment paper.
- Mix all ingredients until well combined. Now, spread this mixture out in an even layer onto the prepared baking sheet.
- Bake about 55 minutes, stirring every 15 minutes. Allow it to cool down at room temperature.
- Afterwards, transfer to an airtight container or serve immediately. Bon appétit!

342. Smoked Tofu with Asian Tomato Sauce

Ready in about 20 minutes
Servings 4

This gourmet tofu with Asian flair is juicy, tasty and extraordinary. Asian chili garlic sauce also adds lavishness and tanginess to this meal.

Per serving: 336 Calories; 22.2g Fat; 12.3g Carbs; 27.6g Protein; 5.5g Sugars

Ingredients

10 ounces smoked tofu, pressed and drained
2 tablespoons olive oil
1 cup leeks, chopped
1 teaspoon garlic, minced
1/2 cup vegetable broth
1/2 teaspoon turmeric powder
Sea salt and ground black pepper, to taste
For the Sauce:
1/2 tablespoon olive oil
1 cup tomato sauce
2 tablespoons red wine
1 teaspoon fresh rosemary, chopped
1 teaspoon Asian chili garlic sauce

Directions

- Pat dry the tofu and cut it into 1-inch cubes. Heat 2 tablespoons of olive oil in a frying pan over a medium heat.
- Then, fry the tofu cubes until they are slightly browned on all sides. Now, add the leeks, garlic, broth, turmeric powder, salt and pepper.
- Cook until almost all liquid has evaporated.
- Meanwhile, make the sauce. Heat 1/2 tablespoon of olive oil in a pan over a medium heat. Add the tomato sauce and cook until heated through.
- Add the remaining ingredients and simmer over a medium-low heat approximately 10 minutes. Serve with prepared tofu cubes. Enjoy!

343. Chia Breakfast Pudding with Plums

Ready in about 5 minutes + prep time
Servings 3

*Don't bother about making breakfast on super-busy days!
Soak chia seeds overnight and add toppings of choice. Easy
peasy lemon squeezy!*

Per serving: 153 Calories; 8g Fat; 11.7g Carbs; 6.7g Protein; 7g Sugars

Ingredients

2 cups almond milk, unsweetened
1/2 cup chia seeds
1/2 teaspoon vanilla extract
1/4 teaspoon cardamom
1/4 teaspoon ground cinnamon
A pinch of salt
2 teaspoons Swerve, powdered
8 plums, pitted and halved

Directions

- Place all of the above ingredients, except for Swerve and plums, in an airtight container.
- Allow it to stand, covered, in your refrigerator overnight.
- Sweeten with powdered Swerve and serve well-chilled with fresh plums. Enjoy!

344. Sautéed Fennel with Basil-Tomato Sauce

Ready in about 20 minutes
Servings 4

*Fennel is among the healthiest foods in the world, it is a
great source of vitamins, minerals, and fiber. Fennel can
lower blood pressure, improve digestion and maintain
bone health. Enjoy!*

Per serving: 135 Calories; 13.6g Fat; 3g Carbs; 0.9g Protein; 1.1g Sugars

Ingredients

2 tablespoons olive oil
1 garlic clove, crushed
1 fennel, thinly sliced
1/4 cup vegetable stock
Sea salt and ground black pepper, to taste

For the Sauce:
2 tomatoes, halved
2 tablespoons extra-virgin olive oil
1/2 cup scallions, chopped
1 cloves garlic, minced
1 ancho chili, minced
1 bunch fresh basil, leaves picked
1 tablespoon fresh cilantro, roughly chopped
Sat and pepper, to taste

Directions

- Heat olive oil in a pan over a moderately high heat. Sauté the garlic for 1 to 2 minutes or until aromatic.
- Throw the slices of fennel into the pan; add vegetable stock and continue to cook until the fennel is softened. Season with salt and black pepper to taste. Heat off.
- Brush the tomato halves with extra-virgin olive oil. Microwave for 15 minutes on HIGH; be sure to pour off any excess liquid.
- Transfer cooked tomatoes to a food processor; add the remaining ingredients for the sauce. Puree until your desired consistency is reached.
- Serve with sautéed fennel. Bon appétit!

345. Autumn Oven-Roasted Vegetables

Ready in about 45 minutes
Servings 4

If you are looking for just the right recipe for sensational roasted veggies, look no further. Don't forget to slice your veggies into similarly sized pieces and drizzle them generously with olive oil. So good, right?

Per serving: 165 Calories; 14.3g Fat; 10.2g Carbs; 2.1g Protein; 3.7g Sugars

Ingredients

1 red bell pepper, deveined and sliced
1 green bell pepper, deveined and sliced
1 orange bell pepper, deveined and sliced
1/2 head of cauliflower, broken into large florets
2 zucchinis, cut into thick slices
2 medium-sized leeks, quartered
4 garlic cloves, halved
2 thyme sprigs, chopped
1 teaspoon dried sage, crushed
4 tablespoons olive oil
4 tablespoons tomato puree
1 teaspoon mixed whole peppercorns
Sea salt and cayenne pepper, to taste

Directions

- Preheat your oven to 425 degrees F. Sprits a rimmed baking sheet with a nonstick cooking spray.
- Toss all of the above vegetables with seasonings, oil and apple cider vinegar.
- Roast about 40 minutes. Flip vegetables halfway through cook time. Bon appétit!

346. Creamed Eggplant and Cashew Soup

Ready in about 1 hour 20 minutes
Servings 4

Take your basic roasted vegetable soup to the next level by making this creamy eggplant soup. The best thing about eggplant, besides its amazing nutritional value, is the way it carries other flavors.

Per serving: 159 Calories; 9.4g Fat; 17.9g Carbs; 4.2g Protein; 5.6g Sugars

Ingredients

1 pound eggplant, cut it in half.
2 ripe tomatoes, chopped
2 shallots, chopped
2 garlic cloves, peeled
1 tablespoon olive oil
1/2 teaspoon dried oregano
1/2 teaspoon dried basil
1/2 teaspoon dried marjoram
3 cups water
3 vegan bouillon cubes
1/3 cup raw cashews, soaked
Salt and pepper, to taste

Directions

- Start by preheating your oven to 390 degrees F.
- Arrange the eggplant on a parchment lined baking sheet. Drizzle olive oil over eggplant.
- Roast about 35 to 40 minutes or until tender. Scoop eggplant from the skin and transfer to a pot.
- Add the remaining ingredient, except for cashews. Let it simmer, covered, for 40 minutes. Puree the soup with a hand blender.
- Drain your cashews and blend them with 1 cup water in a blender until smooth. Add the cashew cream to the soup; stir well and serve immediately.

347. Chocolate and Butternut Squash Smoothie

Ready in about 5 minutes
Servings 2

This luscious, creamy smoothie is worth making! It looks like the perfect snack to bridge the gap between two meals.

Per serving: 71 Calories; 2.3g Fat; 9.1g Carbs; 4.3g Protein; 5g Sugars

Ingredients

2 ½ cups almond milk
1/2 cup baby spinach
2 tablespoons cocoa powder
1/2 cup butternut squash, roasted
1/2 teaspoon ground cinnamon
A pinch of grated nutmeg
A pinch of salt

Directions

- Mix all ingredients in a blender or a food processor.
- Serve well-chilled in tall glasses. Enjoy!

348. Raspberry and Peanut Butter Smoothie

Ready in about 5 minutes
Servings 1

Smoothies are one of the best grab-n-go foods of all time! You can use fresh or frozen strawberries and even 1/2 medium-sized peach in this recipe.

Per serving: 114 Calories; 8.2g Fat; 7.9g Carbs; 4.2g Protein; 3.1g Sugars

Ingredients

1/3 cup raspberries
1/2 cup baby spinach leaves
3/4 cup almond milk, unsweetened
1 tablespoon peanut butter
1 teaspoon Swerve

Directions

- Place all ingredients in your blender and puree until creamy, uniform and smooth.
- Pour into a tall glass. Serve well-chilled.

349. Cremini Mushroom and Broccoli Delight

Ready in about 30 minutes
Servings 4

Cooking satisfying keto food is as simple as recreating a favorite dish. Toss your favorite vegetables in a baking dish, add a few sprinkles of your favorite spices and let the magic happen!

Per serving: 113 Calories; 6.7g Fat; 11.6g Carbs; 5g Protein; 4.2g Sugars

Ingredients

Nonstick cooking spray
1 head broccoli, cut into florets
8 ounces cremini mushrooms, halved
2 garlic cloves, smashed
2 ripe tomatoes, pureed
1/4 cup vegan butter, melted
1 teaspoon hot paprika paste
1/4 teaspoon marjoram
1/2 teaspoon curry powder
Coarse salt and black pepper, to taste

Directions

- Begin by preheating your oven to 390 degrees F. Brush a baking dish with a nonstick cooking oil.
- Next, arrange broccoli and mushrooms in the baking dish. Scatter smashed garlic around the vegetables. Add pureed tomatoes.
- Then, drizzle with melted butter and add hot paprika paste, marjoram, curry, salt, and black pepper.
- Roast for 25 minutes, turning your baking dish once. Serve with a fresh salad of choice. Bon appétit!

350. Crunchy-Topped Vegetable Bake

Ready in about 40 minutes
Servings 4

A vegetable bake is a perfect dish for your busy weeknights. This comfort food version is just as tasty as the vegetable dishes you grew up loving.

Per serving: 242 Calories; 16.3g Fat; 11.6g Carbs; 16.3g Protein; 2.3g Sugars

Ingredients

2 tablespoons olive oil
1 cup shallots, chopped
1 celery, chopped
2 carrots, grated
1/2 pound Brussels sprouts, quartered
1 cup roasted vegetable broth
1 teaspoon turmeric
Sea salt and ground black pepper, to taste
1 teaspoon paprika powder
1/2 teaspoon liquid smoke
1 cup vegan parmesan
2 tablespoons fresh chives, roughly chopped

Directions

- Start by preheating your oven to 360 degrees F. Brush a baking dish with olive oil.
- In a heavy-bottomed skillet, heat olive oil over a moderately high heat. Now, sweat the shallots until they are softened.
- Add the celery, carrots and Brussels sprouts. Cook an additional 4 minutes or until just tender. Transfer the vegetable mixture to the baking dish.
- Mix roasted vegetable broth with turmeric, salt, black pepper, paprika, and liquid smoke. Pour this mixture over the vegetables.
- Top with vegan parmesan cheese and bake approximately 30 minutes. Serve garnished with fresh chives.

351. Artichoke and Tofu Stir Fry

Ready in about 30 minutes
Servings 4

Stir-fry is an ultimate comfort food, critical for success in your keto diet. In addition, this rich and restaurant-style meal is ready in 30 minutes.

Per serving: 138 Calories; 8.9g Fat; 11.9g Carbs; 6.4g Protein; 2.6g Sugars

Ingredients

1 pound whole baby artichokes, cut off stems and tough outer leaves
2 tablespoons olive oil
2 blocks tofu, pressed and cubed
2 garlic cloves, minced
1 teaspoon Cajun spice mix
1 teaspoon deli mustard
1 bell pepper, chopped
1/4 cup vegetable broth
Salt and pepper, to your liking

Directions

- Cook artichokes in a large saucepan of lightly salted water for 15 minutes or until they're tender; drain.
- Heat olive oil in a wok that is preheated over medium-high heat; add tofu cubes and cook about 6 minutes, gently stirring.
- Add garlic and cook until aromatic or 30 seconds or so.
- Add the remaining ingredients, including reserved artichokes, and continue to cook 4 more minutes or until heated through. Serve warm on individual plates. Bon appétit!

EGGS & DAIRY

352. Genoa Salami and Vegetable Frittata...................... 198

353. Two Cheese Omelet with Pimenta and Chervil... 198

354. Asiago and Sausage Egg Cups 199

355. Madras and Asparagus Cheesy Frittata................ 199

356. Colby Cheese and Sausage Gofres 200

357. Mushroom, Cheese and Tomato Rolls 200

358. Eggs with Crabmeat and Sour Cream Sauce 201

359. Easy Breakfast Muffins 201

360. Dill Pickle, Cheese, and Cauliflower Balls 202

361. Easy Two-Cheese Omelet 202

362. Spicy Cheese Crisps 203

363. Three-Cheese Party Balls 203

364. Sriracha Egg Salad with Scallions 204

365. Easy Vegetarian Cheese Tacos............................... 204

366. Sopressata and Blue Cheese Waffles 205

367. Festive Eggs with Cheese and Aioli 205

368. Kid-Friendly Avocado Boats 206

369. Cheesy Cauliflower Fritters.................................... 206

370. Parmesan and Mushroom Burger Patties 207

371. Tinga and Queso Manchego Frittata.................... 207

372. Two-Minute Eggs in a Mug 208

373. Scrambled Eggs with Kale Pesto 208

374. Spicy Sausage with Eggs 209

375. Three-Cheese and Salami Stuffed Avocado 209

376. Baked Cheese Balls Salad 210

377. Two-Cheese and Roasted Pepper Dip 210

378. Greek-Style Cheese Balls.. 211

379. Egg Mug Muffins... 211

380. Ham, Cheese and Eggs Balls.................................. 212

381. Colby and Tuna Stuffed Avocado........................... 212

382. Cheese and Scallion Stuffed Tomatoes................. 213

383. Cheese Sticks with Roasted Red Pepper Dip........ 213

384. Curried Pickled Eggs 214

385. Easy and Yummy Scotch Eggs............................... 214

386. Traditional Egg Soup with Tofu 215

387. Zucchini Boats with Sausage and Eggs................. 215

388. Creamy Gruyère Egg Bites 216

389. Classic Egg Salad 216

390. Mom's Pepper Jack Cheese Soup........................... 217

391. Alfredo, Kale and Cheese Dip 217

392. Italian Salami and Cheese Casserole 218

393. Panna Cotta with Roasted Cartos and Basil........ 218

394. Stuffed Peppers with Cheese and Pork Rinds....... 219

395. Flavored Asiago Cheese Chips 219

396. Keto Mac and Cheese 220

397. Vegetable and Cheeseburger Quiche.................... 220

398. French-Style Eggs with Appenzeller Cheese 221

399. Two-Cheese and Walnut Logs............................... 221

400. Omelet with Bacon and Blue Cheese.................... 222

401. Mini Ham Frittatas with Swiss cheese.................. 222

402. Salami and Cheese Balls... 223

352. Genoa Salami and Vegetable Frittata

Ready in about 25 minutes
Servings 4

For weeknight dining, family gathering, or a rich Sunday breakfast, a frittata is always a good idea. Enjoy!

Per serving: 310 Calories; 26.2g Fat; 3.9g Carbs; 15.4g Protein; 1.9g Sugars

Ingredients

1/2 stick butter, at room temperature
1/2 cup scallions, chopped
2 garlic cloves, minced
1 serrano pepper, chopped
1 carrot, chopped
8 Genoa salami slices
8 eggs, whisked
Salt and black pepper, to taste
1/2 teaspoon dried dill weed

Directions

- Melt the butter in a pan that is preheated over a moderately high heat. Now, sauté the scallions for 4 minutes, stirring periodically.
- Add garlic and cook for 1 minute or until it is fragrant. Add serrano pepper and carrot. Cook an additional 4 minutes.
- Transfer the mixture to a baking pan that is lightly greased with a nonstick cooking spray. Top with salami slices.
- Pour the eggs over vegetables and salami; season with salt, pepper, and dill. Bake approximately 18 minutes. Eat warm with a dollop of full-fat Greek yogurt.

353. Two Cheese Omelet with Pimenta and Chervil

Ready in about 15 minutes
Servings 2

An ultimate comfort food you deserve. Chervil will bring a fresh kick when added on top. You will go crazy for this breakfast!

Per serving: 490 Calories; 44.6g Fat; 4.5g Carbs; 22.7g Protein; 2.7g Sugars

Ingredients

2 tablespoons avocado oil
4 eggs, beaten
Salt and black pepper, to taste
1/4 teaspoon Pimenta, ground
1/4 teaspoon cayenne pepper
1/2 cup Asiago cheese
1/2 cup Boursin cheese
2 tablespoons fresh chervil, roughly chopped

Directions

- Heat the oil in a pan that is preheated over a moderately high heat.
- Season the eggs with salt, black pepper, ground Pimenta, and cayenne pepper. Add the seasoned eggs to the pan; tilt the pan to spread the eggs out evenly.
- Once set, top your eggs with cheese. Slice the omelet into two halves.
- Serve garnish with fresh chervil. Bon appétit!

354. Asiago and Sausage Egg Cups

Ready in about 10 minutes
Servings 3

Here's a perfect meal on-the-go! A smoked beef-pork sausage or Berliner sausage work well for these cups.

Per serving: 423 Calories; 34.1g Fat; 2.2g Carbs; 26.5g Protein; 0.9g Sugars

Ingredients

1 teaspoon butter, melted
6 eggs, separated into yolks and whites
Coarse salt and freshly ground black pepper, to taste
1/2 teaspoon smoked paprika
1/2 teaspoon dried sage
1 cup Asiago cheese, freshly grated
3 beef sausages, chopped

Directions

- Begin by preheating your oven to 420 degrees F. Lightly grease a muffin pan with melted butter.
- Now, beat the egg whites with an electric mixer until stiff peaks form. Add seasonings, cheese, and sausage.
- Pour into muffin cups and bake for 4 minutes.
- Now, add an egg to each cup. Bake for 4 more minutes. Leave the cups to cool down for a few minutes before serving time. Bon appétit!

355. Madras and Asparagus Cheesy Frittata

Ready in about 20 minutes
Servings 4

Enjoy this fresh from the oven frittata, inspired by Indian curry paste and freshly grated semi-hard American cheese.

Per serving: 248 Calories; 17.1g Fat; 6.2g Carbs; 17.6g Protein; 1.1g Sugars

Ingredients

2 tablespoons avocado oil
1/2 cup shallots, chopped
1 cup asparagus tips
8 eggs, beaten
1/2 teaspoon jalapeno pepper, minced
1 teaspoon Madras curry paste
Salt and red pepper, to your liking
3/4 cup Colby cheese, grated
1/4 cup fresh cilantro, to serve

Directions

- In an ovenproof frying pan, heat avocado oil over a medium flame. Now, sauté the shallots until they are caramelized.
- Add the asparagus tips and cook until they're just tender.
- Stir in the eggs, jalapeno pepper and Madras curry paste; season with salt and pepper. Now, cook until the eggs are nearly set.
- Scatter the cheese over the top of your frittata. Cook in the preheated oven at 375 degrees F for about 12 minutes, until your frittata is set in the middle.
- Cut into wedges and serve garnished with fresh cilantro.

356. Colby Cheese and Sausage Gofres

Ready in about 30 minutes
Servings 6

Don't overcook the eggs because they will come out dry and tasteless. These waffles should be fluffy and moist but not runny.

Per serving: 316 Calories; 25g Fat; 1.5g Carbs; 20.2g Protein; 1.2g Sugars

Ingredients

6 eggs
6 tablespoons whole milk
1 teaspoon Spanish spice mix
Sea salt and ground black pepper, to taste
3 fully-cooked breakfast sausage links, chopped
1 cup Colby cheese, shredded
Nonstick cooking spray

Directions

- In a mixing bowl, beat the eggs, milk, Spanish spice mix, salt, and black pepper.
- Now, stir in chopped sausage and shredded cheese.
- Spritz a waffle iron with a nonstick cooking spray.
- Cook the egg mixture about 5 minutes, until it is golden. Serve immediately with a homemade sugar-free tomato ketchup. Enjoy!

357. Mushroom, Cheese and Tomato Rolls

Ready in about 20 minutes
Servings 4

These wraps will surprise you with their wonderful taste! You won't miss flour in this recipe, trust me.

Per serving: 172 Calories; 14g Fat; 3.4g Carbs; 9.5g Protein; 2.3g Sugars

Ingredients

For the Wraps:
6 eggs, separated into yolks and whites
2 tablespoons full-fat milk
1 tablespoon olive oil
Sea salt, to taste

For the Filling:
1 teaspoon olive oil
1 cup button mushrooms, chopped
Salt and black pepper, to taste
1/2 teaspoon cayenne pepper
6-8 fresh lettuce leaves
4 slices of Swiss cheese
2 small-sized Roma tomatoes, thinly sliced

Directions

- Thoroughly combine all ingredients for the wraps.
- Preheat a frying pan. Pour 1/4 of the mixture into the pan; cook over medium-low heat until thoroughly heated, 4 minutes per side.
- Repeat three more times and set your wraps aside, keeping them warm.
- In another pan, heat 1 teaspoon of olive oil over a moderately high flame. Now, cook the mushrooms until they are softened, about 5 minutes; season with salt, black pepper and cayenne pepper.
- Lay 1-2 lettuce leaves onto each wrap. Divide the mushrooms among prepared wraps. Top with cheese and tomatoes. Enjoy!

358. Eggs with Crabmeat and Sour Cream Sauce

Ready in about 15 minutes
Servings 3

Here is a one-pan family dish that is easy to prepare using basic ingredients. This dish makes a great addition to a family lunch table but is also great for a weeknight dinner.

Per serving: 334 Calories; 26.2g Fat; 4.4g Carbs; 21.1g Protein; 1.2g Sugars

Ingredients

1 tablespoon olive oil
6 eggs, whisked
1 can crabmeat, flaked
1 teaspoon Montreal seasoning

For the Sauce:
3/4 cup sour cream
1/2 cup scallions, white and green parts, chopped
1/2 teaspoon garlic powder
Salt and black pepper to the taste
1/2 teaspoon fresh dill, chopped

Directions

- Heat olive oil in a sauté pan that is preheated over a moderate flame. Now, add eggs and scramble them.
- Add crabmeat and cook, stirring frequently, until everything is thoroughly cooked; sprinkle with Montreal seasoning.
- In a mixing dish, gently whisk all the sauce ingredients.
- Divide egg/crabmeat mixture among 4 plates; serve with the scallion/sour cream sauce on the side. Bon appétit!

359. Easy Breakfast Muffins

Ready in about 20 minutes
Servings 6

Who needs a cheese cake when you can have no-flour muffins loaded with cheese, nuts and fruits?

Per serving: 81 Calories; 3.5g Fat; 10.7g Carbs; 5.5g Protein; 8.4g Sugars

Ingredients

3/4 cream cheese
1/4 cup Greek-style yogurt
3 eggs, beaten
2 tablespoons hazelnuts, ground
4 tablespoons erythritol
1/2 teaspoon vanilla essence
1/3 teaspoon ground cinnamon
1 apple, cored and sliced

Directions

- Preheat your oven to 360 degrees F. Treat a muffin pan with a nonstick cooking spray.
- Then, thoroughly combine all of the above ingredients. Divide the batter among the muffin cups.
- Bake for 12 to 15 minutes. Transfer to a wire rack to cool slightly before serving. Serve garnished with apples and enjoy!

360. Dill Pickle, Cheese, and Cauliflower Balls

Ready in about 3 hours 15 minutes
Servings 6

Serve these balls with cocktails at your next party! They are kid-friendly too.

Per serving: 407 Calories; 26.8g Fat; 5.8g Carbs; 33.4g Protein; 1.5g Sugars

Ingredients

4 cups cauliflower rice
1/2 pound pancetta, chopped
6 ounces Cottage cheese, curds, 2% fat
6 ounces Ricotta cheese
1 cup Colby cheese
1/2 cup dill pickles, chopped and thoroughly squeezed
2 cloves garlic, crushed
1 cup grated Parmesan cheese
1/2 teaspoon caraway seeds
1/4 teaspoon dried dill weed
1/2 teaspoon shallot powder
Salt and black pepper, to taste
1 cup crushed pork rinds
Cooking oil

Directions

- Thoroughly combine cauliflower rice, pancetta, Cottage cheese, Ricotta cheese, Colby cheese, dill pickles, garlic, and 1/2 cup of grated Parmesan.
- Stir until everything is well mixed and shape cauliflower mixture into even balls. Now, transfer to your refrigerator for 3 hours.
- Now, in a mixing bowl, thoroughly combine the remaining 1/2 cup of Parmesan cheese, caraway seeds, dill, shallot powder, salt, black pepper and crushed pork rinds.
- Roll cheese ball in Parmesan mixture until they are completely coated.
- Then, heat about 1-inch of oil in a skillet over a moderately high flame. Fry cheeseballs until they are golden brown on all sides.
- Transfer to a paper towel to soak up excess oil. Serve immediately or at room temperature. Enjoy!

361. Easy Two-Cheese Omelet

Ready in about 15 minutes
Servings 2

Tomato is the perfect garnish to this omelet but you can use sour cream, pickles, and red onions as well.

Per serving: 307 Calories; 25g Fat; 2.5g Carbs; 18.5g Protein; 1.6g Sugars

Ingredients

4 eggs
Salt, to taste
1/4 teaspoon black peppercorns, crushed
1 tablespoon sesame oil
1/4 cup Blue Cheese, crumbled
1/4 cup Appenzeller cheese, shredded
1 tomato, thinly sliced

Directions

- Whisk the eggs in a mixing bowl; season with salt and crushed peppercorns.
- Heat the oil in a sauté pan over medium-low heat. Now, pour in the eggs and cook, using a spatula to swirl the eggs around the pan.
- Cook the eggs until partially set. Top with cheese; fold your omelet in half to enclose filling.
- Serve warm, garnished with tomato. Bon appétit!

362. Spicy Cheese Crisps

Ready in about 10 minutes
Servings 4

Try this top-rated keto snack today! It couldn't be simpler. It features basic ingredients and takes under 10 minutes to make.

Per serving: 205 Calories; 15g Fat; 2.9g Carbs; 14.5g Protein; 0.7g Sugars

Ingredients

2 cups Swiss cheese, shredded
1/2 teaspoon garlic powder
1/4 teaspoon shallot powder
1 rosemary sprig, minced
1/2 teaspoon chili powder

Directions

- Preheat an oven to 400 degrees F. Coat two baking sheets with parchment paper or Silpat mat.
- Then, thoroughly combine Swiss cheese with seasonings.
- Then, form 1 tablespoons of cheese mixture into small mounds on the baking sheets.
- Bake for 6 minutes and let them cool before serving. Enjoy!

363. Three-Cheese Party Balls

Ready in about 10 minutes
Servings 10

If you like even fatter and richer balls, simply roll your balls in prosciutto crumbles. Refrigerate up to 3 days.

Per serving: 105 Calories; 7.2g Fat; 2.8g Carbs; 7.5g Protein; 0.5g Sugars

Ingredients

1 ½ cups Ricotta cheese, at room temperature
3/4 cup Monterey Jack cheese, shredded
3/4 cup goat cheese, shredded
1/3 cup black olives, pitted and chopped
1 ½ tablespoons tomato paste
1 teaspoon cayenne pepper
Salt and freshly ground black pepper
20 fresh basil leaves

Directions

- In a bowl, thoroughly combine the cheese, olives, tomato paste, cayenne pepper, salt and black pepper. Then, shape the mixture into 20 balls.
- Place 1 basil leaf on top of each ball and secure with a toothpick. Serve and enjoy!

364. Sriracha Egg Salad with Scallions

Ready in about 15 minutes
Servings 8

Packed with flavors, this family classic is a practical way to use up leftover hard-boiled eggs! Sriracha is an amazing flavor enhancer.

Per serving: 174 Calories; 13g Fat; 7.7g Carbs; 7.4g Protein; 2.4g Sugars

Ingredients

10 eggs
3/4 cup mayonnaise
1 teaspoon Sriracha
1 tablespoon whole grain mustard
1/2 cup scallions
1/2 stalk of celery, minced
1/2 teaspoon fresh lime juice
1/2 teaspoon sea salt
1/2 teaspoon ground black pepper, to taste
1 head Romaine lettuce, torn into pieces

Directions

- Place the eggs in a pan and cover them with at least 1-inch of water; bring to a boil. Then, remove from heat, cover, and let them sit approximately 10 minutes.
- Chop the eggs coarsely and add them to a salad bowl.
- Add the remaining ingredients and gently stir until everything is well incorporated. Place in the refrigerator until ready to serve. Bon appétit!

365. Easy Vegetarian Cheese Tacos

Ready in about 10 minutes
Servings 6

Once you ditch carbs, it opens a whole new perspective on nutrition and dieting. You will love these ketogenic tacos!

Per serving: 370 Calories; 30g Fat; 4.9g Carbs; 19.5g Protein; 1.2g Sugars

Ingredients

1/2 pound Cheddar cheese, grated
1/2 pound Colby cheese, grated
1 teaspoon taco seasoning mix
1 ½ cups guacamole
1 cup sour cream
A small-sized head of lettuce

Directions

- Combine both types of cheese with taco seasoning mix.
- Then, preheat a pan over a moderate flame.
- Scatter the shredded cheese mixture all over the pan, covering the bottom. Fry for 4 to 5 minutes, turning once.
- Top with guacamole, sour cream and lettuce, roll them up and serve immediately. Bon appétit!

366. Sopressata and Blue Cheese Waffles

Ready in about 20 minutes
Servings 2

These are the fluffiest waffle iron omelets in the world! If you don't have Sopressata on hand, you can use Pepperoni or leftover pork instead.

Per serving: 470 Calories; 40.3g Fat; 2.9g Carbs; 24.4g Protein; 1.7g Sugars

Ingredients

2 tablespoons butter, melted
Salt and black pepper, to your liking
1/2 teaspoon parsley flakes
1/2 teaspoon chili pepper flakes
4 eggs
1/2 cup blue cheese, crumbled
4 slices Sopressata, chopped
2 tablespoons fresh chives, chopped

Directions

● Combine all ingredients, except for fresh chives, in a mixing bowl. Preheat your waffle iron and grease with a cooking spray.
● Add the omelet mixture and close the lid.
● Fry about 5 minutes or until desired consistency is reached. Repeat with the remaining batter. Serve garnished with fresh chives and eat warm.

367. Festive Eggs with Cheese and Aioli

Ready in about 20 minutes
Servings 8

Turn leftover hard-boiled eggs into a festive family dinner! Crush peeled garlic in a mortar and pestle just like grandma used to make.

Per serving: 285 Calories; 22.5g Fat; 1.8g Carbs; 19.5g Protein; 1g Sugars

Ingredients

8 eggs, hard-boiled
2 cans tuna in brine, drained
1/2 cup Bibb lettuces, torn into pieces
1/2 cup red onions, finely chopped
1/2 goat cheese, crumbled
1/3 cup sour cream
1/2 tablespoon yellow mustard
For Aioli:
1 egg
2 medium cloves garlic, minced
1 tablespoon lemon juice
1/2 cup olive oil
Salt and black pepper, to taste

Directions

● Peel and chop the eggs; transfer them to a serving bowl. Add tuna, lettuce, onion, cheese, sour cream and yellow mustard.
● To make aioli, beat the egg, garlic, and lemon juice with an immersion blender. Add oil, salt and pepper, and blend again until everything is well mixed.
● Add prepared aioli to the bowl and gently stir until everything is well incorporated.
● Serve with pickles or bell peppers. Bon appétit!

368. Kid-Friendly Avocado Boats

Ready in about 20 minutes
Servings 4

Stuffed avocado brings comfort like nothing else in the world. There's no better way to surprise your little ones today!

Per serving: 342 Calories; 30.4g Fat; 9.5g Carbs; 11.1g Protein; 0.8g Sugars

Ingredients

2 avocados, halved and pitted, skin on
2 ounces blue cheese, crumbled
2 ounces Colby cheese, grated
2 eggs, beaten
Salt and pepper, to taste
1 tablespoon fresh cilantro, chopped

Directions

- Preheat your oven to 360 degrees F.
- Arrange avocado halves in an ovenproof dish.
- In a mixing dish, combine both types of cheeses, eggs, salt and pepper. Divide the mixture among avocado halves.
- Bake for 15 to 17 minutes or until everything is thoroughly baked. Serve garnished with fresh cilantro. Enjoy!

369. Cheesy Cauliflower Fritters

Ready in about 35 minutes
Servings 6

Cauliflower fritters are SO versatile and SO easy to prepare! These fritters are actually loaded with two types of cheese, which add them an extra flavor and nutrition value. Enjoy!

Per serving: 199 Calories; 13.8g Fat; 7.8g Carbs; 13g Protein; 2.1g Sugars

Ingredients

1 ½ tablespoons olive oil
1 shallot, chopped
1 garlic clove, minced
1 pound cauliflower, grated
6 tablespoons almond flour
1/2 cup Swiss cheese, shredded
1 cup parmesan cheese
2 eggs, beaten
1/2 teaspoon dried dill weed
Sea salt and ground black pepper, to taste

Directions

- Heat the oil in a cast iron skillet over medium heat. Cook the shallots and garlic until they are aromatic.
- Add grated cauliflower and stir with a spatula for another minute or so; set aside to cool to room temperature so you can handle it easily.
- Add the remaining ingredients; shape the mixture into balls, then, press each ball to form burger patties.
- Bake in the preheated oven at 400 degrees F for 20 minutes. Flip and bake for another 10 minutes or until golden brown on top. Bon appétit!

370. Parmesan and Mushroom Burger Patties

Ready in about 20 minutes
Servings 4

Full of flavor, these vegetarian burgers are elegant, toothsome and incredible! Cremini mushrooms and Portobello are perfect for this recipe.

Per serving: 370 Calories; 30g Fat; 7.7g Carbs; 16.8g Protein; 1g Sugars

Ingredients

1/2 stick butter, softened
2 garlic cloves, minced
2 cups brown mushrooms, chopped
4 tablespoons blanched almond flour
4 tablespoons ground flax seeds
4 tablespoons hemp seeds
4 tablespoons sunflower seeds
1 tablespoon Cajun seasonings
1 teaspoon deli mustard
2 eggs, whisked
1/2 cup parmesan cheese

Directions

- Melt 1 tablespoon of butter in a pan that is preheated over medium-high heat. Now, sauté the garlic and mushrooms until mushrooms lose their water.
- Add almond flour, flax seeds, hemp seeds, sunflower seeds, Cajun seasonings, mustard, eggs and Parmesan cheese.
- Form the mixture into 4 burger patties with lightly oiled hands.
- Melt the remaining butter in a pan; fry your patties for 6 to 7 minutes. Then, carefully flip them over with a wide spatula. Cook another 6 minutes. Serve warm.

371. Tinga and Queso Manchego Frittata

Ready in about 25 minutes
Servings 6

Bursting with Tinga paste, two types of cheese and fresh vegetables, this Mexican-style frittata is sure to please. Make it tonight for an easy protein-packed family dinner.

Per serving: 225 Calories; 17g Fat; 5.1g Carbs; 13.2g Protein; 2.3g Sugars

Ingredients

10 eggs
1 teaspoon seasoned salt
1/4 teaspoon ground black pepper, or more to taste
1/3 cup chive & onion cream cheese, room temperature
1 heaping tablespoon lard, room temperature
1 leek, chopped
1 teaspoon garlic paste
1 red bell pepper, chopped
1/2 green bell pepper, chopped
1 teaspoon Mexican Tinga paste
1 ½ cups baby spinach
1/2 cup Queso Manchego, shredded

Directions

- Begin by preheating the oven to 370 degrees F.
- Whisk the eggs with salt, pepper and cream cheese.
- Melt the lard in an oven-safe skillet over a moderately high heat. Sauté the leeks until they are aromatic.
- Now, stir in garlic paste, bell peppers, and Tinga paste, and continue sautéing an additional 3 to 4 minute or until they are softened
- Add baby spinach and cook for 1 to 2 minutes more. Stir in the egg/cheese mixture. Shake your skillet to distribute the mixture evenly and transfer to the oven.
- Bake about 8 minutes or until your frittata is golden brown on top but still slightly wobbly in the middle.
- Top with shredded Queso Manchego and bake an additional 3 minutes or until the cheese melts completely
- Cut into 6 wedges and serve warm. Enjoy!

372. Two-Minute Eggs in a Mug

Ready in about 5 minutes
Servings 2

Breakfast that takes less than 5 minutes. Seriously? In addition, you can use whatever you have in your refrigerator – any type of cheese, ham, bacon, pickles, etc.

Per serving: 197 Calories; 13.8g Fat; 2.7g Carbs; 15.7g Protein; 2.2g Sugars

Ingredients

4 eggs
1/4 cup full-fat milk
1/4 cup Asiago cheese, freshly grated
1 garlic clove, minced
1/4 teaspoon dried basil
1/4 teaspoon turmeric powder
Sea salt and red pepper flakes, to taste

Directions

- In a mixing bowl, thoroughly combine the eggs, milk, cheese, garlic, salt and pepper.
- Spritz 2 microwave-safe mugs with a nonstick spray. Pour in the egg mixture.
- Now, microwave for 30 to 40 seconds. Stir with a spoon and microwave for 60 to 70 seconds more or until they're set.

373. Scrambled Eggs with Kale Pesto

Ready in about 15 minutes
Servings 4

This is one of the most nutritious breakfasts you'll ever eat on a keto diet. Eggs are loaded with high-quality protein, as well as 13 essential vitamins and minerals. Kale is packed full of vitamins, minerals, and fiber. Enjoy!

Per serving: 495 Calories; 45g Fat; 6.3g Carbs; 19.5g Protein; 1.6g Sugars

Ingredients

2 tablespoons ghee
8 eggs, well beaten
1/4 cup full-fat milk
Salt and ground black pepper, to your liking

For the Kale Pesto:
2 cups kale
1 cup parmesan cheese, grated
2 garlic cloves, minced
1/2 cup olive oil
2 tablespoons fresh lemon juice

Directions

- Melt the ghee in a heavy-bottomed sauté pan over moderately high heat. Whisk the eggs with milk, salt, and pepper.
- Now, cook this egg mixture, gently stirring, until the eggs are set but still moist and tender.
- Put all the ingredients for the pesto, except the olive oil, in your food processor or blender.
- Pulse until roughly chopped. With the machine running, slowly pour in the olive oil until you get the desired consistency.
- Serve over warm scrambled eggs. Bon appétit!

374. Spicy Sausage with Eggs

Ready in about 20 minutes
Servings 2

A rich and satisfying, this dish is guaranteed to make your meals so much better. Serve as a romantic dinner on blustery winter days.

Per serving: 462 Calories; 40.6g Fat; 7.1g Carbs; 16.9g Protein; 1.1g Sugars

Ingredients

2 tablespoons olive oil
1/2 cup leeks, chopped
1 teaspoon smashed garlic
1 teaspoon habanero pepper, deveined and minced
Salt and black pepper to the taste
6 ounces sausage, crumbled
4 eggs, whisked
1 thyme sprig, chopped
1/2 teaspoon dried marjoram, chopped
1/2 cup ripe olives, pitted and sliced

Directions

● Heat the oil in a nonstick skillet over medium heat; now, sauté the leeks until they are just tender, about 4 minutes.
● Add the garlic, habanero pepper, salt, black pepper, and sausage; cook, stirring frequently, for 8 minutes longer.
● Now, pour in the eggs and sprinkle with thyme and marjoram; cook an additional 4 minutes, stirring with a spoon. Serve with sliced olives and enjoy!

375. Three-Cheese and Salami Stuffed Avocado

Ready in about 15 minutes
Servings 6

A delicate and smooth flavor of avocado makes a perfect counterpoint for savory salami and tangy cheese. If you won't serve this dish immediately, make sure to drizzle each avocado halve with a fresh lemon juice and place in the refrigerator.

Per serving: 308 Calories; 27g Fat; 9g Carbs; 8.8g Protein; 1.1g Sugars

Ingredients

3 avocados, cut into halves and pitted
1/3 cup Cottage cheese
1/3 cup Neufchatel cheese
1/3 cup Queso Fresco, crumbled
1 cup salami, chopped
1 teaspoon Dijon mustard
Salt and ground black pepper, to your liking
1/2 teaspoon paprika
1/4 teaspoon hot sauce

Directions

● Scoop out avocados and place avocado flesh in a mixing bowl.
● Add the remaining ingredients and stir until everything is well combined.
● Divide the mixture between avocado halves. Taste, adjust the seasonings and serve. Bon appétit!

376. Baked Cheese Balls Salad

Ready in about 20 minutes
Servings 6

This reach and healthy salad is both dinner-worthy and vegetarian lunch option. Don't be shy about seasonings and enjoy experimenting with them.

Per serving: 234 Calories; 16.7g Fat; 9.9g Carbs; 12.4g Protein; 3.4g Sugars

Ingredients

For the Cheese Balls:
3 eggs
1 cup goat cheese, crumbled
1/2 cup Parmesan, shredded
1 cup almond flour
1 tablespoon flax meal
1 teaspoon baking powder
Salt and ground black pepper, to taste

For the Salad:
1 head Romaine lettuce
1/2 cup cucumber, thinly sliced
2 small Roma tomatoes, seeded and chopped
1/2 cup red onion, thinly sliced
1/2 cup radishes, thinly sliced
1/3 cup mayonnaise
1 teaspoon brown mustard
1 teaspoon paprika
1 teaspoon oregano
Salt, to taste

Directions

- Start by preheating your oven to 390 degrees F. Line a baking sheet with a piece of parchment paper.
- In a mixing dish, thoroughly combine all ingredients for the cheese balls. Then, shape the mixture into balls.
- Arrange the balls on the prepared baking sheet. Bake until crisp, approximately 10 minutes.
- In a large-sized salad bowl, arrange lettuce leaves. Now, add cucumbers, tomatoes, red onion and radishes.
- In a small mixing bowl, whisk the mayonnaise, mustard, paprika, oregano and salt to taste. Drizzle this mixture over the vegetables.
- Top with baked cheese balls and serve immediately.

377. Two-Cheese and Roasted Pepper Dip

Ready in about 35 minutes
Servings 10

This spicy, cheesy and peppery dip comes together in the twinkling of an eye! Poblano peppers are not too spicy and not too mild, which makes them a perfect addition to this dipping sauce. Serve warm dip with fresh vegetable sticks or cocktail wieners.

Per serving: 228 Calories; 17.2g Fat; 8.7g Carbs; 10.2g Protein; 4.8g Sugars

Ingredients

10 ounces mascarpone cheese, room temperature
1 cup mayonnaise
1 jar (17-ounce) roasted red peppers, drained and chopped
2 pickled poblano peppers, drained and finely chopped
1 ¼ cups Asiago cheese, grated
Salt and black pepper, to taste

Directions

- Begin by preheating your oven to 360 degrees F. Spritz a baking dish with a nonstick cooking spray.
- Thoroughly combine all ingredients and transfer to the prepared baking dish.
- Bake for 25 to 35 minutes, turning the dish once or twice. Bon appétit!

378. Greek-Style Cheese Balls

Ready in about 5 minutes
Servings 6

Bite into this cheese ball and it will bring you the flavors of the Mediterranean. With just a few ingredients, these fat balls are a real crowd pleaser!

Per serving: 217 Calories; 18.7g Fat; 2.1g Carbs; 9.9g Protein; 0.8g Sugars

Ingredients

4 ounces pancetta, chopped
4 ounces Feta cheese, crumbled
1/4 cup aioli
1/2 cup green olives, pitted and chopped
1/2 teaspoon red pepper flakes
2 tablespoons parsley, finely chopped

Directions

- Thoroughly combine pancetta with feta cheese and aioli in a mixing dish. Now, add green olives, red pepper flakes and fresh parsley.
- Taste and adjust the seasonings. Shape the mixture into 10 balls.
- Serve right away or keep in your refrigerator up to 3 days. Bon appétit!

379. Egg Mug Muffins

Ready in about 5 minutes
Servings 2

There's more than one way to cook scrambled eggs. However, when you want to please your beloved one for breakfast, mug muffin is a must.

Per serving: 244 Calories; 17.5g Fat; 2.9g Carbs; 19.2g Protein; 2.2g Sugars

Ingredients

4 eggs
4 tablespoons milk
1/4 cup Asiago cheese, shredded
1/2 teaspoon cayenne pepper
Kosher salt and black pepper, to taste
2 tablespoons scallions, chopped

Directions

- Thoroughly combine all of the above ingredients, except for scallions.
- Spritz two microwave-safe mugs with a nonstick cooking spray. Spoon the egg mixture into the mugs.
- Place in the microwave and cook for 1 minute. Serve garnished with fresh scallions. Bon appétit!

380. Ham, Cheese and Eggs Balls

Ready in about 5 minutes
Servings 6

These balls are a dangerously addictive snack! Hard-boiled eggs are a great addition to this healthy, make-ahead meal.

Per serving: 156 Calories; 12.2g Fat; 1.6g Carbs; 9.7g Protein; 1.2g Sugars

Ingredients

6 ounces smoked ham, chopped
6 ounces Chive & onion cream cheese
A pinch of salt
1/4 teaspoon ground black pepper, or more to taste
1 ½ tablespoons fresh parsley, chopped
2 hard-boiled eggs, chopped

Directions

- Mix all of the above ingredients until everything is well incorporated. Shape into 12 balls.
- Arrange on a serving platter and serve well-chilled. Enjoy!

381. Colby and Tuna Stuffed Avocado

Ready in about 25 minutes
Servings 4

This is the kind of recipe you would eat for a family dinner or a fancy meal in a 5-star restaurant. If tuna isn't your cup of tea, try adding ham or bacon.

Per serving: 286 Calories; 23.9g Fat; 9g Carbs; 11.2g Protein; 0.9g Sugars

Ingredients

2 large-sized avocados, halved and pitted
4 ounces Colby cheese, freshly grated
2 ounces canned tuna, flaked
2 tablespoons scallions, chopped
Salt and freshly ground black pepper, to taste
2 tablespoons fresh cilantro, chopped
1/2 cup radicchios, sliced

Directions

- Begin by preheating your oven to 360 degrees F. Place avocado halves in an ovenproof dish.
- Now, thoroughly combine Colby cheese, tuna, scallions, salt and pepper in a mixing bowl. Stuff avocado halves with cheese/tuna mixture.
- Divide the mixture among avocado halves. Bake approximately 18 minutes and top with fresh cilantro. Garnish with radicchio and serve immediately. Bon appétit!

382. Cheese and Scallion Stuffed Tomatoes

Ready in about 45 minutes
Servings 5

This is another super-easy low-carb recipe, bursting with amazing aromas and flavor. The fresh flavors of scallions and ripe tomatoes pair with the soft flavor of cream cheese and Monterey-Jack cheese. Enjoy!

Per serving: 306 Calories; 27.5g Fat; 4.4g Carbs; 11.3g Protein; 1g Sugars

Ingredients

Nonstick cooking spray
5 vine-ripened tomatoes
1 cup cream cheese, at room temperature
1 ½ cups Monterey-Jack cheese, shredded
1/4 cup sour cream
1 egg, whisked
1 clove garlic, minced
4 tablespoons fresh scallions, chopped
Salt and ground black pepper, to taste
2 teaspoons butter

Directions

- Preheat your oven to 360 degrees F. Lightly grease a rimmed baking sheet with a nonstick cooking spray.
- Slice tomatoes into halves horizontally and discard the hard cores; scoop out pulp and seeds.
- In a mixing bowl, thoroughly combine cheese, sour cream, egg, garlic, scallions, salt, pepper, and butter.
- Divide the filling between tomatoes and bake in the preheated oven for 30 to 35 minutes. Allow them to cool on a wire rack for 5 minutes; serve with fresh rocket leaves. Bon appétit!

383. Cheese Sticks with Roasted Red Pepper Dip

Ready in about 40 minutes
Servings 8

Crunchy cheese sticks go perfectly with tangy and spicy fire-roasted red pepper dip. Keto cheese sticks are so delicious that you won't miss the real breading with breadcrumbs. Moreover, you will love these sticks even more.

Per serving: 200 Calories; 16.9g Fat; 3.7g Carbs; 9.4g Protein; 9.4g Sugars

Ingredients

2 (8-ounce) packages Monterey Jack cheese with jalapeno peppers
3/4 cup Parmigiano-Reggiano cheese, grated
2 tablespoons almond flour
1 tablespoon flax meal
1 teaspoon baking powder
Salt and red pepper flakes, to serve
1/3 teaspoon cumin powder
1/2 teaspoon dried oregano
1/3 teaspoon dried rosemary
2 eggs

For Roasted Red Pepper Dip:
1 cup cream cheese
1/3 cup Greek yogurt
3/4 cup jarred fire-roasted red peppers, drained and chopped
1 tablespoon Dijon mustard
1 chili pepper, deveined and minced
2 garlic cloves, chopped
Sea salt and pepper to taste

Directions

- Cut cheese crosswise into sticks.
- In a shallow bowl, combine the dry ingredients. In another bowl, whisk the eggs.
- Dip each stick into the eggs, and then roll in the dry mixture. Place cheese sticks on a wax paper-lined baking sheet; place in your freezer for about 30 minutes.
- Deep fry cheese sticks until the coating is golden brown and crisp about 5 minutes. Transfer to the pepper towels to drain excess oil.
- Then, make the dipping sauce by mixing all ingredients for the roasted red pepper dip. Bon appétit!

384. Curried Pickled Eggs

Ready in about 20 minutes
Servings 5

There are so many ways to eat eggs! Egg lovers will be absolutely delighted with this recipe!

Per serving: 145 Calories; 9g Fat; 2.8g Carbs; 11.4g Protein; 1.4g Sugars

Ingredients

10 eggs
1/2 cup onions, sliced
3 cardamom pods
1 tablespoon yellow curry powder
1 teaspoon yellow mustard seeds
2 clove garlic, sliced
1 cup cider vinegar
1 ¼ cups water
1 tablespoon salt

Directions

● Boil the eggs until hard-cooked; peel them and rinse under cold, running water. Add peeled eggs to a large-sized jar.
● Add all remaining ingredients to a pan that is preheated over a moderately high heat; bring to a rapid boil.
● Now, turn the heat to medium-low; let it simmer for 6 minutes. Spoon this mixture into the jar.
● Keep in your refrigerator for 2 to 3 weeks. Bon appétit!

385. Easy and Yummy Scotch Eggs

Ready in about 20 minutes
Servings 8

This recipe for keto scotch eggs opens the door to endless possibilities. You can use sausage, lamb, pork or turkey meat. You can skip parmesan or use coconut flour. It is a good idea to wrap the eggs in smoked bacon or salami slices. Amazing!

Per serving: 247 Calories; 11.4g Fat; 0.6g Carbs; 33.7g Protein; 0.3g Sugars

Ingredients

8 eggs
1 ½ pounds ground beef
1/2 cup parmesan cheese, freshly grated
1 teaspoon granulated garlic
1/2 teaspoon shallot powder
1/2 teaspoon cayenne pepper
1 teaspoon dried rosemary, chopped
Salt and pepper to taste

Directions

● Boil the eggs until hard-cooked; peel them and rinse under cold, running water. Set aside.
● In a mixing bowl, thoroughly combine the other ingredients. Divide the meat mixture among 8 balls; flatten each ball and place a boiled egg on it.
● Shape the meat mixture around egg by using your fingers.
● Add the balls to a baking pan that is previously greased with a nonstick cooking spray.
● Bake in the preheated oven, at 360 degrees F for 18 minutes, until crisp and golden. Bon appétit!

386. Traditional Egg Soup with Tofu

Ready in about 15 minutes
Servings 3

Here's a traditional Chinese soup made of beaten eggs, seasonings and homemade stock. You can add scallions, spinach, zicai or tomatoes if desired.

Per serving: 153 Calories; 9.8g Fat; 2.7g Carbs; 15g Protein; 1.2g Sugars

Ingredients

2 cups homemade chicken stock
1 tablespoon tamari sauce
1 teaspoon coconut oil, softened
2 eggs, beaten
1/2 teaspoon turmeric powder
1-inch knob of ginger, grated
Salt and ground black ground, to taste
1/4 teaspoon paprika
1/2 pound extra-firm tofu, cubed

Directions

- In a pan that is preheated over a moderately high heat, whisk the stock, tamari sauce and coconut oil; bring to a rolling boil.
- Stir in eggs, whisking constantly, until it is well incorporated.
- Now, turn the heat to medium-low and season with turmeric, ginger, salt, black pepper and paprika.
- Add tofu and let it simmer another 1 to 2 minutes
- Ladle into individual soup bowls and eat warm. Bon appétit!

387. Zucchini Boats with Sausage and Eggs

Ready in about 35 minutes
Servings 3

Fresh zucchinis are loaded with sausage, mustard, and eggs. You can top these boats with grated cheese to finish.

Per serving: 506 Calories; 41g Fat; 4.5g Carbs; 27.5g Protein; 1.3g Sugars

Ingredients

3 medium-sized zucchinis, cut into halves
1 tablespoon deli mustard
2 sausages, cooked and crumbled
6 eggs
Salt, to taste
1/4 teaspoon black pepper, or more to taste
1/4 teaspoon dried dill weed

Directions

- Scoop the flesh from each zucchini half to make shells; place zucchini boats on a baking pan.
- Spread the mustard on the bottom of each zucchini half. Divide crumbled sausage among zucchini boats.
- Crack an egg in each zucchini half, sprinkle with salt, pepper, and dill.
- Bake in the preheated oven at 400 degrees F for 30 minutes or until zucchini boats are tender. Bon appétit!

388. Creamy Gruyère Egg Bites

Ready in about 20 minutes
Servings 5

Serve as a protein-packed, cold appetizer on a cocktail party. Gruyere is Swiss yellow cheese that can be replaced with any type of hard yellow cheese in this recipe.

Per serving: 177 Calories; 12.7g Fat; 4.6g Carbs; 11.4g Protein; 2.1g Sugars

Ingredients

10 eggs
1/4 cup mayonnaise
1 tablespoon tomato paste
2 tablespoons celery, finely chopped
2 tablespoons carrot, finely chopped
2 tablespoons scallion, minced
2 tablespoons Gruyère cheese, grated
1/2 teaspoon paprika
Salt and black pepper, to taste

Directions

● Place the eggs in a wide pot; cover with cold water by 1 inch. Bring to a rapid boil. Now, turn the heat to medium-low; let the eggs simmer for a further 10 minutes.
● Peel the eggs and rinse them under running water.
● Slice each egg in half lengthwise and remove the yolks. Thoroughly combine the yolks with the remaining ingredients.
● Divide the mixture among egg whites and arrange deviled eggs on a nice serving platter. Bon appétit!

389. Classic Egg Salad

Ready in about 20 minutes
Servings 4

Egg salad is an ultimate comfort food and it is sure to satisfy the whole family. Try this top-rated classic today!

Per serving: 284 Calories; 21.3g Fat; 6.8g Carbs; 16.7g Protein; 2.2g Sugars

Ingredients

8 eggs
1/3 cup mayonnaise
1 tablespoon minced shallot
1/2 teaspoon brown mustard
1 ½ teaspoons lime juice
Salt and black pepper, to taste
10 lettuce leaves
1/2 cup bacon crumbs

Directions

● Place the eggs in a single layer in a pan; cover with 2 inches of water.
● Bring to a boil over a high heat; now, reduce the heat and cook, covered, for 1 minute.
● Remove from heat and leave your eggs for 15 minutes; rinse. Peel and chop the eggs.
● Transfer them to a mixing bowl along with the mayonnaise, shallots, mustard, lime juice, salt and black pepper.
● Mound on fresh lettuce leaves; sprinkle with bacon crumbs and serve.

390. Mom's Pepper Jack Cheese Soup

Ready in about 20 minutes
Servings 4

Go ahead and top your soup with spicy cheese! If you don't feel like eating spicy food, simply omit jalapeno chili peppers.

Per serving: 296 Calories; 14.1g Fat; 7.4g Carbs; 14.2g Protein; 5g Sugars

Ingredients

2 tablespoons ghee
1/2 cup scallions, chopped
1 celery stalk, chopped
1 jalapeno pepper, finely chopped
1 teaspoon garlic paste
1 ½ tablespoons flaxseed meal
2 cups water
1 ½ cups milk
6 ounces Pepper Jack cheese, shredded
Salt and black pepper, to taste
A pinch of paprika, to garnish

Directions

- Warm ghee in a deep pan over a moderately high heat.
- Now, sauté the scallions, celery and jalapeno until they are softened and aromatic.
- Add garlic paste, flaxseed meal, water, and milk and reduce the heat to medium-low. Let it simmer, partially covered, 10 minutes more or until thoroughly cooked.
- Afterwards, fold in shredded cheese, heat off and stir until the cheese is melted and everything is homogenous. Season with salt and pepper to taste.
- Taste and adjust the seasonings. Ladle into individual bowls, sprinkle with paprika and serve. Eat warm.

391. Alfredo, Kale and Cheese Dip

Ready in about 30 minutes
Servings 12

Keto dishes are a cinch to make when you have the right recipe! From now onwards, you can take your keto dishes to the next level and make amazing, homemade dipping sauces for parties and gatherings.

Per serving: 154 Calories; 13g Fat; 3.3g Carbs; 6.2g Protein; 0.2g Sugars

Ingredients

2 tablespoons butter
6 ounces heavy cream
Salt and ground black pepper, to taste
2 egg yolks
2 cloves garlic, chopped
1 ½ cups kale, chopped
3/4 cup sour cream
1/2 cup Swiss cheese, grated
1 cup Cottage cheese, softened
1/2 cup smoked ham, roughly chopped

Directions

- To make an Alfredo-style sauce, melt butter in a pan over medium heat. Now, cook heavy cream, stirring constantly. Add the salt and pepper; whisk in egg yolks.
- Turn the heat to medium-low; cook for a further 4 minutes, stirring continuously. Transfer to a casserole dish.
- Add the remaining ingredients and stir to combine well.
- Bake in the preheated oven at 360 degrees F, approximately 25 minutes. Bon appétit!

392. Italian Salami and Cheese Casserole

Ready in about 1 hour
Servings 4

*Here is a simple trick for cooking like an Italian nonna –
pick high-quality Italian cold cuts and you can't go wrong!*

Per serving: 334 Calories; 23g Fat; 6.2g Carbs; 25.5g
Protein; 2.9g Sugars

Ingredients

Nonstick cooking spray
8 eggs
Coarse salt, to taste
1 cup Mozzarella cheese, grated
1/2 cup Ricotta cheese
1 bell pepper, chopped
1 poblano pepper, deveined and chopped
1/2 teaspoon dried dill weed
1 teaspoon Dijon mustard
4 slices pepperoni, chopped
4 slices pancetta, chopped

Directions

- Begin by preheating your oven to 360 degrees F.
  Generously grease a casserole dish with a nonstick
  cooking spray.
- Beat the eggs, salt and cheese on medium-high speed
  until everything is well incorporated. Spoon the mixture into the casserole dish.
- Add the remaining ingredients; gently stir with a
  spoon. Place a roasting pan with 6 cups of hot water
  in the middle of the preheated oven. Lower the casserole dish into the roasting pan.
- Bake about 1 hour. Allow it to cool down for a couple
  of minutes before cutting it into squares. Serve warm
  and enjoy!

393. Panna Cotta with Roasted Cartos and Basil

Ready in about 40 minutes
Servings 8

*Serve warm with a sprinkling of hot paprika or parsley
flakes. Shaved Parmigiano-Reggiano also works as an
eye-catching garnish.*

Per serving: 155 Calories; 12.7g Fat; 6.2g Carbs; 4.6g
Protein; 1.9g Sugars

Ingredients

4 large carrots, sliced
1 tablespoon coconut oil, melted
1/4 cup fresh basil, chopped
1 cup heavy cream
1/2 cup creme fraiche
1 cup Ricotta cheese
2 teaspoons powdered unflavored gelatin
2-inch   section of fresh rosemary stem,
chopped
Celery salt, to taste
1/4 teaspoon onion flakes
1/2 teaspoon fennel seeds
1/2 teaspoon mixed peppercorns, crushed
1/2 teaspoon cayenne pepper

Directions

- Drizzle carrot slices with melted coconut oil. Roast
  carrots in the preheated oven approximately 30 minutes, stirring once.
- Transfer carrots to a blender. Pulse until creamy and
  smooth.
- Meanwhile, heat a saucepan over low heat; cook fresh
  basil with cream for 4 minutes. Add the remaining
  ingredients and cook until completely melted, 4 to 6
  minutes longer.
- Fold in pureed carrots and stir to combine well.
  Spoon mixture into 8 ramekins. Transfer to your
  refrigerator and let it sit overnight or until set.
- Run a thin knife around edge of each panna cotta; flip
  ramekin onto serving plate. Bon appétit!

394. Stuffed Peppers with Cheese and Pork Rinds

Ready in about 45 minutes
Servings 4

These peppers are definitely one of the best options to make you luncheon a delicious pleasure. You can substitute pasta sauce for pureed tomatoes but be careful with hidden carbs in store-bought sauces.

Per serving: 359 Calories; 29.7g Fat; 6.7g Carbs; 17.7g Protein; 2.6g Sugars

Ingredients

4 bell peppers
6 ounces cream cheese, room temperature
6 ounces blue cheese, crumbled
1/2 cup pork rinds, crushed
2 cloves garlic, smashed
1 ½ cups pureed tomatoes
1/2 teaspoon dried oregano
1 teaspoon dried basil
Salt and ground black pepper, to taste
1/2 teaspoon cayenne pepper

Directions

- Parboil the peppers in salted water for 4 to 6 minutes.
- Preheat the oven to 360 degrees F. Lightly grease the sides and bottom of a casserole dish with a nonstick cooking spray.
- In a mixing bowl, thoroughly combine cream cheese, blue cheese, pork rinds, and garlic.
- Stuff the peppers and transfer to the prepared casserole dish.
- Then, mix pureed tomatoes with oregano, basil, salt, black pepper and cayenne pepper. Pour the tomato mixture over stuffed pepper; cover the dish with foil.
- Bake for 40 minutes and serve warm. Bon appétit!

395. Flavored Asiago Cheese Chips

Ready in about 18 minutes
Servings 2

Did you know that Asiago cheese can make a crispy and salty snack? When it comes to the baking, a non-stick Silpat or a silicone baking mat work well too.

Per serving: 100 Calories; 8g Fat; 0g Carbs; 7g Protein; 0g Sugars

Ingredients

3 cups Asiago cheese, freshly grated
1/3 teaspoon salt
1/2 teaspoon garlic powder
1/2 teaspoon cayenne pepper
½ teaspoon dried rosemary
1/3 teaspoon chili powder

Directions

- Preheat your oven to 420 degrees F. Now, line a baking sheet with a parchment paper.
- Then, thoroughly combine grated Asiago cheese with spices.
- Then, form 2 tablespoons of cheese mixture into small mounds on the baking sheet.
- Bake approximately 15 minutes; your chips will start to get hard as they cool.

396. Keto Mac and Cheese

Ready in about 15 minutes
Servings 4

Turmeric was considered an exotic ingredient not so long ago. Now, it is widely available in any supermarket. This pungent condiment will add a vibrant yellow color and earthy flavor to your mac and cheese.

Per serving: 357 Calories; 32.5g Fat; 10.9g Carbs; 8.4g Protein; 4.8g Sugars

Ingredients

1 large-sized head cauliflower, broken into florets
2 tablespoons butter
Salt and pepper, to taste
1/2 cup milk
1/2 cup heavy whipping cream
1 cup cream cheese
1/2 teaspoon turmeric powder
1 teaspoon garlic paste
1/2 teaspoon onion flakes

Directions

● Begin by preheating your oven to 450 degrees F. Brush a baking sheet with a nonstick cooking spray.
● Toss cauliflower florets with melted butter, salt, and pepper. Place the cauliflower florets on the prepared baking sheet; roast about 13 minutes.
● Heat the remaining ingredients in a heavy-bottomed saucepan, stirring frequently. Simmer over medium-low heat until cooked through.
● Toss cauliflower with creamy cheese sauce and eat warm.

397. Vegetable and Cheeseburger Quiche

Ready in about 45 minutes
Servings 6

If you're eating low-carb, this recipe might become your favorite! Serve with mustard and pickles.

Per serving: 310 Calories; 18.3g Fat; 3.8g Carbs; 30.7g Protein; 1.7g Sugars

Ingredients

1 pound ground beef
1 onion, chopped
1 garlic clove, chopped
1 bell pepper, chopped
1/2 teaspoon coarse salt
1/4 teaspoon black pepper, or more to taste
2 zucchinis, thinly sliced
2 tomatoes, thinly sliced
1/4 cup whipping cream
8 eggs
1/2 cup Cheddar cheese, grated

Directions

● Preheat an oven to 360 degrees F. Brush a baking dish with a nonstick cooking spray.
● Then, in a heavy-bottomed skillet, brown ground beef along with the onion, garlic and bell pepper. Season with salt and pepper.
● Spread the meat layer on the bottom of the baking dish. Layer zucchini slices on top. Top with tomato slices.
● After that, whisk whipping cream, eggs and cheese in a mixing bowl. Spoon this creamy mixture on the top of the vegetables.
● Bake for 40 to 45 minutes, until it is browned around the edges. Bon appétit!

398. French-Style Eggs with Appenzeller Cheese

Ready in about 20 minutes
Servings 5

Get inspired by flavorsome and satisfying ketogenic food! Kick off your day with this amazing, protein-packed recipe.

Per serving: 444 Calories; 35.3g Fat; 2.7g Carbs; 29.8g Protein; 0.9g Sugars

Ingredients

1 tablespoon olive oil
4 slices Jambon de Bayonne, chopped
1/2 cup scallions, chopped
1/2 cup broccoli, chopped
1 clove garlic, minced
1 teaspoon fines herbes
1/4 cup chicken broth
5 eggs
1 ½ cups Appenzeller cheese, shredded

Directions

- Heat the oil in a nonstick frying pan; cook Jambon de Bayonne about 4 minutes, until browned and crisp; set it aside.
- In the same pan, cook scallions in pan drippings. Add the broccoli and garlic and continue to cook, stirring periodically, until they are softened. Add fines herbes and chicken broth and cook an additional 6 minutes.
- Now, make 5 holes in the vegetable mixture to reveal the bottom of your pan. Crack an egg into each hole.
- Scatter shredded cheese over the top and cook an additional 6 minutes. Remove from heat and top with reserved Jambon de Bayonne.

399. Two-Cheese and Walnut Logs

Ready in about 10 minutes + chilling time
Servings 15

If you are in a hurry, place the mixture in the freezer for 30 minutes. After that, shape it into two logs. Enjoy your party.

Per serving: 209 Calories; 18.9g Fat; 3.7g Carbs; 6.6g Protein; 3g Sugars

Ingredients

14 ounces cream cheese, at room temperature
14 ounces sharp American cheese
1/2 cup full-fat mayonnaise
1 (1-ounce) package ranch dressing mix
1 teaspoon lime juice
1/2 cup walnuts, finely chopped

Directions

- Combine cream cheese and sharp cheese with an electric mixer.
- Stir in mayonnaise, ranch dressing mix, and lime juice; mix well. Place in your refrigerator for 3 to 4 hours or until solid and firm.
- When firm, shape the mixture into two logs; roll in walnuts. Serve well-chilled.

400. Omelet with Bacon and Blue Cheese

Ready in about 10 minutes
Servings 2

You will love this super-easy breakfast recipe. It features basic ingredients and takes under 10 minutes to make.

Per serving: 431 Calories; 33.1g Fat; 2.7g Carbs; 30.3g Protein; 1g Sugars

Ingredients

4 slices cooked bacon, crumbled
4 eggs, beaten
1 teaspoon rosemary, chopped
1 teaspoon parsley, chopped
Sea salt and black pepper
4 ounces blue cheese

Directions

- Add the bacon to the frying pan; cook until sizzling.
- Then, mix in the eggs, rosemary, parsley, salt, and black pepper.
- Crumble the cheese over the eggs; fold in half. Cook an additional 1 to 2 minutes or until everything is heated through.

401. Mini Ham Frittatas with Swiss cheese

Ready in about 40 minutes
Servings 5

Go ahead and try this totally different way to enjoy eggs for breakfast. Serve with cabbage kimchi.

Per serving: 261 Calories; 16g Fat; 7.6g Carbs; 21.1g Protein; 3.2g Sugars

Ingredients

1 tablespoon avocado oil
1 red onion, chopped
1 bell pepper, chopped
1 cup mustard greens
6 slices ham, chopped
8 eggs, whisked
1 cup Swiss cheese, shredded
Salt and pepper, to taste
1/4 teaspoon tarragon
1/2 teaspoon ancho powder
1/2 teaspoon Korean red pepper flakes
1 tablespoon fresh parsley, chopped

Directions

- Start by preheating your oven to 390 degrees F. Add cupcake liners to your muffin pan.
- Heat avocado oil in nonstick skillet and sweat the onions for 5 to 6 minutes. Add bell pepper and mustard greens, and continue to cook an additional 4 minutes, stirring frequently.
- Add ham and cook an additional 3 minutes. Stir in the remaining ingredients; stir until everything is well incorporated.
- Transfer the mixture to the lined muffin pan and bake for 23 minutes or until set. Allow the muffins to cool for a couple of minutes before removing them from the cups. Enjoy!

402. Salami and Cheese Balls

Ready in about 15 minutes
Servings 8

These cheese balls could not be easier to make. If you like spicy food, you can use pimentón in this recipe.

Per serving: 168 Calories; 13g Fat; 2.5g Carbs; 10.3g Protein; 0.2g Sugars

Ingredients

1 egg
6 slices Genoa salami, chopped
6 ounces Ricotta cheese
6 ounces Colby cheese
Salt and ground black pepper, to taste
1/4 cup almond flour
1 teaspoon baking powder
1 teaspoon garlic powder
1 teaspoon Italian seasoning

Directions

- Begin by preheating an oven to 420 degrees F.
- Whisk the eggs vigorously; add the remaining ingredients and mix to combine well.
- Divide the mixture into 16 balls; arrange the balls on a baking sheet lined with parchment paper or a silicone mat.
- Bake approximately 13 minutes or until they are crisp and golden brown.

DESSERTS

403. Frozen Cocoa and Almond Dessert 225

404. Chocolate and Coconut Truffles 225

405. Almond Dessert Bars.. 226

406. Espresso and Coconut Delight 226

407. Chocolate and Orange Mousse 227

408. Melt-in-Your-Mouth Chocolate Squares 227

409. Cheesy Coconut Cake 228

410. Coconut Apple Cobbler 228

411. Summer Keto Frappe Dessert.............................. 229

412. Cheesecake Cupcakes with Vanilla Frosting 229

413. Easy Almond Fudge.. 230

414. Peanut Ice Cream 230

415. Coconut Chia Pudding.. 231

416. Festive Cake with Cream Cheese Frosting 231

417. Sinfully Delicious Whiskey Chocolate Bites........ 232

418. Vanilla Walnut Cheesecake................................. 232

419. Chocolate Cream Cheese Muffins........................ 233

420. Chocolate and Orange Mousse 233

421. Cashew Butter Fat Bombs 234

422. Vanilla Keto Pudding.. 234

423. Brownie Pecan Cupcakes 235

424. Nutty Mother's Day Cake 235

425. Luscious Key Lime Curd 236

426. The Best Walnut Truffles Ever 236

427. Avocado and Peanut Butter Pudding 237

428. Caramel Macchiato Candies.................................. 237

429. Blueberry and Chocolate Holiday Candy 238

430. Peanut Butter Cup Cookies.................................. 238

431. Homemade Hazelnut Chocolate 239

432. Orange-Star Anise Custard Pudding..................... 239

433. Melt-in-Your-Mouth Hazelnut Chocolate 240

434. Chocolate Lover's Dream Fudge 240

435. Creamy Mint Jello 241

436. Butterscotch Ice Cream 241

437. Silky Peanut and Coconut Bark............................ 242

438. Decadent Pistachio Truffles 242

439. Walnut and White Chocolate Fudge..................... 243

440. Cappuccino Ice Candy 243

441. Orange Panna Cotta 244

442. Christmas Walnut Penuche 244

443. Coconut and Peanut Butter Flan.......................... 245

444. Berry and Coconut Cup Smoothie 245

445. Quick Chocolate and Walnut Cookies.................. 246

446. Coconut Creamsicle Chia Pudding 246

447. Cheesecake Bars with Raspberry Topping............ 247

448. Simple Strawberries Scones 247

449. Coconut and Avocado Mousse.............................. 248

450. Chocolate Cake with Almond-Choc Ganache..... 248

451. Melt-in-the-Mouth Blueberry Meringues 249

403. Frozen Cocoa and Almond Dessert

Ready in about 10 minutes + chilling time
Servings 6

This easy almond recipe comes together quickly and freezes for a couple of hours. A real feast for everyone who has a sweet tooth!

Per serving: 84 Calories; 8.9g Fat; 1.5g Carbs; 0.8g Protein; 0.2g Sugars

Ingredients

1/2 stick butter, melted
1/2 teaspoon vanilla paste
10 drops liquid stevia
2 tablespoons cocoa powder
2 tablespoons almonds, chopped

Directions

- Melt the butter, vanilla paste, and liquid stevia in a pan that is preheated over a moderate heat.
- Stir in cocoa powder and stir well to combine.
- Spoon the mixture into 12 molds of a silicone candy mold tray. Scatter chopped almonds on top. Freeze until set. Enjoy!

404. Chocolate and Coconut Truffles

Ready in about 15 minutes + chilling time
Servings 16

When it comes to a dessert table, you cannot go wrong with truffles. These delectable balls look and taste wonderful!

Per serving: 90 Calories; 6.3g Fat; 4.9g Carbs; 3.7g Protein; 4g Sugars

Ingredients

1 ½ cups bittersweet chocolate, sugar-free, broken into chunks
4 tablespoons coconut, desiccated
1/2 stick butter
1 cup double cream
3 tablespoons xylitol
1/2 teaspoon pure almond extract
1 teaspoon vanilla paste
A pinch of salt
A pinch of freshly grated nutmeg
1 tablespoon cognac
1/4 cup unsweetened Dutch-processed cocoa powder

Directions

- Thoroughly combine the chocolate, coconut, butter, double cream, xylitol, almond extract, vanilla, salt, and grated nutmeg.
- Microwave for 1 minute on medium-high; let it cool slightly. Now, stir in cognac and vanilla.
- Place in your refrigerator for 2 hours. Shape the mixture into balls; roll each ball in cocoa powder and enjoy!

405. Almond Dessert Bars

Ready in about 30 minutes
Servings 8

Almond lovers will love these fantastic low-carb dessert bars. This recipe is pretty adaptable. You can add walnuts and hazelnuts instead of almonds. You can add chunks of sugar-free chocolate too.

Per serving: 241 Calories; 23.6g Fat; 3.7g Carbs; 5.2g Protein; 0.4g Sugars

Ingredients

2 cups almond flour
3/4 teaspoon baking powder
1/2 cup Swerve
1/2 teaspoon ground cinnamon
A pinch of sea salt
A pinch of grated nutmeg
1 stick butter, melted
3 eggs
1/2 cup Swerve
1 teaspoon vanilla paste
3/4 cup heavy whipping cream
1/2 cup almonds, chopped

Directions

- Preheat your oven to 360 degrees F. Then, line a baking pan with parchment paper.
- In a mixing bowl, thoroughly combine almond flour, baking powder, Swerve, cinnamon, salt, and nutmeg.
- Now, stir in the melted butter, eggs, Swerve, and vanilla paste. Next, stir in the heavy cream to create a soft texture.
- Fold in the chopped almonds and gently stir until everything is well incorporated. Spoon the batter into the baking pan.
- Bake approximately 27 minutes. Allow it to cool completely before serving. Bon appétit!

406. Espresso and Coconut Delight

Ready in about 10 minutes + chilling time
Servings 6

This dessert always turns out great and it looks spectacular on your dining table. You can cut back on the carbs and eat well!

Per serving: 218 Calories; 24.7g Fat; 1.1g Carbs; 0.4g Protein; 0.6g Sugars

Ingredients

4 ounces coconut oil
4 ounces coconut cream
2 teaspoons butter, softened
1 teaspoon instant espresso powder
3 tablespoons confectioners Swerve
A pinch of salt
1 teaspoon pure vanilla extract

Directions

- Melt coconut oil in a double boiler over medium-low heat.
- Add the remaining ingredients. Remove from heat; stir until everything is well combined.
- Pour into a silicone mold and freeze overnight. Bon appétit!

407. Chocolate and Orange Mousse

Ready in about 15 minutes
Servings 4

This fancy mousse dessert can be served on any occasion. And it takes 15 minutes to put together. Serve with fresh berries if desired.

Per serving: 154 Calories; 13g Fat; 9.1g Carbs; 5.3g Protein; 0.6g Sugars

Ingredients

2 egg yolks
3/4 cup heavy cream
3 ounces Ricotta cheese, at room temperature
1 tablespoon freshly squeezed orange juice
1 ½ teaspoons orange zest
1/2 teaspoon ground cinnamon
1/4 cup granulated stevia erythritol blend
1/4 cup unsweetened cocoa powder

Directions

- Beat egg yolks with your electric mixer until thick and pale.
- Heat the cream in a pan over medium heat. Gradually stir hot cream into egg yolk mixture.
- Turn the heat to low and cook for about 5 minutes, stirring constantly, until your mixture is thickened.
- Now, beat the remaining ingredients with your electric mixer until everything is creamy.
- Fold this mixture into cream mixture and serve well chilled.

408. Melt-in-Your-Mouth Chocolate Squares

Ready in about 25 minutes + chilling time
Servings 10

Slightly sweetened with stevia, these chocolate squares are going to be great for a family dessert or midnight snack. A chocolate explosion in your mouth!

Per serving: 119 Calories; 11.7g Fat; 9.2g Carbs; 1.1g Protein; 0.8g Sugars

Ingredients

1/2 cup coconut flour
1 cup almond flour
2 packets stevia
1/4 teaspoon cardamom
1/2 teaspoon star anise, ground
1/2 teaspoon coconut extract
1 teaspoon pure vanilla extract
1 tablespoon rum
A pinch of table salt
1/2 stick butter, cold
1 ½ cups double cream
8 ounces bittersweet chocolate chips, sugar-free

Directions

- Preheat an oven to 330 degrees F. Now, line a baking dish with parchment paper.
- Add flour, stevia, cardamom, anise, coconut extract, vanilla extract, rum and salt to your food processor. Blitz until everything is well combined.
- Cut in cold butter and process to combine again.
- Press the batter into the bottom of the prepared baking dish. Bake about 13 minutes; transfer to a wire rack to cool slightly.
- To make the filling, bring double cream to a simmer in a pan. Add the chocolate and whisk until uniform. Spread over crust; cut into squares and serve well-chilled. Enjoy!

409. Cheesy Coconut Cake

Ready in about 30 minutes
Servings 12

This cake mixes up fast and easy and bakes while you have dinner. It has a sophisticated flavor and lighter-than-air texture.

Per serving: 246 Calories; 22.2g Fat; 6.7g Carbs; 8.1g Protein; 1.9g Sugars

Ingredients

10 ounces almond meal
1 ounce coconut, shredded
1 teaspoon baking powder
1/8 teaspoon salt
4 eggs, lightly beaten
3 ounces stevia
1/2 stick butter
5 ounces coconut yogurt
5 ounces cream cheese

Directions

- Start by preheating your oven to 350 degrees F. Spritz 2 spring form pans with a nonstick cooking spray.
- In a mixing bowl, thoroughly combine the almond meal, coconut and baking powder. Stir in the salt, eggs and 2 ounces of stevia.
- Combine the 2 mixtures and stir until everything is well incorporated.
- Transfer the mixture into 2 spring form pans, introduce in the oven at 350 degrees F; bake for 20 to 25 minutes.
- Transfer to a wire rack to cool completely. In the meantime, mix the other ingredients, including the remaining 1 ounce of stevia.
- Place one cake layer on a plate; spread half of the cream cheese filling over it. Now, top with another cake layer; spread the rest of the cream cheese filling over the top. Bon appétit!

410. Coconut Apple Cobbler

Ready in about 30 minutes
Servings 8

Warm apples topped with crispy topping makes a delicious fruit dessert! Kids of all ages will enjoy this cobbler.

Per serving: 152 Calories; 11.8g Fat; 10.7g Carbs; 2.5g Protein; 7.4g Sugars

Ingredients

2 ½ cups apples, cored and sliced
1/2 tablespoon fresh lemon juice
1/3 teaspoon xanthan gum
1 cup almond flour
1/4 cup coconut flour
3/4 cup xylitol
2 eggs, whisked
5 tablespoons coconut oil, melted

Directions

- Start by preheating your oven to 360 degrees F. Lightly grease a baking dish with a nonstick cooking spray.
- Arrange the apples on the bottom of the baking dish. Drizzle with lemon juice and xanthan gum.
- Then, in a mixing bowl, mix the flour with xylitol and eggs until the mixture resembles coarse meal. Spread this mixture over the apples.
- Drizzle coconut oil over topping. Bake for 25 minutes or until dough rises. Bon appétit!

411. Summer Keto Frappe Dessert

Ready in about 2 hours
Servings 2

Whit its lighter-than-air texture and rich flavor, this dessert will give you more than you could expect from keto recipe!

Per serving: 371 Calories; 37.8g Fat; 10.1g Carbs; 3.4g Protein; 5.1g Sugars

Ingredients

2 teaspoons instant coffee
4 drops liquid Stevia
1 tablespoon cacao butter
1/4 cup cold water
16 raspberries, frozen
1 cup almond milk
2 tablespoons coconut whipped cream

Directions

- Combine instant coffee, Stevia, cacao butter and cold water. Shake with a drink mixer for 20 seconds.
- Place frozen raspberries in dessert glasses. Pour the coffee mixture over it. Add almond milk and ice cubes, if desired.
- Now, freeze for at least 2 hours or until firm. Serve topped with coconut whipped cream. Enjoy!

412. Cheesecake Cupcakes with Vanilla Frosting

Ready in about 30 minutes + chilling time
Servings 8

These silky-smooth cupcakes literally melt on your tongue. Kids will be thrilled!

Per serving: 165 Calories; 15.6g Fat; 8.4g Carbs; 5.2g Protein; 0.2g Sugars

Ingredients

For the Muffins:
3 tablespoons coconut oil
10 ounces Ricotta cheese, at room temperature
1 tablespoon rum
2 eggs
2 packets stevia
1/8 teaspoon ground cloves
1/4 teaspoon ground cinnamon
1/8 teaspoon nutmeg, preferably freshly grated

For the Frosting:
1/2 cup confectioners' Swerve
1/2 stick butter, softened
1 teaspoon vanilla
1 ½ tablespoons full-fat milk

Directions

- Preheat your oven to 360 degrees F; coat muffin cups with cupcake liners.
- Thoroughly combine coconut oil, Ricotta cheese, rum, eggs, stevia, cloves, cinnamon and nutmeg in your food processor.
- Scrape the batter into the muffin tin; bake for 13 to 16 minutes. Now, place in the freezer for 2 hours.
- In the meantime, combine confectioners' Swerve with butter and vanilla with an electric mixer.
- Slowly pour in milk in order to make a spreadable mixture. Frosts chilled cheesecake cupcakes. Bon appétit!

413. Easy Almond Fudge

Ready in about 3 hours
Servings 8

Store your fudge in an airtight container; it does not need to be kept refrigerated.

Per serving: 180 Calories; 18.3g Fat; 4.5g Carbs; 1g Protein; 0.5g Sugars

Ingredients

3/4 cup almond butter, sugar-free, preferably home-made
1 stick butter
1/3 cup coconut milk
1/4 cup xylitol
1/8 teaspoon salt
1/8 teaspoon grated nutmeg
3 tablespoons xylitol
3 tablespoons butter, melted
1 teaspoon vanilla essence
3 tablespoons cocoa powder

Directions

- Microwave almond butter and regular butter until they melt.
- Add coconut milk, 1/4 cup xylitol, salt, and nutmeg; stir to combine well and press into a well-greased glass baking dish.
- Refrigerate for 2 to 3 hours or until set.
- In a mixing bowl, make the sauce by whisking 3 tablespoons xylitol, 3 tablespoons of butter melted, vanilla essence and cocoa powder.
- Spread the sauce over your fudge. Cut into squares and store in an airtight container.

414. Peanut Ice Cream

Ready in about 10 minutes + chilling time
Servings 4

This is probably only ice cream recipe you'll ever need on a ketogenic diet! This is extremely versatile recipe because you can experiment with different flavors. Consider adding frozen berries, fresh mint or walnuts.

Per serving: 305 Calories; 18.3g Fat; 4.5g Carbs; 1g Protein; 0.5g Sugars

Ingredients

1 ¼ cups almond milk
1/3 cup whipped cream
17 drops liquid stevia
1/2 cup peanuts, chopped
1/2 teaspoon xanthan gum

Directions

- Combine all of the above ingredients, except for xanthan gum, with an electric mixer.
- Now, stir in xanthan gum, whisking constantly, until the mixture is thick.
- Then, prepare your ice cream in a machine following manufacturer's instructions.
- Serve directly from the machine or store in your freezer.

415. Coconut Chia Pudding

Ready in about 30 minutes
Servings 4

If you like a richer coconut flavor, you can replace the vanilla extract with pure coconut extract. In addition, serve topped with shredded coconut.

Per serving: 270 Calories; 24.7g Fat; 10.7g Carbs; 4.6g Protein; 2.1g Sugars

Ingredients

1/3 cup chia seeds
1/2 cup water
1 cup coconut cream
1/2 cup sour cream
1/3 teaspoon vanilla extract
1 teaspoon key lime zest
1/4 teaspoon ground cinnamon
2 tablespoons granular Swerve

Directions

- In a bowl, place all ingredients and stir well; let it sit at least 30 minutes.
- Divide among individual bowls to serve.
- Can be stored in the refrigerator up to 3 days.

416. Festive Cake with Cream Cheese Frosting

Ready in about 40 minutes + chilling time
Servings 10

Konjac root fiber, also known as Konjac glucomannan powder, is a water-soluble fiber, it is also a gluten-free and fat-free ingredient. Some good alternatives are psyllium husk, agar-agar, and xanthan gum.

Per serving: 241 Calories; 22.6g Fat; 4.2g Carbs; 6.6g Protein; 2.9g Sugars

Ingredients

2/3 cup coconut flour
1 ½ cups almond flour
1/2 teaspoon baking soda
1/2 teaspoon baking powder
A pinch of salt
A pinch of grated nutmeg
1/2 teaspoon Konjac root fiber
1 cup Swerve
1 teaspoon fresh ginger, grated
2 ½ tablespoons ghee
4 eggs
1 cup coconut milk, sugar-free
1 teaspoon rum extract
1 teaspoon vanilla extract

For the Cream Cheese Frosting:
10 ounces cream cheese, cold
1/3 cup powdered granular sweetener
3 ounces butter, at room temperature
1 teaspoon vanilla
A few drops chocolate flavor

Directions

- Start by preheating your oven to 360 degrees F. Line a baking pan with parchment paper.
- In a mixing bowl, combine coconut flour, almond flour, baking soda, baking powder, salt, nutmeg, Konjac root fiber, Swerve, and ginger.
- Microwave ghee until melted and add to the dry mixture in the mixing bowl. Fold in the eggs, one at a time, and stir until combined.
- Lastly, pour in coconut milk, rum extract, and vanilla extract until your batter is light and fluffy.
- Press the mixture into the prepared baking pan. Bake for 28 to 33 minutes or until a cake tester inserted in center comes out clean and dry.
- Let it cool to room temperature.
- Meanwhile, beat the cream cheese with an electric mixer until smooth. Stir in powdered granular sweetener and beat again. Beat in the vanilla until it is completely incorporated.
- Add the butter, vanilla, and chocolate flavor; whip until light, fluffy and uniform. Frost the cake and serve well-chilled. Bon appétit!

417. Sinfully Delicious Whiskey Chocolate Bites

Ready in about 10 minutes + chilling time
Servings 8

This silky and luscious chocolate dessert can be used as the base for any keto treat you can dream up. You can try adding nuts, instant coffee, flavored whipped cream, and so on.

Per serving: 70 Calories; 3.4g Fat; 10.5g Carbs; 2.4g Protein; 1.8g Sugars

Ingredients

1 cup chocolate chunks, sugar-free
3 tablespoons cocoa powder
3/4 cup buttermilk
1/2 cup milk
2 tablespoons whiskey
1/4 teaspoon grated nutmeg
1/8 teaspoon ground cloves
1/8 teaspoon cinnamon powder
1/2 teaspoon vanilla paste

Directions

- Melt chocolate, along with cocoa and buttermilk in a microwave-safe bowl, on high for 70 seconds.
- Stir in the other ingredients. Pour the mixture into silicone molds.
- Refrigerate at least 1 hour 30 minutes. Bon appétit!

418. Vanilla Walnut Cheesecake

Ready in about 1 hour
Servings 14

You can enjoy this silky and sophisticated cheesecake all year long. Keep this recipe in your back pocket.

Per serving: 393 Calories; 38g Fat; 4.1g Carbs; 9.8g Protein; 0.4g Sugars

Ingredients

8 ounces walnuts, chopped
8 packets stevia
1/4 teaspoon grated nutmeg
A pinch of salt
1/2 cup butter, melted
For the Filling:
22 ounces cream cheese, at room temperature
30 packets stevia
4 eggs
1 teaspoon vanilla essence
1 teaspoon pure almond extract
14 ounces sour cream

Directions

- Combine all ingredients for the crust until well mixed; press the crust mixture into a springform pan. Set aside
- Now, beat cream cheese on low speed until creamy and fluffy.
- Add stevia and eggs, one at a time; mix on low speed. Add the remaining ingredients until well mixed.
- Bake in the preheated oven at 300 degrees F for 55 minutes. Let it cool on a wire rack. Serve well chilled.

419. Chocolate Cream Cheese Muffins

Ready in about 25 minutes
Servings 12

If you have just found out that you can make great keto muffins at home, you probably feel great! These muffins are so easy to make in your own kitchen and they follow keto principles.

Per serving: 134 Calories; 12.5g Fat; 3.3g Carbs; 4.6g Protein; 0.7g Sugars

Ingredients

7 tablespoons butter, melted
5 eggs
2 ounces cocoa powder
1 teaspoon pure vanilla extract
1 teaspoon maple flavor
1/3 teaspoon baking powder
6 ounces Neufchatel cheese, at room temperature
1/4 cup xylitol

Directions

- Beat all ingredients with an electric mixer.
- Place a paper baking cup in each of 12 muffin cups. Fill each cup 2/3 full.
- Bake at 360 degrees F about 23 minutes. Allow your muffins to cool completely; frost as desired and serve.

420. Chocolate and Orange Mousse

Ready in about 15 minutes + chilling time
Servings 6

This rich and tasty mousse is easy to make and fun to eat. It is an elegant and guilt-free dessert that you can serve on any occasion. To serve, top with whipped cream and garnish with grated orange peel

Per serving: 158 Calories; 15.7g Fat; 7.2g Carbs; 2.2g Protein; 1.5g Sugars

Ingredients

2 cups heavy cream
3 tablespoons confectioners Swerve
3 1/3 tablespoons cocoa powder, unsweetened
Fresh juice and zest of 1/2 orange
1/4 teaspoon sea salt
A pinch of grated nutmeg
1/4 teaspoon ground cloves
1/4 teaspoon ground cinnamon
6 ounces sugar-free chocolate chunks

Directions

- Whip heavy cream and Swerve with an electric mixer.
- Add the cocoa powder and beat again. Now, add the remaining ingredients and beat again until everything is well combined.
- Place in your refrigerator until ready to serve. Bon appétit!

421. Cashew Butter Fat Bombs

Ready in about 40 minutes
Servings 12

These amazing balls will satisfy your nut craving! Many store-bought cashew butters contain an added sweetener so be careful or make your homemade one.

Per serving: 114 Calories; 10.6g Fat; 3.4g Carbs; 3.1g Protein; 0.3g Sugars

Ingredients

1/2 cup almonds
1/3 cup walnuts
1/2 cup cashew butter
1/2 stick butter
2 tablespoons cocoa powder, unsweetened
10 drops liquid stevia
1 teaspoon vanilla extract
1/4 cup unsweetened peanut flour

Directions

- Chop the almonds and walnuts in your food processor.
- Transfer to a mixing bowl; add the other ingredients.
- Scoop out tablespoons of batter onto a cookie sheet lined with a wax paper.
- Place in your freezer approximately 30 minutes. Store in your refrigerator up to 1 week.

422. Vanilla Keto Pudding

Ready in about 1 hour
Servings 6

Sometimes you just have a craving for vanilla... This comfort-food recipe is sugar-free and guilt-free!

Per serving: 248 Calories; 20.8g Fat; 12g Carbs; 4.6g Protein; 4.6g Sugars

Ingredients

3 avocados, pitted, peeled and mashed
1 tablespoon vanilla extract
1 cup xylitol
1/8 teaspoon xanthan gum
1 teaspoon lemon juice
1 cup buttermilk
1 cup full-fat milk

Directions

- Mix all ingredients in your blender or a food processor.
- Refrigerate for 1 hour before serving. Enjoy!

423. Brownie Pecan Cupcakes

Ready in about 25 minutes
Servings 12

Here's a perfect dessert for any potluck! If there is something better than brownie cake then it's a brownie cupcake.

Per serving: 251 Calories; 21.5g Fat; 8.6g Carbs; 6.4g Protein; 4.3g Sugars

Ingredients

3/4 cup butter, melted
5 eggs
4 ounces cocoa powder
1/2 cup pecans, ground
1 teaspoon vanilla paste
3/4 teaspoon baking powder
1/4 teaspoon ground cloves
3 ounces cream cheese
3 ounces sour cream
2 tablespoons stevia powder

Directions

- Preheat your oven to 360 degrees F. Place a baking cup in each of 12 regular-size muffin cups.
- Thoroughly combine all ingredients in your food processor. Spoon the batter into the muffin cups.
- Bake for 18 to 22 minutes. Transfer to a wire rack to cool completely before serving. Bon appétit!

424. Nutty Mother's Day Cake

Ready in about 30 minutes + chilling time
Servings 10

Make your keto dessert a little more excessive by adding crunchy toasted nuts. This is one of those cakes that taste better the second day.

Per serving: 211 Calories; 19g Fat; 4.4g Carbs; 7g Protein; 4.4g Sugars

Ingredients

For the Crust:
4 tablespoons peanut butter, room temperature
1 cup almond meal
2 tablespoons almonds, toasted and chopped

For the Filling:
10 ounces cream cheese, room temperature
2 eggs
1/2 teaspoon Stevia
1/2 teaspoon vanilla essence
1/2 teaspoon sugar-free caramel flavored syrup
1 teaspoon fresh ginger, grated
A pinch of salt
A pinch of grated nutmeg

Directions

- Begin by preheating your oven to 360 degrees F. Line a baking pan with parchment paper.
- Thoroughly combine peanut butter with almond meal. Then, press the crust mixture into your baking pan and bake for 7 minutes.
- Then, make the filling, by mixing all the filling ingredients with an electric mixer.
- Spread the filling onto the prepared crusts; bake for a further 18 minutes.
- Transfer it to the refrigerator to chill. Garnish with chopped, toasted almonds; cut into squares and serve well-chilled. Bon appétit!

425. Luscious Key Lime Curd

Ready in about 10 minutes + chilling time
Servings 6

When life gives you limes, make a lime curd! This is one of the favorite keto desserts of all time.

Per serving: 180 Calories; 17.6g Fat; 5.2g Carbs; 2.8g Protein; 1g Sugars

Ingredients

2 eggs, well whisked
1 egg yolk, well whisked
10 ounces fresh key lime juice
1 heaping tablespoon key lime zest
1 ½ cups Swerve
A pinch of salt
1 stick butter, softened

Directions

- Whisk the eggs in a pan that is preheated over a moderate flame.
- Stir in the remaining ingredients and cook for 6 minutes more, whisking constantly.
- Turn the heat to low and continue whisking 2 minutes longer. Remove from heat.
- Cover with a plastic wrap and chill overnight. Serve chilled and enjoy!

426. The Best Walnut Truffles Ever

Ready in about 1 hour
Servings 10

Once shaped, these truffles can be rolled in unsweetened cocoa powder, coconut, matcha powder, and so forth. This is a great idea for the next party, just be sure to make a double batch!

Per serving: 162 Calories; 14.6g Fat; 5.9g Carbs; 2.3g Protein; 4.4g Sugars

Ingredients

1/2 stick butter
4 ounces heavy cream
1/4 cup Sukrin Icing
1 tablespoon brandy
1/2 teaspoon pure almond extract
1/2 cup chopped toasted walnuts
1/2 cup chocolate chips, sugar-free
4 tablespoons walnuts, coarsely chopped

Directions

- Melt the butter in a double boiler, stirring constantly.
- Then, stir in the cream and Sukrin icing; stir to combine well. Remove from heat and add brandy, almond extract and chopped walnuts.
- Now, allow it to cool at room temperature. Shape into 20 balls and chill for 40 to 50 minutes.
- In a double boiler, melt chocolate chips over medium-low heat. Dip each ball into the chocolate coating.
- Afterwards, roll your truffles in chopped walnuts. Keep in an airtight container in your refrigerator. Enjoy!

427. Avocado and Peanut Butter Pudding

Ready in about 15 minutes
Servings 4

This nutritionally dense pudding is naturally sweetened with stevia and enriched with crunchy peanut butter. For this pudding, use ripe avocados that are soft but still firm.

Per serving: 288 Calories; 27.3g Fat; 8.9g Carbs; 6.2g Protein; 2.4g Sugars

Ingredients

1 ½ cups avocado, peeled, pitted, and diced
1/2 cup crunchy peanut butter
50 drops liquid stevia
1/2 cup canned coconut milk
1 teaspoon pure vanilla extract
1/4 teaspoon ground cloves
1 tablespoon lime juice
1/2 cup coconut whipped cream

Directions

- Process avocados, peanut butter, stevia and coconut milk in a blender.
- Now, add vanilla extract, cloves, and lime juice.
- Refrigerate until ready serve. Garnish with coconut whipped cream and enjoy!

428. Caramel Macchiato Candies

Ready in about 10 minutes + chilling time
Servings 8

Once you taste how good these candies are, they will become a must make dessert! These candies are kid-friendly and guilt-free.

Per serving: 145 Calories; 12.8g Fat; 6.9g Carbs; 0.9g Protein; 6.1g Sugars

Ingredients

3 tablespoons cocoa butter
3 tablespoons butter
3 ounces dark chocolate, sugar-free
1 teaspoon cold brew coffee concentrate
1 teaspoon sugar-free caramel flavored syrup
6 drops liquid stevia

Directions

- Microwave cocoa butter, butter, and chocolate for 1 minute or so.
- Stir in the remaining ingredients. Pour into candy-safe molds. Refrigerate until hard. Enjoy!

429. Blueberry and Chocolate Holiday Candy

Ready in about 15 minutes + chilling time
Servings 10

These sugar-free chocolate candies are incredibly simple to make, and they look so festive. Store in an airtight container for up to 2 weeks.

Per serving: 334 Calories; 37g Fat; 5.3g Carbs; 1.6g Protein; 1.4g Sugars

Ingredients

1 cup freeze-dried blueberries
1 stick butter
1 cup coconut oil
4 ounces unsweetened chocolate, roughly chopped
1 teaspoon vanilla crème stevia

Directions

- Crush dried blueberries with a pestle and mortar until you get a powder consistency; reserve.
- Heat a pan over a moderate heat; melt butter, coconut oil, chocolate and vanilla crème stevia, stirring continuously.
- Now, transfer the chocolate mixture to a parchment-lined baking sheet.
- Sprinkle blueberries and gently press them down into the melted chocolate. Swirl with a knife and transfer to your freezer.
- Let them cool and harden completely before breaking into pieces.

430. Peanut Butter Cup Cookies

Ready in about 40 minutes
Servings 10

Get all of the rich flavors of peanut butter cake in these bite-sized pecan pie cookies. If you prefer an extra-silky texture, use a smooth peanut butter instead.

Per serving: 266 Calories; 28.1g Fat; 2.6g Carbs; 3.3g Protein; 1.2g Sugars

Ingredients

1/2 cup coconut oil
1/2 cup butter
1/2 cup crunchy peanut butter
3 tablespoons heavy cream
1 tablespoon granular Swerve

Directions

- Simmer all of the above ingredients in a pan over medium-low heat; stir continuously until everything is well incorporated.
- Divide the batter among muffin cups lined with cupcake wrappers.
- Allow them to harden at least 30 minutes in your freezer. Bon appétit!

431. Homemade Hazelnut Chocolate

Ready in about 15 minutes + chilling time
Servings 8

You've got to love this homemade chocolate. If you like a crunchier texture, simply add coarsely chopped hazelnuts.

Per serving: 184 Calories; 16.9g Fat; 9.2g Carbs; 1.8g Protein; 6.6g Sugars

Ingredients

1 stick butter, room temperature
1/4 cup cocoa powder, unsweetened
1/4 cup granulated Swerve
1/2 cup hazelnuts, finely chopped
A pinch of salt
A pinch of ground cloves

Directions

- Melt butter in a pan over a moderate heat. Now, stir in cocoa powder and Swerve. Heat off and mix well.
- Add hazelnuts, salt and ground cloves; stir until everything is incorporated.
- Line a baking dish with a piece of aluminum foil. Spoon the mixture into the baking dish and let it sit in your refrigerator until completely set.
- Broken into pieces and serve. Keep in the refrigerator.

432. Orange-Star Anise Custard Pudding

Ready in about 1 hour
Servings 5

Silky and sophisticated, this pudding is a must-have for Sunday afternoon! Be sure to use natural sweeteners on your keto diet.

Per serving: 205 Calories; 16.4g Fat; 6.5g Carbs; 7.4g Protein; 0.5g Sugars

Ingredients

3/4 cup Swerve
1 ½ cups whipping cream
3/4 cup water
6 eggs
1 teaspoon orange rind, grated
1/4 teaspoon orange essence
1/2 teaspoon vanilla essence
1/4 teaspoon ground cloves
1 teaspoon star anise star ground

Directions

- Melt Swerve in a pan on medium-low until it is richly browned.
- Spoon caramelized Swerve into the bottom of a baking dish; set aside.
- Then heat the cream and water in a pan, bringing to a boil.
- In a mixing bowl, whisk the remaining ingredients until everything is well combined. Stir warm cream mixture into this egg mixture. Cook, stirring frequently, for a further 3 minutes.
- Spread this mixture over the Swerve layer. Place baking dish in a larger baking pan that is filled with boiling water.
- Bake at 330 degrees F for 1 hour. Invert your pudding onto a serving plate and serve. Bon appétit!

433. Melt-in-Your-Mouth Hazelnut Chocolate

Ready in about 25 minutes
Servings 8

An easy keto hazelnut chocolate recipe made from pungent cacao butter, Swerve, and roasted hazelnuts. It is kid-friendly and perfect for your keto diet.

Per serving: 140 Calories; 14g Fat; 8.1g Carbs; 2g Protein; 4.2g Sugars

Ingredients

4 ounces cacao butter
1 tablespoon extra-virgin coconut oil
8 tablespoons cocoa powder
1/4 cup Swerve
1/4 teaspoon hazelnut extract
1 teaspoon pure vanilla extract
1/8 teaspoon coarse salt
1/4 teaspoon grated nutmeg
1/2 cup roasted hazelnuts, chopped

Directions

- Melt the cacao butter and coconut oil in a microwave for 1 minute or so.
- Now, stir in cocoa powder, Swerve, hazelnut extract, vanilla extract, salt and nutmeg.
- Pour the mixture into an ice cube mold. Add the roasted hazelnuts and place in your freezer for 20 minutes or until solid. Enjoy!

434. Chocolate Lover's Dream Fudge

Ready in about 15 minutes + chilling time
Servings 8

This dessert is chock-full of rich low-carb chocolate, thick cream, and condensed milk. Did you know that National Fudge Day is June 16?

Per serving: 220 Calories; 20g Fat; 7g Carbs; 1.7g Protein; 1.4g Sugars

Ingredients

1 cup condensed milk, sugar-free
3/4 Sukrin chocolate, broken into pieces
1 stick butter
2 tablespoons coconut oil
4-5 drops Stevia
1/2 cup heavy cream

Directions

- Microwave condensed milk and Sukrin chocolate for 70 seconds; spoon into a baking dish and freeze until firm.
- Melt butter in a small-sized pan; stir in melted coconut oil, Stevia, and heavy cream; whisk to combine well or beat with a hand mixer.
- Spread the cream mixture over the fudge layer in the baking dish. Transfer to the refrigerator or freezer until solid. Bon appétit!

435. Creamy Mint Jello

Ready in about 45 minutes
Servings 10

Here's a classic dessert, simple and surprisingly delicious! Kids will be delighted by this impressive treat.

Per serving: 56 Calories; 5.5g Fat; 0.4g Carbs; 1.5g Protein; 0.4g Sugars

Ingredients

2 envelopes unflavored gelatin
5 tablespoons Swerve
1 teaspoon peppermint oil
1 teaspoon pure vanilla essence
3/4 cup boiling water
1 ¼ cups heavy cream

Directions

- Combine the gelatin, Swerve, peppermint oil, and vanilla extract in a heatproof dish.
- Pour in boiling water and stir well until the gelatin is dissolved.
- Stir in heavy cream; whisk to combine well. Pour the mixture into paper cups sprayed with a nonstick cooking spray.
- Place in your refrigerator for 30 minutes or until they are firm. Unmold before serving and enjoy!

436. Butterscotch Ice Cream

Ready in about 15 minutes + chilling time
Servings 8

Creamy and flavorsome. this is the perfect dessert for a hot summer day. It scoops well after freezing too.

Per serving: 89 Calories; 9.3g Fat; 1.5g Carbs; 0.8g Protein; 0.5g Sugars

Ingredients

3/4 cup heavy cream
1/2 cup coconut milk
1 tablespoon butterscotch flavoring
25 drops liquid stevia
1/3 teaspoon pure vanilla extract
A pinch of salt
1/4 cup sour cream

Directions

- Cook the heavy cream and coconut milk in a pan that is preheated over a medium-low flame. Let it simmer, stirring constantly, until there are no lumps.
- Allow it to cool at room temperature; mix in the remaining ingredients.
- Blend with an electric mixer until your desired consistency is reached. Transfer to your freezer for about 5 hours. Enjoy!

437. Silky Peanut and Coconut Bark

Ready in about 10 minutes + chilling time
Servings 12

Everyone loves a bark! If you prefer slightly salty bark, add a pinch of crushed Maldon sea salt to the mixture.

Per serving: 316 Calories; 31.6g Fat; 4.6g Carbs; 6.6g Protein; 1.3g Sugars

Ingredients

3/4 cup peanut butter
3/4 cup coconut oil
1 cup Swerve
1 teaspoon pure vanilla extract
1/2 teaspoon pure almond extract
1/2 cup coconut flakes

Directions

- Combine all ingredients in a pan over a moderate heat; cook, stirring continuously, for 4 to 5 minutes.
- Spoon the mixture into a parchment-lined baking sheet. Refrigerate overnight and break your bark into pieces. Serve.

438. Decadent Pistachio Truffles

Ready in about 25 minutes + chilling time
Servings 6

Indulge in these melt-in-your-mouth truffles bursting with toasted pistachios. It is wonderful for potlucks, family gatherings and holidays!

Per serving: 113 Calories; 8.5g Fat; 8.9g Carbs; 1.7g Protein; 0.4g Sugars

Ingredients

3 bars sugar-free chocolate spread
1/2 cup heavy cream
1 teaspoon vanilla essence
1/4 teaspoon ground cinnamon
1/2 cup toasted pistachios, finely chopped

Directions

- Melt chocolate spread with heavy cream in your microwave for 1 minute or so.
- Add the vanilla and ground cinnamon; transfer to your refrigerator for 8 hours or until firm enough to shape.
- Shape the chocolate mixture into balls. Freeze for 20 minutes.
- Afterwards, roll the balls into the chopped pistachios. Keep refrigerated until ready to serve.

439. Walnut and White Chocolate Fudge

Ready in about 15 minutes + chilling time
Servings 12

For this fudge, don't overheat the butter and walnut butter, they should have a semi-soft consistency. If you are able to, use a homemade walnut butter.

Per serving: 202 Calories; 21.3g Fat; 2.3g Carbs; 2.4g Protein; 0.6g Sugars

Ingredients

3/4 cup butter, softened
1 ¼ cups walnut butter, sugar-free
3 ounces sugar-free white chocolate
1/3 cup coconut milk, unsweetened
2 tablespoons xylitol
1/8 teaspoon coarse sea salt
1/4 teaspoon grated nutmeg
1/4 teaspoon ground star anise
1/4 teaspoon lemon peel zest

Directions

- Microwave butter, walnut butter, and white chocolate until they are melted. Add the butter mixture to your food processor.
- Now, add the other ingredients and mix again until everything is well incorporated. Scrape the mixture into a parchment lined baking pan.
- Place in the refrigerator for 3 hours. Cut into squares and serve. Bon appétit!

440. Cappuccino Ice Candy

Ready in about 10 minutes + chilling time
Servings 8

Have you ever wondered how delicious avocado, espresso, and heavy cream can be together? Try this recipe and you will be delighted!

Per serving: 117 Calories; 11.2g Fat; 5g Carbs; 1.3g Protein; 1.4g Sugars

Ingredients

1 ½ cups avocado, pitted, peeled and mashed
1 cup brewed espresso
2 tablespoons cocoa powder
1 cup heavy whipping cream
3 tablespoons erythritol
1/2 teaspoon cappuccino flavor extract
A pinch of salt
A pinch of grated nutmeg

Directions

- Throw all of the above ingredients into your food processor; mix until everything is well combined.
- Pour the mixture into an ice cube tray. Freeze overnight, at least 6 hours. Serve well-chilled.

441. Orange Panna Cotta

Ready in about 10 minutes + chilling time
Servings 10

Make this Italian dessert and amaze your guests. The hardest part of this recipe will be keeping your kids away from this attempting dessert. Yes, it's difficult to wait for it to harden, but it is worth waiting for.

Per serving: 221 Calories; 21.5g Fat; 13.8g Carbs; 4.3g Protein; 11.8g Sugars

Ingredients

1 ½ teaspoons gelatin, unflavored
1 ½ cups coconut milk
1/4 cup erythritol
1 teaspoon Blood orange juice
1 teaspoon blood orange zest

Directions

- Place gelatin and coconut milk in a pan; let it sit for 2 minutes. Add the remaining ingredients.
- Simmer the mixture over low heat until gelatin is dissolved, about 3 minutes.
- Pour the mixture into 4 molds. Place in your refrigerator until set, at least 6 hours.
- To serve invert over a small plate. Enjoy!

442. Christmas Walnut Penuche

Ready in about 2 hours
Servings 8

Make this crunchy, buttery penuche in your own kitchen! You can use these wonderfully inspirational sweets to create DIY presents for Christmas.

Per serving: 167 Calories; 17.1g Fat; 8.8g Carbs; 2.4g Protein; 7g Sugars

Ingredients

1 cup xylitol
1 cup condensed milk, unsweetened
1 stick butter
1/2 teaspoon vanilla paste
2 ounces toasted walnuts, chopped
1/4 teaspoon orange rind, grated
A pinch of salt

Directions

- Combine xylitol and milk in a pan that is preheated over a moderate heat. Simmer, stirring often, for 5 to 6 minutes.
- Stir in butter and vanilla. Cream with an electric mixer at low speed; beat until very creamy.
- Fold in chopped walnuts, orange rind, and salt; stir again. Afterwards, spoon into a baking dish and freeze until firm, about 2 hours. Bon appétit!

443. Coconut and Peanut Butter Flan

Ready in about 40 minutes + chilling time
Servings 4

Flan is a light an elegant dessert for a weeknight treat or to serve as a midnight snack. For the best ketogenic experience, make sure to use a homemade peanut butter.

Per serving: 304 Calories; 27.7g Fat; 6.6g Carbs; 11.6g Protein; 3.1g Sugars

Ingredients

1 cup coconut cream, unsweetened
4 eggs
1/2 cup peanut butter
1/2 cup granulated Swerve
1/4 teaspoon ground mace
1/2 teaspoon pure vanilla extract
1/2 teaspoon pure almond extract

Directions

- Begin by preheating your oven to 340 degrees F. Place 4 ramekins in a deep baking pan. Pour boiling water to a depth of about 1 inch.
- In a saucepan, bring coconut cream to a simmer. In a mixing dish, whisk the remaining ingredients until eggs are foamy.
- Slowly and gradually pour egg mixture into warm coconut cream, whisking constantly.
- Spoon the mixture into prepared ramekins and bake for 35 minutes, or until a tester comes out dry.
- Allow it to cool about 4 hours. Can be stored in refrigerator up to 3 days. Bon appétit!

444. Berry and Coconut Cup Smoothie

Ready in about 10 minutes
Servings 4

There's no such thing as a bowl of a thick and rich berry smoothie. We added an almond butter to achieve a better, silky texture but you can use peanut or walnut butter as well.

Per serving: 274 Calories; 26.8g Fat; 7.5g Carbs; 3.9g Protein; 3.2g Sugars

Ingredients

1/2 cup raspberries, frozen
1 cup coconut milk
2 tablespoons almond butter
1/4 cup coconut shreds
1 teaspoon vanilla paste
4 drops liquid stevia
2 tablespoons hemp seeds

Directions

- Pulse frozen berries in your food processor to desired consistency.
- Add coconut milk, almond butter, coconut, vanilla and stevia. Blend until everything is well incorporated.
- Dived between 4 individual bowls; top with hemp seeds and serve immediately.

445. Quick Chocolate and Walnut Cookies

Ready in about 30 minutes
Servings 10

It's tea time! Whether you're on a keto diet or not, try these cookies with a cup of tea today!

Per serving: 157 Calories; 14.8g Fat; 3.5g Carbs; 4.5g Protein; 0.1g Sugars

Ingredients

1 stick butter
1/2 teaspoon pure almond extract
2 eggs
15 drops liquid stevia
1/8 teaspoon kosher salt
1 ¾ cups almond flour
1/2 teaspoon baking powder
1/4 teaspoon ground cinnamon
1/2 cup walnuts, chopped
1/3 cup sugar-free baker's chocolate, cut into chunks

Directions

- Heat the butter in a pan that is preheated over a moderate flame; stir and cook until it is browned.
- In a mixing bowl, beat the pure almond extract with the eggs, stevia, and salt.
- Add the melted butter, along with the other ingredients.
- Preheat your oven to 350 degrees F. Line a cookie sheet with a parchment paper. Spritz with a nonstick cooking spray.
- Bake for 25 minutes and transfer to a wire rack to cool before serving.

446. Coconut Creamsicle Chia Pudding

Ready in about 20 minutes
Servings 4

Sometimes the best dessert recipes are not difficult at all. You can fix up this pudding in advance because it can be stored in your refrigerator up to 3 days.

Per serving: 226 Calories; 17.9g Fat; 11g Carbs; 5.9g Protein; 5g Sugars

Ingredients

1 cup water
1 cup heavy cream
1 cup coconut milk, unsweetened
1 teaspoon vanilla extract
1 cup chia seeds
1/4 cup coconut shreds, unsweetened
2 tablespoons erythritol
1/4 teaspoon ground cloves
1/2 teaspoon ground anise star

Directions

- Thoroughly combine all of the above ingredients in a mixing dish.
- Allow it to stand at least 20 minutes, stirring periodically.
- Divide among four individual cups to serve. Enjoy!

447. Cheesecake Bars with Raspberry Topping

Ready in about 30 minutes
Servings 6

Luscious cheesecake bars with only 8.3 grams of carbs per serving! Give yourself a special treat, you deserve it.

Per serving: 333 Calories; 28.4g Fat; 8.3g Carbs; 11.7g Protein; 6.9g Sugars

Ingredients

For the Cheesecake Bars:
1 stick butter, melted
4 eggs
1 cup mascarpone cheese
1 teaspoon vanilla paste
1/4 teaspoon star anise, ground
3 tablespoons Swerve
1/3 teaspoon baking powder

For the Raspberry Topping:
3/4 cup, frozen raspberries
1 ½ tablespoons erythritol
1/2 teaspoon lemon juice
A pinch of salt
1 ½ tablespoons water

Directions

- Thoroughly combine all ingredients for the cheesecakes with a hand mixer. Line a baking pan with parchment paper or Silpat mat.
- Bake in the preheated oven at 330 degrees F, approximately 25 minutes. Transfer to a wire rack to cool completely.
- Meanwhile, place all of the ingredients for the topping in a pan that is preheated over a moderate heat; bring the mixture to a boil.
- Now, reduce heat and let it simmer until the sauce has thickened.
- Cut cheesecake into squares. Spoon about 2 tablespoons of the raspberry sauce over each cheesecake square. Enjoy!

448. Simple Strawberries Scones

Ready in about 25 minutes
Servings 10

Just like the name says, these scones are simple, fruity and chewy. Further, they have zero sugar, as well as less saturated fat and fewer carbs than classic ones. How could it be any better than this?

Per serving: 245 Calories; 21.6g Fat; 10.4g Carbs; 3.8g Protein; 0.8g Sugars

Ingredients

1 cup coconut flour
1 cup almond flour
1 teaspoon baking powder
A pinch of salt
1 cup strawberries
2 eggs
1 ½ sticks butter
1 cup heavy cream
10 tablespoons liquid stevia
1 teaspoon vanilla extract

Directions

- Start by preheating your oven to 350 degrees F.
- In a mixing bowl, thoroughly combine the flour with baking powder, salt and strawberries.
- In another mixing bowl, beat the eggs with butter and cream. Stir in liquid stevia and vanilla extract; stir to combine well.
- Combine the 2 mixtures and stir until you obtain a soft dough. Knead gently and avoid overworking your dough.
- Shape into 16 triangles and arrange on a lined baking sheet. Bake for 18 minutes and serve your scones cold.

449. Coconut and Avocado Mousse

Ready in about 15 minutes+ chilling time
Servings 6

With its high-fat content and a dense, creamy flesh, avocado makes an excellent addition to a keto mousse recipes. You will love this sophisticated mousse and its airy texture.

Per serving: 303 Calories; 30g Fat; 8.1g Carbs; 3.5g Protein; 3.3g Sugars

Ingredients

1 cup coconut milk
1 ½ cups avocado, pitted, peeled and mashed
A pinch of salt
A pinch of grated nutmeg
1 cup heavy cream
1/2 cup softened cream cheese
2 tablespoons confectioners Swerve

Directions

- In a deep pan, warm coconut milk over medium heat.
- Stir in avocado, salt, and nutmeg and cook, stirring continuously, about 5 minutes or until the mixture bubbles up.
- Then, beat heavy cream, cheese, and Swerve with an electric mixer on medium-high speed. Reserve roughly 4 tablespoons of this cream mixture to top mousse before serving.
- Afterwards, place in your refrigerator to set for a couple of hours.
- Serve with a dollop of cream mixture on top. Bon appétit!

450. Chocolate Cake with Almond-Choc Ganache

Ready in about 50 minutes + chilling time
Servings 10

A decadent chocolate cake with nutty ganache, you'll want the moment to last forever.

Per serving: 313 Calories; 30.7g Fat; 7.5g Carbs; 7.3g Protein; 1g Sugars

Ingredients

1/2 cup water
3/4 cup granulated Swerve
14 ounces unsweetened chocolate chunks
2 sticks butter, cold
5 eggs
1/2 teaspoon pure almond extract
1/4 teaspoon ground nutmeg
1/4 teaspoon ground cardamom
A pinch of salt

For Almond-Choc Ganache:
3/4 cups double cream
9 ounces sugar-free dark chocolate, broken into chunks
1/4 cup smooth almond butter
A pinch of salt
1/2 teaspoon ginger powder
1/2 teaspoon cardamom powder

Directions

- Begin by preheating your oven to 360 degrees F. Line a baking pan with parchment paper.
- Now bring water to a rolling boil in a deep pan; add Swerve and cook until it is dissolved.
- Microwave the chocolate until melted. Add butter to the melted chocolate and beat with an electric mixer.
- Add the chocolate mixture to the hot water mixture. Now, add the eggs, one at a time, whipping continuously.
- Add almond extract, nutmeg, cardamom, and salt; stir well. Spoon the mixture into the prepared baking pan; wrap with foil.
- Lower the baking pan into a larger pan; add boiling water about 1 inch deep.
- Bake for 40 to 45 minutes. Allow it to cool completely before removing from the pan.
- Meanwhile, place double cream in a pan over a moderately high heat and bring to a boil. Pour hot cream over dark chocolate; whisk until chocolate is melted.
- Add the remaining ingredients for the ganache and whip until it is uniform and smooth. Finally, glaze a cooled cake and serve well-chilled. Enjoy!

451. Melt-in-the-Mouth Blueberry Meringues

Ready in about 2 hours
Servings 10

Meringues must be one of the most popular desserts in the world. The reason is obvious – they are affordable, simple to make, and just irresistible!

Per serving: 51 Calories; 0g Fat; 4g Carbs; 12g Protein; 0g Sugars

Ingredients

3 large egg whites, at room temperature
1/2 teaspoon vanilla paste
A pinch of salt
1 teaspoon finely grated lemon zest
1/3 cup Swerve
3 tablespoons freeze-dried blueberry, crushed with a pestle and mortar

Directions

- Preheat an oven to 200 degrees F.
- Now, beat the egg whites, vanilla, salt, and lemon zest with an electric mixer on medium-high speed. Add Swerve and continue mixing on high until stiff and glossy.
- Add crushed blueberries and mix until everything is well incorporated.
- Drop the meringue, about 2 inches apart, on the parchment-lined baking sheets; you can use a pastry tube here.
- Bake about 2 hours. Leave the meringues in the turned-off oven for several hours.

OTHER KETO FAVORITES

452. Mediterranean-Style Garlic Aioli............................ 251

453. Juicy & Flavorful Lamb Cheeseburgers................. 251

454. Chocolate and Cashew Chia Pudding................... 252

455. Prosciutto, Egg and Brie Cups.............................. 252

456. Colby and Carrot Meatballs.................................. 253

457. Italian-Style Prosciutto and Mascarpone Balls..... 253

458. Apple Pie Granola 254

459. Spicy and Savory Tuna Mousse 254

460. Cheese and Garlicky Chicken Fillets.................... 255

461. Camembert, Gruyere and Provolone Fondue 255

462. Grilled Feta Cheese and Eggs Plate...................... 256

463. Family Short Ribs with Bell Peppers 256

464. Mascarpone and Caramel Balls............................ 257

465. Extraordinary Pizza Dip....................................... 257

466. Spring Sour Cream Omelet................................... 258

467. Baked Chicken Skin Chips with Cheesy Sauce 258

468. Must Make Cheese Sauce 259

469. Creamy Walnut Bars... 259

470. Creole Crawfish Frittata 260

471. Reblochon and Bacon Party Balls......................... 260

472. Pimiento-Cheese Bites
     with Carrot Pepper Chips 261

473. Mushroom Panna Cotta.. 261

474. Fajita Beef Sausage with Vegetables...................... 262

475. Three-Cheese Fried Pizza with Peppers................ 262

476. Easy Pumpkin and Cheese Mousse 263

477. 5-Minute Egg and Salami Breakfast...................... 263

478. Turkey and Bacon Meatloaf Cups......................... 264

479. French-Style Strawberry Omelet........................... 264

480. Crêpes with Butter-Rum Syrup 265

481. Mustard Rolled Turkey with Prosciutto 265

482. Pancetta, Cheese and Egg Muffins........................ 266

483. Perfect Tuna Pâté... 266

484. Hemp Heart Porridge with Brazil Nuts................ 267

485. Pancetta and Asiago Waffles 267

486. Greek-Style Berry Pancakes.................................. 268

487. Mexican-Style Pan Pizza 268

488. Homemade Bread with Herbs and Seeds.............. 269

489. Blue Cheese and Cauliflower Purée...................... 269

490. Ham and Broccoli with Queso Quesadilla 270

491. Keto Iced Coffee 270

492. Cheese Flat Bread with Salami 271

493. Baked Avocado Stuffed with Grapes and Cheese 271

494. Smoked Bacon and Gorgonzola Muffins 272

495. Almond Coconut Cream Pie 272

496. Queso Oaxaca and Avocado Fat Bombs 273

497. Chia Egg Balls.. 273

498. Star Anise and Pecan Porridge 274

499. Sour Cream and Chocolate Donuts....................... 274

500. Chèvre Custard with Sautéed Morels 275

452. Mediterranean-Style Garlic Aioli

Ready in about 10 minutes
Servings 8

Olive oil, fresh dill, and garlic are wonderfully combined in this fresh, silky and addictive Mediterranean dipping sauce. Serve with fish, seafood or hard-boiled eggs.

Per serving: 116 Calories; 13.2g Fat; 0.2g Carbs; 0.4g Protein; 0g Sugars

Ingredients

- 1 tablespoon balsamic vinegar
- 1 egg yolk, at room temperature
- 1 clove garlic, crushed
- 1/2 teaspoon sea salt
- 1/2 cup olive oil
- 1/4 teaspoon ground black pepper
- 1/4 cup fresh dill, chopped

Directions

- Add vinegar, egg yolk, garlic and salt to a blender; pulse until creamy and smooth. Turn to low setting.
- Slowly drizzle in olive oil and mix until the oil is well incorporated.
- Add ground black pepper and dill; gently stir to combine. Store in the refrigerator and garnish with fresh snipped chives to serve.

453. Juicy & Flavorful Lamb Cheeseburgers

Ready in about 20 minutes
Servings 6

These tender and juicy burgers are loaded with tho kinds of cheese, scallions and a high-quality ground meat. How could it be any better than this?

Per serving: 252 Calories; 15.5g Fat; 1.2g Carbs; 26g Protein; 0.2g Sugars

Ingredients

- 1 pound ground lamb
- 1/2 cup scallions, chopped
- 2 garlic cloves, finely chopped
- 1/4 teaspoon ground black pepper, or more to taste
- Sea salt and cayenne pepper, to taste
- 2 ounces mascarpone cheese
- 3 ounces Asiago cheese, grated
- 2 tablespoons olive oil

Directions

- In a mixing bowl, combine ground meat, scallions, garlic, black pepper, salt and cayenne pepper.
- Shape the meat mixture into 6 balls; flatten to make 6 patties.
- In another mixing bowl, combine mascarpone with grated Asiago cheese.
- Divide cheese mixture among prepared patties. Wrap the meat mixture around the cheese until the filling is sealed inside.
- Heat the oil in a heavy-bottomed skillet over a moderately high heat. Cook your burgers 5 to 6 minutes per side, until thoroughly cooked. Serve with fresh or pickled salad. Bon appétit!

454. Chocolate and Cashew Chia Pudding

Ready in about 35 minutes
Servings 4

Like a creamsicle but a little bit tastier! You can eat this chia pudding as a snack, breakfast or dessert.

Per serving: 93 Calories; 5.1g Fat; 9.2g Carbs; 4.4g Protein; 2.4g Sugars

Ingredients

3/4 cup cashew milk, preferably homemade
1/4 cup water
2 tablespoons almond butter
1/2 cup chia seeds
20 drops liquid stevia
1/2 teaspoon maple extract
3 tablespoons orange flower water
2 tablespoons cocoa powder, unsweetened

Directions

- Place cashew milk, almond butter, chia seeds, stevia, maple extract, orange flower water, and cocoa powder in a mixing bowl.
- Allow it to stand for 30 minutes, stirring periodically.
- Divide among 4 serving bowls and garnish with hemp seeds.

455. Prosciutto, Egg and Brie Cups

Ready in about 20 minutes
Servings 6

These cups are perfect when you need a protein hit. Prepare big batch as they freeze well.

Per serving: 268 Calories; 18.3g Fat; 0.7g Carbs; 26.2g Protein; 0.4g Sugars

Ingredients

24 small and thin slices of prosciutto
6 eggs, beaten
Coarse salt and freshly ground black pepper, to taste
1/4 cup fresh cilantro, coarsely chopped
2 ounces cream cheese
2 ounces Brie, chopped

Directions

- Start by preheating your oven to 390 degrees F.
- Line each muffin cup with 2 slices of prosciutto so that they circle each mold.
- In a mixing dish, thoroughly combine the remaining ingredients. Fill each prosciutto lined muffin cup 3/4 of the way with the egg/cheese mixture.
- Bake for 15 minutes or until your cups don't jiggle. Serve immediately and enjoy!

456. Colby and Carrot Meatballs

Ready in about 35 minutes
Servings 5

This recipe is a smart way to get children to eat veggies! You can mix in shallots, zucchini, and tomatoes. Enjoy!

Per serving: 342 Calories; 23.7g Fat; 4.3g Carbs; 31.7g Protein; 1.7g Sugars

Ingredients

1 egg, beaten
1 pound ground turkey
1 carrot, grated
2 garlic cloves, minced
1 onion, chopped
1 tablespoon Italian mixed herbs
Salt and freshly ground black pepper, to taste
2 tablespoons olive oil
1 cup Colby cheese, shredded

Directions

- Preheat your oven to 360 degrees F.
- Mix all of the above ingredients, except for cheese, until everything is well incorporated.
- Then, shape this mixture into 20 meatballs; arrange on a parchment-lined baking sheet.
- Bake for 25 minutes, turning once. Scatter cheese over the balls and bake an additional 7 minutes or until it melts completely. Bon appétit!

457. Italian-Style Prosciutto and Mascarpone Balls

Ready in about 15 minutes
Servings 4

This is another super-easy keto balls recipe, bursting with delicious flavor. The smoky notes of prosciutto and aromatic flavors of seasonings really brighten the gentle flavor of mascarpone.

Per serving: 88 Calories; 6.5g Fat; 0.7g Carbs; 6.5g Protein; 0.4g Sugars

Ingredients

4 prosciutto slice
1/2 cup mascarpone cheese
1/2 teaspoon smoke flavor
1/2 teaspoon maple flavor
1/4 teaspoon apple cider vinegar
1 teaspoon shallot powder
1/2 teaspoon garlic powder
1 teaspoon red pepper flakes

Directions

- In a mixing bowl, thoroughly combine prosciutto, mascarpone cheese, smoke flavor, maple flavor and apple cider vinegar.
- After that, add the remaining ingredients and stir to combine well.
- Form into 4 balls with a spoon.
- Serve right away or refrigerate up to 3 days. Bon appétit!

458. Apple Pie Granola

Ready in about 35 minutes
Servings 8

This granola will give you more than you could expect! When it comes to the nuts, pecans, macadamia and Brazil nuts, have fewer carbs than cashews, almonds and pistachios.

Per serving: 281 Calories; 26.6g Fat; 7.7g Carbs; 5.4g Protein; 1.4g Sugars

Ingredients

3 tablespoons coconut oil
1/4 cup stevia
1 cup shredded coconut, unsweetened
3/4 cup pecans, chopped
1/2 cup cashews, chopped
1/2 cup pumpkin seeds
1/3 cup sunflower seeds
1 teaspoon apple pie spice mix
A pinch of salt

Directions

- Start by preheating your oven to 300 degrees F.
- Heat the coconut oil in a pan over a moderate heat, add stevia and stir until everything is well combined.
- In a large bowl, combine the remaining ingredients. Add the mixture to the pan; stir to combine.
- Spread this mixture on a lined baking sheet. Bake for 30 minutes, stirring once or twice. Leave your granola to cool down before serving. Enjoy!

459. Spicy and Savory Tuna Mousse

Ready in about 20 minutes + chilling time
Servings 5

This fancy recipe will amaze your guests! It is a total stunner that you can eat for an elegant dinner whilst it goes perfectly on an open-faced sandwich.

Per serving: 100 Calories; 5.8g Fat; 4.1g Carbs; 8g Protein; 0.6g Sugars

Ingredients

1 ½ teaspoons gelatin, powdered
3 tablespoons water
2 ounces mascarpone cheese
3 tablespoons mayonnaise
1 teaspoon Dijon mustard
3 ounces canned tuna, flaked
1/4 cup shallots, finely chopped
1 garlic clove, minced
1 teaspoon jalapeno, minced
1/2 teaspoon celery salt
1/4 teaspoon black pepper, preferably freshly ground
1/3 teaspoon fresh ginger, grated

Directions

- Dissolve gelatin in water; allow it to stand for 10 minutes.
- Now, melt mascarpone in a pan over moderate heat; stir in gelatin and whisk vigorously until well blended.
- Allow this mixture to cool to room temperature. Add the other ingredients and mix again until everything is well incorporated.
- Divide the mixture among 5 mousse molds and place in your refrigerator overnight. To serve, invert the mold over a plate and enjoy!

460. Cheese and Garlicky Chicken Fillets

Ready in about 20 minutes
Servings 4

Chicken tastes better with cheese and garlic. These chicken fillets are cooked just the way you like it.

Per serving: 416 Calories; 26g Fat; 3.2g Carbs; 40.7g Protein; 1.2g Sugars

Ingredients

1 tablespoon butter
1 pound chicken fillets, sliced
2 garlic cloves, minced
1/2 cup heavy cream
1/3 cup vegetable broth
2 tablespoon tomato paste
1 cup Colby cheese, shredded

Directions

- Heat the butter in a pan that is preheated over a moderate heat; fry the chicken with garlic for 4 minutes, stirring periodically; reserve.
- Now, whisk in the heavy cream, vegetable broth, and tomato paste; cook until it is thickened.
- Add the reserved chicken back to the pan; scatter shredded cheese over it. Cover and let it sit for 5 to 10 minutes or until the cheese is melted. Bon appétit!

461. Camembert, Gruyere and Provolone Fondue

Ready in about 15 minutes
Servings 10

Serve this fondue right out of the oven with keto-friendly veggies. If you have a fondue pot, it will be a hit for sure.

Per serving: 148 Calories; 10.2g Fat; 1.5g Carbs; 9.3g Protein; 0.5g Sugars

Ingredients

1/3 pound camembert cheese, chopped
1/3 pound Gruyere cheese, shredded
1/2 cup Provolone, freshly grated
1 tablespoon xanthan gum
1/2 teaspoon granulated garlic
1 teaspoon onion powder
3/4 cup Sauvignon blanc
1/2 tablespoon lemon juice
Ground black pepper, to taste
1 Roma tomato, chopped

Directions

- Preheat the broiler.
- In a cast-iron skillet, combine cheese with xanthan gum, granulated garlic, and onion powder; stir to combine well.
- Now, add the wine and lemon juice. Season with black pepper to taste and stir again.
- Then, place the skillet under the broiler for 6 to 7 minutes, until the cheese begins to brown.
- Garnish with chopped tomatoes and serve hot. Bon appétit!

462. Grilled Feta Cheese and Eggs Plate

Ready in about 20 minutes
Servings 4

Aromatic, soft cheese with fluffy and creamy eggs. This recipe is super satisfying and quick to prepare; it is a great idea for breakfast or brunch.

Per serving: 542 Calories; 46.4g Fat; 11.2g Carbs; 23.7g Protein; 5.5g Sugars

Ingredients

1 (12-ounce) piece of Feta cheese
3 teaspoons olive oil
1 teaspoon dried Greek seasoning blend
1 tablespoon butter
6 eggs
1/2 teaspoon sea salt
1/4 teaspoon crushed red pepper flakes, or more to taste
1 ½ cups avocado, pitted and sliced
1 cup grape tomatoes, halved
4 tablespoons walnuts, coarsely chopped

Directions

- Heat your grill to a medium-low. Place the Feta in the center of a piece of heavy-duty foil. Now, drizzle with the oil and season with Greek seasoning blend.
- Seal the foil to form a packet. Grill for 15 minutes; after that, slice into four pieces.
- Meanwhile, melt 1 tablespoon of butter in a frying pan; then, cook the eggs over a medium-high heat. Gently stir with a spatula to form large, soft curds.
- Season with salt and pepper.
- To serve, place the eggs and grilled cheese on a plate. Serve with avocado and tomatoes, garnished with chopped walnuts.

463. Family Short Ribs with Bell Peppers

Ready in about 15 minutes
Servings 4

A perfect mix of flavors and textures in this classic beef recipe will amaze your family and friends. Boneless short ribs go wonderfully with garlic and bell peppers.

Per serving: 490 Calories; 44g Fat; 5.5g Carbs; 16.9g Protein; 3.1g Sugars

Ingredients

1 pound boneless short ribs, cut into serving pieces
1/4 teaspoon ground black pepper
1 teaspoon paprika
Garlic salt, to taste
1 tablespoon tallow, at room temperature
2 garlic cloves, smashed
2 bell peppers, deveined and thinly sliced
2 tablespoons chives, chopped

Directions

- Season short ribs with black pepper, paprika and garlic salt. Melt the tallow in the pan that is preheated over a moderately high heat.
- Then, brown short ribs for 3 minutes per side or until no longer pink; reserve. Cook garlic and peppers in pan drippings until tender and fragrant.
- Serve with reserved short ribs, garnished with fresh chives.

464. Mascarpone and Caramel Balls

Ready in about 5 minutes
Servings 4

You no longer have to miss rich and fatty food. These balls are loaded with good fats and amazing flavors, as well as they are extremely versatile. They might become a staple in your household.

Per serving: 180 Calories; 17.3g Fat; 3.4g Carbs; 5.3g Protein; 0.8g Sugars

Ingredients

3 ounces mascarpone
3 ounces pine nuts, chopped
1/2 teaspoon caramel flavor
1/4 teaspoon allspice

Directions

- Mix all ingredients in a food processor until uniform and smooth.
- Form mixture into 8 balls and serve well chilled.

465. Extraordinary Pizza Dip

Ready in about 20 minutes
Servings 10

With this extraordinary recipe, you won't crave pizza, trust me. And the best of all – you can have this dish assembled in one single dish, in less than five minutes.

Per serving: 160 Calories; 12.7g Fat; 2.4g Carbs; 8.9g Protein; 0.6g Sugars

Ingredients

8 ounces salami, chopped, a few slices reserved
8 ounces Ricotta cheese, room temperature
2 ounces Colby cheese, shredded
1 cup ripe tomato, pureed
1 teaspoon garlic paste
1/4 teaspoon chipotle powder
1/2 teaspoon red pepper flakes, crushed
1 teaspoon shallot powder
1 teaspoon porcini powder
1/2 teaspoon dried oregano
1/2 teaspoon dried basil
Flaky sea salt and freshly ground black pepper, to taste
1/2 cup Kalamata olives, to garnish

Directions

- Preheat an oven to 360 degrees F.
- Place all ingredients, except for Kalamata olives, in a casserole dish. Mix until everything is well combined.
- Top with reserved salami slices and Kalamata olives. Bake for 15 minutes or until it is done to your liking. Serve warm and enjoy!

466. Spring Sour Cream Omelet

Ready in about 15 minutes
Servings 2

When it comes to the perfect omelet recipe, it all boils down to versatility. You can invent your own fillings, savory and sweets. You can come up with your unique combo of seasonings. Or you can use leftovers from yesterday's lunch.

Per serving: 319 Calories; 25g Fat; 10g Carbs; 14.9g Protein; 4.4g Sugars

Ingredients

2 teaspoons butter
2 spring onions, chopped
2 spring garlic, chopped
4 eggs, beaten
1 (8-ounce) carton sour cream, divided
2 medium-sized tomatoes, sliced
1 piquillo pepper, minced
2 tablespoons chervil, chopped
Kosher salt and freshly ground black pepper, to taste

Directions

- Melt the butter in a pan that is preheated over a moderate flame. Sauté spring onion and garlic until they are just tender and fragrant.
- Then, whisk the eggs with sour cream. Add the egg mixture to the pan and gently smooth surface with a wide spatula; cook until the eggs are puffy and lightly browned on bottom.
- Place tomatoes, piquillo pepper and chervil on one side of the omelet. Season with salt and pepper.
- Fold your omelet in half. Slide omelet onto a warm serving plate and cut into wedges. Bon appétit!

467. Baked Chicken Skin Chips with Cheesy Sauce

Ready in about 15 minutes
Servings 4

Don't even think about throwing poultry skins in the trash! Chicken crips are incredibly easy to make and they are absolutely delicious.

Per serving: 119 Calories; 10.5g Fat; 1.1g Carbs; 5.1g Protein; 0.1g Sugars

Ingredients

Skin from 4 chicken thighs
1/4 cup Cottage cheese
2 tablespoons sour cream
1 tablespoon ghee, at room temperature
1/2 teaspoon ground cumin
2 tablespoons green onions, finely chopped
Sea salt and ground black pepper, to taste

Directions

- Start by preheating your oven to 360 degrees F. Then, bake skins for 10 to 12 minutes until they are browned and crispy.
- Allow chicken skins to cool slightly; then, cut them into bite-sized pieces.
- In a mixing bowl, thoroughly combine the remaining ingredients to make the spread. Serve with prepared chicken skins.

468. Must Make Cheese Sauce

Ready in about 15 minutes
Servings 6

Here's the perfect keto sauce for vegetables, seafood, zoodles… Gouda is a Dutch yellow cheese that can be replaced with Monterey Jack, Asiago or Appenzeller cheese.

Per serving: 110 Calories; 10.5g Fat; 0.7g Carbs; 3.4g Protein; 0.5g Sugars

Ingredients

1/3 cup heavy cream
1 ½ tablespoons ghee
1/2 cup Neufchatel cheese
1/3 cup Gouda, grated
3 tablespoons water
1 teaspoon shallot powder
1/3 teaspoon hot paprika

Directions

- Heat the cream with ghee in a sauté pan over a moderate flame. Once it is heated, add Neufchatel to the pan.
- Then, stir in the other ingredients. Cook approximately 4 minutes, stirring continuously. Serve right away!

469. Creamy Walnut Bars

Ready in about 20 minutes
Servings 4

Without added sugar, these bars are perfect for everyday snack and breakfast on the go. Such a creative way to eat your daily dose of nuts!

Per serving: 278 Calories; 30.1g Fat; 2.2g Carbs; 2.2g Protein; 1.1g Sugars

Ingredients

1 cup double cream
1/4 teaspoon cardamom
2 tablespoons coconut oil
2 tablespoons walnut butter
A pinch of coarse salt
A pinch of grated nutmeg
1/2 cup walnuts, coarsely chopped

Directions

- Line a baking pan with foil.
- In a mixing bowl, thoroughly combine double cream and cardamom. Scrape the mixture into the prepared pan.
- In a separate bowl, whisk together the coconut oil, walnut butter, salt, and nutmeg. Spread this glaze over the creamed mixture.
- Scatter chopped walnuts over the top. Place it in the freezer for 15 minutes.
- Cut into squares and enjoy!

470. Creole Crawfish Frittata

Ready in about 25 minutes
Servings 3

Make sure to check your frittata occasionally to avoid over-baking. This frittata should have the texture of custard.

Per serving: 265 Calories; 15.8g Fat; 7.1g Carbs; 22.9g Protein; 5.2g Sugars

Ingredients

1 tablespoon olive oil
1 red onion, chopped
4 ounces crawfish tail meat, chopped
1 teaspoon Creole seasoning blend
6 large eggs, slightly beaten
1/2 cup yogurt

Directions

- Preheat your oven to 350 degrees F.
- Heat the oil in a large oven-proof non-stick skillet that is preheated over medium-high heat.
- Sauté the onions until they are softened; add crawfish and cook for 2 minutes longer. Sprinkle with Creole seasoning.
- Make sure your ingredients are evenly distributed across the bottom of the skillet.
- Now, whisk the eggs with yogurt. Pour the egg mixture into the skillet.
- Transfer the skillet to the preheated oven and bake approximately 18 minutes or until eggs are thoroughly cooked. Cut into wedges and serve warm. Bon appétit!

471. Reblochon and Bacon Party Balls

Ready in about 15 minutes
Servings 5

These fat-bombs are a delightful combination of a soft French cheese and crunchy fried bacon. The balls will melt in your mouth thanks to their creaminess.

Per serving: 206 Calories; 16.5g Fat; 0.6g Carbs; 13.4g Protein; 0.3g Sugars

Ingredients

3 ounces bacon
6 ounces Reblochon
1 jalapeño pepper, seeded and finely chopped
1/4 teaspoon parsley flakes
1/2 teaspoon paprika

Directions

- Cook the bacon in a frying pan over a moderately high flame. Cook until it is well browned; then, finely chop the bacon into small pieces.
- In your food processor, blend other ingredients until everything is well incorporated. Allow the mixture to chill in your refrigerator.
- Shape well-chilled mixture into 10 balls.
- Place crushed bacon in a shallow plate. Roll your balls around to coat all sides.
- Serve immediately or refrigerate up to 3 days. Bon appétit!

472. Pimiento-Cheese Bites with Carrot Pepper Chips

Ready in about 25 minutes
Servings 8

Pimientos, also known as cherry peppers, are a key ingredient in this fantastic ketogenic recipe. They'll give an exotic touch to each bite!

Per serving: 177 Calories; 12.9g Fat; 6.8g Carbs; 8.8g Protein; 3.5g Sugars

Ingredients

1 cup Pepper-Jack cheese, shredded
1/2 cup Greek yogurt
1 cup Romano cheese, freshly grated
2 tablespoons tomato paste
1/2 teaspoon dried rosemary leaves, crushed
1 teaspoon dried thyme leaves, crushed
2 tablespoons pimientos, chopped
Coarse salt and freshly ground black pepper, to taste

For Carrot Pepper Chips:
1 pound carrots, cut into sticks
2 tablespoons sesame oil
1 teaspoon black pepper, preferably freshly cracked
Coarse salt, to taste

Directions

- Thoroughly combine cheese, yogurt, tomato paste, rosemary, thyme, pimientos, salt, and black pepper in a mixing bowl.
- Place in foil liners - candy cups and keep in the refrigerator until ready to serve.
- Now, preheat your oven to 430 degrees F.
- Toss carrots with sesame oil, pepper, and salt. Place them in a single layer on a cookie sheet.
- Bake about 20 minutes, tossing once or twice. Dip carrot pepper chips in pimiento-cheese cups. Bon appétit!

473. Mushroom Panna Cotta

Ready in about 15 minutes + chilling time
Servings 6

Everyone will love this fancy Italian classic. Make family dinner time stress-free and prepare this panna cotta in the morning; it'll take less than 15 minutes.

Per serving: 489 Calories; 47.4g Fat; 6.9g Carbs; 12.7g Protein; 1.3g Sugars

Ingredients

1 tablespoon butter
2 ounces fresh mushrooms, chopped
2 teaspoons powdered unflavored gelatin
1 1/3 cups heavy cream
1 cup sour cream
8 ounces blue cheese
1 teaspoon Herbes de Provence
1/4 cup pecan halves

Directions

- Melt butter in a pan over high heat; now sauté the mushrooms for 4 minutes, stirring continuously.
- Add gelatin and heavy cream and cook, bringing to a boil.
- Remove from heat; add the sour cream, cheese, and Herbes de Provence. Pour this mixture evenly into 6 glasses. Refrigerate at least 6 hours or overnight.
- Serve garnished with pecan halves.

474. Fajita Beef Sausage with Vegetables

Ready in about 25 minutes
Servings 4

If you are searching for an authentic flavor, Fajita seasoning mix is the right choice for this skillet. Doubtless, Zahtar works well too.

Per serving: 227 Calories; 18g Fat; 9g Carbs; 7.1g Protein; 4g Sugars

Ingredients

1 tablespoon lard
2 smoked beef sausage links, sliced
1 teaspoon crushed garlic
2 zucchinis, sliced
1 carrot, sliced
1 teaspoon fajita seasoning
1 piquillo pepper, minced
2 bell peppers, sliced
1/2 teaspoon saffron

Directions

- Warm the lard in a wok that is preheated over a moderate heat.
- Now, brown chicken sausage along with garlic approximately 8 minutes.
- Add the other ingredients and cook, stirring periodically, for 13 minutes more. Eat warm.

475. Three-Cheese Fried Pizza with Peppers

Ready in about 15 minutes
Servings 4

You will be surprised how much this keto dish tastes like real thing! You can add ripe olives and fresh Mediterranean herbs if desired.

Per serving: 266 Calories; 23.6g Fat; 6.6g Carbs; 9g Protein; 3.7g Sugars

Ingredients

2 tablespoons olive oil
1/2 cup Pepper Jack cheese, shredded
1 ¼ cups mozzarella cheese, shredded
1/2 cup cream cheese
2 tablespoons sour cream
2 garlic cloves, chopped
1 red bell pepper, sliced
1 green bell pepper, sliced
10 cherry tomatoes, halved
1 teaspoon oregano
Salt and black pepper, to taste

Directions

- Heat the olive oil in a pan that is preheated over a moderate flame.
- Add cheese and make sure to cover the bottom; cook about 5 minutes until it is golden brown and crispy.
- Spread sour cream and garlic over the crust. Add bell peppers and tomatoes; cook for a further 2 minutes.
- Sprinkle with oregano, salt, and pepper and serve warm.

476. Easy Pumpkin and Cheese Mousse

Ready in about 15 minutes + chilling time
Servings 6

Looking for an easy mousse recipe? This simple but incredibly rich and flavorful pumpkin mousse will remind you of a pumpkin pie. Life is beautiful!

Per serving: 368 Calories; 33.7g Fat; 5.6g Carbs; 13.8g Protein; 2.1g Sugars

Ingredients

1 ½ cups heavy cream
1/2 cup cream cheese
1/2 cup erythritol
3 eggs
1 ¼ cups canned pumpkin
1/2 teaspoon ground cloves
1/2 teaspoon ground cinnamon
1/4 teaspoon grated nutmeg
A pinch of coarse salt

Directions

- In a pan, combine heavy cream, cream cheese, and erythritol, and bring it to a boil; whisk frequently.
- Whisk the eggs; slowly add 1/2 of the hot heavy cream mixture to the beaten eggs. Add the mixture back to the pan. Cook another 2 to 4 minutes, or until mixture is thickened.
- Heat off; stir in pumpkin, cloves, cinnamon, nutmeg, and salt. Divide the mixture among serving bowls and place in the refrigerator.
- Serve well-chilled. Bon appétit!

477. 5-Minute Egg and Salami Breakfast

Ready in about 5 minutes
Servings 3

Breakfast in a mason jar? Don't believe in words and try this EGGcellent recipe.

Per serving: 303 Calories; 22.4g Fat; 3.6g Carbs; 21.6g Protein; 2.2g Sugars

Ingredients

3 teaspoons butter, melted
6 eggs
1/2 cup American yellow cheese, shredded
1/2 cup cottage cheese
3 slices Genoa salami, chopped
Coarse salt and ground black pepper, to taste
1 teaspoon yellow mustard

Directions

- Grease 3 mason jars with melted butter.
- Crack two eggs into each jar. Divide the other ingredients among the two jars.
- Cover and shake until everything is well incorporated.
- Remove lids and microwave for 2 minutes on high. Eat warm and enjoy!

478. Turkey and Bacon Meatloaf Cups

Ready in about 30 minutes
Servings 6

These meatloaf cups promote the best of a keto diet – ground meat, bacon, eggs and cheese. With a negligible amount of carbs, they are obviously perfect for your diet!

Per serving: 276 Calories; 18.3g Fat; 1.2g Carbs; 29.2g Protein; 0.2g Sugars

Ingredients

2 tablespoons shallot, chopped
1 teaspoon garlic, minced
1 pound ground turkey
2 ounces cooked bacon, chopped
1 egg, beaten
1 teaspoon brown mustard
Coarse salt and ground black pepper, to taste
1/2 teaspoon crushed red pepper flakes
1 teaspoon dried basil
1/2 teaspoon dried oregano
4 ounces Brie cheese, cubed

Directions

- Thoroughly combine the shallot, garlic, ground turkey, bacon, egg and mustard in a mixing bowl.
- Season with salt, black pepper, red pepper, basil and oregano.
- Mix until everything is well incorporated. Divide the mixture among muffin cups. Insert one cube of Brie into each meatloaf cup. Seal the top to cover the Brie by using your fingers.
- Bake at 350 degrees F for about 20 minutes, or until the meatloaf cups are golden brown. Allow them to cool for 10 minutes before removing from the muffin pan.

479. French-Style Strawberry Omelet

Ready in about 10 minutes
Servings 1

For an elegant touch, don't fail to add warmed cognac to finish. Crème de cassis and Grand Marnier (a French, orange-flavored liqueur) work well too.

Per serving: 488 Calories; 42g Fat; 8g Carbs; 15.3g Protein; 4.4g Sugars

Ingredients

2 eggs, beaten
2 tablespoons heavy cream
1/2 teaspoon ground cloves
1 tablespoon coconut oil
2 tablespoons cream cheese
6 fresh strawberries, sliced
1 tablespoon Cognac

Directions

- Whisk the eggs with heavy cream and ground cloves.
- Next, melt coconut oil in a pan that is preheated over medium-high heat. When hot, add the egg mixture; cook for about 3 minutes until the base is thoroughly cooked.
- Tip the omelet out onto a plate; top with cheese and strawberries. Roll it up; add warmed Cognac over your omelet and flambé. Bon appétit!

480. Crêpes with Butter-Rum Syrup

Ready in about 25 minutes
Servings 6

Is there anything better than the smell of fresh, homemade crepes on Sunday morning? Make these delicious and fluffy crepes from scratch, in less than 25 minutes, with common and easy-to-find keto ingredients.

Per serving: 243 Calories; 19.6g Fat; 5.5g Carbs; 11g Protein; 4.7g Sugars

Ingredients

For Crêpes:
6 ounces cream cheese, softened
6 eggs
1 ½ tablespoons granulated Swerve
1/4 cup almond flour
1 teaspoon baking soda
1 teaspoon baking powder
1/2 teaspoon apple pie spice mix

For the Syrup:
3/4 cup water
1 tablespoon butter
3/4 cup Swerve, powdered
1 tablespoon rum extract
1/2 teaspoon xanthan gum

Directions

- Combine all ingredients for the crepes using an electric mixer. Mix until everything is well incorporated.
- Grease a frying pan with melted butter; fry your crepes over a moderate heat until the edges begin to brown.
- Flip and fry on the other side until it is slightly browned.
- Whisk the water, butter, and Swerve in a pan over medium heat; simmer about 6 minutes, stirring continuously.
- Add the mixture to a blender along with rum extract and 1/4 teaspoon of xanthan gum; mix to combine.
- Add the remaining 1/4 teaspoon of xanthan gum and let it stand until the syrup is thickened. Serve with warm crepes and enjoy!

481. Mustard Rolled Turkey with Prosciutto

Ready in about 50 minutes
Servings 6

The simple combo of whole grain mustard, tarragon and chili pepper will spice up boring turkey breasts and take your family dinner to the next level.

Per serving: 275 Calories; 9.5g Fat; 1.3g Carbs; 44.5g Protein; 0.1g Sugars

Ingredients

6 (4-ounce) turkey fillets
1 tablespoon herb-infused olive oil
3 tablespoons whole grain mustard
2 tablespoons fresh parsley, roughly chopped
3 garlic cloves, chopped
1 jalapeno pepper, chopped
1 teaspoon tarragon
Salt and ground black pepper, to taste
1 teaspoon hot paprika
6 slices prosciutto

Directions

- Preheat your oven to 390 degrees F. Flatten turkey fillets with a meat mallet.
- Rub herb-infused olive oil and mustard all over the turkey breasts.
- Place fresh parsley on each fillet. Divide chopped garlic, jalapeno pepper, tarragon, salt, black pepper and paprika among fillets.
- Roll the fillets in the prosciutto. Place in a glass baking dish and transfer to the preheated oven.
- Bake for 35 to 45 minutes (until the internal temperature reaches 180 degrees F). Bon appétit!

482. Pancetta, Cheese and Egg Muffins

Ready in about 30 minutes
Servings 9

Here're scrambled egg muffins loaded with eggs, pancetta, and Monterey Jack cheese. Make sure not to overcook your muffins! You can have the best ingredients ever but an overcooked muffin is dry and tasteless.

Per serving: 294 Calories; 21.4g Fat; 3.5g Carbs; 21g Protein; 1.7g Sugars

Ingredients

9 slices pancetta
9 eggs
A bunch of scallions, chopped
1/2 cup Monterey Jack cheese, shredded
1/4 teaspoon garlic powder
1/2 teaspoon dried dill weed
Sea salt and ground black pepper, to taste

Directions

- Start by preheating your oven to 390 degrees F.
- Then, brush a 9-cup muffin pan with oil; line each cup with one slice of pancetta.
- In a mixing bowl, thoroughly combine the remaining ingredients.
- Divide the egg mixture among muffin cups. Bake in the preheated oven for 20 minutes. Bon appétit!

483. Perfect Tuna Pâté

Ready in about 10 minutes + chilling time
Servings 12

Versatile and easy, this tuna pâté is a great idea for any occasion, from a luxury dinner party to the school lunch box. Serve with pickles or fresh vegetable sticks.

Per serving: 64 Calories; 2.9g Fat; 1.3g Carbs; 7.9g Protein; 0.2g Sugars

Ingredients

1 (14-ounce) tuna in brine, drained
1/2 cup Ricotta cheese
1/4 cup sour cream
2 tablespoons mayonnaise
1/2 teaspoon country Dijon mustard
2 ounces cilantro, finely chopped
Coarse salt and freshly cracked mixed peppercorns, to your liking
1/2 teaspoon smoked paprika

Directions

- Add all ingredients to a mixing bowl.
- Mix with a wide spatula until everything is well incorporated.
- Pour into a greased mold; chill for 6 hours or overnight. Unmold onto a serving platter and enjoy.

484. Hemp Heart Porridge with Brazil Nuts

Ready in about 20 minutes
Servings 4

Less than 7 grams of carbohydrates in every bowl, it sounds like a perfect keto breakfast. This is an endlessly inspiring porridge, you can add pepitas, sunflower seeds, berries, etc.

Per serving: 405 Calories; 37g Fat; 6.6g Carbs; 14.8g Protein; 1.5g Sugars

Ingredients

2 tablespoons coconut oil, room temperature
4 eggs, lightly whisked
1/4 cup hemp hearts
1/4 cup flax seed, freshly ground
20 drops liquid stevia
1/4 teaspoon pinch psyllium husk powder
1 teaspoon pure vanilla extract
1/4 teaspoon coarse salt
A dash of ground cinnamon
16 Brazil nuts

Directions

- Preheat a sauté pan over medium-low heat. Add coconut oil, eggs, hemp, flaxseed, stevia, and psyllium husk powder.
- Stir, uncovered, until the mixture is well combined; raise the heat to medium and stir in vanilla, salt, and cinnamon. Cook until the porridge starts to boil lightly.
- Divide warm porridge among four serving bowls. Top each serving with 4 Brazil nuts and eat warm.

485. Pancetta and Asiago Waffles

Ready in about 20 minutes
Servings 3

These waffles will melt in your mouth, we bet you won't miss the flour. You can even skip pancetta in this recipe.

Per serving: 453 Calories; 37g Fat; 4.5g Carbs; 25.6g Protein; 2.4g Sugars

Ingredients

6 large-sized eggs, separate egg whites and egg yolks
1/2 teaspoon baking powder
1/2 teaspoon baking soda
4 tablespoons ghee
Kosher salt, to taste
1/2 teaspoon dried oregano
3 tablespoons tomato paste
3 ounces pancetta, chopped
3 ounces Asiago cheese, shredded

Directions

- Thoroughly combine egg yolks, baking powder, baking soda, ghee, salt, and oregano in a mixing bowl.
- Now, beat the egg whites with an electric mixer until pale. Gently mix egg whites into the egg yolk mixture.
- Generously grease a waffle iron. Heat you waffle iron and pour in 1/4 cup of the batter. Cook until golden, about 3 minutes. Repeat until you run out of batter; you will have 6 thin waffles.
- Add one waffle back to the waffle iron; spread 1 tablespoon of tomato paste onto your waffle; top with 1 ounce of pancetta and 1 ounce of shredded cheese.
- Top with another waffle; cook until cheese is melted. Repeat with remaining ingredients. Serve right away!

486. Greek-Style Berry Pancakes

Ready in about 20 minutes
Servings 4

You can adapt this recipe according to your preferences and use only strawberries or blueberries for the topping. Some of the coconut flour (2-3 tablespoons) works well if you have it on your hand.

Per serving: 237 Calories; 16.3g Fat; 8.5g Carbs; 14.5g Protein; 4.1g Sugars

Ingredients

For the Batter:
5 eggs
6 ounces Ricotta cheese, room temperature
1 teaspoon baking powder
A pinch of salt

For the Topping:
2 tablespoons coconut oil
1 cup fresh mixed berries
1/4 teaspoon freshly grated nutmeg
2 tablespoons Swerve
1/2 cup Greek yogurt

Directions

- Thoroughly combine all the batter ingredients with an electric mixer.
- Heat up a small amount of coconut oil in a frying pan over medium heat.
- Spoon some of the batter into the pan and cook approximately 3 minutes on each side.
- Divide fresh berries among prepared pancakes; sprinkle with grated nutmeg and Swerve, and top with a dollop of Greek yogurt.
- Serve immediately!

487. Mexican-Style Pan Pizza

Ready in about 15 minutes
Servings 2

With a killer crusty base and melt-in-your-mouth topping, this pizza is super quick to prepare and it is ideal for when you're just making two personal pizzas.

Per serving: 397 Calories; 31g Fat; 8.1g Carbs; 22g Protein; 3.1g Sugars

Ingredients

For the Crust:
4 eggs, beaten
1/4 cup sour cream
2 tablespoons flax seed meal
1 teaspoon chipotle pepper
1/4 teaspoon cumin seeds, ground
1/2 teaspoon dried coriander leaves
Salt, to taste
1 tablespoon garlic-infused olive oil

For the Toppings:
2 tablespoons tomato paste
2 ounces 4-cheese Mexican blend, shredded

Directions

- Thoroughly combine all ingredients for the crust, except for the oil.
- Heat 1/2 tablespoon of garlic-infused oil in a pan over moderately high heat. Now, spoon 1/2 of crust mixture into the pan and spread out evenly.
- Cook until the edges are set; then, flip the pizza crust and cook on the other side. Turn the broiler on high.
- Heat the remaining 1/2 tablespoon of oil in the pan. Repeat with another pizza crust. Spread tomato paste over the top of each of the prepared pizza crusts.
- Divide Mexican cheese blend among these two pizza crusts.
- Broil them on high until the cheese is completely melted. Eat warm and enjoy!

488. Homemade Bread with Herbs and Seeds

Ready in about 40 minutes
Servings 6

Everyone loves the smell of homemade bread baking. It's simply adorable.

Cook's note: The dough shouldn't stick to your hands; if the dough is too sticky, just add more flour.

Per serving: 109 Calories; 10.2g Fat; 1g Carbs; 3.9g Protein; 0.2g Sugars

Ingredients

5 eggs, separated
1/2 teaspoon cream of tartar
2 cups almond flour
1/2 stick butter, melted
3 teaspoons baking powder
1 teaspoon sea salt
1 teaspoon dried basil
1/2 teaspoon dried oregano
1 tablespoon poppy seeds
2 tablespoons sesame seeds

Directions

- Preheat your oven to 360 degrees F. Lightly oil a loaf pan with a nonstick cooking spray.
- Mix the eggs with cream of tartar on medium-high speed until stiff peaks form.
- Add the flour, butter, baking powder and salt to your food processor; blitz until everything is well mixed.
- Now, stir in the egg white mixture; gently stir to combine well. Spoon the batter into the prepared loaf pan.
- Sprinkle dried basil, oregano, poppy seeds and sesame seeds on the loaf and bake for 35 minutes. Serve with butter and enjoy!

489. Blue Cheese and Cauliflower Purée

Ready in about 15 minutes
Servings 4

Looking to surprise your guests with an unusual recipe, but don't know what to prepare? This extraordinary purée combination is sure to amaze them.

Per serving: 230 Calories; 17.7g Fat; 7.2g Carbs; 11.9g Protein; 3g Sugars

Ingredients

1 ½ pounds cauliflower, broken into florets
2 tablespoons olive oil, divided
1 teaspoon crushed garlic
1 rosemary sprig, chopped
1 thyme sprig, chopped
2 cups blue cheese, crumbled
1/2 teaspoon paprika
Freshly ground black pepper, to taste

Directions

- Boil cauliflower in a deep pan of salted water over moderately high heat about 8 minutes.
- Transfer cooked cauliflower florets to a casserole dish.
- Pulse 1/2 of the cauliflower in your food processor. Add 1 cup of the cooking liquid and 1 tablespoon of oil to the food processor.
- Repeat with the remaining cauliflower, water and 1 tablespoon of olive oil.
- Afterwards, add the remaining ingredients and stir to combine well.

490. Ham and Broccoli with Queso Quesadilla

Ready in about 15 minutes
Servings 4

In this recipe, use the back fat. Unlike hydrogenated lard, it has a slightly porky flavor. Queso Quesadilla is Mexican cheese that can be replaced with mild cheddar and Monterey Jack cheese. Enjoy!

Per serving: 323 Calories; 24g Fat; 7.4g Carbs; 18.8g Protein; 1.8g Sugars

Ingredients

1 tablespoon lard
1/2 pound ham, cut into strips
1 pound broccoli, broken into florets
1/4 cup sour cream
3/4 cup heavy whipping cream
1 teaspoon smashed garlic
2 tablespoons apple cider vinegar
1/2 cup Queso Quesadilla, shredded

Directions

- Warm the lard in a frying pan over a moderate heat; brown the ham, stirring frequently, about 3 minutes. Set it aside.
- Now, cook broccoli in pan drippings until the broccoli florets are tender.
- Pour the sour cream and whipping cream into the frying pan. Add the garlic and vinegar; cook until it is thoroughly warmed.
- Add reserved ham back to the pan. Fold in shredded Queso Quesadilla and cook for a further 2 minutes, or until cheese is completely melted. Bon appétit!

491. Keto Iced Coffee

Ready in about 10 minutes
Servings 4

This iced coffee is a true indulgence: rich and refreshing with a touch of cinnamon flavor. Enjoy!

Per serving: 161 Calories; 13.7g Fat; 11.4g Carbs; 0.7g Protein; 7.5g Sugars

Ingredients

4 cups strong brewed coffee, cooled
4 teaspoons coconut oil
1/4 cup coconut milk
4 teaspoons granular Swerve
1/4 teaspoon ground cinnamon
4 tablespoons heavy cream

Directions

- Pour coffee into a large bowl and mix with remaining ingredients, except for the cream.
- Place ice cubes in 4 tall glasses. Divide coffee among these glasses.
- Add cream on top of each glass without stirring. Serve right away.

492. Cheese Flat Bread with Salami

Ready in about 30 minutes
Servings 6

These flatbreads are soft and pliable so they're perfect for wraps and sandwiches. Take your breakfast or brunch to the next level.

Per serving: 464 Calories; 33.6g Fat; 9.1g Carbs; 31.1g Protein; 5.4g Sugars

Ingredients

10 ounces Mascarpone cheese, melted
2 ½ cups Provolone cheese, shredded
4 large eggs, beaten
3 tablespoons Romano cheese, grated
1/2 cup pork rinds, crushed
2 ½ teaspoons baking powder
A pinch of sea salt
A pinch of grated nutmeg
1/2 cup tomato puree, preferably homemade
12 large slices of salami

Directions

● Mix Mascarpone cheese and Provolone cheese with eggs. Stir in grated Romano cheese, pork rinds, and baking powder.
● Season with salt and nutmeg; stir until everything is well combined.
● Preheat a nonstick pan over a moderately high heat. Cook each flatbread about 2 minutes per side. Spread tomato puree over each flatbread; top with 2 slices of salami and serve warm.

493. Baked Avocado Stuffed with Grapes and Cheese

Ready in about 25 minutes
Servings 4

Have you ever heard about roasted grapes?! Get ready for these amazing avocado, loaded with cheese, nuts and fruit – it'll knock your socks off.

Per serving: 264 Calories; 24.4g Fat; 11g Carbs; 3.7g Protein; 3.5g Sugars

Ingredients

1 teaspoon grapeseed oil
1/2 cup red grapes, seedless
2 avocados, halved and pitted
3 ounces cream cheese
8 almonds, slivered

Directions

● Start by preheating your oven to 425 degrees F.
● Arrange seedless grapes on a baking pan that is previously greased with grapeseed oil.
● Roast approximately 15 minutes or until they are caramelized on the outside; sprinkle with a pinch of salt and reserve.
● Decrease the oven temperature to 360 degrees F.
● Add cream cheese and slivered almonds to avocado halves and bake approximately 18 minutes. Top with roasted grapes and serve at room temperature.

494. Smoked Bacon and Gorgonzola Muffins

Ready in about 25 minutes
Servings 5

The aroma of smoked bacon mixed with eggs and cheese is enough to make anyone salivate. It is perfect for Sunday breakfast or served as finger food at a cocktail party.

Per serving: 240 Calories; 15.3g Fat; 10g Carbs; 16.1g Protein; 0.4g Sugars

Ingredients

4 slices smoked back bacon
4 eggs, beaten
1/2 cup coconut flour
1 teaspoon baking powder
1 cup gorgonzola cheese, diced
A pinch of kosher salt
A pinch of grated nutmeg

Directions

- Preheat a frying pan over a moderately high heat. Now, cook the bacon, turning with tongs, until it is crisp and browned on both sides; drain your bacon on paper towels.
- Chop the bacon and combine it with the other ingredients; stir to combine well.
- Grease muffin molds. Fill the prepared molds with batter (3/4 full). Bake in the preheated oven at 390 degrees F for 15 minutes. Bon appétit!

495. Almond Coconut Cream Pie

Ready in about 30 minutes
Servings 6

There are many pie recipes out there but keto pies have something special indeed. They are airy, fluffy and incredibly delicate!

Per serving: 305 Calories; 30.6g Fat; 9.7g Carbs; 4.6g Protein; 5.8g Sugars

Ingredients

For the Crust:
1/2 stick butter
1/3 cup erythritol
3/4 cup almond flour
1/3 cup coconut shreds, unsweetened

For the Custard
1 ¼ cups double cream
3 egg yolks
1/3 cup almond flour
3/4 cup water
1/2 teaspoon ground cinnamon
1/2 teaspoon star anise, ground
1/2 teaspoon vanilla paste
1/2 teaspoon pure almond extract
1/3 cup erythritol
For the Topping
1 cup double cream
2 tablespoons almonds, toasted and chopped

Directions

- Melt your butter in a pan that is preheated over medium-low. Add erythritol and cook, stirring frequently, until it has dissolved completely.
- Stir in almond flour and coconut shreds and cook 2 minutes longer. Scrape the crust mixture into the bottom of a baking dish. Transfer to your refrigerator.
- Now, heat up the pan; add 1 ¼ cups of double cream and cook over medium-low heat. Fold in egg yolks and whisk until well combined.
- Whisk in almond flour and water until it is thickened. Add cinnamon, anise star, vanilla, pure almond extract, and erythritol.
- Cook until the mixture is thickened. Allow it to cool about 10 minutes; spread over the crust. Refrigerate for a couple of hours.
- Beat 1 cup of the cream just until the cream reaches stiff peaks. Top the cake with the cream. Scatter toasted almonds on top and serve well chilled.

496. Queso Oaxaca and Avocado Fat Bombs

Ready in about 20 minutes + chilling time
Servings 8

If you cannot find Queso Oaxaca, feel free to use Mozzarella cheese because it is white cheese made from cow's milk as well. It has a similar texture, moisture, and taste.

Per serving: 145 Calories; 12.6g Fat; 3.7g Carbs; 5.5g Protein; 0.1g Sugars

Ingredients

6 ounces avocado pulp
6 ounces Queso Oaxaca, softened
2 ounces smoked bacon, cooked and crumbled
1/2 teaspoon chipotle powder
1/4 teaspoon ground bay leaf
1 tablespoon red pepper flakes

Directions

- Stir all ingredients, except for red pepper flakes, in a mixing bowl; whisk until everything is well combined.
- Shape the mixture into 8 balls. Place in the refrigerator until they are solid.
- Roll each ball into red pepper flakes. Serve well-chilled. Bon appétit!

497. Chia Egg Balls

Ready in about 35 minutes
Servings 6

These egg balls are incredibly delicious and so versatile. If you don't like pork products, use anchovy fillets or canned tuna instead.

Per serving: 174 Calories; 15.2g Fat; 4.3g Carbs; 5.9g Protein; 0.7g Sugars

Ingredients

3 eggs
1/2 stick butter, at room temperature
8 black olives, pitted and coarsely chopped
3 tablespoons mayonnaise
Salt and crushed red pepper flakes, to taste
3 slices cooked ham, chopped
2 tablespoons chia seeds

Directions

- Place the eggs, butter, olives, mayonnaise, salt and pepper in your food processor. Pulse until everything is well combined but not over blended.
- Add the chopped ham; stir again.
- Transfer to your refrigerator approximately 30 minutes. Shape the mixture into balls.
- Place chia seeds on a plate; roll your balls through to coat evenly. Refrigerate in an airtight container up to 4 days. Bon appétit!

498. Star Anise and Pecan Porridge

Ready in about 25 minutes
Servings 2

Porridge is an ultimate, everyday comfort food that is delicious and super easy to make. Turmeric is a powerful addition to this porridge – it has antioxidant and anti-inflammatory properties.

Per serving: 430 Calories; 41.1g Fat; 9.8g Carbs; 11.4g Protein; 6.5g Sugars

Ingredients

3 eggs
3 tablespoons Swerve
1/2 cup double cream
1 ½ tablespoons coconut oil
1/2 teaspoon star anise
1/4 teaspoon turmeric powder
1/4 cup pecans, chopped

Directions

- Thoroughly combine eggs with Swerve and double cream in a mixing bowl.
- Melt coconut oil in a pot over moderately high heat; stir in egg/cream mixture and cook until they are warmed through.
- Take off the heat and stir in star anise and turmeric.
- Divide the porridge among individual bowls, scatter chopped pecans on top and serve.

499. Sour Cream and Chocolate Donuts

Ready in about 25 minutes
Servings 6

Forget fried and oily donuts like your grandma used to make. Try new-fashioned, fresh from the oven donuts! Sprinkle the glazed donuts with chopped hazelnuts or toasted coconut for a kid's birthday party.

Per serving: 218 Calories; 20g Fat; 10g Carbs; 4.8g Protein; 2.4g Sugars

Ingredients

2/3 cup coconut flour
1/4 cup xylitol
1 teaspoon baking powder
1/2 teaspoon baking soda
1 teaspoon cinnamon, ground
A pinch of salt
A pinch of ground cloves
1/2 stick butter, melted
1/2 cup sour cream
1 eggs
1 teaspoon pure vanilla extract

For the Frosting:
1 cup double cream
1 cup sugar-free chocolate, broken into chunks

Directions

- Begin by preheating your oven to 360 degrees F. Generously spritz a donut pan with a nonstick cooking spray.
- In a mixing bowl, thoroughly combine the coconut flour, xylitol, baking powder, baking soda, cinnamon, sea salt and cloves.
- In another mixing bowl, mix together the butter, sour cream, egg, and vanilla extract. Add the wet mixture to the dry mixture.
- Spoon the batter evenly into the donut pan. Bake approximately 17 minutes or until done.
- In the meantime, heat double cream in a pan over a moderate flame; let it simmer for 2 minutes.
- Fold in the chocolate chunks; mix until all the chocolate is melted. Frost your donuts and serve. Bon appétit!

500. Chèvre Custard
with Sautéed Morels

Ready in about 45 minutes
Servings 6

The delicate and smooth flavor of this cheese custard make a perfect counterpoint for savory sautéed morels. Pure hedonism!

Per serving: 263 Calories; 22.4g Fat; 6.1g Carbs; 10g Protein; 4.4g Sugars

Ingredients

1 ½ cups double cream
4 ounces Chèvre cheese, crumbled
3 eggs, beaten
Salt and ground black pepper, to taste
1 tablespoon butter, softened
4 ounces morels, chopped
1 garlic clove, smashed

Directions

- Preheat your oven to 320 degrees F. Lower 6 ramekins into a large pan. Pour boiling water into the pan to a depth of about 1-inch.
- Heat double cream over a moderately high heat. Turn the heat to a simmer; add Chèvre cheese and stir until it is completely melted.
- Place the beaten eggs in a bowl and add 3 tablespoons of the hot cream mixture; mix well. Add the mixture back to the pan with hot cream/cheese mixture.
- Season with salt and ground black pepper to taste. Spoon the mixture into ramekins. Bake for 40 minutes or until center is set. The custard should wiggle like firm jello.
- Meanwhile, warm the butter in a sauté pan that is preheated over a moderately high heat. Now, sauté the morels along with garlic until they are tender and fragrant.
- Top each custard with morels and serve immediately. Bon appétit!

Made in the USA
Lexington, KY
21 August 2018